# The Successful Writers and Editors Guidebook

# The Successful Writers and Editors Guidebook

Compiled and edited by

**ROBERT WALKER**

**Editor, *Christian Life***
**President, Creation House**
**President, Christian Writers Institute**

**JANICE FRANZEN**

**Executive Editor, *Christian Life, Christian Bookseller***
**Executive Editor, Creation House**
**Director of Studies, Christian Writers Institute**

**HELEN KIDD**

**Registrar, Christian Writers Institute**

**Creation House • Carol Stream, Illinois**

*Design: Wendell Mathews*



*Published by Creation House, 499 Gundersen Drive, Carol Stream, Illinois 60187*
*Distributed in Canada: Beacon Distributing Ltd.*
*104 Consumers Drive, Whitby, Ontario L1N 5T3*
*Distributed in Australia: Oracle Australia, Ltd.*
*18-26 Canterbury Road, Heathmont, Victoria 135*

*Biblical quotations from the* New American Standard Bible © *1971*
*are used with permission from the Lockman Foundation.*

*ISBN 0-88419-014-5*

*Library of Congress Catalog Card Number 76-062692*

*Printed in the United States of America*

# Contents

## SECTION II. THE WRITER'S DISCIPLINE

## SECTION III. THE WRITER BEGINS

## SECTION V. THE WRITER'S TECHNIQUES

## SECTION VI. THE WRITER'S PITFALLS

## SECTION VII. THE WRITER AND THE EDITOR

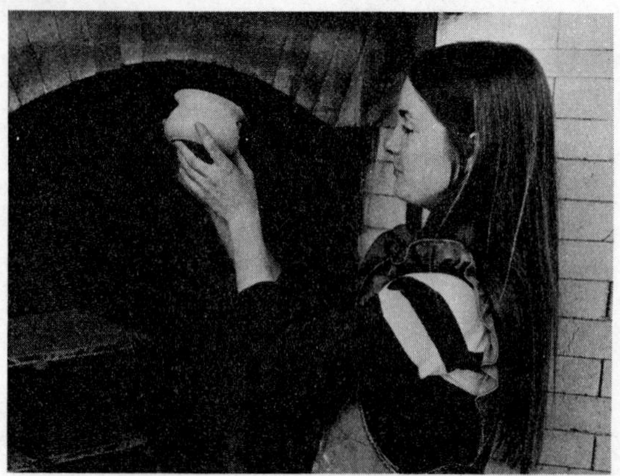

## SECTION VIII. THE WRITER DECIDES THE TYPE OF WRITING

needs of the Sunday school.

*Christian Education Markets*

53 **WRITING FOR TODAY'S WOMAN** 293
Katie Fortune

Writing for women can have a broader impact than speaking to women.

*Women's Markets*

54 **WRITING FOR THE FAMILY** 298
Lois Curley

Families are looking for answers. Curly makes some basic recommendations for writing for the family.

*Examples: "Pat and Shirley Boone, How We Raised Our Girls;"*
*"One by One by One."*

*Family Markets*

55 **WRITING FOR A DENOMINATIONAL PUBLICATION** 313

G. Roger Schoenhals

Editors want the best they can get for their readers. They are as anxious about mail delivery as writers are.

*Denominational Markets*

56 **WRITING FOR ROMAN CATHOLICS** 327
Richard Scheiber

Writing for Roman Catholics is not the same as it was ten years ago. The field is tough but rewarding.

*Roman Catholic Markets*

57 **WRITING FOR THE CHARISMATIC MARKET** 335
Viola Malachuk

The primary qualification for good writing aimed at the charismatic market is a contrite heart. The message is not, "I speak in tongues," but "Jesus is Lord."

58 **SELLING YOUR CHURCH** 338
Winfield C. Arn, Jr.

The difference between selling a bottle of Alka Selt-

## SECTION X. WRITING IN THE FIELD OF MUSIC

covered I not only have a desire to write, but I also have a determination. I think I'm hooked.

77 TO CONFERENCE—TO CONFERENCE 441
Jan Franzen

Conferences are a place to receive specific help, encouragement and inspiration.

*Writers Conferences*

78 HOW TO START A WRITERS CLUB 449
Catherine Brandt

Workshop criticism, comparison of output and report of sales combine to encourage a writer, beginning or established.

*Writers Clubs*

## SECTION XII. THE CARE AND FEEDING OF WRITERS BY EDITORS AND PUBLISHERS

79 HOW TO FIND CAPABLE WRITERS 457

To succeed, an editor/publisher must begin with the certainty that there is a given market or group of people who are waiting to receive information on a given subject.

80 TRAINING WRITERS 460

Often an editor will keep a manuscript because he has no choice. He wants an article on that particular

# How to use this book

The book that you now hold in your hands can help you succeed in the field of Christian writing.

But before you read this book, please remember that you, the writer, have to participate as well. There are always two sides in success. We've done our part. Your part is to read the book, not just parts of it.

While you are reading, take notes. There is marginal space just for that purpose. We've included some notes in the margins already. So please add to them.

The more than three hundred markets are listed categorically and appear right after each correlating article. Read through them carefully. We have also included those who do not wish to have free-lance material. This is for your benefit as well as theirs. The many abbreviations within the market listings are explained in the appendices.

To avoid unneccessary rejection slips, abide by the prerequisites listed for each market.

Get acquainted with the markets before you send your query or manuscript. Send for a sample copy of the magazine as well as for editorial requirements. Maybe you should even consider subscribing to a few different magazines to get acquainted with slant, content, etc.

If you have a book in mind, go to the public library after you've received the editorial requirements. Look up some of the books published by your target market. Scan them. Try to read them from a publisher's viewpoint.

There are many pieces of advice given in this book—advice worth taking—because it comes from people who know. Learn from them.

Your part is now to heed the advice, know your markets, and practice, practice, practice.

May God bless your journey of writing.

# Section I
# The Writer's Opportunity

1

# Why be a writer?

SHERWOOD ELIOT WIRT
Editor Emeritus, *Decision* Magazine

If I were a young Christian, eager to make an impact on today's world for Jesus Christ, I would not enroll in a seminary to learn how to preach. I would not take courses in mass communications or speech or linguistics. I would not try to start another denomination or parachurch super-organization. I would not try to get on television.

I would become a writer.

C. S. Lewis influenced more people for Christ than any other Christian of the 20th century, and he couldn't even type. But he could write. What the world needs in the decades ahead, until the Lord comes, is writers who can lay it on for Christ.

Why? Because if a person can write, he can do all these other things. They come with the package.

So here are my suggestions to young would-be writers today:

**Suggestions for would-be writers**

First, get to know your Bible. Take some solid Bible courses. Become involved in regular Bible study under a good teacher, so that the Word of God is continually irrigating your thoughts.

Become grounded in your language. Take survey courses in English literature under instructors who know and love the masters of the language. Study French or some other language, so that you can appreciate good literature in another tongue.

Take a course or two in journalism. Learn the rules of fairness, accuracy, objectivity, brevity, clarity. Study the writings of top-flight journalists.

If you find someone whose writing you admire and who is popularly received today, make a special study of that author. If it comes naturally to you, endeavor to imitate his style.

Learn what the live, exciting issues of the day are and immerse yourself in them. But don't become known as a writer of trivia. Major on the great themes—faith, love, suffering, prayer, life, salvation.

Join an organization of writers, preferably Christian. In a small critique group you will have an opportunity to submit your material for criticism. Make sure you can take it!

Attend writing schools and become acquainted with publishers, editors and other writers. Discuss your ideas with them. Once you get a foothold with an editor or publisher, hang on. If he suggests a line of development for your writing, follow his advice. Accept all his suggestions until you are well established as a published writer.

Build a system for collecting and classifying material—illustrations, quotations and topical references. Make use of familiar and appropriate illustrations in your writing.

Greatest theme of all

Stay close to the greatest theme of all, Jesus Christ. And may the Holy Spirit breathe through your words.

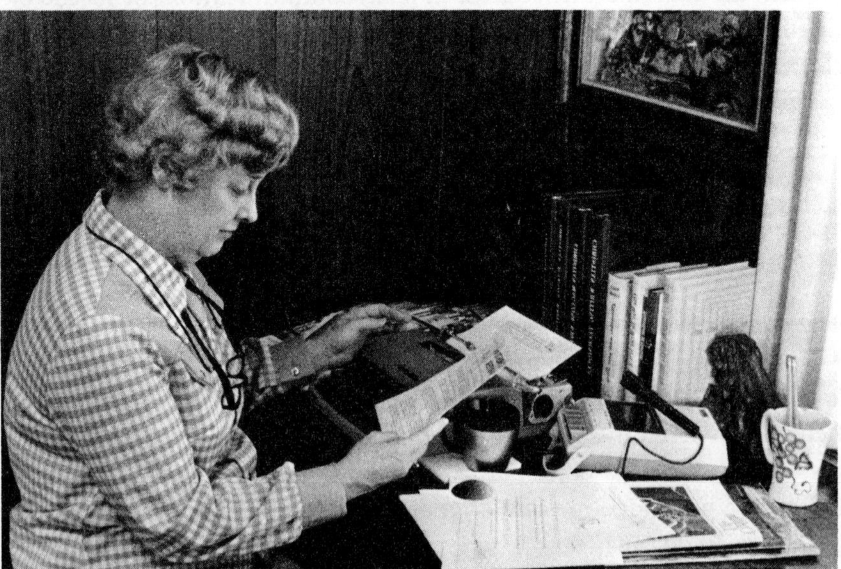

*The kingdom of God needs writers who have His message for these times.*

# 2

# You can have a writing ministry

LESLIE B. FLYNN
Pastor, Conservative Baptist Church
Nanuet, NY

Everyone should have a hobby. Writing is an excellent avocation. Here are some reasons, compensations and advantages of a writing ministry.

**Advantages of a writing ministry**

*It can be done part-time.* You won't have to quit your job to enter the ministry of writing. In fact, writing will probably have to be on a part-time basis.

*Writing combines well with other occupations.* You can be a housewife and a writer; a carpenter and a writer; a secretary and a writer; a pastor or missionary and a writer. You can write whenever or wherever you wish—perhaps after hours, when no one is around.

*And it pays too!* Money may seem a mundane motive and if it's the only motive, one cannot be a Christian writer. But remuneration is a Biblical principle for "a laborer is worthy of his hire." The writer can expect to be paid just as the preacher.

*Writing satisfies a creative urge.* Made in God's image, we all have these urges to make something whether by knitting a sweater, painting a picture, designing a house, or writing an article.

*Writing gives us an opportunity to meet people.* Through the years, in the course of writing, I have met, among others, a heavyweight boxing champion of the world, famous preachers, and missionaries from the third world countries. I even recall spending hours with Jim Vaus, a former gang leader, on the location of his work in Spanish Harlem.

*Writing widens your ministry.* The average preacher may preach to only two hundred or three hundred people during the week but an article may reach over thirty thousand people at one time.

**Advantages of the printed message**

Your typewriter can become a pulpit from which to preach. The printed message has some advantages over the spoken message. It can be read and reread at one's leisure. It works while we sleep and sometimes even after we die. The printed message can get into places we cannot and it travels cheaply.

There are over two hundred religious markets requiring articles each week. The Christian writer should take advantage of this situation. The missionary, for example, would be able to write true adventure articles.

*Writing can be done by mail.* As a student in seminary preparing for the ministry, I received letters from my girlfriend (now my wife) who would send me the notes from her journalism class. She jotted down notes, diagrams, etc. and I read them devotionally and read between the lines. This is how I started in the Christian writing field.

As Robert Walker, president of *Christian Life* magazine says, "If you can think, you can write."

*Many writers work full time at something else and find that their vocation provides the ideas, knowledge and experience for their writing. One such writer is Dr. J. Richard Chase, president of Biola College.*

# 3

# Everybody has a story

CARLTON L. MYERS
Free-lance writer

If you're a typical human being, sometime in your life you've thought, "I could have written an article (or book) as good as that one I just read!"

Well—why don't you? It's easier than you imagine. I can say that because I'm just an ordinary guy who went the whole route. That is, I read an article one day that didn't say anything new to me. *I can write as good as that,* I decided. So I applied the seat of my pants to the chair in front of my typewriter (stick-to-it-tiveness is one of the main requirements for success in writing) and I started in.

I'll tell you later how I finally was able to see my by-line (by Carlton L. Myers) in such magazines as *Christianity Today, Church Administration, Eternity, Home Life, Sunday School Builder, War Cry* and many other publications. First, I know you have a stack of unanswered questions like; How do you learn to write? Does it pay? Can you make a living as a writer? Are writers born or made?

I discovered that editors are always looking for new writers. *The Successful Writers and Editors Guidebook* lists the editorial needs of more than 300 publications. And it is by no means complete. The Sunday School Board of the Southern Baptist Convention, for example, has more than 100 weeklies, monthlies, quarterlies, graded

**Editors are always looking for new writers**

*People from other countries often have stories worth telling.*

publications, special study units and supplementary items that could not be listed in a small book. And they do not require that writers belong to their denomination!

Homemakers, businessmen, doctors, educators, pastors, laymen and ordinary people like you and me write for these Christian periodicals. They write articles, books, poems and stories.

Of course not every manuscript that is sent in is accepted. I have enough rejection slips (those polite little form letters that tell you your manuscript didn't make it) to paper the walls of our house. But my sales have made me regard rejections as challenges, not deterrents.

Learning to be a writer

How do you learn to be a writer? You sit regularly in front of your typewriter and let *nothing* bother you: telephone calls, discouragement, lack of inspiration, other distractions. You write. You write because you know you have something that must be said, something somebody else needs. You learn through trial and experience,

*Some writers find stories by getting to know people with unusual occupations. (Israeli Art-Craft)*

and you learn through success and failure. These all have a part.

An old saw claims that everybody has a story. I'm convinced that's right!

I couldn't sell a single article fifteen years ago. I know why now. As I reread those first futile attempts, they look like the first sermons of a student pastor. I couldn't afford the expensive writing corre-

*An ordinary person may have a unique hobby. Writers need to develop an interest in people and a listening ear. (The Center)*

spondence courses offered by schools across the country, and almost gave up. Then I noticed an advertisement by the Christian Writers Institute.

Before I had finished my first course from CWI, I had sold an article and some devotions to *Home Life* and *Open Windows*. I wished I had known about these courses years before.

Many annual workshops in Christian writing are listed, among which are the CWI annual Conference and Workshop, and the *Decision* magazine workshop.

Making a living by writing

Can you make a living by writing for Christian publications?

Norman Rohrer, in the July 1970 *Writer's Digest,* had an article, "Make a 5-figure Income as a Full-time Free-lancer in the Religious Field." That's at least $10,000 a year! To do that, Rohrer writes articles for small religious magazines, writes for a religious news service syndicate, and ghost writes books.

I don't make that much. My full-time career is that of a minister of education and music. But the satisfaction I get from writing cannot be measured in dollars and cents.

Most of my checks run from $12.50 to $60. A few publications, like *Christian Life,* for example, pay up to $175 per article. But those articles have to include top-notch photos, and must require only a little editing!

From my checks I must deduct income tax. But my expenses—typewriter, ribbons, paper, etc.—are tax deductible. A reasonable amount of "rent" for the room I set aside for writing purposes—my office, in other words—also can be deducted.

Now that I have been selling regularly to Christian publications, I am aiming toward secular magazines. It's not mainly because they pay much better—although that would be a nice bonus. But through them I can reach a large number of readers who rarely, if ever, have been confronted with the need of committing their lives to Jesus Christ. According to *Writer's Market,* there are more than 4,000 such markets just waiting—I hope!—for the manuscript I will someday send to them!

How may Christians are writing full-time or part-time? The graduates of Christian Writers Institute alone number in the thousands. They write for local papers, Sunday School publications, magazines and books. Most are part-time writers, of course. Most Christian publications pay about 2¢ a word. That means a $20 check for 1,000 words, a $40 check for 2,000 words. Many magazines prefer shorter articles. So your checks might run as little as $15. Figure it out for yourself. You'd have to produce a lot of saleable manuscripts each week to earn any kind of a living. (As a beginner, you might have as many as 50 percent of your manuscripts rejected.)

How long does it take to write an article, story or poem? That depends on the person. You have to get the idea, do research, write several drafts and type the manuscript.

Figuring one saleable manuscript per day worth $20, you'd make $5,200 per year; one a day worth $25 would add up to $6,550 per year; one a day worth $45 would produce an annual income of $11,700. This is based on five working days a week, 52 weeks per year.

Of course the picture would be a lot different if you were writing for secular publications. Their pay scale ranges from around $150 to $5,000 per article. Payment often depends as much upon quality as quantity, however.

Way back in 1957, Larston Farrar wrote a book *How To Make $18,000 a Year Free-Lance Writing*. He started with $106 the first year and worked up to his present (at that time) salary, and claimed that there were 20,000 full-time free-lance writers in the U.S.

Books, of course, are quite a different matter. Some authors come up with a winner on the first try. Most need help. But there is a wide-open market for book-length manuscripts. And with the world as topsy-turvy as it is today, there are a lot of exciting and helpful things to write about. Because of the importance of book-length fiction (the novel) the Christian Writers Institute has a specialized course in that technique.

An important requirement for all writers

There is one basic, very important requirement for all writers that seems almost too obvious to mention. But in case you overlooked it, it is simply this: a writer must read, read, read! Everything. All types of material. Extensively and intensively. And especially every issue possible of the magazine he wants to write for.

Now I'm not necessarily advising you to write without training, but let's say you have an article you want to write *right now*. How do you go about it?

Hints for writing

First, you look over the magazines that you are familiar with. Which one uses material of a similar nature? (*Moody Monthly* would have little interest in an article favoring the National Council of Churches.) You will want to "slant" your article for the readers of the magazine to which you are going to send it.

If the article is going to require a lot of research, you'll want to send a letter to the editor of your "target" publication to get a tentative go-ahead so you don't do a lot of time-consuming research for nothing.

After you have all your facts and figures and human interest stories about people (these are called anecdotes), you organize your material. This was one place I fell down badly before I took my courses with CWI.

After the material is organized, you sit down by your typewriter. All manuscripts must be typewritten on plain white paper, double-spaced, with wide margins. Top and bottom margins should be about 1½ inches on all pages but the first. That first page should begin almost half way down with the title and your name under it. In the upper left-hand corner goes your name and address (single spaced). The approximate number of words should be typed in the upper right-hand corner.

You should always enclose a stamped, self-addressed envelope for the return of the manuscript if the editor cannot fit it into his editorial schedule.

**Make time to write**

When do you have time to write? If you're an active Christian, you won't have time. But you'll make time—or take it! It may be at 4 a.m. before anyone else is up. It may be at 10 a.m. when the children are off to school. Or it may be at midnight after the rest of the family has turned off the TV and gone to bed.

If you are writing for the Lord, why not write on Sunday afternoons? Preachers preach on Sunday.

I make time for writing like I do for everything else I really want to do. You can, too. Large blocks of time are best, but shorter ones will do. If you cannot write at least a few minutes each day, never let a week go by without writing something, even if it is only a query letter.

**Rewards of writing**

The rewards? Maybe just a few small checks several times a year. Maybe much more. In either case, what you write—if it is published—is sure to change the lives of countless unseen readers. It already had an impact on the editors, or they wouldn't have accepted it. And who can measure the satisfaction of seeing your "brain child" in print!

And at last, after having ministered to others through the written word, you are eligible to receive the Divine Editor's "well done, thou good and faithful servant."

You can't beat that!

(Reprinted from *Christian Life* magazine)

# 4

# Actualize your potential

ANNE HARRINGTON
Editor, *Freeway;* Instructor,
Christian Writers Institute

One of my CWI students recently wrote of her lifelong urge to write. "There is no one who has a greater desire to write than I," she explained, "and perhaps no one who is more aware of her inadequacies."

I know how she feels.

Like many another new writer, I once thought all I had to do was rush to my typewriter and eagerly bang out a first draft. I learned the hard way that this only results in wasted time and frustration.

Much later I discovered that, like the pro, a beginning writer must learn to use his working time for the most profitable production. But I also discovered there are things even more important to the would-be writer than organizing a work schedule. Visualizing goals, for instance, and developing confidence and creativity are also essential.

**Build self-esteem**

You can't devalue yourself and be creative, for you become creative by building self-esteem. Consider God's true evaluation, and put your talents in His hands. Added to His bountiful resources, your little becomes a lot!

**Utilize your talents**

Utilizing the talents God has given you, of course, requires a great deal of planning and discipline.

E. B. White, the author of *Elements of Style,* has stated in this book that while some writers found that ideas just seemed to come to them,

"They never come to me. I have to go after them."

So do I. Few of us become writers by inspiration. Good writing takes time, hard work, and tenacity.

According to author Terry Morris, "Freelancing demands strong self-motivation, widely variegated interests, a keen awareness of current trends on all levels and, perhaps most of all, curiosity and a zest for life."

**Keep in touch with the news**

It is important, therefore, that we keep in touch with the news. Read a newspaper every day, then start an idea file.

Noted author Samm Sinclair Baker explains that the pro is always looking, listening, digging, using what comes his way. The beginning writer too often has his eye focused so far out that he misses the opportunities at his feet.

As Christian authors, we are mediators between God's help and man's hurt. We are mirrors of the good news of God, and each of us has a story to tell.

**Test your idea**

Once you have an idea, test it. Does it say something big? Is it complete? Does it answer a question a lot of people are asking? Does it *feel* big?

Then wait awhile. Before you get to your typewriter, give your idea a chance to grow—or leave!

**Live up to your potential**

If you really are committed to writing, and believe God has called you to write, you *have* to write. And unless you are utilizing the talent God has given you, you are not living up to your potential. So don't waste time worrying about what you can't do; just do your best with what you have. Get a handle on your talent and get moving toward your goal—one step at a time.

# Section II
# The Writer's Discipline

5

# Writing is risking

DAVID AUGSBURGER
Author; Assistant Professor,
Northern Baptist Seminary

If I crystallize the experience of this moment in writing, I may in the next moment, come to disagree with its content, and wish to disown the thought. But there it is. In print. Published. Permanent.

I have written numerous little books in the past decade. Some of them I'd love to eat. (Not that I think they would be sweet to the taste or less than sour to the stomach.) But I've come to thoroughly disagree with their contents, as I no longer agree with their author, the young preacher prescribing simplified solutions to painfully complex problems.

**The pilate problem**

The Pilate problem—living with what has been written—may freeze a writer's ink, block the flow of expression of deeper feelings and emerging convictions. "What I have written, I have written" may be an affirmation that I will stand by my statements, Dutchboy-like, and thumb the dike of defensiveness if my views don't hold water (to continue the simile).

"I have not changed my views on any issue since I entered the ministry 23 years ago," a pastor told me with humilipride. (No risk involved if he should write. No Pilate problem.)

The liquid stream of life flexes in ever-changing patterns for those of us who view ourselves not as static statements—restatements of consistent character but as a flowing sequence of growing experiences.

(I am not a network of unchanging traits which were determined by my genes and chromosomes, prewired in my brain cell matrix, and played out in spite of the givens of my genetic inheritance.)

**Free to change perspective**

I am free in this moment to change my perspective of the last. I am the thinker, but I am not the thought. In the next moment I can be challenged by another, and correct the thought (repentance it is called). I am the writer but not the item written. I am free in the next moment to grow beyond what I write now—if your feedback challenges my viewpoint and stimulates me to enrich or radically alter my thinking.

"What I write is me," a writer with deep identification with his product once told me. My writing was an expression of the me living in the moment of authoring, but I am not my past. "Disidentification" is the name given this realization of separate identity from my past thoughts, emotions, expressions, experiences, and any record of them. Roberto Assaggioli, the great counselor from Florence, Italy, has contributed these disidentification discoveries to the world of therapy.

I am not my past. I covet the freedom to affirm this for many people I have known whose yesterdays continue to invade and tyrannize their todays, stifling growth and mocking their hopes of repentance and the freedom to be who they are here and now.

I pick up a copy of my first book, *Seventy Times Seven*, and note that it has virtually nothing to say about forgiveness (supposedly the subject). If an editor were to pencil out "forgive" in each reference and substitute the word "love" throughout the entire book, nothing would be lost. As I see it now, the whole book is about restoring one's attitude of love, not about forgiveness. Loving is a prerequisite to forgiving, but they are not the same. So, thoroughly disagreeing with the author, I affirm that the book, as an expression of my 1966 awareness of faith has its own right to exist, and perhaps be of some use to others.

**Writing is risking**

Writing is risking. But the venture of pouring your perspectives and emotions into the mold of words is to reach out to others in open self-disclosure. The self-disclosed will reach new closures in the next moment. Thus to write, and to invite another to read, is to bid them grow along with me. Mutual risk. If you're still with me, we've both just taken it, and for me, at least, it is good.

---

(Reprinted by permission from
*Festival Quarterly,* Lancaster, Pennsylvania)

6

# An author's limitation

ELISABETH ELLIOT
Author; Visiting Professor,
Gordon-Conwell Seminary

Writing must be a personal expression of what the writer himself perceives as truth.

The book of Isaiah is introduced as "the vision of Isaiah the son of Amoz *which he saw*" (italics mine). Jeremiah says, "Now the word of the Lord came *to me*." Ezekiel says, "*I saw* visions of God."

**Firsthand knowledge**

God limited Himself to the ability of individual men to apprehend a particular facet of truth. The men who received these revelations had to be willing to lay down their lives—their own reputations, prior frames of reference, their security—and to put down faithfully what they saw, without fear of the labels which might mark them or the accusations which must have come from some of their readers.

Christian writers must be willing to write what they know firsthand without trying to please a constituency, without fear of what the truth may lead to, without rigid categories into which the truth must somehow be fitted.

**Unobscured perception**

One cannot create so long as he is preaching (that is, reiterating axioms which he has not actually lived). To make something meaningful to another, a writer's perception must be personal, and unobscured by the "conditioned reflex" of pat phraseology.

Too much that goes by the name of Christian writing postulates a knowledge of the answers. The author assumes that he already knows the solution to the ultimate mysteries, and therefore has no incentive to question, search, or contemplate the truth with humility and purity of heart.

It is this, I believe, which has hindered Christians from producing anything in recent generations which is worthy of the name of truly great art. Christian readers too often feel threatened when honest questions are raised. Anxiously they can scan their favorite periodicals for the shibboleths which assure them that they are on familiar ground—for familiar ground to them is "safe" ground. They have not been willing to "leave behind the elementary teaching about Christ and go forward to adult understanding," but have insisted on laying "over again the foundation truths."

**A writer's virtues**

A writer should be mature enough, honest, humble and courageous enough, to admit that there is a vast area beyond the "foundation truths" which he does not know, questions of the most fundamental nature which he cannot possibly answer.

The writer who, in the integrity of his heart, presents only what he perceives at a given time, without attempting to fill in all the gaps by drawing on someone else's vision, probably will be charged with one-sidedness. Jeremiah must have been so charged in his day. He wrote the word that came to him—pessimistic and shocking as it was. But he did not consider his own reputation or the consequences.

Not only is it cowardly to evade the truth because of what it may do to us or to our work, it is immoral. It is the sheerest casuistry to apply the pragmatic test to truth—to ask, What will this do to our work?" or "Where might this lead?" when the only valid question is, "Is this true?"

The Apostle Paul said to the Corinthians, "I earnestly want you to find the right answer even if that should make me no real Christian.... We can make no progress against the truth, we can only work for it."

**Facing the truth**

May God grant us courage to face the truth as we perceive it and to take whatever risks may be necessary to state it. We may be mistaken, but it is infinitely better to be mistaken than to bluff. We may be ignorant, but the admission of ignorance has sometimes cleared the way for the statement of truth. The reader recognizes common ground with the writer and is more likely to receive the message.

None of us is big enough to contemplate, let alone to write, the whole truth. For God Himself is Truth. What we see of it or of Him at a given moment is what we are responsible to reproduce.

# 7

# You have to surprise me

ALEX LIEPA
Editorial Director,
Religion, Doubleday

You want to know what it is that makes a publisher reach out and accept your manuscript?

Well, of course, you must have the ability to write well—clearly and pleasantly. But from where I sit, it seems almost as if we were living in an age when there are more people able to write well than there are people willing to read or at least to *buy* the many books that are being written.

**Crossing the decisive barrier**

Good writing is no longer enough. To cross the decisive barrier that separates the good but unpublished writers from the published authors, you must also have a fresh, even startling idea that will make an editor sit up and say: "Now this is something that ought to be said and has not been said before"—and, second, make people tell other people, "You must read that book. It will tell you something new."

Could I give you samples of such new ideas? No. If I had that good an idea, I'd probably be off somewhere in a quiet and beautiful setting writing *my own* best seller. So all I can tell you is what I tell all beginning writers, namely, don't send me your manuscript. Tell me about it and about your own qualifications to write it in a letter—a letter that should be no longer than three or four typewritten pages; a letter that must make me, your potential editor, sit up and say, "Now, indeed, here is something new. Here is an idea or a concept that surprises me pleasantly."

You say this is tough. You say you aren't that good at writing letters. But professional authors are good letter writers, and we know *you* are trying to compete with them—aren't you?

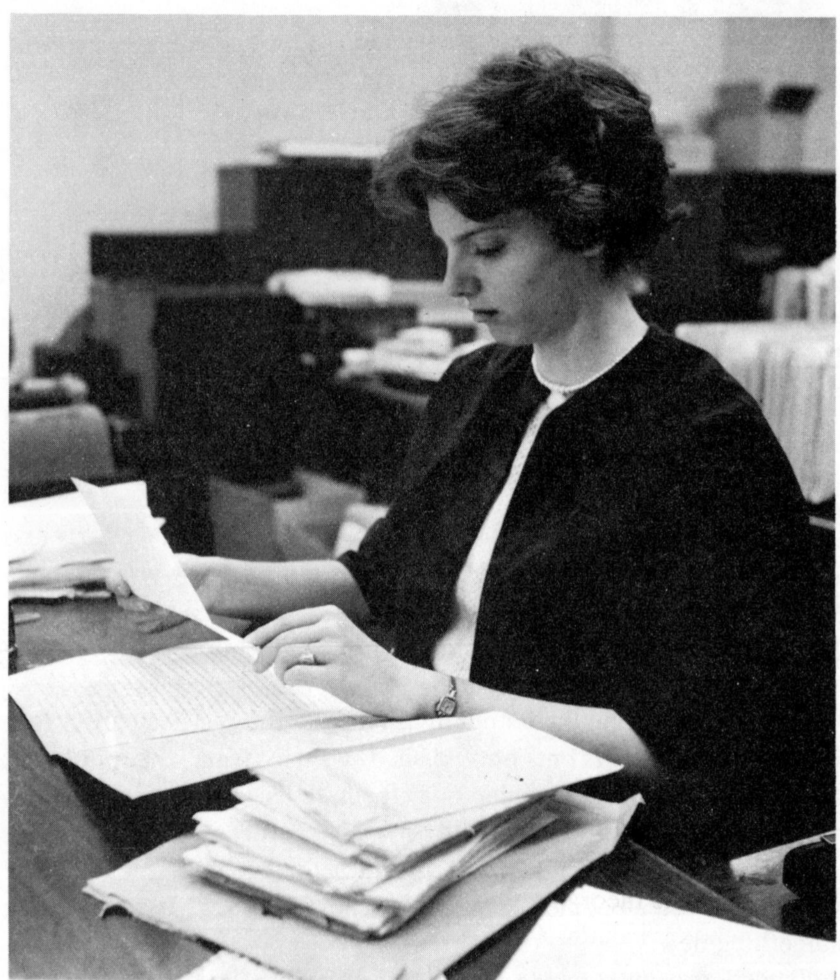

*As editors wearily plow through mountainous stacks of manuscripts and queries, somehow something you say must arrest their attention and capture their fancy.*

8

# The writer's discipline

ROBERT WALKER
Editor, *Christian Life* Magazine

"How can I learn to become a writer?"

As a former free-lance writer, college instructor in journalism and now as editor, publisher, lecturer on print communications, I have had this question put to me many times.

"It's so simple you won't believe me," is my usual reply.

And they don't.

**Anyone can write**

The reason is my conviction that writing is primarily a matter of discipline. Anybody who wants to become a successful writer badly enough can do so. It may take blood, sweat and tears for the average person. But it's still possible.

What do I mean by discipline?

Learning to write is like learning to swim. You can read all the books available on the theory of swimming. But until you get into the water and apply the principles, you'll never learn. The same goes for writing. And the more you swim, just as the more you write, the more proficient you become.

**Principles of discipline**

In disciplining yourself as a writer, the first principle is to determine that you will spend a given amount of time writing each day. I don't recommend less than one-half hour. An hour is better. And be sure that you spend that full hour writing—not dreaming about writing.

Start by setting a picture postcard up in front of you. Then write five hundred words describing the scene. Or recount a dramatic incident which you may have witnessed in the past week. Be sure to use as much dialog as possible.

Second, in order to make this discipline of writing work, you must set a precise time in which you will write. Some people can do this at the end of the day. I must do mine in the early morning hours. This means rising an hour or more earlier than normal for me; it may mean disciplining yourself to staying up an hour later. The point is: set a time and stick to it whether it is once a day or once a week.

Third, you must discipline yourself to come to the typewriter fully prepared to write. Your research must be done in advance so when you sit down at the typewriter, you have material on which to work. Obviously this takes more time—at interviewing, checking other sources for facts, statistics, etc., reading up on the subject in other books, periodicals, etc.

Fourth, to be a successful writer you must discipline yourself to study the markets available to you. It is not enough simply to prepare a manuscript on the subject which is appealing to you or your friends. Instead you should check the periodical or book market to see what has already been done on the subject, and which publication or publisher would be most likely to use what you are about to write.

You must also query the publishers who it appears might most likely be interested in your subject.

Thus when your manuscript is completed, you will be able to send it

*Walker demonstrates some essential steps in becoming a writer: 1) sit before typewriter 2) insert paper 3) write.*

out to the most likely market rather than on a hit or miss basis.

Fifth, you must stay everlastingly at it. Don't become discouraged when a rejection brings a manuscript back to you.

If you have done your research well, then you are convinced that the subject is an important one. If you have studied the markets carefully, then you will most likely have another publisher in mind to whom you can send the manuscript in the event the first market rejects the manuscript. Above all, don't toss your manuscript in the drawer and forget it.

Remember, the time you have spent in researching and writing is a matter of stewardship. If you have given yourself and your talents to the Lord, then He has a place in which they can be effectively used. Your job, at this point, is to find out when and where.

**Time is stewardship**

Sixth, discipline yourself to be looking continually for new ideas, new trends, new evidence of what and how the Lord is working in your life and in the lives of mature Christians.

The Bible—both the Old Testament and the New Testament—is a record of God's dealing with men and women in another age. You as a writer are God's interpreter of the way in which He is working today. Resist the temptation to become lethargic, to think you've seen it all, to assume that God works only in certain ways. And be willing to listen to and observe even the person who might seem to be the most unlikely source of information—especially if there is evidence that God is working through him.

**Listen and observe**

Seventh, remember that God delights in faithfulness. Again, the Scriptures are replete with accounts of men and women who kept relentlessly at the call which they believed God had for them. The very fact that you are reading this book is an indication that you believe in some way God is calling you to communicate through print media. Never lose sight of this conviction. Discouragements are bound to come. Frustrations bug all of us.

But just as God Himself is faithful, so He honors faithfulness in members of His family. As you exhibit faithfulness in disciplining yourself as a writer, so God will enlarge your opportunities and successes.

**God's promise**

You can indeed become a successful writer if you are in God's will. How do I know? Simply on the basis of God's promise in Mark 11:24: "All things for which you pray and ask, believe that you have received them, and they shall be granted you."

# 9

# Stop dreaming

FLOYD THATCHER
Executive Editor, Word Books

Obviously, there are times when our minds just run down completely, and we need to recharge our mental batteries.

Subtle devices

The mortal enemy of every writer is that foxy and deceitful little demon whose name shall be called "Dreamer." And as with most demons, Dreamer pollutes the atmosphere with half-truths, partial truth, and whenever he thinks he can get away with it, no truth at all. But for the Christian writer Dreamer reserves the subtlest of the devices in his sulphuric bag of tricks: pious rationalizations sprinkled with the "in" jargon of the elect.

For example, you have an assignment to write an article. You're at the typewriter—fingers poised over the keys, eyes glued almost hypnotically on a blank sheet of paper, your stomach is knotted with apprehension and a touch of panic, but nothing comes. At that moment Dreamer slips up on your blind side and whispers, "Come on now; you're rushing things. You aren't ready yet. Take it easy. Settle back in the rocker . . . meditate a little . . . dream a while . . . relax . . . *you know He'll give you inspiration at just the right time. After all, you're doing this for the Lord, so it's His responsibility to give you the words."*

And so, to the rocker you go; the paper remains blank for another day. You've been had!

*To think creatively, to write effectively, you must dream, but you must also act upon those dreams.*

Why? That's the paradox! There is a minus to dreaming, to thinking, to meditating—but there's also a plus . . . the half-truth in Dreamer's advice. Obviously, there are times when our minds become constipated, and we need to recharge our mental batteries. Certainly no writer should approach the typewriter without having dreamed and meditated and thought through his ideas.

Recharge mental batteries

But then there's the time to act—anything else is a cop-out. Dreaming, sharpening pencils, shuffling papers, dusting the desk . . . all destroys creativity and results in blank paper.

Thought is action

To think creatively, to write effectively, you must dream, but you must also act. Thought is action. We mold much of our future in our imaginations. Our world—yours and mine—is the result of our dreams and inner beliefs. But nobody will know about them if we don't communicate in concrete form.

Thoreau put it well: "If one advances confidently in the direction of his dreams and endeavors to live the life which he has imagined, he will meet with unexpected success." And another writer in our time says, "The secret of success is to trust God and to exercise your God-given imagination. It is to dream and be willing to struggle."

Willing to struggle

But there's the rub: *willing to struggle*. There comes a time to stop dreaming and act. For it is in doing that we learn to write better . . . it is in doing that we become energized and exciting people . . . it is in doing that the Lord can speak to and through us.

I like this definition: "An irresistible writer feels and expresses enthusiasm. He has energy. He is excited by life—eager for the experiences of life. There is nothing antiseptic, flaccid, passive, sterile, about him. He has the guts to be a participant, not a spectator."

In a speech in Boston, Clare Boothe Luce said, "A great man is one sentence. . . . History has no time for more than one sentence, and it's always a sentence that has an active verb."

Supreme model

In writing our sentence Dreamer tempts us with passive verbs. But the supreme Model for doing and acting is in the Gospels. . . . His sentence had an active verb. What about yours and mine?

10

# Paying the price to have something to say

WIGHTMAN WEESE
Editor, Victor Books

A recent issue of the Research Institute of America's *Management Action* explained why some business meetings are still going long after they should have been adjourned. An unwise chairman may force a member into empty chatter simply by looking at him or by asking if he has anything to say. Invariably, when put on the spot like that, the non-participator will conjure up something to say whether it is worth hearing or not.

In much the same way, some writers, simply because they have become known as writers, put themselves under the same pressure to say something, even when they have nothing to say. They simply can't stand to think of their typewriter standing idle for several hours. Or they can't bear to think that they haven't published anything for such a long time.

A story is told of Sir Winston Churchill being called on to give a speech for a certain banquet gathering. He rose and said, "I have nothing to say at this time." And sat down. Wise man that he was, with nothing to say, he said nothing.

Even the best writers sound bad when they are trying to say the same old tired things in slightly different terms. Unfortunately, most people aren't willing to pay the price good writing demands.

**Three price tags**

Good writing usually involves three key words and each has its own price tag.

The first word is *insight*—that spark of originality that crackles between two or more facts when their relationship becomes clear in your own mind. The price is the time it takes to research the facts and to cultivate the mind to make it a fertile field for new, original growth.

The second word is *experience*—the truths you have learned, often the hard way, the contributions your own life can bring forth to advance universal truth. The price is your willingness to learn from experience and the willingness to risk your pride to make hard-won wisdom believable.

The last is *validity*. Original thoughts must be well-grounded and justifiable; they must be relevant, useful and meaningful; their conclusions must be correctly derived from premises. It will cost your emotional life to be brought under control long enough for reason to prevail. Our greatest struggles over the truth are often emotional battles within our own soul as we seek to reconcile our heart and our minds, our feelings and our faith.

Perhaps too much has already been written about the too-hasty writer, but all of us who attempt to write should be wary lest we commit this error. When our writing passes the tests of having insight, of relating experiences that only we can discuss, and of being genuinely valid, we are ready to write, and people will appreciate what we have to say.

When good writing is praised, the honor is often misplaced—more praiseworthy than the good writing is the price a person has paid to write well.

# Section III
# The Writer Begins

11

# What constitutes good writing

FLOYD THATCHER
Executive Editor, Word Books

Very shortly I'll wrap up my 28th year in the Christian writing and publishing world. I not only love it, I like it. But I'm going to criticize Christian writing now because as I see it, it is characterized by a rather appalling mediocrity. Most Christian writing seems so often to miss the point when it comes to the realities and vigor of life. Why is this so?

**Mediocrity in christian writing**

One reason, I believe, is because we've retired and retreated to our doctrinaire, theological ghettos, and are comfortable only with people who look and think and talk the way we do. We live in a beige world. We have baptized our prejudices into Christian convictions and have fallen into a rather musty and safe, gray-flanneled, orthodox uniformity . . . never risking . . . seldom venturing . . . hiding behind our spiritual masks. In short, we seem to have lost an authentic lust for life. We have lost the art of living New Testament Christianity.

**Read the Gospels with candor**

An unfair indictment? I don't think so. To read the Gospels with unvarnished candor, without the manmade trappings and speculation that have robbed them of their original flavor and gusto, is to discover a throbbing account of earthy and gutsy people. It is also to rediscover that the central character was not a bland, platonic Jesus but the supreme model of *life* . . . a person who could not rest when someone else had a need . . . a person who did not spend all of His time in the synagogue or temple . . . one who said, "Inasmuch as you have done it unto the least of these, you have done it unto me . . . " . . . a person who didn't get His kicks out of arguing theology or nit-picking over some obscure passage in 2 Chronicles.

**Jesus—the supreme model**

There is powerful argument from the sketchy accounts we have that Jesus was a person of passion and feeling and caring. He was at odds with the orthodox bigotry of the accepted and respected and orderly and conservative church leadership of his time. Jesus didn't clink a coin into the temple collection plate as a means of paying off his debt to suffering and needy humanity. He was acutely aware of people who were hungry—He did something about it. He felt deeply enough about the physically sick, the lonely, the bereaved, the mentally ill, even about a woman who was caught in bed with a man who wasn't her husband, to reach out and identify with them—not judge them. Jesus liked to party; He liked to be with people who *lived*, and we read instances where the nice religious establishmentarians of His time disapproved of some company He kept.

Jesus lived in full measure and in stark contrast to our apparent middle class mediocrity. In a personal conversation with Adela Rogers St. John—that irrepressible lady who created "Tell No Man" and who is one of the best short story writers of our time—she made this statement: "Some of the best, most earthy writing of all time is found in the New Testament." And she proceeded to tell me that in her opinion the best short story ever written was found in the Gospels. It was told by Jesus Himself. What an incredible statement! What was it? The story of the prodigal son . . . just 488 words long, but an electric account of feeling, of passion, of caring. Then to cap it off, she quoted from a *New York Times* piece of several years ago: "The greatest news story ever written is the Sermon on the Mount."

And so, in the Gospel accounts we have our models for feeling and living and writing. And the Jesus who really knew how to live is credited with the best short story and the greatest news story ever written. This is in stark contrast to so much of the pallid, bias-ridden, and "other-worldly" prose which appears in print under the Christian label.

**Earning the right to be read**

Writers don't automatically deserve the right to be read—we earn it. The style and depth of our writing is determined by what we really are—not in public behavior but behind closed doors. The quality of our personhood determines the quality and lasting, redemptive, impact of what we write. Our writing will not be better than we are.

Paul Tournier has greatly influenced my own life and thought. He has said, "What I want, in fact, is to put into a book not only my ideas, but my person." And he does that! One does not read any of Tournier without becoming acutely conscious of his greatness, his humility, his feeling capacity, as a person.

In talking about love this remarkable man has said, "To love is to will good for another. Love may mean writing with enough care so that our correspondent can read without spending time deciphering; that is, it may mean taking the time to save his time." What amazing insight! Godlike caring has no time or place for the superficial, faddish writing which clutters both minds and bookshelves. It is Paul Tournier's caring that has made him not only a world-renowned medical doctor and psychiatrist but a sensitive, articulate writer and interpreter of the Christian faith.

**Writers must be people of deep feeling**

It is just not possible then for me to overstress the profound belief that as writers we must be people of deep feeling, otherwise we're wasting hours at the typewriter that could be better spent elsewhere. A good writer must know how to cry . . . to feel the hurt and anguish and despair of other people. As a boy in Sunday school, I was trained to give a flip, rote answer to the meaningless and senseless question, "What is the shortest verse in the Bible?" But I'm only now beginning to catch a glimmer of the deep meaning of "Jesus wept."

There is a book on the market written by one of today's Christian leaders which illuminates the intense crisis of world hunger. The jacket contains a photograph of an emaciated child looking out at the reader. Here is a poignant account of the suffering of people who have feelings just as I have. They're not statistics—they're flesh and blood people with dreams and hopes and feelings just like mine. But these dreams are smothered by wrenching hunger and slow, agonizing death by starvation.

It is reported that in some areas this book is rejected because of the picture of the emaciated child on the jacket—occasional comments hve filtered through that we don't want to face the stark reality pictured there because it demands action and produces guilt.

Writing will never be stronger or deeper or more profound than we are as persons—not when we're in church but in the solitude of our alone moments.

The effective writer knows how to live with gusto and feeling. He or she is a risker who is able to think and feel and believe "outside the boundaries."

The selling writer, whether it be in fiction or nonfiction, cares deeply about persons and conditions . . . cares deeply enough to respect the integrity of readers.

The caring writer has his or her spiritual priorities sorted out . . . we come to know what is really important and don't get sidetracked. I was enormously pleased this past week while working on a manuscript by my long time friend, Richard Halverson, to see him emphasizing the central truth of the great commission of Jesus, "Go . . . penetrate the world . . . witness *there* and live the Good News of the Gospel." But, we've gotten derailed on a spur track with our razzle-dazzle gimmicks and tricks to herd people into the Sunday school classroom or into the sanctuary twice on Sunday and at least once during the week. This is not going *into* and *penetrating* the world in response to the great commission of Christ. Far too often our energies have been deflected into headhunting and statistics gathering expeditions.

In one way or another this indictment applies to those of us who write. We need constantly to gauge our priorities by the raw edge of the Gospel. Dr. Donald Larson of Bethel College put it well when he said, "Men do not meet Christ in buildings, but in people; not in concerts but in performers; not in believers but in doers."

There's an appalling amount of arrogance in much of Christian writing. *We* decide what readers need without ever giving thought to the notion that we need to listen. I'm convinced that one of the greatest witnessing opportunities in our harried culture is that of creative listening. We Christians are bad listeners—we're so busy broadcasting that we don't know how to or have time to receive. My appeal then is: learn to listen; it is vital to good writing.

**Creative listening**

Writing is not like an automated factory. It is still in the handcraft stage. People have to do it themselves. And it is wretched taste for them to be satisfied with the commonplace when the excellent lies at their hand. I agree readily with Harper Lee's indictment, "Most writers are too easily satisfied with their work."

We don't seem to care enough to sweat out rewrites and engage in endless word sleuthing. We try to ramrod an article a month or a book a year, irrespective of the novelty of our ideas or the excellence of our writing.

I referred earlier to Adela St. John. It took her four years, I believe, to write *The Honeycomb.* And she ended up with 1700 pages of manuscript. Her editor insisted that it had to be cut to 1100 pages. She worked a solid year on that cut. She cared enough to have it right!

**Living copy**

It is this meticulous and sweat-producing attention to what and how we write that produces living copy. In addition to ideas, it is this intense preoccupation with words—words which inflame and pierce the soul—which makes the difference in the lasting impact of what we write. Truman Capote has been known to spend a whole day searching for just the right word. This is, indeed, one of the fine arts of writing practices honed down to a razor edge.

**Writers' tools**

I am a notebook fanatic. My verb notebook is a constant companion and invaluable tool. I know that verbs are the keys to convincing and energized writing. If readers are to see and touch and hear and taste and smell what I want them to see and feel and hear and taste and smell, it will only happen if I use verbs which incite those emotions. And so, on the completion of a piece, if I'm at my best, I try always to go back over that piece and examine every verb against the verb notebook, eliminating wherever possible any form of the verb "to be."

Another notebook always in standby contains a collection of unique expressions which come from my reading. The *Readers Digest* people call this "picturesque" speech. Now, the fact that I have these doesn't give me the right to steal them, but here's what happens: they help trigger usable variations. For example, here is a delightfully descriptive phrase from one of my favorite writers, Abba Eban: "Every time the foreign minister of Egypt opens his mouth, he subtracts from the sum total of human wisdom" (*Eban* by St. John, Doubleday).

In addition, my cliche and jargon notebook is an invaluable deterrant to even an unconscious slippage into one of the most subtle of writing sins. Those of us who write from the Christian arena impregnate our material so frequently with "Protestant Latin." We use "in" words and phrases which are meaningless to anyone who isn't "in." These become badges of orthodoxy rather than tools to communicate life-changing truth. What a waste!

**Writers are mind shapers**

Writers influence our ways of thinking and living. I love people who are dedicated to the art of writing. Nothing here is intended to be destructively critical of Christian writing, or writers. My appeal rather is to excellence. Let's not represent the exciting, living message of the Gospel in a shabby, mediocre fashion.

(Reprinted from *Christian Bookseller.*)

# 12

# On getting article ideas

ROGER PALMS
Editor, *Decision* Magazine

Are you going dry? Do you find yourself staring at a blank sheet of paper, the panic building because nothing is coming through? It happens to every writer, but there are ways to jog ourselves out of it and keep the ideas flowing.

**Keeping ideas flowing**

Be observant and keep a notebook handy to record every observation, no matter what it is—a snatch of conversation in the supermarket, a description of children, an idea that comes in the middle of the night—put it down.

Walk the streets. Leave your car in the garage and wander someplace. Vary your route. Observe the people, the houses, the activity. Talk to strangers. Feel what is happening. Smell the smells. Watch the animals.

Go to new places. You don't have to travel far. Take a bus to the shopping center and just stand some place and watch. Take notes on what you see. Take your laundry to the laundromat. Listen to the talk of the people there or start your own conversations. Thumb through the magazines scattered on the tables.

Walk around a local campus. Sit on the curb near some students or drink coffee in the student union and listen. Read the campus newspaper. Visit places where the high school students hang out after school. Sip a coke and hear what they say, and how they say it. Read newspapers, even small town papers. Go to your library. Read foreign publications. Study small or obscure magazines, newsletters, and company house organs. Read signboards, advertising, even street signs.

Strike up conversations in the bank line. Sit somewhere on an airplane where you can talk to the stewardess. Visit with the barber. Find out what people are struggling with, worrying about, commenting on. They are facing what most people are facing, but each person has a particular way of phrasing it.

Pray. Not so much for an idea but for God's message. Very often we are in a blank time because we have been staying too long in the study with our own thoughts, and our praying has been more for a particular article than for God's stimulation or personal teaching.

**Type of communication**

As I write this, I am interrupted. The person interrupting me communicates through words, feelings, body language and attitudes. Everything that comes from my interrupter is an idea and may be the beginning of an article. Each minute of every day—like a drop of pond water—is as warm. The ideas are there, and multiplying.

*Out of ideas? Go to new places, meet new people, talk to them about their work and their interests. (Union University)*

# 13

# Do you have a good idea?

HAROLD LINDSELL
Editor, *Christianity Today*

**Definition of an idea**

Ideas are preliminary plans, patterns, concepts that have not yet become reality. Nothing original or creative has ever come into being without first existing in someone's mind as an idea. The idea of the telephone existed in the mind before it was developed in the laboratory. The airplane as an idea has been around since the days of the Greeks and their mythology of waxed wings for flight. Thus we may say that all writing has in it at least three elements: the idea, the development of the idea, and the execution of it. Perhaps one might even add a fourth: the acceptance and publication of the idea in its written form.

How do you know if you have a good idea? You may not. It may be simply an illusory dream that never matures. It is interesting that a million ideas will do you no good unless you find people who want to read about them. Therefore, ideas that reach the reading stage must be ideas that are reciprocal, i.e., ideas that others recognize as valid and useful to them and for which they will pay money and spend time to mull over. I think it was Johnson who said that anybody who doesn't write for money is a fool. There is some truth in that statement. Behind the aphorism lies the truth that if no one will pay you for what you write "you should have stood in bed."

When you get an idea you should develop it in your own mind, check

**Developing your idea**

it out with others and discover its publishable possibilities. You will save your time and that of editors. Then you need to do the hard work of thinking through the idea, outlining its composition, and perform the reading and research essential to its execution. And then you begin to write. Writing is *very* easy. It is the rewriting that is hard. That is what separates the men from the boys, or the women from the girls.

In a sense there are no new ideas. And anything you know about can become the base for an article or a book. Good and evil are perennial topics. But it is how the subject is treated, and what new insights and applications are drawn that gives it life and usefulness.

What makes literature possible is the fact that old themes always need re-exploring, for life changes and new applications of truth to changing situations are called for. Yesterday it may have been the Middle Ages with its peculiar structures, then the Victorian era, then the flapper age of the 1920s, then the post-war era of the sixties, and now the day of the Marxist dream. What you need to do is take old ideas and run with them in new ways. Relate them to life in the present, and let the intended reader see himself, his culture, and the future through your eyes in such a way that he will be assisted in his own struggle to live a satisfying and constructive life.

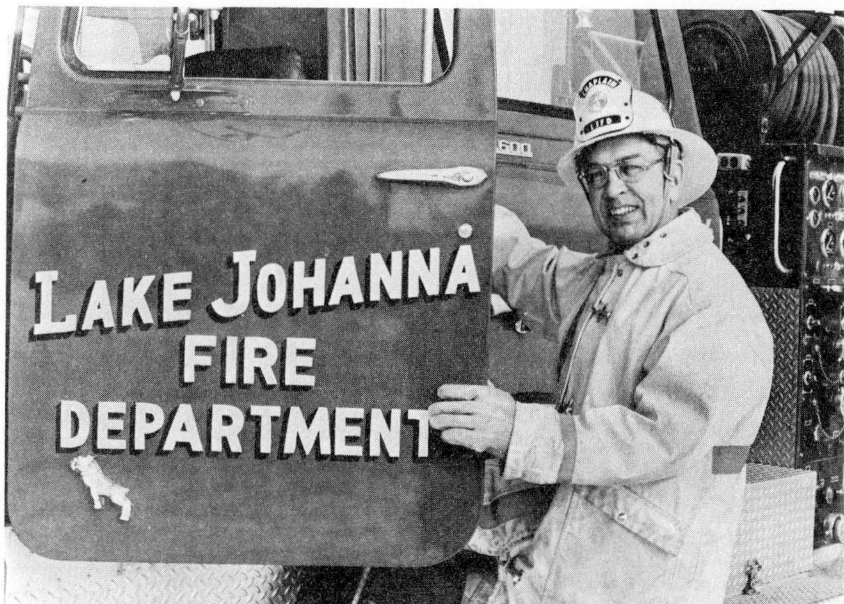


*Your community and its workers are valuable sources of ideas. Has some Christian found an effective way to express his faith on his job?* (Religious News Service)

# 14

# What's the big idea?

MELVIN E. LORENTZEN
Professor of English, Wheaton College

A good idea is almost as rare as a red rhinoceros. Editors prize them even above the S.A.S.E. Without them, a writer might as well trade in his typewriter for a tub of wallpaper paste to mount all his rejection slips.

Little wonder, then, that the misty-eyed beginner's first question of the flinty-eyed professional is, "Where do you get your ideas?" Wrong question. You don't "get" an idea. You "beget" one—bring it to birth, complete with labor pains. All that you "get," usually, is a thought, a notion, a fancy, or even a gut instinct. You then have to *develop* that into an idea.

**Beget an idea**

The difference between a passing thought and a workable idea is the difference between the sizzle and the steak. The first tantalizes you, the second nourishes you. Back in the 1930s during Hitler's rise to power in Germany, a self-exiled intellectual named Herman Kantorowicz pointed out to American audiences that while men possess thoughts, ideas possess men. A forceful and effective writer is thus "possessed," is in the grip of something that craves expression. His thoughts have generated an idea.

For this to happen, three steps are necessary:

1. ACCUMULATION. Other things being equal (like command of language fundamentals and a will to work hard), the more a writer knows, the more likely he is to be seized by good ideas. The reservoir of knowledge can be filled with first-hand personal experiences, with careful observation of the experiences of others, with broad reading and deep reflection. There must be prolific intake if there is to be good outgo. **Accumulation**

2. ASSIMILATION. It's not enough for a writer to cram his head full of information or raw data. He must give it time to become a part of him so that when he writes about it, he can do so with the ring of conviction to his words. In this subconscious assimilative process, thoughts need to be variously regarded: **Assimilation**

Some thoughts are like seeds: put them underground and "forget" them while they germinate;

Some are like soup: let them simmer, stirring occasionally, adding seasoning as needed;

Some are like eggs: sit right over them, keeping them warm while you brood over them;

Some are like nuts: remove the outer shell to get to the usable kernel inside;

Some are like cherry pits: discard them as unpalatable and unproductive.

3. ARTICULATION. This is that "90 percent perspiration" stage when the writer must struggle to find the right words and put them in the right order to get his idea across to his readers. His task will be simplified if he has worked through to the precise thing he wants to say before he even begins to write. That process is something like this: **Articulation**

Area: Parents
Subject: Parent-child relationships
Topic: Parental discipline
Title: "How I Spank My Six-Foot High Schooler"
Angle: Creative discipline of teen-agers.

Zero in on a specific idea that makes a significant point, and editors and readers will bless you for it!

# 15

# Finding ideas

TED GRIFFIN
Assistant Editor, Tyndale House

Question: Where can a Christian writer get good ideas for his articles or books? Answer: Where can't he?

Ideas, worthwhile ones, interesting ones, constantly surround each of us. Most of them go unrecognized. As writers, we face the challenge of being able to see and use not only good ideas but the best ones to communicate truth, drama, inspiration, emotion to our intended readership.

**Watch for ideas**

We should make a habit of watching for ideas—in situations we ourselves experience (or have experienced), in things others say (to us or someone else), in situations we see (even on the tube or in the daily newspaper). If we're not looking for ideas, we won't find them (obviously).

A rush-hour cab ride, changing a flat tire in the rain, a TV drama plot which could be adapted by the injection of Christian values, a child's humorous (to us) comments about God, emotional reactions to a thunderstorm, a nation's refusal of assistance after a major earthquake, trends we see in church life, a friend's deliverance from one addiction or another, practical application of a Bible verse or passage, the death of a loved one, a frightening drive through a severe snowstorm, poignant memories, brief encounters on a commuter train, vacation experiences, our most imaginative "what ifs," etc., etc., etc.—these are all possibilities for our writing.

**Read**

Then too, it is important for Christian writers to be readers. Books, articles (and not just those in evangelical magazines!), brochures, and the 101 other forms of literature in our society are all treasure chests full of ideas. We should even purposely read material we know we can in no way accept. This will not only confirm the truth in us, but will make us more aware of ways to communicate that truth to those who don't believe it.

We don't have to be 100 percent original. We don't want to steal or plagiarize, but we can adapt and remodel. We bump into an amazing number of mediocre ideas which can be remade into powerful, new, fresh ones.

**Jot down ideas**

Being human, most writers have a common problem—forgetfulness. To combat this, jot down ideas as they come to you and store your memos somewhere for later use. Whether you use office memos, or the back of a business card or church bulletin, or a napkin in a restaurant, or whatever, write the idea down! And go back through your idea file *often*.

**Set aside time**

Deliberately set some time aside to be alone (though not really alone—ask God to stimulate your thinking), to mull over possible ideas for your writing, to consider needs you would like to meet through this ability God has given you, to set goals for yourself, and perhaps to run through your idea file.

**Evaluate and eliminate**

There is a process of evaluation and elimination which is second cousin to idea-gathering. Not all ideas, even good ones, are good for you. Believe it or not, you are not qualified to write about *everything*. As ideas come your way, evaluate them. If they aren't worth doing, or aren't something you personally can handle, don't waste time on them.

Ask yourself whether the idea has any merit to begin with, whether it would help readers, whether it is a topic or principle or story or whatever, that really means something to you. (If it doesn't and you write it up anyway, it will be as cold as an obituary and as dull as the White Pages.) Also consider whether the idea is something the markets you're interested in would use. Be brutally honest with yourself. If an idea isn't worth the bother, don't bother, and thus save yourself the pain of one more rejection slip later.

Ideas? They're all around us. It's up to us to find them and put them to use. Keep your eyes open and mind alert.

# 16

# One idea—four articles

PAUL SCHROCK
Book Editor, Herald Press

Perhaps you find less time for writing than you'd like. In spite of your best intentions you are fortunate to complete an occasional article suitable for publication.

**Efficiency in research**

True, your own self-discipline and a regular time for writing are crucial. But a wise writer looks for legitimate ways to squeeze more efficiency out of his research efforts.

Here's a useful hint to keep in mind. Excess material gathered for one article can usually be shaped and slanted for several publications.

Careful research inevitably yields more good material than you can use effectively in a single story. Why not deliberately plan from the outset to record more facts, quotations, and anecdotes than you can incorporate in your original article?

Your first article will be stronger than if your research were more limited, and you will have plenty of material left over to use in a second, third, or even fourth article.

The extra effort you put into research for the bonus articles will be considerably less that the energy you would expend on developing articles in unrelated subject areas.

"Okay," you say. "I think I understand your suggestion. But can you give me an example?"

Fair enough. Suppose Pastor Yoder and his family have just returned from a ten-day tour of evangelical churches in Mexico.

Pastor Yoder, his wife, their 17-year-old son, and twin daughters, age 10, speak enthusiastically of their experiences.

**Sketch out ideas**

You arrange to interview the Yoders for an article. But wait. Why not sketch out several ideas before you meet to question them?

1. A Christian family magazine may be interested in an article telling how to plan a family trip to a foreign country. You might include a checklist of things to remember and pitfalls to avoid. Interlace these suggestions with anecdotes still fresh in the memory of the Yoders.

2. Develop one of their most significant encounters with Mexican Christians into an informative, inspirational article for an adult Sunday school handout paper.

3. Probe for leads from the son or the twins that might work as articles in church periodicals for youth or juniors.

4. Spend extra time with Pastor Yoder probing how his perception of the church in Mexico has changed as a result of his trip. Such an article may appeal to his denominational journal.

Well, you get the idea. The list could be extended to include a travelog piece for the magazine section of your nearest big-city newspaper. Or how about a feature news story for your local weekly newspaper? Or . . . you take it from there.

To provide perspective and depth for your articles you will need to do some library research on the areas where the Yoders visited churches. Trace their progress on a map. Read some recent accounts of the current status of evangelical Christianity in Mexico.

**Background material**

Here again, the background material will serve a multiple purpose. Drawing from your newly acquired expertise for several articles will be more efficient than researching entirely separate subjects.

So, the next time you decide to prepare an article, pause to sketch out several related pieces. With practice you'll find that you can develop a second, third, or even fourth article with little extra effort.

17

# Whatcha gonna do when the well runs dry?

GEORGE HARPER
Free-lance writer

It's very easy to think—when you have a few courses in journalism, or have even graduated from "J" school—that now you are a full-fledged journalist. Like the fellow who said, "I always wanted to be a writer. And today I are a writer."

I doubt if there is a single journalist who did not, at one time, fall into this trap of thinking, "Boy, I'm really a journalist. I know what it's all about."

Sometimes later, and sometimes sooner, the realization dawns that all of a sudden one has run out of new ways to approach a story.

What happened? Nine times out of ten you will find that the fledgling writer had not bothered to enrich either his life or his vocabulary since he finished his formal training. To put it plainly, the well has run dry. He's run out of words, ideas, approaches, new ways to dramatize the story he wants to tell. Instead of copy that "sings," he turns out copy that is gasping for breath.

What can you do about this? Here are a few suggestions:

**Read books**

*Read books.* Set up a schedule that enables you to read one book a month . . . or week . . . or whatever. But read! It's tough, with so many things that demand our attention. But just as we must *take* time to be holy we must *make* time to read. And we're not talking strictly about religious books, but about any kind of book that presents new ideas, fresh approaches, dramatic vocabulary and important subject matter. Don't shy away from the secular, but obviously you ought to exercise some discretion here. You won't find any new ideas in a trash can.

**Read the bible**

*Read the Bible.* Nowhere will you find literature that approaches the majesty of this book. Whether in proverbs or parables, you'll find its words and approaches to telling a story without equal.

**Read the dictionary**

*Read the dictionary.* True, the plot is weak. But pick out five or ten new words a few times a week. Learn what they mean, and try to use them in your writing. Zero in on active words, the kind that scintillate when you use them. You will be amazed at the improvement in your copy and your new ability to say things not only more interestingly but also more concisely.

**Read periodicals**

*Read periodicals.* Know what is going on in the world other than in your own pea patch. React to story presentations. And there is nothing wrong with "lifting" approaches you can adapt to your own situation.

**Set your priorities**

*Set your priorities.* What is more important at this point—more fun time or sharpening your writing skills? Could you skip just one set of tennis, or nine holes, or a coffee klatch—or whatever takes your leisure time—to improve your communications skills? It takes some sacrifice but it is worth the effort.

Communication, no matter what form it takes, should be *fun.* If it isn't, you're in the wrong business. And it is rewarding. For what greater sense of accomplishment can we have than to feel that we have influenced the minds of men?

Whatcha gonna do when the well runs dry? What you do will determine whether you become a prize-winning author or a "hack writer."

# 18

# How to get started when writing an article

THOMAS S. PIPER
Managing Editor,
*Good News Broadcaster*

Those first scrambling, frenzied steps in a foot race in some ways resemble the first few lines in the lead of an article. There, the writer must set the tone, and give hints of why he's writing and how he'll develop his ideas. In these few lines he will also establish a "feel" for the style of his article.

**Developing a lead**

But how does one think of a lead? Should he take out a ball-point and paper and wait for a vision?

Two basic steps greatly affect one's ability to write a good lead and an article that will sell and help people. In a race the quality of the run depends greatly on the runner's previous training. Similarly, the production of a good article takes just the right kind of preparation. One thing I can promise you: although it may be enjoyable, it will also be very hard work.

**Develop language proficiency**

New writers must first develop a proficiency in the language they'll be using. The knowledge and ability to use good grammar, spelling and writing style come only by hard study and practice. There are many places from which a person can get this training—courses in school, correspondence courses (how I started), reading books on the subject, subscribing to writers' magazines, using a dictionary frequently to check spellings, and so forth. The inexperienced writer should begin with the more organized methods of study first.

**Choose a familiar topic**

When choosing a topic, consider one on a familiar subject. It may be in an area of real, personal interest, but it should also be in an area of knowledge and expertise. Then you will be able to zero in on the details in a way that will be believable and helpful to the reader. If you write for Christians, it will be important to know exactly where you stand on what the Bible says. A Bible college training would be excellent. One can also get help through good Bible correspondence courses, a Bible teaching church, Biblical magazines and books.

**Know your proposed market**

Before one can begin to write he must be familiar with his proposed market—magazines, tracts, tabloids or others. Write for samples of the publication, study its purpose and style, try to visualize its audience and theological position. For which publication would you be the most comfortable writing? Then think about what else needs to be said in that publication's field, keeping in mind today's trends and how they are related to the subject.

Then write to the editor of that magazine and explain your idea. Try to sell him on it. Tell why you are knowledgeable in the area and qualified to write on this. Or write editors telling of your availability

*Choose subjects within your area of expertise. After her conversion Eugenia Price immersed herself in the Scriptures. She has published several highly successful books applying Biblical principles to everyday living.*

**Query the editor**

and ask for subjects of coming issues for which they may need articles. If a particular publication states that "query letters" are not wanted, then skip this step.

When you are able to "touch base" with an editor, you are on your way. But WATCH OUT! Too many promising writers blow it at this point. Remember that now you are just to the place where you will be "allowed" to run in the race. Your article isn't written or sold until you perform. So be extremely careful to find out *exactly* what the editor wants or what he likes about your idea.

**Sketch an outline**

Getting the article from the intriguing idea stage down onto the paper is the hardest part. It helps me to make a sketchy, three- or four-point outline in my head. I include the basic points and the order I think I will follow. I put this on scratch paper and begin to develop the progression of thought that is so critical to every article. I try to envision some of the ways I will lead from one point to the next. I jot down rough ideas for illustrations, examples and anecdotes that I may wish to incorporate. I sometimes rewrite this outline a few times, adding more details as I think of them. I do research on some of the details of the article.

**Creative thinking**

Between the stages of development of the idea, and especially when other needs of family living come up, I feel free to set aside the outline, rather than chance getting bogged down. I find it helpful to carve out blocks of time of at least one hour to do creative thinking on the article.

When you are pretty happy with your ideas, you might wish to send a copy to the editor. He will probably be glad to let you know if there are some other aspects of the subject he would like you to include. When you have progressed to this point, you are finally ready to write that lead.

When I think of what to write in a lead, I find it helpful to think the article through as carefully as possible and then just write the first words that seem to begin it best. But I need to keep myself in kind of a speculative or flexible mood when I am making this initial approach. This keeps my mind open to improve my first ideas. I keep trying to say them better. When I can think of a better way, I cross out the inappropriate words, recopy the remaining words and try to go further into the article. Once the lead is rewritten and polished into an effective unit, the rest of the article will fall into line quite easily.

The only serious problem you will face then is how to end it all. But that's another article altogether.

# 19

# Ideas—the essential factor

JAMES ADAIR
Editorial Director, Victor Books;
Editor, Power/line Papers

You may be the finest sort of word carpenter, but unless you consistently come up with good ideas you'll never have a high batting average in sales.

**Tune your mind to ideas**

Start by tuning your mind to ideas. Remember the story of two men walking along a busy city street? Suddenly one of the men stopped, cupping his ear. "I hear a cricket chirping," he said. The other man wrinkled his brow in astonishment. How could his friend hear a cricket amid all of the sounds of traffic, clicking heels, and conversation? The answer was simple: the man was from the country and his ear was tuned to the sound of a cricket. A little later the other man stopped and turned abruptly, looking down. He had heard a coin striking the sidewalk. His ear was tuned to quite another sound!

Tune your mind—your *idea* ear—to ideas that fit certain publications. Get to know several publications well. Read them regularly. Learn to think like the editors of these publications. Then you'll recognize good ideas as you meet them—ideas that you otherwise might pass by without even tipping your hat to them.

**Sources of ideas**

Ideas come your way down many avenues. I have found them by *reading*. One morning some years ago on my way to work I read a news item about a young murderer who had met God in prison. Later I made a trip to prison to see the young man. A story that exalted Jesus Christ resulted, and I sold it to *Pageant* magazine, which used it as the lead article in a spring issue to tie in with Easter.

I've written articles as a result of *observation.* As my daughters have grown up, I've sensed stories in some of their adventures. Only the other day they rescued a turtle from the street in front of our home and phoned me at the office to take them and the turtle to the park lagoon.

The next day our local paper pictured a turtle making its way across a busy street. "Why did the turtle cross the road?" the caption of the special interest picture asked. I quickly put two and two together. Obviously the turtle the girls had found was the same turtle, for the picture had been taken a block east of our home. I pounded out a little feature story on my daughters and the turtle, answering the question of the caption. The story appeared a few days later in the paper.

I've enjoyed writing other stories about their adventures: hatching an egg in a little incubator that they won selling seeds; finding and caring for a baby bird until it could fly. Both of these stories appear in *The Hairy Brown Angel and Other Animal Tails* (Victor Books).

It even pays to listen closely to sermons, apart from spiritual reasons. Sometimes your minister or another speaker may mention something that will give you a good idea for an article, story, or even a book.

Years ago I heard a minister tell the story of Edward Spencer, a young ministerial student who rescued a number of people from the sinking *Lady Elgin* in Lake Michigan. I researched the story carefully and sent it in to the *Chicago Tribune Magazine.* I got a quick acceptance. The editor had just assigned the story to a feature writer to tie in with the hundredth anniversary of the *Lady Elgin* tragedy, but my story came in time for him to call off the assignment.

By listening closely to a speaker, you might possibly even end up authoring a book. Many speakers with something vital to say need an alert writer to step into the picture and get sample chapters of a message series into the hands of a book publisher. However, make sure you have something fresh and new. Few publishers want a book of run-of-the-mill sermons.

I asked my staff members who edit *Power*/line Papers to give me input regarding ideas. "A pro writer is always listening and digging for ideas. Look around you as well as far out," says Anne Harrington, publication editor of *Free Way.* "Keep in touch with the news. Read

God's Word. Read a newspaper daily. Read magazines. Talk to people. Keep an idea file."

Don Crawford, executive editor of *Power*/ line Papers, says it isn't so much getting the ideas as it is testing the ideas. Most alert writers have more ideas than they can work with. Here are some test questions that Mr. Crawford has found helpful:

**Questions to test your idea**

Who cares? Will enough people care? Will it help? Does the idea have enough meat for complete development? Has it been done—is it different? Will it bring honor to Christ?

Here's hoping you get the idea!

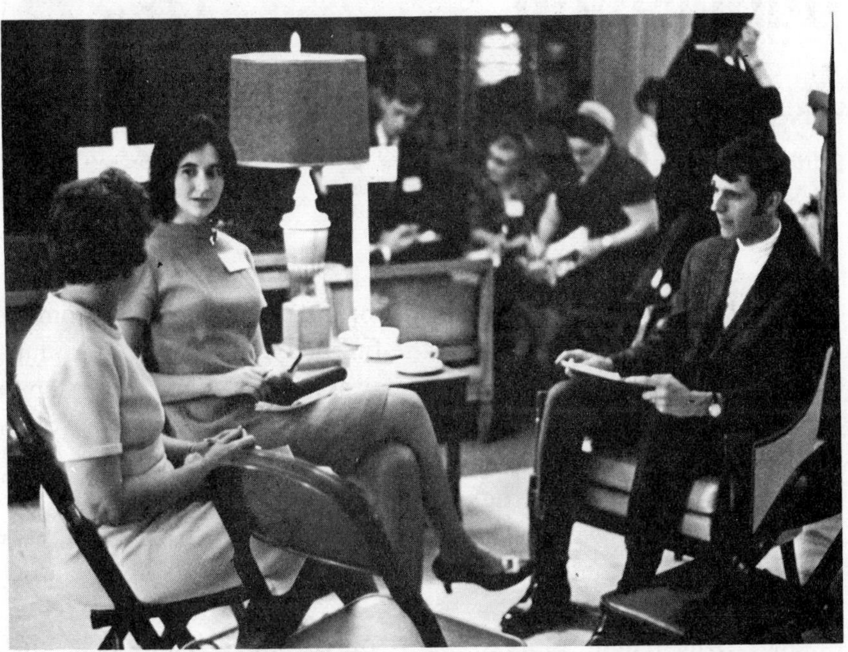

*Attend a writers conference or join a writers club. Test your ideas on other writers.*

# 20

# Idea to publication

ROBERT WALKER
Editor, *Christian Life* Magazine

Five basic steps trace the life of an ordinary manuscript—from the beginning of an idea through to the finished and published product. The real pros in the writing game may skip or glide over one step or another, but basically they, along with the rest of us, ultimately cover all the bases.

**An idea is born**

In the beginning must come the idea.

Too often young writers endued with the desire to communicate don't take time enough at this point to come up with a good enough idea. As a result, they fail.

Successful writers resort to many sources for their idea. The most obvious, of course, is simple observation of the needs of men and women around them.

Let's say, for instance, that you have observed that in your church a great need is for an audio-visual program. Perhaps the church or Sunday school possesses several projectors—16mm. as well as 35mm. But no one uses them. Moreover, you frequently hear Sunday school teachers say "I wish we had an audio-visual program in our Sunday school."

Here then is the initial idea for an article: "How to get an audio-visual program started in your Sunday school."

Often first ideas are too big or too general to enable you to do a good job with it. This may be the situation here. In the first place, this subject has probably been written about by many different writers. In addition the general idea of an audio-visual program may have been tried before without success. Hence, if you could come up with some new or different twist on this general idea, you might have an article concept which the editor of a Christian magazine might be more interested in.

So you begin to research the subject. You talk with the Sunday school superintendent and some of the teachers. One of the things you discover is that when an audio-visual program was set up at an earlier date, the first and continuing problem was to find a source for films. In fact, it was the lack of good films that finally bogged the whole program down.

Now you are warming up on the idea with the additional refinement: "How to keep your audio-visual program going."

In your further research you discover that the best source for additional films to keep the program going is your local Christian bookstore. He not only has a film—he has a whole library of Christian films. That is, 16 mm. films which can be rented and many different 35 mm. film titles which can be purchased at a modest price.

Thus, you now have the beginnings of a solid article based on a practical problem.

**Finding a market**

Your next step is to find a market for the article. With a short piece like this you can always take the chance by sending it directly to the editor without prior contact with him. On short articles of 1,000 words or so this is quite proper and correct. However, with longer articles it is much better to query the editor as to his interest in the subject, eliciting from him any suggestions which may help you slant the article to meet his specific needs.

What does a good query letter sound like?

Basically it must sell the editor on the fact that your idea is good and that you know enough about it to write an interesting article on it.

(Poor Example)

Dear Mr. Jones:

As you, of course, know, many churches and Sunday schools do not have an adequate audio-visual program. Hence, I propose to write an article on this subject.

If you would like to have this article for your magazine, I shall be glad to send it to you. I am sure that your readers will find it most interesting and helpful.

Please let me know if you want this article.

Cordially yours,
Joe E. Dokes

(Better Example)

Dear Mr. Jones:

Why do so many audio-visual programs in churches and Sunday schools fail?

In a recent survey which I made of half a dozen Sunday schools and churches in various parts of the country I discovered that the reason is a simple one. Most churches have both 16 mm. and 35 mm. projectors. Most churches believe that they should have an effective audio-visual program. But they don't—and the reason is that they do not know where to get an adequate supply of films.

Another survey which I have also made recently has revealed the fact that several churches with fine and effective audio-visual programs have discovered that the Christian bookstore in their community provided just the sort of help that enabled them to get the type of film they wished. This film plus the inspiration and help of bookstore personnel spelled success for these audio-visual programs.

I believe that an article could be written on this subject around 1,000 words in length. I have several photographs with which to illustrate it. If you are interested I shall be glad to send it along and, of course, will appreciate any suggestions you may have as to how you might prefer to have this article treated.

Cordially yours,
Joe E. Dokes

**Slanting the article**

Next big step in preparing your idea is to slant it for the market or publication for which you are writing. This means you must study the publication carefully, read many copies of it so that you understand the whole tone and approach the editor is taking towards his readers. As a beginning writer it will even be helpful for you to copy on the typewriter several pages of article material from the publication. This will give you a feel for the approach which the editor wishes.

**Writing the article**

Assuming that you have done an adequate amount of research, the next and probably the biggest and most important step is the actual job of writing. Here you will do well to follow the formulas outlined in the courses offered by the Christian Writers Institute. Lacking this, you should search for a similar type of article in a successful secular publication and seek to follow its organization. Organization is the key. If your article is properly organized, you stand the greatest possibility of success.

After you have typed your first draft, your next task is to edit it. This means correcting grammar, spelling and tightening up both sentences and paragraphs. Cut out unnecessary words—particularly articles "a" and "the."

Also attempt to substitute active verbs for forms of the verb "to be."

When you have completed the editing of your first draft you are ready to make a final draft to be sent to the publication.

In the upper left-hand corner place your name, street address, and city. In the upper right-hand corner put the word "Approximately" and underneath it the number of words. Be sure that this is an approximation—to the nearest 50, nothing else.

Two thirds of the way down the first page put the title of your manuscript in caps. Beneath it place the by-line; that is, the word "By" and your name. Then begin the manuscript, leaving one-inch margins on both the left hand and the right hand side as well as a one-inch margin at the bottom. At the bottom of the first page and each page thereafter except the last page, place the word "more" in parenthesis.

On succeeding pages place the number of the page in the upper left hand corner, followed by a dash and your last name. Observe the one-inch margins on all pages.

On the last page of the manuscript place the word "The End" or some other similar marks such as "-30-", or "###" which indicates the end of the manuscript.

## EXAMPLES OF EDITED ARTICLES

*On the following pages is a portion of a manuscript showing the editor's markings. A writer can gain valuable insights into what an editor wants by comparing his original manuscript with the published version.*

5910 Sheldon Rd.
Blissfield, MI 49228

From Strangers to Angels

By Mary Ellen Porter

Yesterday was my 51st birthday. Among the greeting cards I received was one addressed to "Mum," postmarked London. It sent "tons of love and a BIG hug from other daughter Pancha." Pancha is our red-haired Chilean daughter, the first exchange student to whom we opened our hearts and homes. Since then, we've learned to love and appreciate Reza from Turkey, Lars from Sweden, Saeko from Japan, Janick from France and most recently, Marty from Ecuador.

Hosting exchange students is an avenue of Christian service which is often overlooked by many families. The recent experiences of our family has encouraged me to write this article with the prayer that the Holy Spirit will use it to open many other hearts and homes in America to this ministry.

~~Our latest opportunity came very unexpectedly~~, as ~~God's calls often do.~~ [Begin →] It was a Friday evening in mid-August, three days after we had said goodbye to our daughter-for-a-month, Janick, [an exchange student from France.] We were all tired; in no way receptive to invasion by another stranger; in no mood for further problems or obligations. ~~July had been crammed with showing an appreciative French girl what America is all about.~~ We had thoroughly enjoyed ~~the experience and loved~~ Janick, a sweet sensitive artist ~~who was~~ the same age as our older daughter Deanna, a college junior. But

~~But now~~ we were all looking forward to a two-week rest before school resumed. ~~for us all: high school sophomore Jean; college junior Deanna; husband Lyle, social studies teacher; and myself, a high school counselor.~~ We had barely had time to catch our breath when I answered the telephone to hear Mr. Larry, the International Cultural Exchange official, say,

"We have an emergency situation, ~~here.~~ Mrs. Porter. Fifteen girls from Ecuador are here for a year's stay in the U.S. with passages all paid and no homes. There has been some kind of a mix-up and we hate to send them ~~home now that they're actually here.~~ back. Could you see your way to opening your home to another student, this time for a year?"

Contradictory thoughts flooded my mind. "No. No. I'm too tired....What if this is a call from God for service?...~~For a whole year?....You know how it bothers me to have extra people around.~~...I don't even have time for the necessary tasks, much less time for reading, sewing....How can I add extra work for an entire year?.... Think what we would all have missed if we hadn't known Janick, Frances, Reza, Saeko and the others....But a month, a week-end, even ten weeks is different from a whole year....Be not afraid to entertain strangers, for thereby you entertain angels unaware....I was a stranger and ye took me not in!!!!

These last words were drowning out all the others in my consciousness and I know that we would have to have a family conference and pray together about it.

I had long admired a cousin who for 35 years has taken newborns from the hospital and given them Tender Loving Care until they are ready for adoption. With a steady stream of 80 babies, she hasn't known a night's uninterrupted sleep or a vacation from diapers or bottles for those same 35 years. It was she who said to me once, "God has a job for everyone. It's right under your feet if you only look for it."

And my principal who copes with teenager's problems all day and then goes home to the problems of four foster children in his home. I knew I didn't have the patience or the courage to do what these people were doing, but was there any good reason why I couldn't do this? No real reason except a few selfish ones like more demands on my schedule, another lunch to pack, clothes to wash, a re-adjustment of schedules for us, someone always around, no privacy. I knew Steve, away at law school halfway across the continent, wouldn't be using his room upstairs.

But this was a decision which involved the entire family, one about which we must all agree. As we held our conference, these words from the Scripture came to

## PHOTO ESSAY—
## After your manuscript is accepted

*The designer meets with editorial to go over the manuscripts for the next issue of the magazine. They decide on the titles, the types of visuals to use, and the order in which the articles will appear in the magazine.*

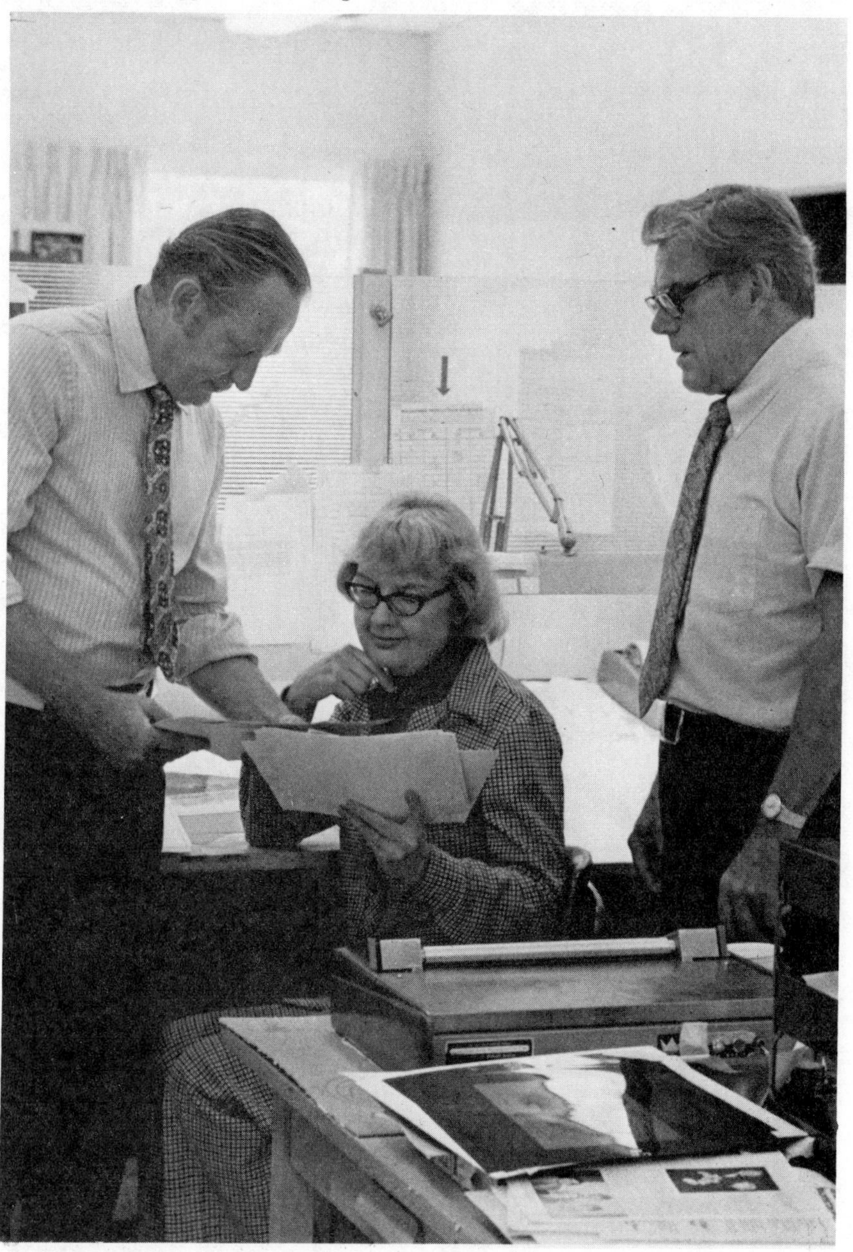

*The designer goes then to the drawing board and works out ten to twenty possible layouts for each article. He chooses one to present to editorial.*

*Detail of the thumbnail layouts prepared by the designer.*

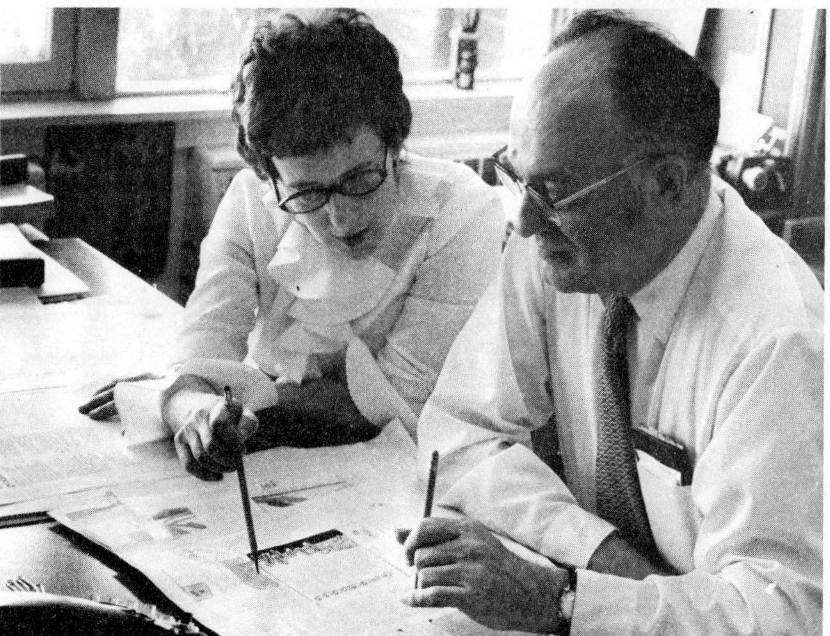

*Layouts go to editorial for approval and suggestions. (Scripture Press)*

*The typesetters convert edited copy to camera-ready copy. The typesetting department also provides galleys of the copy for the editors to proofread.*

*Today magazines tend to use photographs for illustration rather than art. When photos are unavailable or special effects desired, the illustration may be assigned to an artist. (David C. Cook Publishing)*

*The keyliners paste up the camera-ready copy according to the layout "dummy" provided by the designer. After this step the material is ready for the camera.*

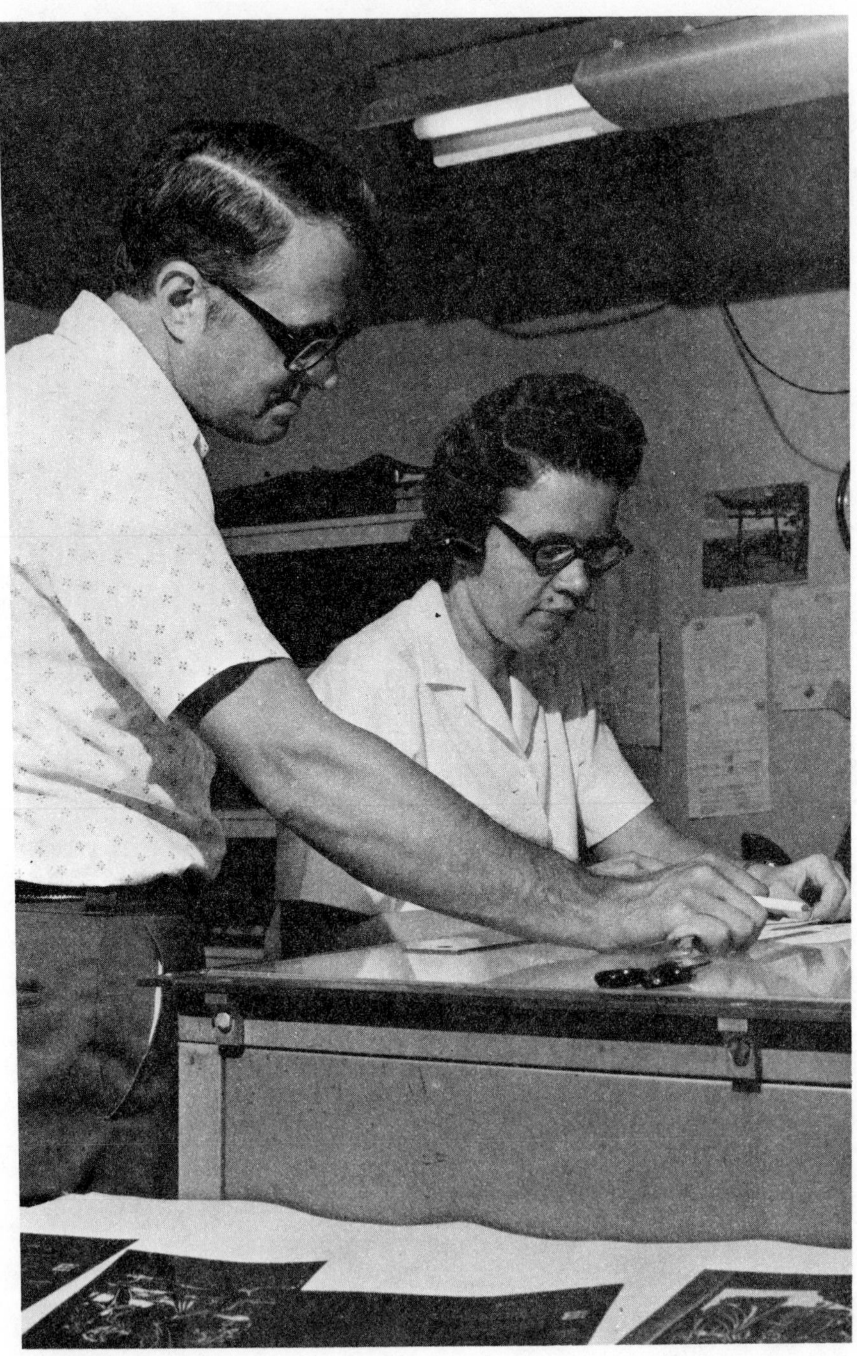

*This is no Brownie! A gigantic camera prepares the negatives which go to the printer for plate-making.*

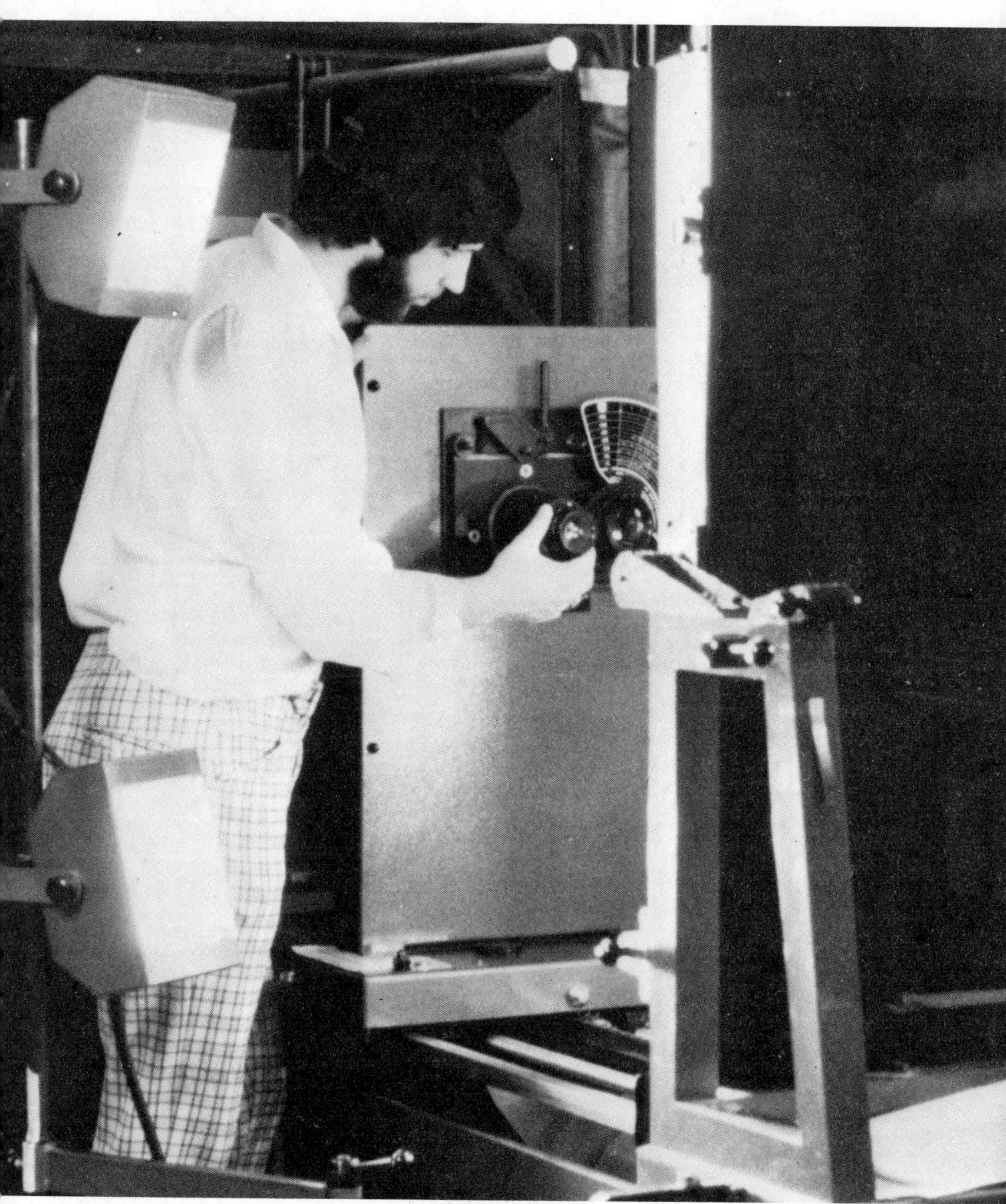

An editor checks pageproofs against original copy. (Scripture Press)

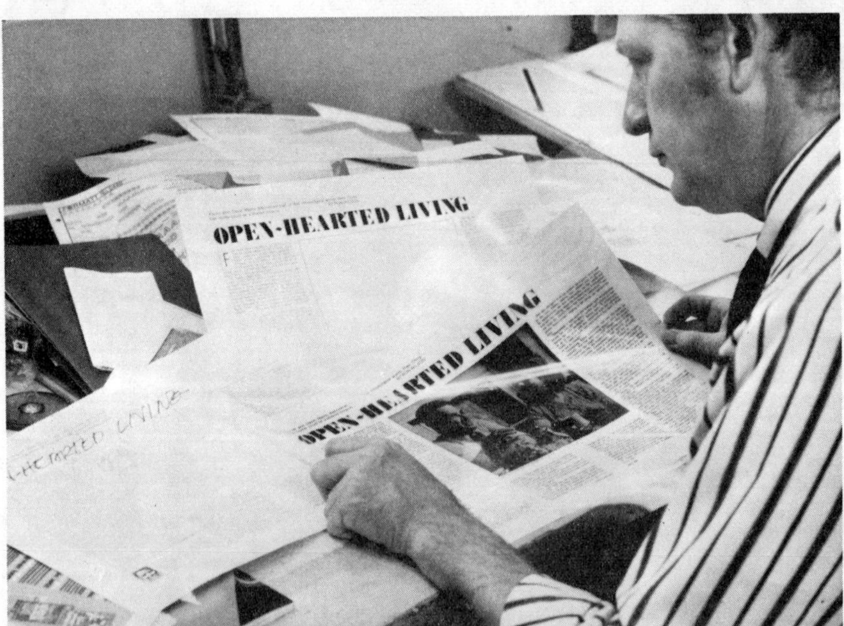


The designer checks the photo density and the use of color on the film and compares the film with design and paste-up copies.

*Magazine article copy, ads and photographs have now become a magazine, covered, stapled and ready for delivery.*

*The circulation department attaches address labels, sorts the magazines according to zip code and sends the publication on its way to the reader.*

# Section IV
# The Writer's Organization

21

# Organization—a must for the successful writer

WM. CAREY MOORE
Managing Editor, *Logos Journal*

At Christmastime and on birthdays a familiar scene is enacted in our home. Usually one of the children has received a bicycle or my wife has purchased some item of children's furniture or a home appliance. All that remains is for someone to assemble the thing. And that someone is usually me.

Experience has taught me to do two things. First, I spread out the pieces and parts to be assembled on a clean surface where I will do the work. And then I read the "How to Assemble" instructions. These are never easy to understand, and the task is made all the more difficult by one child's conversation with me and the baby's climbing up on my back while I squat on the floor. But sooner or later, the thing begins to take shape and, if I'm lucky, I won't have to go back and undo something; the instructions lead me step by step until no more pieces are on the floor and all of them are incorporated in the assembled item.

**Organization is a must**

The process of writing is similar, be it a magazine article, a news story, a term paper or a book. Organization is a must. The shorter the written piece, the less organizing necessary; but, every writer has a method for organizing and if this process is given scant attention, the resulting manuscript usually shows it.

When I was assistant editor of *United Evangelical Action*, I remember facing the formidable monthly task of putting together an in-depth story on the major news event. I remember one story having to do with the church-state separation issue, particularly the question of federal assistance to private education. I had amassed quotes from several persons, statements from two or three Supreme Court decisions, historical references, dates, some current information and a few interesting facts that I thought might add some color.

*The key to organizing is direction. The writer must know where he is going; he must know what he is trying to accomplish with his writing.*

I found then, and I still find, that it helped me to spread out the raw material on the desk, and even on the floor around the typewriter, so that I could refer to it as I put the story together. Usually I jotted down on a sheet of paper any of the pertinent data that I thought would ultimately be a part of my story. This would be just a bare word or a line to bring to mind the fact or quotation; I could turn to the raw material for the substance when it was needed. On this sheet, after some thought, I tried to write a sort of outline, listing steps in the order in which I expected to present them.

**Key to everything**

The key to organizing is direction. The writer must know where he is going; he must know what he is trying to accomplish with what he writes. Many of us fail right here. We launch some written piece, perhaps in a fit of emotion, and we just soar for a few paragraphs. But without some organizing purpose to energize the story all along the way, it falls to the ground—or to the wastebasket—where it lies, void of life.

**Organization and the idea**

Organizing begins with the initial idea, the seed of the article or book. Before a writer conducts an interview he should know what he wants to do with the interview material; otherwise, he will return to his typewriter bewildered by a vast collection of all kinds of matter, unable to "get a handle on it". He will probably have to go back and do some of the interview over, if he can and if he dares.

The thrust of what the writer is going to say formulates gradually in the mind. I have found it helpful to get at least the nub of this organization down on paper beside me. Then the task of assembling the manuscript can proceed. The writer may scrap the first three leads he attempts, but once he gets on the way, the attention given to organizing will keep him on course and lead him through to a satisfying conclusion.

22

# How do you find time to write?

RICHARD SCHNEIDER
Managing Editor, Chosen Books;
Roving Editor, *Guideposts*

I was in the midst of writing a book and had struggled to that part of the mountain where the top seemed absolutely inaccessible. If the phone wasn't ringing, or the grass didn't need cutting, I'd slump down to the typewriter and sink into a gray miasma, hoping the phone *would* ring to give me an excuse to turn away from what has become ultimate drudgery.

Finally, I kissed my wife and children goodbye, put the typewriter into the back seat of my car and drove up to Blue Mountain Christian Retreat in Pennsylvania. There in the quiet of a woodland cabin, I put in two days of uninterrupted writing and was able to get enough of the book done to have that comfortable feeling that someday it *would* be finished.

*Time* was the key.

We all reach that stage where our fingers wander idly over recalcitrant keys. Usually the cause is that we've been trying to write in fits and starts, fitting it in between home chores and PTA meetings and starting all over again when we've seen what we've produced under such conditions.

Of course, most of us usually cannot even steal those few days in a cabin to get that book started.

After some years of writing under a variety of conditions, here are a few tips that have helped me.

**Pray**

First, pray when you sit down at the typewriter. Ask for God's guidance and help. He has never failed me. Somehow the fingers fly and phrases materialize when you know God is looking over your shoulder.

**Stick to a regular time**

Try to set aside a regular period for writing each day, and *stick to it.* Perhaps it is three hours in the evening while the rest of the family is watching TV, or an early hour in the morning. There is no such thing as waiting until inspiration strikes. Under this delusion I have stared at white paper for hours trying to get just the right start to a story.

In this fix, the best remedy is to simply start writing your thoughts as they come to you. Once you've started the train of thought moving, you've overcome the inertia, your faculties will regroup behind the subject at hand, and the copy will begin to form.

When is your best time for writing? Early in the morning? Late at night after the family is asleep? This varies with people. But when you find yours, reserve those hours and stick to them.

**Set a goal**

Vitally important, set a goal for your writing. There is no greater incentive than a target to shoot at. Three pages a day? An article done in three days? A book chapter a week? Whatever, set it and fight to reach it. One of Satan's greatest devices is to whisper: "Relax, you've got all the time you need."

You don't, and the souls of those waiting to be touched by what you write certainly don't.

For example, when I write a book, perhaps my outline shows it to be fifteen chapters. I'll block out time for each chapter. Two weeks a chapter? All right, that gives me thirty weeks. Some I might finish in a week; but that gives me more time for the difficult ones. Into your schedule add a few weeks to allow for interruptions such as trips, unexpected guests, special events.

The point is, you have a deadline. Most writers perform best when facing one.

**Don't let feelings affect your work**

While writing, don't let your feelings about your work affect you too much. One of my best articles was written when I felt I was putting out poor material. Another time, when the prose seemed to flow and I felt like Hemingway, the story was a bummer. When you feel you're struggling up a steep grade, keep slogging ahead, doing the best you can. "Whatsoever thy hand findeth to do, do it with all thy might."

Let's face it. Most of us have to sandwich our writing time in between our regular work and personal responsibilities. And this in itself can be very good. For it is our very involvement in everyday living that can provide the color and background to which the average reader can relate.

Pray for ample writing time, yes. But when that interruption comes, don't bewail it. In it might be the lesson that the Lord wants you to pass on to others.

God be with you!

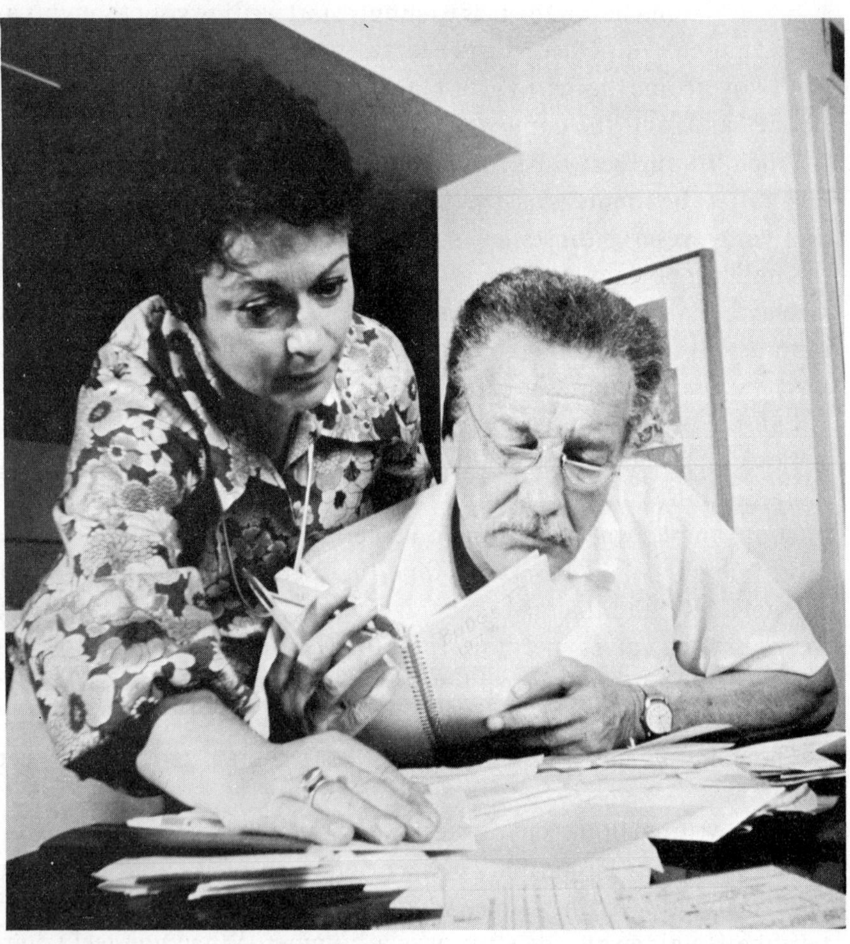

*Most of us have to sandwich our writing time in between our regular work and personal responsibilities. (Family Films)*

23

# Keep your records straight

GRACE FOX
Publications Editor, *Counselor*

So once again you forgot to put down the name of the publisher to whom you'd sent your article about aphids! You just found a new magazine to send it to. Now what do you do?

Well, if you don't want a hassle with an editor, and I'd advise making friends with them whenever possible, you'll just have to wait until the article is returned or accepted before sending it out again—if at all.

As an editor, I've seen the other side of a writer's failure to keep good records. One time we purchased all rights to a story. (In other words, the author could not sell it to anyone else without our permission and then only on second rights basis.) But just as the story was to appear in print, I picked up a competitor's publication and what did I see but the very same story by the same author.

I wrote to the author and asked what had happened. "I guess I just forgot to record the sale," was her reply. I continued to buy her stories because I make mistakes too, but I tended to check her data more carefully after that.

**Your credibility**

You see, carelessness can cause an editor to doubt your credibility. And in some instances, your honesty. So do set up some system, some way of knowing where your manuscripts are, whether or not they've been purchased, under what rights, by whom, and for how much. (You need to maintain good relations with Uncle Sam too!)

**Record systems**

My own system is the simplest because I don't do much free-lance writing. I simply put the carbons of an article I send out in an envelope with the manuscript title on the outside of the envelope. Attached to the carbon is a carbon of the covering letter which mentions the name of the publisher, the date sent, etc. When a story is purchased, I simply add that information to the letter and record the title, sale price, and date in a small notebook—for income tax purposes.

However, if you do quite a bit of writing and have several items out at a time, you should either keep a notebook or a 3 x 5 card file on your material. If you choose a notebook, pick a small ring binder with an alphabetical index. Make out a separate sheet for each title and file it alphabetically by title.

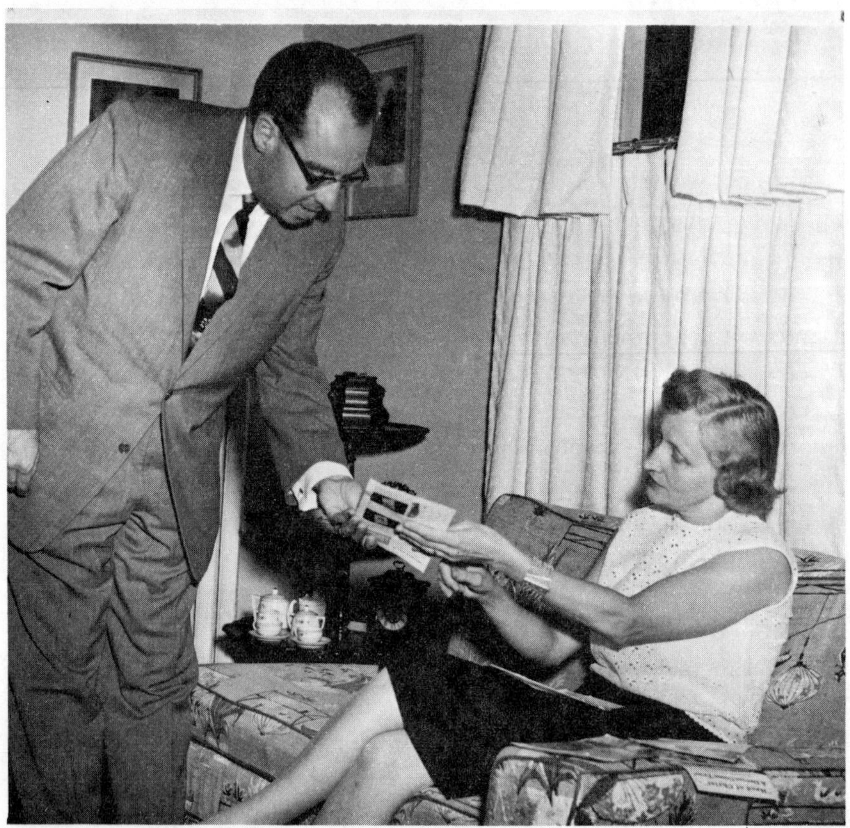

*Bernice Flynn has found an anecdote for her husband Leslie to use. The Flynns keep well-organized files for their writing, even an extensive anecdote file.*

Below the title, write in the name of the publisher and date you send it to him. If it is returned, add a brief reason and the date returned. If purchased, you might have a second section in the notebook where you file purchased manuscript pages alphabetically. Under the title, add purchase date, name of purchaser, and rights that were bought.

You still need a running list of items purchased, the date purchased, and sale price so you have a record for tax purposes. Such a list can go at the back or front of your notebook.

If you prefer a 3 x 5 card file, arrange it in the same way suggested for the notebook with an alphabetical section for new titles sent out and one for manuscripts purchased as well as separate lists for yearly sales.

You may think of some other divisions you want to make. If you submit a lot of material, you might even want to break down your titles under such headings as stories, how-to articles, poems, etc.

The main thing is, do keep accurate records—for your own sake, for good working relations with editors, and by all means for accurate tax records. A Christian author should be able to show good workmanship all along the line and a clean, neat, record system may some day be a good testimony to the watchful eye of the Internal Revenue Department.

# Section V
# The Writer's Techniques

24

# Those all-important queries

JAN FRANZEN
Executive Editor, *Christian Life*

Writer Josie Doakes had a great idea for an article. In her town lived Sam Glutz, a preacher's kid with a velvet voice. Sam made it to the big time, then hit the skids. He began popping pills; beat up his wife (to whom he also was unfaithful); and contemplated suicide. Then he found Jesus; rather, Jesus found him. Now Sam (stage name: Harry Hopskip) sings only for the Lord.

So Josie decided to query *Christian Life* about a possible article. Her letter went something like this:

Dear Madam: A really tremendous singer lives in my town. He sings only for Jesus. He's really handsome. Best of all, he lives next door. I would like to write about him for *Christian Life*. Please tell me what kind of an article you would like. Also, how long would you like to have it? Sincerely, Josie Doakes.

Did she get a go-ahead?

No. She got a polite note saying, "We are sorry that we cannot tell from your brief query whether or not we can use the article you suggest . . ."

**Query essentials**

What was wrong with Josie's letter? Maybe you've figured it out already. I hope so. Here are some of the missing ingredients: Name of the subject. Some of the big-time shows in which he sang. Credentials of the author. Name of Sam's recording company, and titles of his records. An anecdote or two showing that Sam is interesting as a person and a truly committed Christian.

In other words, by giving specific information, Josie's query letter should have made me want to see her article.

An editor is interested in possible photos, too. And he certainly would appreciate knowing that you read his publication—if not every month, at least often enough to know his slant (in this case, *Christian Life* prefers to have the ministry, not the man, highlighted; wants an anecdotal approach; and is looking for the philosophy/beliefs/ Christian commitment of the person rather than just his life story).

**A time saving tip**

One time-saving tip: usually it is wise to query only when research and/or an interview is required. If the material already is on hand, or if you plan to write a short story or true adventure where style, suspense, characterization, etc., enter in, just send the manuscript without a previous query. (And, by the way, a covering letter is *not* necessary unless you need to verify the fact that you are an authority on a certain subject.)

Always remember that an editor wants to work with any author who knows how to communicate, and who has something to say which will minister to his readership. So don't be afraid to query. Only make sure that your letter doesn't sell you short.

*The wise writer will learn how to write a good query.*

# 25

# How to conduct a successful interview

ANNE HARRINGTON
Editor, *Freeway;* Instructor,
Christian Writers Institute

If you're starting in a writing career, your ability to draw facts and opinions out of people during an interview is very important. The art of asking the right question at the right time largely makes an interview successful. Though methods vary according to the person, place and time, some interviews always seem to go better than others. But you can count on a number of good interviews if you follow these ten rules:

**Right question at right time**

**Ten rules for interviewing**

1. Plan the interview in advance. Set up an appointment at least a week ahead of time. This gives the subject a chance to think over what he wants to say. Meanwhile, find out all you can about your subject. The more you know about him, the better your interview will be.

2. Make out a list of at least a dozen specific questions. Ask questions about his job, his interests, his hobbies, to put the subject at ease. Once rapport has been established, ask tougher questions.

3. Try to make the interview leisurely. Explain the nature of the interview, and let the person know why he is there. You must seem relaxed in order to put your subject at ease. As you warm up to each other, it becomes easy to guide the conversation.

4. Keep your reportorial regalia to a minimum. While some journalists use a tape recorder, most consider it an "electronic albatross" that inhibits informal give-and-take. If you use a recorder, use a small,

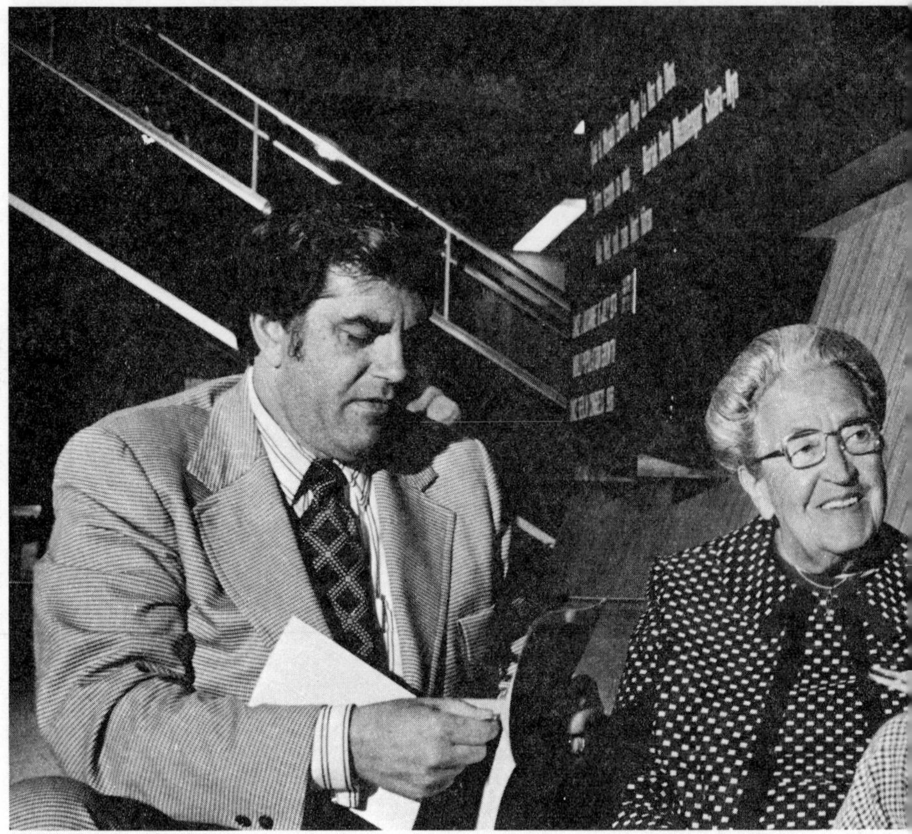

*Walker interviews Corrie ten Boom and World Wide Pictures president, Bill Brown.*

unobtrusive microphone. Explain that the tape is only to help your bad memory, and that he will have a chance to check the article so he won't be misquoted.

Avoid too obvious note-taking. Use a small, spiral-bound notebook or a piece of copy paper folded twice such as reporters use. Say, "I hope you won't mind if I take a few notes." Write down only key words and fill in the details as soon as possible.

5. Go after anecdotes. These add spice to your article and give you dialog which makes for easy reading. Ask questions such as, "What were some of the most amusing things that happened to you? What did you enjoy most? Least? What do you value most from your experience?"

6. Allow an hour, then leave. Usually the subject is a very busy person; don't impose on his time. Soak up everything during that hour—the subject's hands, dress, surroundings, books, favorite words,

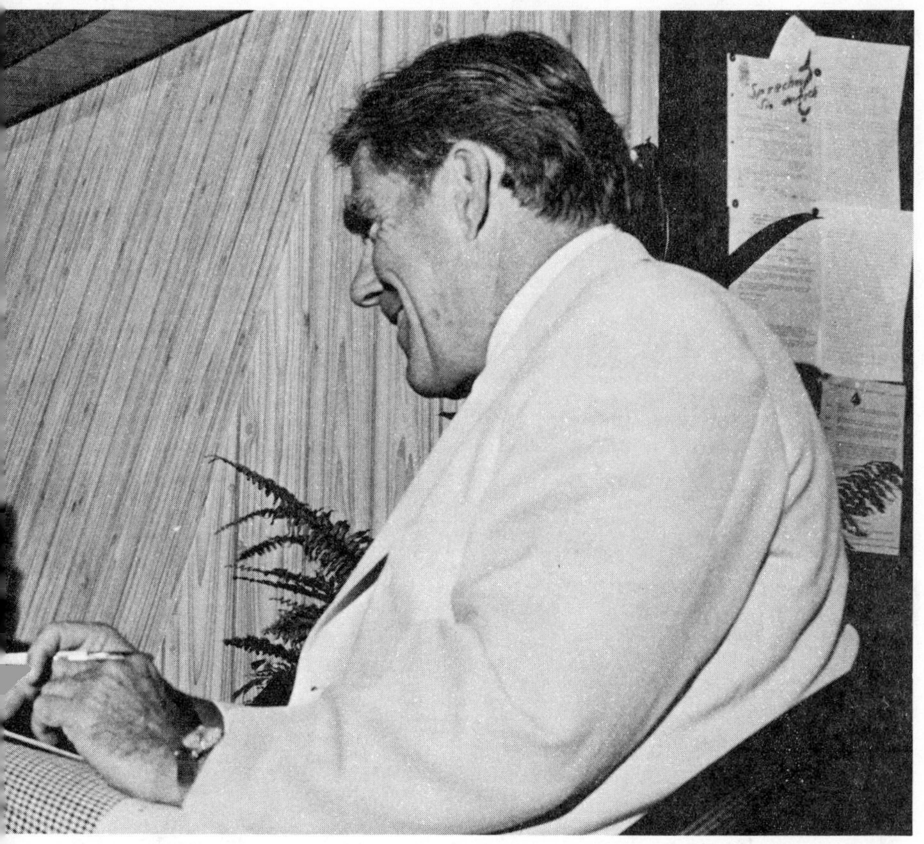

mannerisms, mood and his sense of humor.

7. Take your own photos. Take your camera along and get both the interview and the photos with one trip. By capturing your subject in his own environment you will reflect his interests and tastes. Also, you will get what you want that way.

8. Listen carefully during the last few minutes. Usually I learn more after I've put my notebook away and am on my way out the door. Then my subject is relaxed and has decided I'm not such an ogre after all. From these off-the-cuff comments, I've often gleaned my best anecdotes.

9. Get to your typewriter while the interview is still fresh. Write the lead in your head on the way home; often the rest of the article will fall into place.

10. Remember, a good interview can be a happy experience for both parties. Prepare for it, and enjoy it.

# 26

# Dialog is a two-way street

ESTHER VOGT
Free-lance author; Novel Instructor, Christian Writers Institute

Dialog is literally a "talking together," a conversation between two people. It's a most important facet of any short story or novel, acceptable and useful even in nonfiction.

Writing dialog is not merely framing in quote marks something a character has said. It takes skill to write good dialog. Pay close attention—eavesdrop, if you must—to the everyday world, and you'll discover the key to good dialog. Blessed is the author with the perceptive ear for human speech patterns and rhythms, for of such is the kingdom of good writing. But to get this across to the reader through the medium of characters is the trick!

**Why use dialog?**

Why use dialog then, if it's hard to master? Because dialog is so basic to good reading. For instance, dialog should, among other things,

- delineate characters
- convey feeling or emotion
- move the plot along
- add sharpness and color and help establish locale
- break up long passages of straight narration or exposition

**Purpose of dialog**

I encourage my novels students to "show" rather than "tell." One of the best ways to do this is to use conversation. Yet dialog must never interrupt the narrative; rather, its purpose is to push the story along. It must always present characters as real people, and your fictional people must stay "in character." If your heroine is gentle, soft-spoken, you can't have her yelling her head off, or behaving like a shrew. A detective, used to brittle, laconic speech, can't suddenly without reason mumble like Casper Milquetoast.

**Dialog in fiction**

In fiction dialog must be kept natural and real. Watch out for stilted, patronizing, overwritten speech. Learn the art of condensing and compressing, and use only the essential ingredients in any conversation. Edit. Throw out each word, each speech that clutters up your paragraph. Toss the inconsequentials, the idle chit-chat, out the window.

On the flip side of the coin, however, don't be too pugnacious in your attempt to squeeze your fictional conversation to the point where your people act and talk like flimsy paper mache puppets. Read your dialog aloud and listen to it, and ask yourself; "Is this really my Selena talking?"

Avoid cliched expressions—unless your character has a fetish for mouthing trite phrases.

Dialog must be easy to read. If the reader is forced to stop and "translate" the sentence to understand its meaning, you've lost him and the illusion is shattered. Stick with plain old U.S.A. English. If your Selena speaks in dialect, don't beleaguer your reader with a maze of mumbo-jumbo; use idiomatic expressions, those bits of characteristic speech from specific locales. This adds color and freshness to your conversation. Remember, dialog is not an end in itself; it's one of your best tools in creating illusion and portraying emotion and action; so handle it with care.

**Speech keys**

What about speech keys? How often must you identify who is speaking? Never let your reader "count back" to see who is saying what. Should you tack on *Joe said—Mary said* at the end of each speech and bore your reader to death? Tone it down by interspersing your conversation with other action or description showing who is speaking. It will add emotion as well.

**Dialog in non-fiction**

How do you employ dialog in nonfiction? By using direct speeches from sources quoted; by highlighting the meat of the article through quotation emphases. Conversation used in a true adventure can be highly effective if used especially to underscore conflict or suspense.

Dialog is a two-way street. It goes somewhere. A fresh viewpoint, a pat on the back, a moment of truth . . . it can lead a reader to God!

# Section VI
# The Writer's Pitfalls

# 27

# It was a fine idea, but...

KENNETH WILSON
Editor, *Christian Herald*

. . . It was too cosmic in scope. There may be places for that, but the effective article is usually focused on some manageable and usually modest aspect of a topic. This small story then represents the large story.

. . . It was, if I may put it gently, over your depth. If we want an expert opinion, we will go to an expert. There are things in which every writer is expert, certainly in his or her own experiences.

. . . You didn't get me excited about the subject. An article may be competently written with the commas in all the right places and the words spelled correctly, but still be pedestrian. There has to be an emotional impact, a touch of entertainment, along with information.

**Appeal to many readers**

. . . The topic did not have sufficiently general interest. Though a magazine aims for a range of subject matter within an issue, each article should have an appeal to many readers rather than to few.

. . . You didn't show how the idea related to me. There may be topics far removed from my interests that I should know about and would even like to know about, but I am most concerned about those which impinge upon my life. Most of them do. Show me.

. . . It came out sounding like a sermon. Sermons are fine in their place, and sometimes their place is in magazines. Perhaps what I really

*The most common problem in manuscripts* Christian Life *editor, Jan Franzen, rejects is mediocrity. The manuscripts say little that is new, fresh, or significant.*

mean is that it sounds preachy because you do not include yourself in the audience.

. . . It is dogmatic. There is a place for dogmatism. But not many people are convinced of something simply because someone says it is true. What is the evidence? Make a case so strong that the reader will agree without your demanding that he do so.

. . . The article didn't add to the fund of knowledge already easily available on the topic. You are like the person announcing breathlessly six months after the election, "Wow! Carter was elected!"

. . . There was no joy in it. What you said was all true, but it left me feeling flat, unresponsive. It did not help me tap divine resources or sense the presence of God.

**Encourage reader to ask questions**

. . . It did not make me want to do anything to help solve the problem. Some fine articles do not offer answers, but at least they should encourage me to ask questions.

. . . You thought it improper to write in first person, when this is the area in which the beginning writer can best compete with professionals. No one else can duplicate your experience. That experience must, of course, have implications for the reader.

. . . You thought the idea was all that was necessary, and that good writing didn't matter.

. . . It came two months after a seasonal deadline, and to buy it will mean holding it for a year.

. . . It had local interest only.

. . . We used a similar article recently.

. . . Unfortunately, you didn't have the resources to deal with the subject adequately. That's not necessarily your fault and may be our fault. Some subjects require a heavy financial investment in research and time.

. . . The query letter, in which you were informal and unself-conscious, was better than the finished article, in which you were very self-conscious and uptight.

# 28

# How to handle rejections

JAMES RUARK
Managing Editor, Zondervan

Every writer who has ever received a rejection slip knows by now that *Jonathan Livingston Seagull* ricocheted around children's departments in a half-dozen or so publishing houses before an adult editor accepted it and came up with a surprise best seller.

Jim Bishop researched *The Day Lincoln Was Shot* for twenty-two years, offered it unsuccessfully to five publishers in turn, and finally persuaded Harper & Row to take a chance with it. The late Bennett Cerf of Random House had rejected it with the remark, "Jim, every kid knows your story. They even know who did it."

Margaret Hill, novelist and short-story writer, conceded that she once sold a story on its one hundred twenty-second submission. An extreme example, but hardly unique.

No writer has escaped the rejection-slip phenomenon. For some, the ratio of hits to misses is simply appalling. And each slip—be it form letter or not—brings a wince of pain to the writer. The object of his hard work, stolen time, and outpoured soul has been coldly dismissed with a peremptory statement that the manuscript "does not meet our publishing needs at this time." Impersonal, undebatable, final—no!

What is a writer to do? What does the rejection slip mean in regard to that piece or the writer's skill as a whole? Should the author try again with that publisher with the same or a different manuscript? Most important, what can a writer learn from his experience to improve his opportunities for acceptance? Though each publisher has his own way of handling rejections, in the end it's not all that difficult to understand his viewpoint and what he is telling the writer, even in an impersonal form. The observant writer will make some educated guesses, adapt, and rescue a rejection out of dejection to a new connection.

**Ask questions**

A rejection should cause a writer to ask questions first of all about his work. It is possible, of course, that the manuscript simply was not suited to the publisher's particular list: the house doesn't do poetry; another work on the same topic is already in progress; the publisher specializes—evangelical Christian books or cookbooks or science textbooks only, for example. Perhaps the publisher won't read unsolicited manuscripts (but remember that he *will* read query letters).

More often than not, however, the reason for rejection lies in the manuscript itself. As Jim Bishop's experience shows, sometimes an editor makes a poor judgment. But publishers are looking for new material day in and day out; if a manuscript gets turned down, it's most likely because the publisher felt it didn't have what it takes.

**Why?**

A rejected writer wants to ask, why? A form return is especially discouraging for this reason. It is futile to ask the publisher for more information. First, an editor has neither the time nor the facilities for explaining every rejection. Second, to persist with an editor may place him in the uncomfortable and unfair position of having to hurt your feelings more than the rejection slip did. The editor wants to make the rejection as tolerable as possible.

John Ciardi wrote of how difficult this can be: "There is this ego facet to us all, and when a poet says, 'Tell me what you think of this poem I have written,' he means, 'Oh, praise me! Praise me!'. . .What you have written is obviously bad, and how can I explain its badness to you, as I must if I am to keep you from making a life-size mistake?. . .Don't think badly of me. I am trying to warn you away from a disastrous gamble." Your work may not be nearly so bad as that poet's; but whatever its weaknesses, the publisher wants you to discover them for yourself.

**Is a publisher's door still open?**

Another question a writer will raise is, how long is a publisher's door open to me after a rejection? The answer is "probably always," as long as an author shows enough talent and wisdom to keep a publisher interested. A publisher will weigh each work on its merits. Writers grow; one work is different from another; publishers are in business to publish. Sometimes a rejection will take the form of a semipersonal letter in which the publisher expresses the hope that the writer will consider him for future submissions. This should be taken at face value: it is an encouraging expression that the publisher sees a measure of talent and potential.

**Is a publisher interested in a manuscript he already rejected?**

Is a publisher interested in a manuscript he has once rejected? Not unless he initiates discussion with the writer, expressing continued interest and suggesting specific revisions.

**Will an editor suggest other publishers?**

Will an editor suggest other publishers for a work he can't accept? Often he could do so, but he won't, with very, very few exceptions. A major reason for this is "professional propriety"—one publisher's

*Free-lance writer, Don Brown, puzzles over the rewrite of a rejected manuscript.*

respect for another. A publisher does not wish to place any obligation on another. Moreover, an author should have the resourcefulness to familiarize himself with the publishing scene and track down the appropriate markets.

One of an editor's greatest assets is "instinct." Given an equal number of pluses and minuses for a manuscript, an editor occasionally resolves his ambiguity by responding to his "gut feelings." His instinct sometimes leads him to accept, but often to reject. It would be disconcerting for a writer to know of this subjective element, yet every good editor knows better than to ignore it. Instinct is intangible, but real and reliable nonetheless.

Ben Hibbs, long-time editor of *The Saturday Evening Post,* was asked on what basis he made decisions regarding manuscripts.

"Intuition," he responded. "People who work on magazines have to have a seventh sense which tells them what great masses of people like to read."

This instinct can work to a writer's advantage. If a new writer shows promise, the editor may write an encouraging letter, asking to see the next work or giving specific suggestions for improvement.

"Every editor is on the lookout for promising newcomers," writes Lawrence P. Ashmead, editorial director of the Doubleday Crime Club, "and it's one of the great joys of publishing when attention and encouragement eventually produce a publishable book."

In the absence of such encouragement, a rejected writer may be tempted to question the publisher's action as unfair. Since rejection sometimes has a lasting sting, an author should be careful, if he chooses to respond to an editor's decision, that he not express hostility and thereby prejudice a publisher against him for the future.

The form that the rejection takes may reveal much to an author. If he feels no sense of encouragement, if he does not feel any sense of personal attention, he should accept the fact that this particular manuscript and that particular publisher are not the right connection.

**Simultaneous submissions**

There is, however, one condition that readily prejudices a publisher against a manuscript—simultaneous submissions. This cardinal rule is for all intents and purposes inviolable: most publishers will not look at a manuscript if they suspect it has been offered to someone else at the same time. The time an editor or a staff of editors invests in a manuscript is too great to justify the gamble a simultaneous submission involves. A serious writer will avoid this practice.

It is not so with query letters. A simple query involves little commitment of time and effort. If a writer chooses to include a synopsis, table of contents, or writing sample, he is asking more of the publisher and, therefore, should safeguard the publisher's interest accordingly by foregoing simultaneous offerings.

**A dog-eared manuscript**

A work that has "been around" for a while, in and out of the hands of publishers, presents another problem for the writer. How much stock does a publisher place in the dog-ears on a manuscript? Generally, not a lot. The dog-ears may indicate that the writing simply isn't worthy of publication.

But publishers acknowledge that manuscripts sometimes do not find the right market quickly; so they are still interested in seeing what the work holds for them. Thus, it is not necessary to retype a manuscript between every submission. If a manuscript is typed according to the standard rules—double-spaced, on one side of good stock, 8½ by 11, with adequate margins—dog-ears will not prejudice an editor against it. The writer must be pragmatic; at the same time he must remember that first impressions endure.

Other questions a writer may ask with rejection slip in hand can be summarized thus: If I am persuaded that my work is worthy of publication, what can I do to get a publisher that I haven't already done? If an article or book has any merit, it will link up with a publisher eventually if the writer is persistent, observant, and teachable.

Dale Copps, who is both editor and author, puts it succinctly, wearing his editorial hat: "We don't approach work with a 'show me' attitude. Rather, the raw material that comes into our hands is deemed innocent, publishable, great, and just-what-we've-always-been-looking for, until it proves itself otherwise. The fact that it does prove itself otherwise time and again never dampens the vigor of our search. That search into the unknown material remains one of the most stimulating aspects of our occupation."

So what if Simon & Schuster wasn't excited when one of their authors "came along with an outline about a crazy captain and a ship's mutiny"? Herman Wouk scooped up his manuscript for *The Caine Mutiny* and had it published elsewhere.

As John J. Geoghegan of Coward, McCann and Geoghegan, said it, "I firmly believe that everything publishable is published in due course"—adding in the same breath, "plus a lot that would be no loss to civilization if it were not."

# 29

# Turn rejects into sales

LOWELL RAYMOND
Free-lance author

A few days ago I received a check for a short story that sold on its 40th trip through the mails.

Financially this wasn't a profitable undertaking, but the editor wrote: "This check is in no sense a remuneration for your story. Your larger compensation will come from the help given our thousands of readers."

Earlier this month an editor accepted another of my stories on its 22nd trip; and today I received from a Christian youth magazine a check for an article that found an editorial home on its 28th submission. Three months ago I received checks for two other manuscripts that were accepted on their 25th journeys.

I cite these experiences because many competent Christian writers figuratively bury a script after it has been rejected only a few times.

Amazing? Hardly! After talking to scores of writers at Christian conferences over the last twelve years, I'm convinced that most of them are failing to perform their full duty to themselves—and to their Lord—by giving up too soon in their selling efforts.

If you have been writing and studying long enough to be reasonably familiar with the basic techniques of writing Christian fiction and articles, and if you have written a manuscript that you like and "feel," and

**At least twenty chances**

that you believe will help someone else, give it at least twenty chances—more if you've received any editorial encouragement.

Many writers who stop too soon seem unaware of the fact that a large number of manuscripts are rejected for reasons other than lack of merit: (1) overstocked, (2) wrong word length, (3) wrong slant, (4) no longer use fiction (or that particular type of article).

And don't panic just because an editor says, "Characters are wooden," "Plot is trite," or "Style needs improvement." Any rejection specifying lack of merit (such as poor characterization, inadequate motivation, unconvincing and unrealistic plot, or stilted dialog) is a rejection based on the opinion of only one editorial office. Another equally competent editor may consider the script excellent. I have seen this demonstrated in many cases. I recall one special script of mine in this category that sold on its 29th trip to one of the better youth magazines. It was even featured on the magazine cover.

And my biggest all-time sale was a manuscript accepted on its ninth trip by the magazine that had rejected it on its first trip for some of these same reasons.

All this explains why the hopes of free-lance writers should not be killed by disparity of editorial opinion, regarding such basics as: Is the story or article convincing? Do the characters come to life? Is the motivation clear and sound?

**Vast editorial differences**

Remember, even if every editor who has judged a manuscript were equally well-trained in editorial work, there still could be vast differences of editorial opinion about the script. The contrariety of judgments would be explained largely by the editor's background differences (religious, educational, occupational, family, temperamental, etc.). In other words, their editorial differences would be explained chiefly by the simple fact that they are human.

**Study each criticism**

The moral of this is: study each editorial criticism honestly and eagerly—but don't let it floor you. (And as I say this, I sincerely join those who believe that nearly all Christian editors are the writers' dedicated, helpful friends!)

Regardless of the number of times you submit a manuscript, you should reread it critically and prayerfully each time to improve it if possible. And retype it if in doubt.

You may sell it more quickly and may receive maximum cash for it. And you will receive that "larger compensation" not measurable in money. Better reach for one of those rejects.

30

# Those publishers called vanity

JAN FRANZEN
Executive Editor, *Christian Life*

Anyone can get his book manuscript published if he has enough money. True or false?

True. And I do mean *published* and not just *printed.*

How? Through a company which likes to be known as a "subsidy publishing house" but which more often is referred to as a "vanity publishing house" (so named because an author's vanity is claimed to be the reason he wants his book to come off the press after a regular publishing house has turned it down).

Before we get into the pros and cons of vanity publishing, let's compare its modus operandi with that of the more typical publishing business.

**Typical publishing houses**

A typical publishing house will not take a manuscript unless it believes there is sales potential. When it sees a book as marketable, it is willing to invest its editors' time in rewriting and/or editing to bring the book up to professional level. It invests in the printing, jacket design, and promotion. In other words, the publishing house shares the risk with the author, who gets a certain percent of the sale price of each book (called a royalty).

**Vanity publishing**

On the other hand, a vanity publisher will take any manuscript submitted. The author pays a stated fee (usually $5,000 to $7,500). The publisher usually does not edit, but merely prints the book. He does design the jacket, and allocates a small percentage of your fee for publicity. Instead of taking from six to twelve months to get your book off the press (as in the case of a regular publishing house), the vanity publisher can have it off the press in two to three weeks.

Now let's see how all this works. When you've decided on the theme of your book, prepared an outline and table of contents, and have at least two chapters written, you're ready to query an editor.

Let's say you've done this — and haven't received even one faint word of encouragement from the ten editors you've queried.

So, convinced that your story is worth telling, you've applied yourself to your typewriter, and you've completed all 200 pages.

You box your brain child and send it off, with a covering letter, to another editor. No interest. Another editor. No interest. Another editor. . . . Finally you reach the point of no return.

Sure, most bonafide publishing houses will pay you 10 percent royalties on your book up to 10,000 sales: 12 percent on sales up to 15,000, etc. Sure, you won't have to pay them one red cent. Sure, they'll advertise your book, jacket it, get articles written about it. Sure, IF they accept it.

But at this point you're discouraged. You see an ad in a reliable magazine, something like: "Looking for a publisher? We can get your bestseller off the press in less than two weeks."

You write the company . . . or several similar companies. You discover that for between $5,000 and $7,500 you can have 3,000 copies of your 192-page book published in record time. You'll receive 40 percent royalties on each book sold. (What you must realize is that even if your book sells 1,500 copies, you are, in effect, paying yourself the royalties.) And, although some 10 percent of your investment is earmarked for advertising and promotion, you'll find that $500 doesn't go very far (not even a page in most publications; sometimes only 4 to 5 inches).

Is it worth it to you? That's a question you'll have to answer.

As one editor of a Christian publication says, "Some people have something to say to a limited market; or have a lot of relatives who would benefit from their book. If they have an extra $5,000 kicking around, this might be a good investment. ."

And once in a while, a subsidy publishing company will come up with a bestseller. This decision demands a lot of prayer and motive-searching. But investigate carefully before you shell out.

31

# Quick way to the "out" tray —cliches

EDITH QUINLAN
Editor, Baptist Publications

*Burning the midnight oil* reviewing freelance manuscripts, I have made a discovery which hit me *like a bolt from the blue.* I'll *call a spade a spade* and say that writers who are misers with words are *few and far between. To add insult to injury,* many writers—especially in the evangelical market—work with worn-out words and expressions. Cliches.

*Needless to say,* my rejection letter urges the writer to *nip in the bud* the temptation to use cliches. Even if he must work into the *wee small hours,* I tell him, he must *employ his utmost capabilities* to delete phrases and expressions which are *better left unsaid.*

I tell this *"diamond in the rough"*—the aspiring writer—that *after all is said and done,* his writing will meet an *untimely end* unless he *keeps abreast of the times* by questioning words and expressions before he uses them. If he will put such *method to his madness,* he will, *in due time,* become *the proud possessor* of a salable manuscript, and he will be *as happy as a lark.* Otherwise, I tell him, he just might some day be a writer who is *as hungry as a bear.*

Frank Sullivan, the *New Yorker's* cliche expert, has been collecting trite expressions for years. Some of those used in these opening paragraphs are from his list of cliches.

"The test of good writing," said Christopher Morley, "is the power to set fire to that damp sponge called the brain."

If writing is liberally sprinkled with worn-out words, it amounts to pouring water rather than fuel on that damp sponge, and it will not ignite.

To have a healthy respect for words is a healthy way to begin. Words! They can be so meaningless—and so meaningful. Words! They can be so frustrating—and so fascinating. Words! They can be like bombs that blast open people's minds, or like empty shells that whizz by indifferent minds. Finding the right word, using it in the right way and in the right place, is a clue to success in expression. This means you eliminate trite phrases from your writing.

**A clue to success in expression**

How do you do this? Start with your first draft. Discipline yourself to detect hackneyed expressions. When you reread your rough draft, underline everything you recognize as a tired and stale expression. Then go to the dictionary, thesaurus or some other source, or your own mind and experience, to pull out a fresh expression that will say what you want to say in a crisp and lively way.

Which of these two replies would you prefer? A writer who was compiling a book wrote to two authors to ask permission to quote from their books. Here are the replies: "It was with great pleasure that I received your letter of August 12th, requesting permission to quote from my book (title). I have considered the matter and decided that such permission shall be granted." The second letter said, "By all means quote from my book—and thanks."

**Develop a way with words**

Our readers are not a captive audience. If we want to keep them turning pages—with interest, rather than tossing the article aside with indifference—we must develop a way with words.

Mark Twain said, "The difference between the right word and the nearly right word is the difference between lightning and the lightning bug." Many writers settle for the lightning bug. They miss the lightning. And so do their readers!

# 32

# Yield not to temptation

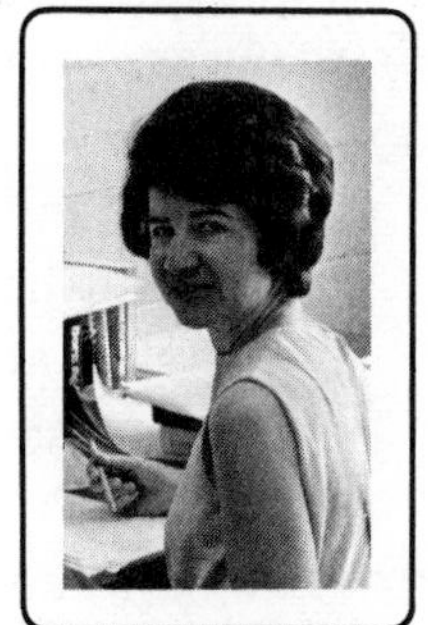

LILA BISHOP
Book Editor, Creation House

So you are a Christian writer. You realize, of course, that this designation is not a license to preach. Obviously, many writers do not. The literature of the Church abounds with warmed-over sermons constructed by individuals who mistook a typewriter for a pulpit.

True, for several centuries most of the writings in the English language had a moral tone. Even public school textbooks had a moral tacked on to each lesson.

But today we live in a different world—a more secular world. People are better educated, more sophisticated, more independent, less inclined to take advice. Preaching turns modern readers off. It is too negative. Writing that spells everything out insults the reader's intelligence and labels the author as an amateur or a hack. And the modern reader more quickly detects a self-righteous attitude on the part of the author.

**Recognize preachiness**

But are you able to recognize preachiness? Can you see it in the examples below?

> It was like Mark had stabbed me the day he said, "Jesus! Jesus! I can't stand to hear that name any more."
>
> A few months later he was asking me to pray with him for

special concerns and for witnessing to his classmates and teachers. He talked about God as easily as discussing the latest football scores.

But that path to the Lord does not lead straight upward. There is much backtracking. Praise the Lord for this awareness. If we shrank back each time there was a critical or angry remark, we would rarely witness. Jesus certainly aroused antagonism and so did His apostles. Many of us felt antagonism toward those who witnessed to us but now we love them all the more because they cared for us.

"Wait a minute," I objected. "How can you possibly tell somebody what he has, or has not experienced—when you weren't in his skin at the time? You can tell him what you think the Scriptures say. But to go beyond that is presumptuous—and dangerous."

Judging another's religious experience is always dangerous, as the Pharisees of Jesus' day, and even Paul, found out. But still we do it.

Pretty obvious, wasn't it? People have far more difficulty spotting unnecessary moralizing in their own writing. One writes an article with the intention of communicating certain truths. He must be sure the reader does not miss these truths.

**Getting your point across**

However, there are many ways to get your point across without preaching. Try humor, irony, or a parable, for example. Spoofing a human weakness or foible makes a strong impression on the reader's mind. Several writings of this type have become classics in English literature, i.e. "To a Louse: On Seeing One on a Lady's Bonnet at Church," and *Gulliver's Travels.*

When C. S. Lewis wanted to encourage Christians to stand fast in their faith during times of spiritual dryness, he did not exhort; he chose letters as the vehicle for his message. He had the devil, under the name of Screwtape, write to one of the demons.

The dryness and dullness through which your patient is now going are not, as you fondly suppose, your workmanship; they are merely a natural phenomenon which will do us no good unless you make good use of it.

> To decide what the best use of it is, you must ask what use the Enemy wants to make of it, and then do the opposite . . .
>
> He (God) leaves the creature (Christian) to stand up on its own legs—to carry out from the will alone duties which have lost all relish. It is during such trough periods, much more than during the peak periods, that it is growing into the sort of creature He wants it to be . . .
>
> —*The Screwtape Letters*

Does the following excerpt sound preachy to you?

> If I am afraid to speak the truth, lest I lose affection, or lest the one concerned should say, "You do not understand," or because I fear to lose my reputation for kindness; if I put my own good name before the other's highest good, then I know nothing of Calvary love.
>
> —*If*

What method is the author, Amy Carmichael, using to communicate a moral truth?

As a rule, resist the impulse to moralize. However, if an insight or understanding is essential to your story, be sure to relate that insight in terms of the thought process of the character in the story, not as an editorial remark. As an illustration, take the first quotation given in this article. After the words "football scores," the writer could have said something like this: "All the hurt from those early encounters with Mark melted away. It was well worth the pain."

Related as an experience of the author, the lesson learned no longer sounds preachy.

**Most effective method to make your point**

Perhaps the most common and most effective way to make your point is to present a positive example which people will want to emulate. The example can take the form of an anecdote, short story, or a whole book.

Note how the following reveals the nature of true Christian love.

> In announcing the death of Princess Alice to the House of Commons, William Gladstone told this moving story.
>
> The little daughter of the Princess was seriously ill with diptheria. The doctors warned the Princess against kissing her

daughter. Breathing the child's infected breath would endanger her own life. On one occasion, when the child was struggling to breathe, the mother took the little one in her arms to keep her from choking to death. Gasping, the child said, "Mama, kiss me!"

Unthinking of self, the mother tenderly kissed her. Princess Alice contracted diptheria and some days later died a sacrificial death.

—*Christian Life*

When using an example such as this, you will never need to tell your readers that they should be more loving, patient, trust God more, or whatever. The actions, words and thoughts of your character forcefully communicate that message.

To sum up, allow me to deliver a two-word sermon of my own. DON'T PREACH.

# Section VII
# The Writer and the Editor

# 33

# Consider a publication's personality

JERRY JENKINS
Managing Editor, *Moody Monthly*

Have you ever told a writer how lucky he or she was to have been published in such-and-such magazine? Or has anyone ever hit *you* with that left-handed compliment?

"Getting published" is hardly the result of luck. Some say, "Luck may have put me in the right place at the right time, and luck may have put my manuscript on the editor's desk just when he needed that type of a story, but it was the work I put into it that made it a sale."

There's a lot of truth to that. The luckiest novice could run into a big time editor somewhere and enjoy the good fortune of discussing a common interest. "We could use an article on that subject," John Editor might say.

"I will turn my file of notes into a manuscript and have it to you by next week," Freida Freelance might respond.

What a break! But where is Freida if the manuscript stinks? She's going to wish she'd never been so lucky. Not only has she missed a great opportunity, but she has also tainted her reputation with what could have become a key market source.

So, luck schmuck. That kind of luck could be an albatross. Give me instead the sort of luck that comes from hard work and careful market research.

**Market research**

Market research? What a sophisticated term for "hoping to get my piece published!" Perhaps, but you'll find that market research is the name of the game. Those writing friends who are so consistently "lucky" are the ones who have learned precisely what their target markets need.

They have considered the personalities of the publications they want to write for.

**No short-cut**

There is no shortcut. You must read the last several issues, as many as it takes for you to get the feel of the magazine. What is the audience? What are the magazine's goals? What is it trying to say? A good publication will make these things clear in each issue, and if it doesn't—if you can read three or four issues and still be in the dark about where it's going—you don't want to write for it anyway.

Consider the Sunday school papers as an example of publications who have separate and distinct personalities. Besides each being aimed at a different age grouping, there are other differences. You know you can write, so why is the publisher rejecting your super idea for an article about Camp Big Trunk?

You've hit the wrong publisher. Sure, it's a great idea. Yes, there is a Sunday school paper publisher out there who might just love it. But if you send it to the one that publishes only people-centered stories, you've missed. Read several recent issues and see if your target publisher runs articles on events, or movements, or happeings, or places. Nope. People. People from places, maybe. People who work at Camp Big Trunk, maybe. But not just a story about a thing.

**Bigger issues to consider**

There are bigger issues to consider, of course. *Moody Monthly* is phasing out its promotional blurbs in the secular writer's market listings. People who are not *born-again, Bible-believing, Christ-centered* individuals see words like that in the listing, and not realizing that their ignorance of such terms should eliminate *Moody Monthly* as a target market for them, send in articles on everything from the Golden Rule to fiction "with a good moral."

Learn the personality of your target market. Read it. Correspond with the editors. Then, when you're ready to query him, blow him out of his chair with an idea so perfect for his readership that he has to give you a green light.

Then be sure that the same "luck" you used getting in the door goes into your writing.

34

# Getting an editor interested

LESLIE H. STOBBE
Editor, Moody Press

Where I grew up we depended on flags. No, not the Stars and Stripes, nor the Union Jack (that's before the Maple Leaf took over in Canada!). One flag was on the mailbox to stop a speeding mail carrier when we had mail out and he had no mail to put in. Another was to let the milk truck driver know we had ten-gallon cans sitting in the cool water of the milk house. And I remember the dispatcher at a nearby station putting out the flag when he had express parcels for the train.

That taught me something about flagging an editor before he attached a rejection slip to my manuscript. Strangely enough, I learned even more about getting an editor interested from a very old book, the Bible. I stumbled across Luke's method for attracting a reader (editor?) only after I had attached a few rejection slips to manuscripts myself. See if you can identify five hints from Luke 1:1-4 that will help you gain an editor's attention.

**Five hints**

Ready?

First, let the editor know that you have a clearly defined target audience in mind. In a day where ethnic barriers were more pronounced than now, Luke targeted his material for Theophilus, a fellow Greek. Of course, he also kept in mind that Theophilus was a new believer, needing "milk" not "meat." So he wrote in a narrative

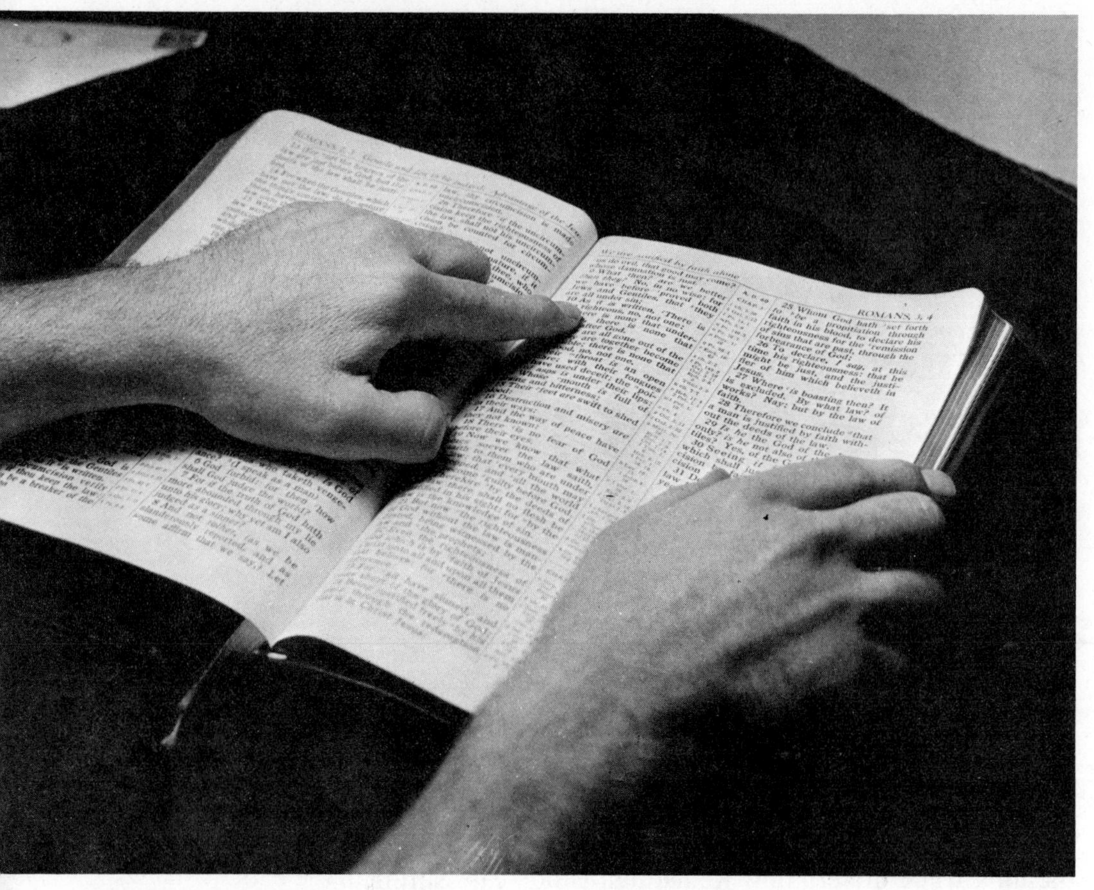

*Believe it or not, the Bible can even offer guidelines to writers.*

style. The narrative style of writing has a built-in interest factor.

**Define target reader**

Who is your target reader? Can you define him so closely that in your mind's eye he sits in front of your desk as you write? If so, give the editor this description—and always keep him in mind as you develop your manuscript.

As a second step, let the editor see that you know about existing literature or formats. Luke had checked already extant materials and came to the conclusion something new was needed for Theophilus. Visit church libraries and local booksellers, check periodical indexes, making sure your idea isn't already in print. And, if it is, be sure the publisher you have in mind hasn't already published an article or book like yours. If you do this, you'll have the instant attention of any jaded editor, provided the subject is one in which he is interested.

Your third step involves research on the topic. Luke writes that he did special research to make his account original in many ways. Normally you do not need to tell an editor you've done original research. Your content will reflect this. Clear negative giveaways are footnotes listing only secondary sources—or a bibliography several years out of date.

**Negative giveaways**

Catch the fourth step? Be selective in materials so that everything focuses on your themes or helps along your plot development. Luke could have written a much larger book, but he picked out those incidents and words of Christ that, under the guidance of the Holy Spirit, would help achieve his goal of an orderly presentation of the life of Christ. Disorganized material, a tendency to go off on tangents, loses the attention of an editor so fast he can't wait to slap a rejection slip on your manuscript.

What have we missed? Purpose. Luke clearly enunciates his purpose. Does your purpose show in your letter, in your material? Or are you fuzzy on your goal?

Recently an eminent theologian and head of a seminary sat down to rewrite his book. Evaluation of his manuscript revealed he had tried to write for both the academic and the lay reader. He also thought he had made a significant new contribution, only to be told much of his material was already available. Not only that, he had a tendency to repeat himself—carrying on his oral teaching habit. In his case his reputation guaranteed him the editor's attention, but it did not prevent the rewrite. Do it right the first time and you'll get the editor's attention even without a "big name."

**Do it right the first time**

Ready to put out your own flags for an editor?

# 35

# Advice for the bookworn

PETER E. GILLQUIST
Religious Book Editor,
Thomas Nelson, Inc.

A great frustration for writers—both new and sometimes even old—comes in wondering exactly how editors think and feel about their manuscripts.

Eight years ago as an unpublished author, I felt the Lord had specifically instructed me to write a book on the grace of God. Many people who had been helped by the material that I taught on the subject enthusiastically agreed. The question was, "How do you bridge the gap between what you *want* to do and what you *need* to do to get your book published?"

The answer is simple: YOU GO TO THE EDITOR. (It's just like evangelism—you can talk about the ten ways to do it or you can do it. In prayer—you can talk about the five ways to pray or you can just pray. In writing—you can figure out three entrees to the editor or you can GO!)

**Three entrees to an editor**

If you need three ways, I suppose you could phone them, write, or visit. I phoned and then I visited. I called the editor, told him what I had in mind, and asked for his suggestions.

Happily, he suggested I come see him and bring with me on paper an outline of what I proposed to do.

During our visit, he not only read over the outline, but asked me to comment on a couple of the chapters in the book from a Biblical point of view. This I did, and he was frankly fired up!

About a year later, *Love Is Now* rolled off the presses.

Okay, that's a success story. All encounters such as this do not end with publication—not by a long shot. But the fact still remains, it's best to begin by going to the people you'd like to be your publisher.

Today as an editor with the Thomas Nelson Publishing Company, we get myriads of what we call "transom manuscripts." They seem to come in over or under the door sometime during the night! Because of the nature of Father Time, we rarely get to give them a fair shake. There are just too many of them. Besides, we have an editorial policy and some goals of our own we are trying to build.

What I appreciate most is the person who gives me a call or drops me a line, letting me know what he or she has in mind. If I like it, I say so; if I don't like it, I say so. And whenever possible, I always try to make constructive comments on how I feel it could be improved.

Don't forget, without manuscripts, editors and publishers would be out of business. They want quality material; they just don't want to be barraged by stacks of unsolicited manuscripts in the morning mail.

So if you've got an idea you feel is from the Lord and you're excited about it, go ahead and drop us a note or give us a call. We can be *very friendly!*

*Many editors would rather read a query than an unsolicited manuscript.*

# Section VIII
# The Writer Decides the Type of Writing

# 36

# What is a plot?

MARY POWELL

Instructor, Christian Writers Institute

Plotting probably is the hardest part of writing fiction. A story without a strong plot may be published because of its emotional impact; however, it won't be satisfying to the reader.

**Definition of a plot**

Simply stated, a plot is the working out of a problem which the main character has. The climax must be satisfying and logical. It may not be happy, it may not be even what you (the author) would like to have happen, but it will satisfy you and the reader because that is the logical solution to *this* problem happening to *this* character.

**Bad plot characteristics**

What isn't a good plot? Only one scene—unless it's a short short story—isn't a good plot.

A story without an ending isn't a good plot either. "The Lady and the Tiger" type of story made it when there wasn't much interesting reading around, but readers now would think you were too lazy to work out an ending. In fact, you'd probably never see the light of print!

Solving the wrong problem is a no-no, too. Sometimes writers have one problem in their opening and the solution to another problem in their climax. And the reader screams, "What happened to the diamond necklace that was stolen on the first page? I'm not interested in the arrival of Gertrude's long lost brother. I want to know what happened to the necklace!"

A general idea isn't a plot; the specific working out of the idea is a plot.

Good plot characteristics

Which brings us to the positive. What is a good plot? It's a series of dramatic scenes, climaxing in the most important scene of the story, which shows the problem solved. A common trait of beginning fiction writers (and some not so beginning) is that the last scene only partially ends the story and they must then use several paragraphs of narrative writing to tell "what happened to the necklace." By that time, your reader couldn't care less.

A good plot is logical. Here's where your characters come into the picture. Really you can't separate characters from plot. Your solution to the problem—and even the problem itself—depends on your characters. The way I'd go about finding a stolen diamond necklace and the way you would probably would be completely different. The way I'd react to a certain situation or certain people would be different from the way you'd react. The solution that would be right for me might not be for you. So be sure the way your protagonist works at solving his or her problem is consistent with his or her personality.

Plotting is hard work. You may beat your head against the wall and cry. But when you're finished you can put that manuscript into an envelope and not be ashamed of its workmanship. And know the Lord won't be either.

## EXAMPLES OF FICTION PLOTS

**As you read the following two short stories, notice how the problem is introduced, then solved; how characters are developed through dialog and description; how scenes move the story forward. Also notice transitions between scenes.**

# Promise of the Forsythia

### RHODA ELIZABETH PLAYFAIR

**N**othing spectacular happened the day Judie came to our hospital to start nursing. I mean—no halo followed her, no trumpets sounded, nothing we could notice—or if there was, we couldn't put a finger on it then.

She came in with an armful of forsythia and put it on the nursing desk. It wasn't blooming. Bare twigs, really, though of course forsythia will break out into yellow blossoms from the barest bits if given half a chance. The thing was, Mrs. Taylor, who's our supervisor, likes the desk uncluttered. Patients who leave us flowers and send us grateful Thank You cards, are not appreciated by Mrs. Taylor.

"It's best to keep things tidy, girls," she tells us in her clipped no-nonsense way. "This is a hospital! Let's have efficiency, and never mind the sentiment!"

I like her, mind. She's fair, and if you keep the rules, you're okay. But that morning, seeing Jude breeze in with the forsythia, I knew that she was in for trouble.

The matter was brought up at once.

"Miss Forster?" Mrs. Taylor's voice was even, not unkind. "I'm told you brought in the forsythia."

"Yes, Mrs. Taylor."

"Take them away, please. We like the desk kept clear. No extras—flowers, cards, nothing of the sort. You understand?"

"Why, yes, of course. I'll move them," Jude said cheerfully and took the vase down to the service room. I thought she'd thrown them out but when I went down later, I saw them—still in the vase, set in a corner on the floor. I grinned. If Mrs. Taylor saw them there—and anyway, what was the sense? They'd never bloom now, stuck off in a corner without light.

We were on evenings, Jude and I. Three to eleven, supper break at six. I kind of took to her. I don't know why. Or, yes—I guess I do. It was her smile. She had a way of smiling when she looked at you that made you think of green pastures. Which is a dumb thing to say, I suppose, but I don't know how else to put it.

Anyway, on her second night there, we were sitting down to supper in the cafeteria when I noticed she was saying a prayer. I glanced around nervously. We were eating by ourselves but I had an uncomfortable feeling that it wouldn't have mattered to Judie if we'd been surrounded by 3B's entire staff. I took the silverware off my tray with a bit more clatter than was necessary. When I looked up again she was grinning at me, as though she knew what I'd been doing, and why. It made me cross.

"You'd better not do that when there's a crowd around," I said.

"Why not?"

"They'll laugh you off your chair!"

She laughed herself at that. "Oh, Pat! But why? I mean—why would they care?"

"Oh—I don't know." I opened up my crackers, broke them into the soup. "Next thing they'd figure you'd be praying on the wards."

"Well?" Judie smiled. Her smile, as I have said, could take you round the world and back, but I was too outraged to notice.

"You don't mean that you *do?*"

"Do what?"

"Pray on the wards!" My voice came out a whisper. What if someone was listening. . . .

But Judie went on eating cream of mushroom soup with equanimity. "Why, yes, of course. What good would I be by myself? Without the Lord to guide me?"

"Judie." I put my spoon down anxiously and just for once forgot to worry about myself. "You're new here. You don't know. But Mrs. Taylor's *dead* on stuff like that. You work to rule, that's all. Just mind your business and you'll be okay."

"This is my business," Jude said mildly.

I shook my head and sighed. I felt pretty certain that Judith's interpretation of minding-your-business was going to be somewhat different from that of Mrs. Taylor's. And of course I was right.

Things went on for a couple of days without much change. Mrs. Taylor didn't seem to notice the forsythia in its gloomy corner and she had no way of knowing about Judie and the prayers, but it was simply the calm before the storm.

It was the fifth day after Judie's arrival that Mr. Cooper died. He was an elderly patient who'd been on ward for six weeks and he knew he was going. He was one of those religious nuts who kept a Bible by his bed and when we went in with meals or medication, he was often reading it.

Don't ask me how he knew that Jude was a Bible freak, too. I swear there's a kind of radar between people like that. In any case, they seemed to recognize each other and chatted every time they got a chance. The night before he died we were fixing up his bed when he looked at Judie and said simply, "You think you could come back and pray with me, a little later on? If you're not too busy?"

I thought, *Oh, brother! This is it!* and rattled the side of the bed to catch Jude's eye. "Remember—Susan's sick tonight, Jude. We're shorthanded. We'll have to go like mad to get things done." And Mr. Cooper said, "Oh, that's okay then," but she didn't seem to hear.

"I'll be right down when everybody's settled. Don't you worry. There is always time."

I was so mad at Judie I could hardly wait until we got out of Mr. Cooper's room to tell her so.

"Are you *trying* to make trouble?" I hissed. "You know Mrs. Taylor's policy! No member of the staff's supposed to get involved with religion on the ward. Oh, Jude! *Why?* I don't want to see her down on you!"

She looked at me, a kind of puzzled look, and sad.

"Pat," she said patiently, "if you saw someone hungry—really hungry, really needing—and you had food to give him, and you didn't . . ."

"That's different," I said crossly, interrupting. "You always make things sound so, so person-to-person, and you can't! You've got to be objective. You're a nurse!"

She paused at the door of the next room down and looked at me strangely.

"I'm a Christian," she corrected. "My field just happens to be nursing. That's all."

"I don't understand you," I moaned. "And if Mrs. Taylor finds out . . ."

Inevitably, of course, Mrs. Taylor did find out. Sooner or later she was bound to, and while with a little luck it might have been later, things didn't work out that way. It was Mr. Cooper himself who mentioned it sometime during the following day before he slipped peacefully away. It was, as a matter of fact, one of the last things he said.

"Tell Miss Forster the Lord's been with me all the way. And thank her for her prayers."

Well! That got back to Mrs. Taylor faster than you could say penicillin and she called Judie to her office. We couldn't hear what was said—she shut the door so nobody could hear—but we could *see* right through the glass partition, and the expression on Mrs. Taylor's face told the story in itself. Worse than that, word was out on the ward now, too, so that everybody knew what was going on. A few status quo types were solidly behind Mrs. Taylor but most of the staff considered it a joke. I stuck close as an adhesive strip to Jude at supper, knowing what she'd be up against.

"Hi, Jude! I hear the dragon's breathing down your neck!"

"Hey, Judie—pray for me tomorrow, willya? I've got a date with this new guy."

"I can't decide between the roast pork and the chicken! You think the Lord might help me out, Miss Forster?"

I was so embarrassed I hung my head over my baked potato, but as supper progressed I could feel myself getting fighting mad.

"How can you *stand* it, Jude? I'd like to push my pudding in their stupid faces!"

She laughed. "Oh, Pat! You know something? They're saying silly things like that, and making jokes, and being mean because they don't yet know what else to do."

"I don't know, either!" I said honestly. "I mean—you're in big trouble, likely to get fired. You're ridiculed by all the staff—and you can laugh?"

"You said I had to be objective, Pat. And so I am. It's just that my point of reference is a little different from that of the others."

The remainder of the week passed quietly. Everybody had had her fun and not much more was said though I knew very well that as far as the staff was concerned, Jude was on probation. As far as Jude herself went, nothing had changed at all. She went on exactly as she'd done before, caring for her patients and caring for the people she worked with. But I knew Mrs. Taylor was waiting for a slip. It was like living in the eye of a hurricane.

Judie was off the night they brought in Mr. Robson. I've been sorry for lots of patients in the years I've been nursing, but I've never felt as sorry for anyone as I did for Mr. Robson. He was 73 years old and he'd fallen off a ladder. He was paralyzed from the neck down and in such bad shape mentally and emotionally that we couldn't do anything with him. We put patients with back injuries like that on something we call a Stryker frame—a kind of revolving bed, with removable parts that let you turn the whole bed over like a pancake when you want the patient to lie face down. He'd been in this thing for over 24 hours by the time Jude came back on duty and he was beside himself. He moaned ceaselessly, called for the nurses and begged pitifully for help when anyone came near him.

It was after supper. Judie and I were making our rounds when we came to his room. We gave him the prescribed medication and did what we could for him, but still his sobbing followed us as we prepared to leave. I could feel Jude hesitate at the door. I grabbed her arm fiercely.

"Come on eh, Jude? We've got to get the others done!"

But Jude just smiled. "Go on without me for a sec. I've gotta talk to Mr. Robson."

"Oh no you don't . . ."

But she was gone as though I hadn't spoken.

The Stryker was in the reverse position so that Mr. Robson was face down. In order to look into his face, Jude had to kneel on the floor beneath him.

"Mr. Robson," she said gently.

The old man sobbed.

"Mr. Robson, we've done everything we can for you, you know. Everything that nurses and doctors and hospitals can do, I mean. But I know Someone else who can help, if you want Him to. Would you like me to pray with you?"

Great Scott! I stood there absolutely paralyzed myself. The picture was unreal. The old man crying, Judie on her knees, and any minute, down the hall. . . . I closed the door and leaned against it in a panic.

The old man seemed to hear. "Oh, would you please?" he said, and Judie's voice, calm and confiding as a friend who talks with friend, began its prayer. I was so scared I couldn't really take in what she was saying—just that she was talking about Mr. Robson to the Lord Jesus as though the three of them were right there together. And then a queer thing happened. Mr. Robson fell asleep. Right there, while Judie was praying. He quit moaning and began snoring, very gently, and quite at peace.

"Judie," I gasped. "Oh Judie—let's get out of here!" and Judie calmly got up off her knees and went on down the ward.

I'm not much given to prayers but even I said one that night in hopes she wouldn't be found out, which only goes to show how little I know about things working together for good!

It was Mr. Robson himself who spread the word. I couldn't blame him. I mean—if you've been lying for all those hours like a tortured animal in a cage without hope, and suddenly—well, suddenly you're a changed man—you've got to talk about it! And Mr. Robson was a changed man. I don't mean he was able to leap off the old Stryker frame and start walking (though he did, in due course, advance to a wheel chair and later to a walker). The change was in the way he *felt*. He'd gone to meet the Lord, and having met Him, was at peace. He was so excited he was babbling to everybody.

The staff was dumbfounded. "What happened to *you*?" Each one would ask on entering his room, and Mr. Robson would tell them gleefully.

The story was up and down the ward and through the hospital so fast it might as well have been put on the intercom: Some nurse up on 3B had put her foot in it again! The puzzling thing was, laughs and jokes aside, this poor old guy who'd been in misery since admitting, was *himself* sharing the laughter and jokes and telling everyone he was a new man! It was too much!

I figured Mrs. Taylor would be waiting for Judie with a scalpel, but when we first came on duty, nothing happened. I knew she had found out. She makes the rounds of every room herself when she comes on, and the change in Mr. Robson would have smacked her in the face the minute she stepped inside his door. So how come she wasn't saying anything?

At supper break I steered Jude to the farthest corner of the cafeteria.

"Has she said anything?"

"Not yet."

"I don't like it! She's playing cat and mouse! I wish she'd get it over with."

Jude looked beyond me with a grin. "I

think she may be going to."

"Oh Jude!" I wailed. "Why can't you ever take things seriously?" and Mrs. Taylor's voice, behind my shoulder, said, "May I sit down?"

I swear my heart stopped beating. Otherwise, why wouldn't I have made a run for it? Instead, I sat there speechless while Mrs. Taylor put her coffee on the table and said to me, "For heaven's sake, Miss Babcock, close your mouth!"

I gulped and looked at Jude, and she was very still. Aware, kind of, and waiting.

"I see that Mr. Robson's outlook," Mrs. Taylor's voice was clipped, no-nonsense, as was customary, "seems considerably improved."

"I'm glad," said Judie simply.

"I hear," her eyes were level, seeking, "you're responsible."

"Not *me*. I only . . ."

"You know what I mean!" Mrs. Taylor said impatiently. She searched Judie's face. "Where did you learn to pray like that?"

"You really want me to tell you?" Judie said slowly.

"I don't know." Mrs. Taylor frowned. "I don't quite know. I know I don't approve—but there is Mr. Robson telling everyone how much better he feels. And I can see he does. As a nurse, I can't explain it. But as a nurse, I can't discount improvement in a patient, either."

"Maybe we don't have to be able to explain it," Judie said. "Not always. I mean, He made blind beggars see, you know. And told the lame to walk. They didn't bother asking how. They just got up and went."

"Well," Mrs. Taylor said. We were for a long moment a small refuge of silence in the echoing bedlam of banging crockery and incessant voices that made up the cafeteria. "Well, now," she said again, and looked at Judie thoughtfully.

"Oh, by the way." She stood up, readying to leave, and I began to breathe again. "While we are on the subject of the inexplicable—those bare bits of forsythia, stuck in a corner of the service room?"

I put my head down in my hands and groaned, but Mrs. Taylor took no notice. "I see they've started blooming in the dark. You'd better put them back out on the desk."



# And Then, On Christmas Eve

## PATRICIA HOUCK SPRINKLE

With a sigh of disgust David Randall shoved his unfinished Christmas sermon across his desk.

"No, no, no," he moaned, clasping his head between his hands. "That's almost exactly what I said last year. Lord, isn't there anything new to say about Christmas?"

He glanced at the digital clock blinking the minutes away. Christmas Eve already, and past noon. In less than 12 hours he would be mounting the high rostrum and peering through candlelight into 2,000 expectant faces to tell them— what?

The biggest crowd of the year, except for Easter, filled the pews of First Memorial Church for the annual Christmas candlelighting service. David knew the sermon wasn't what brought them. Some came for tradition, others for the music, some for the wonder of the tall Gothic sanctuary softened by candlelight, and many for a private time of meditation and prayer.

But a sermon was expected. What could he say that they hadn't heard before?

It wasn't that David was late getting started on the sermon. Since Thanksgiving he had sat in his office and shuffled ideas. But in 15 years at First Memorial he must have said all there was to say about Christmas—several times.

Fifteen years. Had it really been that long? "Such a promising young man," he had overheard one old lady telling another soon after he arrived with the ink still fresh on his doctorate. He wondered what they said now.

Wearily, with an unfamiliar tinge of panic stirring beneath his belt buckle, David pushed back the heavy leather chair and crossed his office to the windows, closed against the noisy street below. As always he admired the leaded casements before he looked at the tiny park across the street. Gothic architecture was heavy for the airy warmth of north Florida, but David loved it. The wavy glass in the diamond panes, the arches, the towering height of the sanctuary reminded him of centuries of history which had brought him and his congregation to this point in time. But what was this point in time? Christmas Eve, and no sermon written.

"Lord, I am so sterile," he confessed, ashamed of a lump that was blocking his throat. "I know it's Christmas, but I feel nothing. We've tried, Lord. We've decorated the chancel tree, we've sung carols. Maybe we're just played out by now. But Lord, I'm so *tired* of Christmas."

There. He'd said it. Thank the Lord he'd only said it privately. For a minister to be tired of Christmas was like a lawyer being tired of justice. Christmas was what it was all about, wasn't it? God coming to earth as a babe in a manger? But it was hard this year to get excited about a plaster babe in a store-bought manger, resting on a red plush carpet under a jeweled window in air conditioned comfort.

Longingly David's eyes rested on the park across from his office. For 15 years he had intended to go sit in that park. When he'd first come to the church he'd envisioned himself composing sermons on the green benches surrounded by playing children and pigeons. The first year, of course, he had deliberately avoided the park. Some parishioners had proved to be acutely conscious of their minister's every activity, and sitting in the park during a work day was hard to explain even if David knew he was working. Then after the first year he had been so busy—a building campaign, an evangelism campaign, a music improvement campaign, a membership drive.

But the little park still waited. Palms and towering oaks reached heavenward while birds home from northern vacations gossiped on every branch. Smug pigeons tottered about hoping for elderly ladies with plastic bags of hoarded crumbs. But where were the people?

Startled, David looked more closely. The park was deserted! Fifteen years ago it had swarmed with children playing games while adults watched from the benches. But today squirrels and birds were sole tenants. When had this desertion begun? Were the green benches beginning to look shabby? He couldn't tell from his second-story perch.

"Well," he decided, "since I can't write my sermon, I might as well go see."

He flipped on the intercom.

"Becky, I'm going across to the park for a while. Hold my calls."

He flipped off the speaker before she could reply. What would she think: The proper Dr. Randall seldom had time for a cup of coffee with his staff, much less to sit in the park. Besides, she knew his sermon wasn't ready—she was waiting overtime to type it. Well, he'd only be in the park for a few minutes, just long enough to collect his thoughts.

Almost defiantly David clumped down the stairs and across the flagstone octagonals of the sidewalk. Jaywalking through Christmas traffic he found himself at last on the very verge of the grass.

"Hallelujah," he breathed, crossing the park in long strides and breathing deeply. It was a day for praise—crisp, warm and slightly breezy. Spanish moss waved from the oaks, and sun streamed through the palms. David chose a bench a short distance from the sidewalk and sprawled on it, eyes closed.

"Ahhh," he sighed. "Why haven't I done this before?"

When he opened his eyes, he was startled to realize that instead of escaping from the church, he now confronted it. Separated from him by sluggish traffic and several yards, the building was slightly unfamiliar.

David considered it through half-closed eyes. "You're a proud old lady," he murmured. "Do you give your members airs, or reflect theirs? And what can I tell you about Christmas that you haven't already heard a thousand times before?"

"Hey, mister, you okay?" The voice was

so unexpected it jerked David's attention to the end of his bench. A small boy of about seven stood there, wearing a dirty blue tee-shirt and jeans.

"Sure I'm okay," said David. "Why?"

The boy wrinkled a freckled, rather dirty nose. "Who you talking to?"

David nodded to the church. "That building over there."

The boy looked from the building to the man. "I never heard a man talking to a building before."

"Oh, I do it all the time. Don't let it bother you." He grinned. "You've only got to worry if you hear it talking to me."

The boy narrowed his eyes, but when he saw David's grin he snickered. "That's a good one, mister. A building talking to a man." He snickered again, then confided, "But you'd better watch who hears you talking to that building. Some folks might think you was . . . " he whirled one finger around his ear.

David nodded gravely. "I'll be careful. Thanks for the warning."

The boy edged his way around the end of the bench and perched on the outside board. "You come here often, mister?"

"This is my first time. Do you?"

"No. I come when I can. It's peace and quiet, you know." He tossed off the adult phrase as though he used it often.

"Peace and quiet?"

"Yeah, you know. No kids yelling upstairs or mama hollering for me to do something or Mrs. Slotts pounding on the floor with her cane." He swung his feet and carefully placed his hands where thin white knees were working their way through his jeans. "What'd you come for, mister? You need peace and quiet too?"

"Sort of. I was working over there . . ." David pointed to the church and the boy's eyes widened.

"You live there? It sure looks neat."

David didn't answer at once, for he had just noticed that the boy's nose was about to spill onto his upper lip. "Need a handkerchief, fellow?" He reached into his back pocket and brought out his own.

The boy took it in amazement. "Cloth kleenex. What they gonna think of next?" He swiped his nose and gave a hefty blow, then wadded the handkerchief and carefully threw it far beyond them across the park.

"Hey!" David's concern for ecology *and* his handerchief made him react automatically. The boy whirled around and, anticipating anger, poised to leave. David forced himself to smile. "Nice throw."

The boy looked pleased. "You ain't seen nothing yet," he said. "I'm gonna play for the Atlanta Braves when I get big, with Hank Aaron. Watch this." He fumbled in the grass for a suitable stick and lobbed it neatly into the street, narrowly missing a red Cadillac.

"You're really good," David admired, "but don't you think you'd do better to practice where people don't get in the way?"

"Aw, there ain't no places to practice around here. Now, mister," he settled himself back on the bench, then paused. "You got a name?"

"Sure. It's . . . " he almost said Dr. Randall—that was what everyone at the church called him except for a few close friends. Why did he hesitate and say to the child, "Call me Dave"?

"Hiya, Dave. I'm Norman." Gravely he put out a grimy palm and they shook. Then he returned to his original sentence. "Now, Dave, tell me," he commanded, hunching himself to the very back of the bench, "do you really live over yonder?"

"No," David told him. "Nobody lives there. It's a church."

"Oh." The boy nodded wisely. "I know all about a church. I went to one once when my grandmama died. They had flowers and music and long couches without cushions all lined up in rows. You got all those things in your church?"

David nodded. "Would you like to see?"

But Norman shrank against the bench. "Naaa. I'd rather sit here and talk. What do you do over there? Do you have to polish all them benches? That must take a lot of time."

Remembering that priests in ancient Israel had indeed devoted their time to tending the temple, David regretted that he had to answer, "No, I work in the office." As he had expected, the boy was unimpressed.

"My ma's a welder," he announced proudly. "There ain't many women welders. Boy, is she good! What do you do in the office?"

"I'm a preacher."

"That sounds like teacher." The boy's tone wasn't at all flattering. "What's a preacher do?"

David thought it over. "Well, I make speeches and I tell people about Jesus to help them when they're sad or sick or dying." How inadequate that was. He tried to think of another way of putting it, but the boy had already seized on one point.

"Is that Jesus like Jesus Christ?" He looked puzzled.

"That's right. Do you know Jesus Christ?"

"Sure." The boy swung his legs and nodded sagely. "I know all about Jesus Christ. Emmanuel says that all the time. Jee-sus *Christ*." His intonation was, David suspected, almost perfect. "Every time Emmanuel falls over my wagon or bumps his head on the back door, that's what he says. Jee-sus *Christ*. Does saying that make people weller?"

David didn't answer, for he was staring at the boy in amazement. Could a child live for seven years in an American city and not know at least the basic stories about Christmas and Easter?

The boy grew impatient. "Well?" he demanded. "Does saying Jee-sus *Christ* make people weller?"

"Who is Emmanuel?" he stalled.

"My mama's boyfriend."

"Oh. So your mom's boyfriend Emmanuel says Jesus Christ all the time." I must remember that line, he told himself.

"Mister, you sure are funny." The child was nearing the limits of exasperation. "First you talk to buildings, then you just say back what I already said. If you don't want to tell me, just say so." He inched himself forward as if to leave, but David put out a hand to stop him.

"No, Norman wait. I'm sorry. You see, I was surprised, because Jesus Christ isn't just something people say. Jesus Christ is a person."

"No joke?" Norman's blue eyes squinted with apprehension. "Boy, he's sure gonna be mad at Emmanuel. You won't tell him, will you? Cause if Emmanuel found out I told you, and if Jesus beat him up, he'd sure come after me with his belt."

"Jesus won't beat Emmanuel up," David assured him. "He's not like that at all. Besides, He's getting ready for His birthday, Christmas."

"Christmas is Jesus Christ's birthday?" Norman beamed. "What d'ya know? It's my birthday, too. Where does he live? Jesus, I mean."

"Well," David hesitated, and then very slowly, picking out every word, he started to tell the story of Christmas—not from a high pulpit surrounded by candlelight, but from a park bench surrounded by traffic and pigeons.

At first the boy was restless. "Another fairy story," he muttered when David was telling about the angel. But when David assured him "Cross my heart and hope to die, it's true," he settled back against the bench and listened intently.

Occasionally he interrupted. "That old hotel manager ought to be beat up. If they'd come to my house we'd a given them my bed." And "Those cows sure musta been surprised, huh? It's a good thing they didn't eat the baby by mistake." And "Those shepherds should a had a tape recorder. I'll bet they coulda sold a billion records of the angels, don't you?" And "Wow, weren't those rich old kings surprised to find they'd come all that way just to see a baby?"

Gradually, too, as the story progressed the boy slowly inched closer and closer to David across the bench. Before the kings reached the manger his small head reached David's armpit and was securely tucked in.

When the story was finished Norman sat quietly for several minutes. When he spoke, his voice was soft with wonder. "God must sure love poor folks," he said. "Looks to me like He'd have had His baby born in a good hotel or a hospital. And rich. Poor people hardly ever get their pictures in the paper. How was anybody gonna know?"

"The stars and the angels," David

reminded him. "Better than newspapers."

"Oh yeah. I forgot. Wouldn't you love to see an angel?"

David nodded. "I sure would. We will when we die, if we love Jesus."

"Do you reckon?" The boy peered up at him. "I heard angels play the harp real good. You reckon any of them play the guitar? I sure would like to learn to pick a mean guitar."

David grinned back at him. "I reckon one or two can."

With a sigh of comfort the boy settled back against David's shoulder, and neither spoke. Their quiet was suddenly filled with bells, the chimes of First Memorial marking the passing of another hour.

The boy jerked up like a shot. "Two o'clock. I musta missed lunch at Mrs. Slotts'. She's gonna skin me." He slid off the bench and took a quick step towards home, then pivoted back.

"Hey, Dave?"

"Yes?"

"Is there more to that story?"

"Sure."

"Well," he hesitated, "maybe I can come back sometime and you can tell me. Think so?"

"I think so."

"Well, when are you gonna be here again?"

Automatically David reached inside his coat pocket for the small black appointment book that ruled his days, but as his eyes met Norman's he withdrew his hand.

"When do you want me to come?"

Norman shrugged his thin shoulder. "I don't know. Sometimes I have to help my mama. How about if I call you under your window?"

David glanced across to his study windows, shut against the noises from below. "Sure," he said. "I'll just keep my window open." Norman nodded as if that was what he had expected.

"Bye, Dave. Thanks." He scampered down the sidewalk and disappeared behind the trees. David watched him go, then stood and slowly stretched.

"Why did I say that, Lord?" he marveled. "You know I can't study with those windows open." He flexed his shoulders. "Boy, I feel like I've been sitting on that bench for hours." Then he grinned. Actually he felt like he'd been on the bench for years. Norman had pulled him from the sidelines of faith and put him back in the ballgame.

Florida Christmas breezes brushed his cheeks as David recrossed the traffic and headed back to his office. He mounted the stairs rapidly, and rushed across his office to fling open the window that faced the park.

"Do you really think he'll come again?" a doubting voice asked, but David knew. Of course he'd come. Not as a small thin boy, perhaps. He might come as a lonely woman in the pew, a dying man in a hospital bed, a saucy little girl in choir. The world was full of Normans who had never been told the Story, or who, told, had never heard.

"And," David hoped wistfully, looking across the street at the empty bench, "he might come back as Norman."

Turning from the park David went to his desk and flipped on the intercom. "Becky?"

"Yessir?"

"Go on home. The sermon came in the park, and I won't need notes."

"Are you sure?" She sounded really concerned. David realized he needed to spend time getting to know her, too—as soon as Christmas was over.

"Go home, Becky," he said. "And don't come back until Monday."

"Why thank you!" He could almost see her gentle smile through the speaker. "Goodbye, then, Dr. Randall. I'll see you at the Christmas service."

Was it his imagination, or did her voice hold a new note of anticipation?

# 37

# Effective devotional writing

MAXIE DUNNAM
World Editor, *The Upper Room*

"I had been wrestling with my dilemma for two weeks. Almost instantly, this morning, the answer was clear."

"I faced my surgery with confidence and hope."

"I'm in the state prison and for the first time I'm confident of God's love!"

These are typical comments from letters that come to my desk daily. A person has read a devotional in *The Upper Room* and, miraculously, it is God's word for that person, that day.

**Don't discount the holy spirit**

How does it happen? First and foremost, don't discount the working of the Holy Spirit. I'm continually amazed at how God uses even weak and inadequate instruments to accomplish His work. John Calvin, writing of the mystery of the Sacrament of Holy Communion, said, "I experience more than I understand." Our words, written and spoken, are often the vehicles used by the Holy Spirit to enter the life of a person. Persons reading and hearing, often experience far more than we even intend to say. So, don't discount the work of the Holy Spirit.

**The personal dimension**

Acknowledging that, there are some recognizable ingredients of effective devotional writing. The *personal* dimension is crucial. In effective writing the "word becomes flesh"—that is, it must come from the flesh of personal experience. The devotionals to which we get the

*Upon his death, V. Raymond Edman left a wealth of devotional books which commanded a large reading audience. Here Edman and his wife were sharing a few quiet moments in the Word.*

most response, are those in which the writer shares a personal experience. Begin your devotional writing with a personal experience. Readers will identify, either because they have had a similar experience, or because in sharing your life you will become a person to them, and thus they will be ready to receive what you have to say.

**Deal with experiences**

Deal not with ideas or concepts, but with experiences. Persons who read devotional books, or magazines, are persons needing guidance and growth. They're looking for spiritual help—primarily, they need a word of hope. You can't give answers, but you can share the source of all answers, Christ—as you share your experience of Him. Norman Cousins said, "An editorial page is an exercise in present tense." Devotional writing should be that—sharing your experience of Christ in the present tense. It is that kind of experience which offers hope.

**Root your words in *the word***

Root your words in *The Word*. God is present in His Word, since it is He Who speaks through Scripture. For that reason our words must be founded in His Word.

Alfred North Whitehead said, "Expression is the one fundamental sacrament." In writing devotionals we are given the opportunity of celebrating the sacrament of expression, and having people whom we don't even know share in that sacrament with us. Our devotionals can be different and powerful if they include these elementary ingredients.

## EXAMPLES OF DEVOTIONAL WRITING

**Anecdotes keep devotional articles from sounding preachy. They add sparkle and human interest. Notice how they are used in the following two articles. Notice, too, how the author zeros in on—and develops—his one basic idea, always relating it to the experiences of the reader.**

# Should We Honor the Mother of Jesus?

LESLIE FLYNN

During a prolonged drought in Australia several years ago, the wild creatures of the bush became so thirsty that they braved even the dangerous dooryards of settlers for a drink of water. The settlers, whose cattle and sheep were dying like flies for lack of water, were constantly on the lookout lest these wild creatures drink what little water was left. Each man hung a loaded gun near his doorway to be used at a moment's notice.

Suddenly one hot summer day, a settler noticed movement in the brush. Instantly he seized his gun and stood ready. Out of the bush a mother kangaroo, with a young one in her pouch, came loping across the brown, arid, open space surrounding the house. Nearer and nearer she came, her beautiful brown eyes fixed beseechingly on the settler. She made her way straight to the tub of water placed there for the use of the few domestic animals that had thus far survived. Still the settler did not shoot.

Reaching the tub, the kangaroo waited, her soft gaze still fixed on the man while the young kangaroo in her pouch drank its fill. Then she turned without taking a drop for herself and loped back across the parched open space and on into the tangled depths of the bush. The settler watched until she disappeared. Then he hung up his gun and, with a catch in his throat, went back to work.

The poet asks, "Whose love can equal the love of a mother?"

Many human mothers have the same spirit of self-sacrifice. Some years ago a woman whose husband had just passed away came to a college town in Kentucky so that her son and a daughter could continue their schooling. She worked all day and half the night to put them through. Just before their graduation, she suddenly died. At the funeral parlor, the son placed his graduation robe and cap at the foot of the casket; the daughter placed her graduation gown and cap at the head.

"We want everyone to know that mother put us through school and that we're grateful," they said.

This month when we honor mothers, how fitting it is to pay tribute to the mother of Jesus. Of all the persons who have lived on this earth, the only one who had the privilege of choosing His own mother was the Lord Jesus Christ. Mary must have been a wonderful girl for Jesus to select her as the human instrument from whom He would be born.

However, we must be careful not to honor Mary more than the Bible does. Over church entrances in Portugal and Italy I have seen paintings of the Trinity—Father, Son and Holy Spirit—crowning Mary "queen of heaven." But nowhere in the Bible is Mary pictured as queen of heaven. Rather, she is presented as being on a subordinate level. For example, one day when Mary and the brothers of Jesus were seeking Him, someone said to Jesus, "Behold, Your mother and Your brothers are outside looking for You."

"Who are My mother and My brothers?"

Jesus answered. "...whoever does the will of God, he is My brother and sister and mother" (Mark 3:32-35).

Another day when a woman in the crowd called out to Jesus, "Blessed is the womb that bore You, and the breasts at which You nursed," Jesus retorted immediately, "On the contrary, blessed are those who hear the word of God, and observe it!" (Luke 11:27,28.) There is no "honor" here.

According to the four Gospels, when the lame, blind or deaf wanted healing, they always asked Jesus, never His mother. And when Jesus was dying, the thief on the cross next to Him asked His forgiveness. He did not go through Mary, even though Mary was standing right there.

After the resurrection, Mary is mentioned only once by name—when she is in the upper room, praying with the disciples (Acts 1:14).

Yet the Bible does say that all generations would call Mary blessed (Luke 1:48).

But for what do we honor Mary—beauty, brains, culture, education, wealth, social status? We are not told that she possessed any of these attributes. Possession of all these qualities would not have immortalized her. What, then, are the qualities for which she should be honored?

First, she was chaste and pure. Nazareth lay in the path of caravans going from Capernaum to seaports. As in all generations, some girls courted affairs with traveling men on the trade routes. Fixing bright ribbons in their hair, they flirted with the merchants. When Mary refused to go, other girls may have told her that she was old-fashioned and missing something. But Mary stuck to her ideals. God honored her because of her purity. And her best-known title today is "The Virgin Mary."

Also, Mary was submissive. When the angel ended his astonishing announcement that Mary was to bear the Son of the Highest who would reign over the house of David forever, and this apart from a husband but by the Holy Spirit, she simply answered, "Behold, the bondslave (or servant) of the Lord; be it done to me according to your word" (Luke 1:38). Her reply spoke of humble obedience.

Mary was a girl who knew her Bible. She was well versed in the Messianic hope. Her Magnificat alludes to several Old Testament books, at least five of them. Making her way to the hill country to visit her cousin Elizabeth, she must have mused on what the angel had told her plus what she knew of Scripture. And when she reached her cousin's home, the famous lines commonly called the Magnificat poured from her heart under the inspiration of the Holy Spirit. What was in her heart came out in her speech.

Mary was a homemaker. From available evidence, neither she nor Joseph came from wealthy families. In Hebrew homes, all members of the family helped in daily tasks. Mary doubtless knew well the meaning of toil, even in pre-marriage years when her hands were likely roughened by winnowing and grinding grain. If she had younger sisters or brothers, the winding of swaddling clothes on a newborn babe may not have been a foreign experience. As wife of Joseph, her full family numbered at least nine. The Bible names four brothers of Jesus, mentions sisters which means there were two at least, plus Jesus, mother and father. This meant nine to feed at every meal, nine to wash and care for, with no automatic washer, dryer, dishwasher, electric oven or modern plumbing. The softly draped figure so often depicting Mary may be a far cry from the hard-working wife of Joseph.

Mary was a secret-keeper. She had the unusual ability of keeping things to herself. Right from the start she had to do this. After the visit of the shepherds she could have bragged to neighbors, "Do you know what happened the night my baby was born? Angels sang. And shepherds told me of the bright light, as well as of the heavenly chorus! My little lad is the promised Messiah." Though Mary knew all this, she didn't talk. The Bible says, "But Mary treasured up all these things, pondering them in her heart" (Luke 2:19).

**After Jesus' interview with the temple doctors at the age of 12, his mother again could have bragged, "My boy—just 12 years old—carried on an intelligent conversation about deep theological subjects with the learned scribes." Instead, she "treasured all these things in her heart" (Luke 2:51). Recital of such exploits by**

a boastful mother would have stirred up jealousy among neighbors plus mockery by unbelieving listeners. Mary possessed the rare grace which enabled her to control her tongue.

Then, Mary was willing to sacrifice her Son so others could be saved. A sword must have pierced her own soul as she watched her boy hanging on the cross, slowly dying. Amazingly, she never raised her voice in His defense.

Did Mary love Jesus less than other mothers love their sons? Hardly. But she knew Him to be different. She recognized Him to be uniquely born, immeasurably wise, miraculously powerful. She willingly let Him die, knowing that He—as the Son of the Most High—was fulfilling His role as Redeemer.

We need mothers who will give their children to the Lord's work so that others might become Christians. Three young men went out to Africa as missionaries just before the turn of this century. They were the pioneers of the Sudan Interior Mission. Two lost their lives through malaria, experiencing a lonely death deep in Africa, far from home. The surviving youth, Roland Bingham, took the belongings of one of the boys to his mother back in America. On learning of her son's death, the mother exclaimed, "Well, Mr. Bingham, I would rather have had my boy go out to the Sudan and die there, all alone, than have him home today, disobeying his Lord."

For these qualities let us honor Mary—qualities worthy of emulation by every woman today—her chastity, her obedience to her Lord, knowledge of the Bible, faithful homemaking, tight-lipped ability to keep secrets, and sacrificial spirit.

But let us not forget that Mary was a sinner like every other human being, and needed a Savior. She put her trust in her Son, and will be in heaven, not because Jesus was her child, but because He was her personal Savior through her faith in Him.



# You Can Stretch Your Day

## PAT KING

"Have you ever had the experience of asking God to give you His love for someone you couldn't love yourself?" Catherine Marshall, well-known author and lecturer, asked me one day. It seemed an odd question, for we were discussing how God is the giver of time.

I nodded, remembering Sonny, an "impossible" neighbor boy who destroyed the trikes and wagons, and daily made all the children cry. Desperately I prayed, "Father, I cannot love him, but I know You love him. Please give me Your love for him."

I can't explain how it happened, but that very day as he began his destructive ways, I found myself going out into the backyard and saying, "Sonny, come in. I want to talk to you." There was no anger—just sort of a loving feeling for him I'd never known before. I marveled at God's answer.

I brought him in, thinking I'd talk to him about the toys he had broken. Instead I said, "Have a cookie." He stuffed one into his mouth, then another and another. "Sonny, are you awfully hungry?"

"Uh huh."

So we made a deal. Anytime he wished, he could come on in and make a peanut butter and jelly sandwich, but he must help me take care of the little children when they were outside.

The evening with Catherine wasn't long enough to share this story, so I just acknowledged I had experienced God giving me His love when I had had none of my own.

"Then," she said, "if we can ask Him for love that is not ours, I believe we can ask Him for time that is not ours."

The most delightful fact of all regarding

time is simply this: The creator of time is also the giver of time. When we have exhausted our supply, used up our 24 hours, and still need time, an amazing thing can happen to those who ask for it. Along with Catherine Marshall, I have discovered that God will give us time. I don't know how it happens, but many people besides myself have experienced it. God can do this for one reason—time belongs to Him.

Who can explain God's ownership of our time better than C. S. Lewis who writes of it in his delightful book, *The Screwtape Letters.* The book is a series of letters supposedly from an experienced demon named Screwtape to his young demon nephew, Wormwood, schooling him in the art of tempting men away from God.

The older demon writes: "You must zealously guard in his [man's] mind the curious assumption, 'My time is my own.'

"You have here a delicate task. The assumption which you want him to go on making is so absurd that if once it is questioned, even we cannot find a shred of argument in his defense. The man can neither make nor retain one moment of time. It all comes to him by pure gift. He might as well regard the sun and moon as his chattels."

No, time is not our own. Just as we belong to the Father, so also does our time. If we can understand this it will give new meaning to our search. For if we will walk in union with Jesus we can ask the Father for anything in His name and He will give it to us (John 14:14).

After I began asking God for more time (and receiving it!) I also asked the Lord to send others across my path who had experienced this phenomenon in their lives. A short while later Nora Tilton, a woman who had heard of my interest in time, called.

One morning, during her sixth pregnancy when she was feeling worn-out before the day had even begun, she had prayed, "Lord, I need to do all the laundry, drive three car pools, make the grapes into juice, and do the beds, kitchen and meals. Please help me."

She was barely back from driving the first car pool when a friend phoned who needed her full attention. Nora had just hung up from that long chat and had started her work when another friend knocked at the door.

"Am I bothering you? I need to talk to someone." Nora put her work aside again. When the friend left, Nora drove the kindergarten car pool and returned home. As she was throwing some laundry into the machine, another friend in need called on the phone.

Nora was not frustrated. "I asked the Lord to help me find the time," she said, "and I knew He would." As soon as she hung up from distraction number three, Nora somehow made the beds, finished the laundry, made the grape juice, began dinner, and finished in time to drive the third car pool.

"I don't know how it happened—I did not have enough time to get all that work done. But when I ask the Lord for time, He always gives it to me," she said.

Another experience came through the mail in a letter from John Sherrill, author of *They Speak in Other Tongues.*

"I made a discovery," the letter said, "some years ago about the task of preparing my income tax. I put the whole process into a framework of prayer. Lord, You know that this is a segment of time which I must set aside for this purpose. Since I must do this, I am simply going to wait until You prepare the time for me. Then I put my income tax papers out on the table. I did this about a month ahead of deadline and I simply waited. Every day I took a look at the papers with no anxiety that I wasn't going to get them done on time. I went about my regular routine without feeling frustrations and conflicts for the use of time. I had a confidence that since the Lord knew of this need, He would supply.

"And that's exactly what did happen. One day an appointment that would have taken a huge chunk of time was cancelled. I 'knew' instantly that this was the Lord's time for my tax. I turned to it with a great sense of continuing relaxation about the time requirement, knowing that if I didn't get through it now, there would be more time available. But most important of all, I thoroughly enjoyed preparing my income tax. It allowed me an opportunity to review nostalgically all the interesting and good things that had happened to Tib and me over the year as they were reflected in the travel, entertainment, etc. Since then I have always found that this dreaded expense of time will yield to this technique."

Another young woman came to the house and asked if I would like to hear her little story about God giving her time. Pat Hogan has three preschool children who seem to need her constant attention. One of the great satisfactions of her life was her Bible study class, but Pat grinned and said, "Three little children and daily time for Bible study are incompatible. At least they were until I prayed a rather curious prayer. Twice a week I needed to sit down at 10:00 and study for 45 minutes. Always it seemed that that was the time when bedlam grew worse and the phone rang and rang. Then one morning I prayed, 'Jesus, please keep this next 45 minutes protected from interruption.'

"I settled the children with something to do and began the lesson. The children played without a quarrel. The house was quiet, no one came or called and I was able to get all my studying done. At the end of the 45 minutes the phone rang, the children began quarreling and needing attention. I said, 'Oh, thank You, Lord, for that protected time.' Then I began to wonder if it was a coincidence. But since then it has happened over and over, enough to show me that Jesus truly is Lord of our time."

Gretchen Earley tells another story of a time when she trusted time-to-get-everything-done to the Lord. "It was Sunday morning and, due to unexpected activities on Saturday, my house was a perfect mess. I had invited my parents for dinner for their wedding anniversary. Although they had to drive a great distance they were well known for always arriving an hour before the appointed time.

"In my mind I outlined what had to be done to the house as well as meal preparation and I felt the 'not enough time' panic closing in. There was an alternative; I could skip church. Then I remembered our weekly Bible study class which was stressing our yieldedness to the Spirit and to His Lordship over everything, even time. So I said, 'Lord, if I go to Your house this morning and yield my hours to You, somehow You will have to make enough time for me to get all these things accomplished. Thank You, Father.' I asked my husband to pray about it also but didn't mention it to my two teenagers who were staying home due to colds.

"By the time I arrived home from church, a slight bit of apprehension was growing again—but to my amazement and joy the house was clean. The children had decided it needed straightening and had pitched in together. My heart overflowed with this unexpected answer to prayer. As a bonus blessing, for the first time my parents were 30 minutes late."

Then came the day when I wondered if maybe I could be wrong about the Lord being the giver of the time we need. My prayer that morning had included the specific request for time during the next two days to write and finish an important article for *Aglow* magazine. Just as I finished the prayer the phone rang. It was Tricia, a woman in our prayer community who runs a communal hospitality house for temporarily homeless people.

"Pat, the baby of a transient family died here last night. Can you take the other six children in the household for me today?"

Even as I was saying I could, I wondered how the Lord was going to give me enough time to finish that article, but I was certain He would. My friend, Virginia, came over and together we made it through the morning with eight preschoolers. I presumed that while the children rested, the Lord would give my writing wings. I settled four of the children in the upstairs bedroom and began to settle the rest in the front room.

"Now you two boys take this davenport and you two girls take . . . oh, oh, where's Monique?"

The three I had just settled got up and we searched the bedrooms, bathrooms and closets, calling her name, looking for her mop of red hair.

"Where could a two-year-old go?" I asked.

"She runs away sometimes," one of the children answered.

Good grief, had she taken the path to the beach or the dangerous road where all the accidents occur? I sent the five-year-olds to the beach with a strong directive not to go into the water, put a four-year-old girl in charge of the little ones while I checked with the neighbors. The neighbors hadn't seen her; the boys came back without her. I called the sheriff and described her. He said they would check the beach first.

Where had she gone? Her family had lost one baby this very day; they couldn't lose another one. I jumped in the car and went down the dangerous road. Half a mile away I saw a head of frizzy red curls. She was walking along the street holding a man's hand. I rolled down the window.

"Monique!"

The man brought her to me, great relief on his face. He had found her heading for the water, had rescued her and had been asking passersby if they knew her. I thanked him (I hope I did, the lump in my throat was almost too big to say anything), and put her in the car. At home I called the sheriff, settled everyone again, and sat down to my desk.

Ten minutes later the school children walked in the door. The day was over—and the time to write was completely gone. I did really wonder why. I knew that I had everything in right order. I knew I could ask for enough time and expect that the Lord would provide it. Now there wasn't enough time. I felt puzzled.

The next morning before the breakfast dishes were even started, a friend called inviting my two boys on an all-day outing. They left at 9:00 with their lunches packed in brown bags. With a whole morning I hadn't counted on, I wrote the two-day article in one day.

Yes, God is the Lord of our time. He does give us time to do the things we need to do. My friend, Virginia, is a woman who walks with the Lord and knows His ways. She insists that God is such a force in the lives of people who will trust Him that He plans their day including *not* providing time for the things He does not want them to do.

"He delays us, puts us in unusual places we couldn't have planned and changes our path. When something comes up to take our time from a previously-planned project, we don't have to feel frustrated because He is in charge of our moments just as surely as He is in control of the universe," she says.

A Bible Study Fellowship teacher, Winnie Dong, told of a time she and her minister husband were driving to an important pastors' convention in Canada when car trouble in a remote little town held them up for several hours while parts were being located. Pastor and Winnie Dong were totally at peace, knowing that since their time was the Lord's, He had allowed this particular delay for a reason. They sat so unconcerned in their car that the service-station owner finally couldn't stand it.

"What's with you people? How can you be so patient? Anyone else would be furious," he said.

"We're Christians," Pastor Dong replied, "and we believe that we can trust the Lord in every circumstance." For the next few hours while they waited for the parts to arrive, Winnie and her husband shared the wonderful truths of salvation with this man who had never heard them before.

They didn't make it to the pastors' convention, but instead turned around for home, praising God the rest of their journey for the young man who had accepted Jesus as his Savior.

Sometimes Jesus has something planned for our time that we don't want to do. My friend, Charlotte, looked forward all week to Sunday afternoon when her husband took their four active children on an outing and left her at home to have some time for herself. She was always especially relieved to get away from her ever-active 10-year-old Larry, who had been unexplainably irritable and rebellious lately. But one Sunday Larry threw a rock at a neighbor's cat and broke a neighbor's window as well as one of Charlotte's rules. Because of this, Charlotte said that this Sunday he positively could not go with his father. No treats for him when he was disobedient.

But as two o'clock came, Larry grew more and more obnoxious. Everything in her wanted to get him out of the house for a few hours so she could just rest. She went into her bedroom to pray. "Jesus, You know I need some time with myself. Would it be all right to let him go?"

The answer came almost before she had finished asking. "No, he needs you to follow through on your punishment."

As Larry balked and pouted, Charlotte remained firm. Hoping to interest him in a pastime, she laid out a table game. He was too irritated to even talk and went out to sit on the back steps. Still Charlotte hoped she could take a nap. She also wished the Lord would do something to this boy to change him but that seemed impossible. Then Larry came back in.

"I'll play the stupid game if you'll play it too," he said defiantly.

As Larry waited for her answer, Charlotte knew the Lord was asking her to give up her special Sunday time. As Charlotte and Larry played the game, the communication that had been closed for weeks opened between them. Larry explained about the rock-throwing incident, apologized for his behavior and admitted that he would have been disappointed if she had let him go.

Charlotte did not get a nap or her time alone that week, but she went to bed that night far more rested from the breakthrough with Larry. She commented to me many years later, "I've found that when we acknowledge our time is the Lord's, we can give it away. When He gives it back, it is not always the way we think it should be, yet it is always right for us."

In the same way, experience has shown Bill and me that we can always trust that Jesus, whom we've made Lord of our time, will not let us down.

Last fall, Paul, one of our teenagers, asked, "If I take care of everything after dinner, could you and Dad drive to the Northgate shopping center by 7:00 because there is a good sale on tennis shoes and a free basketball for the first 250 people to come." We agreed to do it partly because Paul asks so few favors and partly because we had to be close to the center at 9:30 that night. We dashed out of the house and got to Northgate just at 7:00. Amazingly, in view of such a grand sale, we had no trouble getting a parking spot. We hurried into the store and found that we had come on the wrong night.

After a moment's shock it dawned on us both that there must be a reason for it. We sat in the car and asked, "What is it, Lord? What are we supposed to do? Who are we supposed to see?" We were both positive God wouldn't let us waste two-and-a-half hours. I thought of our daughter-in-law, Annette, who lived close by and she was the person who came to Bill's mind too.

When we arrived at Annette's we found her alone with the baby. I don't even know how the conversation started, but within five minutes of our arrival she began sharing how for two weeks she had doubted the worth of Christianity and the reality of God. Bill shared for an hour as she asked question after question. Then we prayed with her and counseled her about the snares of the enemy. Over and over she thanked us for coming. We left for our next commitment rejoicing, knowing that we can count on the Lord to use the time He has given us to His best advantage.

The Lord did not let Paul down either. The next night Annette and Dave went to Northgate and bought Paul's tennis shoes and even managed to get him a free basketball.

We can expect this kind of guidance just as Jesus expected the guidance of the Father as He walked this earth. He was always in the right spot at the right time. He was in Capernaum just when the centurion's son became ill. He was in Nain just as the widow's son's funeral was passing by. He didn't ask, "Whom shall I heal?" He healed Simon's mother-in-law. The crowds came to Him for healing. The Father had given Him a message to teach, but He didn't have to search for people to listen. They sought Him out. He did not apologize for not curing or teaching the crowds while His physical body was being restored and refreshed.

Jesus flowed with the hours of the day. He always had enough time.

So it can be for us.

# 38

# Personality profile

ROBERT WALKER
Editor, *Christian Life* Magazine

Next to God, the most significant factor influencing our lives is people. Virtually everything we do or think about is influenced by the effect which other people have on our lives.

As a result, articles or stories about people can be the most effective way to communicate ideas. Today the market for personality profiles or sketches is wide indeed. Many Sunday school papers feature personality sketches of Christian athletes, statesmen or business executives. Religious magazines also provide a good market for personality sketches.

**Available options**

Meanwhile, the personal experience-biography or autobiography has become a best-selling book type in the religious market; and its popularity has spilled over into the secular market.

One of the first of these was Dave Wilkerson's *The Cross and the Switchblade*, which has sold several million copies. Pat Boone's *A New Song* was a close second. Since then Johnny Cash has written his story, Colonel Harland Sanders has done his. These are well-known personalities, but there are many other lesser-known persons who have either written their own stories or written about other personalities with good success.

Remember, you not only have the opportunity of writing about a personality as a third person, but you may also be able to ghost write with a well-known personality. As a matter of fact, this has become a very important and lucrative ministry for many Christian writers today.

After you have located the personality about whom you are going to write, and determined the market, your next job is to decide how to collect your material.

**Tape recording an interview**

Most writers today favor a tape recorded interview with the principal. Before you go into such an interview—with or without a recorder—be sure that you have a list of key questions. They should follow a sequence which will lead to the clue to the effective life that your principal is living. But keep your questions flexible. In other words, don't hesitate to inject other questions as you go along and where you believe additional information will be necessary to bring

*In his profiles, Wes Pippert, UPI correspondent, utilizes a style common to newspapers. (See profile beginning on page 175.)*

out the personality characteristics of the person whom you are interviewing.

The most important step in getting adequate material from an interview is to get your subject to describe scenes or situations. These will give you insights into the character of the personality and enable you to bring out his unique characteristics.

**Reassure your subject**

In such an interview you often may find your interviewee objecting to the personal note or slant of your question. Or he may hedge with his answer. Reassure him. Tell him that you need to get all of the facts and that you will promise to let him see it before it goes into print. This is important because you want his confidence in you as a writer.

For instance, at one point, Jan Franzen, executive editor of *Christian Life* magazine, was interviewing Dr. Bob Schuller, pastor of the famed Garden Grove Community Church, on his formula for a successful Christian family life, he demurred.

"How do I know you are going to get this right?" he asked.

"I'm listening carefully," Jan replied, "but when I finish the manuscript I'll send it to you. You can check it out for yourself."

Schuller was reassured and proceeded to give Jan one of the finest articles that has ever appeared in *Christian Life* magazine on Christian family living.

**Do your homework**

Before you go into an interview you must do your homework. Read up everything you can on the subject. If he has authored books, read or at least scan them. When you set up the interview in advance—either by telephone or by correspondence—be sure to give the subject opportunity to determine what he thinks he would like to talk about. You may agree with him and follow along. On the other hand, you may think there is some other subject on which he has spoken which has more popular interest.

Start where he wants to start, then direct your questions gradually into the area which you believe is more important. You can never be sure why he has chosen his subject. It may be that he or she is uncertain about his expertise, or he may feel others may be critical of what he might say. Actually his opinion is probably as good as anyone elses, and he will respond when you express confidence in him and in his ideas.

Earlier I mentioned the importance of creating scenes. This means dialog. Be sure to catch the color of your personality's dialog. When tape recording an interview, of course, you have it directly as he speaks it. If you are not taping, jot down words or phrases from time to time that will give you the correct inflection in the dialog. And if you are not taping, don't take too copious notes. As a matter of fact, I prefer not to take any notes whatsoever—but rather to listen intently to what the person is saying. I discover when I do this that I am able to reproduce words and phrases so accurately that the subject is perfectly satisfied with the direct quotes which I use from him.

**Most dramatic means for telling**

Clearly, the personality sketch is one of the most dramatic means for conveying the result of a born-again experience in an individual. This kind of "witness" is most convincing to nonbelievers. Moreover, articles on the mature Christian's walk in the Spirit, can be most encouraging and stimulating to other Christians.

Best of all, there is scarcely a community anywhere in the United States—indeed the whole world—where there is not some person who is worthy of a personality sketch of some sort that is publishable. So look around you. Read your local newspaper. Listen to your local radio and television stations. If you are not aware of such personalities in your community at the present time, it's likely they will be paying your village or city a visit in the near future. These personalities with unique experiences, unusual lifestyles or dramatic conversion experiences, are material for the kind of Christian personality profile which can give you great satisfaction in producing and seeing published.

## EXAMPLES OF PROFILES

**Personality sketches can—and should—make the reader feel that he has come to know a person and how he thinks on current, significant subjects. Notice that neither of the following articles merely relates a life story. Also notice the two styles of presentation: question/answer; reportorial.**

# Mrs. Billy Graham: More Than a Mother

### WESLEY PIPPERT

Poised, cheerful and attractive in a simple light-tan dress with a single strand of pearls, Ruth Bell Graham the other day talked of her world-famous evangelist husband, her children and their relationships in a world which is putting unusual pressure on husband-wife-child-associations. We were seated in her husband's office not far from their rustic-style home on North Carolina's Black Mountain.

To many people, the voice of Billy Graham on the subject of family relationships comes as a welcome antidote to the siren calls for fleshpots of sex or women's lib. But the evangelist speaks only as a male. What would his wife, the mother of five children, have to say? I wondered this as I asked my first question.

*Christian Life*—How do you feel about the women's lib movement?

*Mrs. Graham*—I am a strong believer in women's lib, to this extent: I think women should be liberated from civic responsibility, from having to work for a living, and, unless it's absolutely necessary, from all extracurricular affairs. They need to be liberated from them so they can do . . .

*Christian Life*—From them?

*Mrs. Graham*—From them, right! Delivered from public life so they can devote themselves to their homes.

*Christian Life*—That's the opposite . . .

*Mrs. Graham*—Complete opposite! I heard two women on the Today show who maintained that motherhood is not a full-time job, and I could not disagree more heartily. This is one of the troubles with our children today, that motherhood has become a part-time job. Even if we have one child, that child needs a mother full-time. I say this very reverently, but a mother, like God, needs to be a "very present help in trouble." A child's troubles don't wait for your convenience. When they happen, they happen. They're usually quite temporary, but the child needs his mother there. And when the children come home from school, they should know mother's going to be there.

*Christian Life*—Yet, in a way, you are a very liberated woman. Even advocates of women's lib would acknowledge this.

*Mrs. Graham*—In what sense? You mean I like what I'm doing?

*Christian Life*—Yes.

*Mrs. Graham*—Tremendously! I feel that being a wife and a mother is the most exciting and the most rewarding, as well as the hardest, job in the world. You remember that sorry old joke about "he might as well have et"? Well, when the preacher came to town, his landlady wanted to feed him a big meal, and he said, "No, I never eat before I preach because I want to preach a good sermon." Someone asked her after the sermon, "How was the sermon?" and she said, "He might as well have et." (laughter) Well, I have told my children I don't want anyone putting on my tombstone, "She might as well have traveled."

*Christian Life*—What advice then would you give to the Christian mother and wife who may wonder whether there's a bit of truth in what the women's lib advocates are saying and whether they've been misled through the years?

*Mrs. Graham*—The Bible is our one sure guide in a very unsure world. You can't go wrong if you follow God's directives. And I really believe God's directives are that our husbands are the head of the home. We adjust ourselves to them, not the other way around. That is why I tell young girls who are planning to get married, to marry a man they won't mind adjusting to. I realize there have to be mutual adjustments, but I am talking about the overall picture. The burden of the adjustments rests on the wife, or should.

Of course, there are exceptions to all these statements. But my advice is to go to the Scriptures and to be the type of woman God wants you to be. The only way we can find that out is to study the Scriptures and to pray. The two go hand in hand. Sometimes in prayer we do all the talking. We need to read the Scriptures and listen. I know this is true, because sometimes God speaks to me when I already have my mind made up that something is the right course. When I stop to listen, He hits me with an idea that's absolutely contrary to what I've been thinking.

I remember one time I was convinced

that our oldest son—that's when he was much smaller—needed much stricter discipline than I was giving him. It was very hard for me at the time to really lower the boom.

"Lord," I said, "help me to be tougher, to really bear down on this boy."

And just like that came the words, "Love him more," which was exactly what he needed at that time.

I believe we must study our Bibles consistently and carefully and, as we study, ask the Lord, "Show me how to apply this to my life today." It's no good to study the Bible if we don't ask that. But when we do, we're going to have ideas, thoughts and suggestions on how to handle situations that we would never have had otherwise. That would be my suggestion.

*Christian Life*—Do you think that living in this particular place has made it any easier to raise your children?

*Mrs. Graham*—Mother and Daddy had settled here after they returned from China. When Bill started with Youth for Christ, it meant that he was going to have to be on the road most of the time. I believe that if a husband is going to travel most of the time, his wife should have the privilege of living where she would be the happiest. I felt I would be happier in this general vicinity. It's worked out very nicely because we were near enough to my parents so that, after the children came, I could take occasional trips with Bill and know that, even though I had someone else taking care of the children, the grandparents were across the road to be called on in case of emergency—of which there are quite a few when children are growing up. Psychologically it gives them a sense of security if someone is there, although I haven't been gone that much. Then, too, when I'm here, it's been awfully nice having my parents nearby.

*Christian Life*—Then this decision to live in Montreat was made long ago?

*Mrs. Graham*—Oh, years ago. We were married in 1943. We were almost two years in Western Springs, and then we moved down here. Gigi was born here.

*Christian Life*—Have you always lived on the same spot?

*Mrs. Graham*—No, we lived right next door in the little house where Stephan and Gigi (Tchividjian) are living now. We were with Mother and Daddy for two years, but when Ann was on the way we bought the property next door. It was during the war, so we got an old summer house and lot all for $4,500. That was an enormous amount to us at the time. We had to borrow to get it. Then we remodeled the downstairs, which you could do during the war when you couldn't build a new house, and left the upstairs as it was. Years after we remodeled the upstairs. Really it's a cute little place. When it got too small for us, and also too public—we were on the sightseeing tours, and you can't raise children that way—we moved up the mountain. We're just one mile up.

*Christian Life*—When did you move into that home?

*Mrs. Graham*—Fifteen years ago, I believe.

*Christian Life*—And you built it?

*Mrs. Graham*—Yes.

*Christian Life*—And so it all dates back to your parents settling here?

*Mrs. Graham*—We lived with them for two years. I think this was a financial reason. (laughter) I don't think it's a healthy situation as a rule, but Mother and Daddy have been wonderful in-laws. From the very beginning they have stayed out of our affairs. Otherwise, I think it's much better for young people to be away from both families, especially when they're first married.

*Christian Life*—Tell me about your children.

*Mrs. Graham*—Gigi is the oldest and she's

back here (from Switzerland) temporarily, studying. She is married to Stephan Tchividjian, and they have three children. Ann is married to Dr. Danny Lotz, a dentist, in Raleigh, North Carolina. Bunny is married to Ted Deinert, who is in an advertising agency, and they live in Valley Forge, Pennsylvania. Franklin is in college—well, he's taking a semester off. He said, "Mom, I don't know what I want to do so what's the big rush?" There is something to be said for this, although I am eager for him to get his requirements out of the way. Then he can make up his mind what he wants to do. But last summer he was working on the Wheaton Tours in the Middle East, traveling in London, Greece, Rome, Tel Aviv, Jerusalem. He met Aileen Coleman at a little hospital for chest diseases in Jordan, where she and Dr. Eleanor Soltau—two middle-aged women—are doing a really fantastic work among the Bedouin. He was so impressed with Aileen that he came home and conned his daddy into getting a Land Rover for the hospital. Then he talked his roommates from LeTourneau into going back with him. They picked up the Land Rover in London. It usually takes a year to get one, but this shows how God was really in the whole project. They were able to get one in a week, equipped for the desert. They drove that thing across France, Switzerland, Austria, Yugoslavia, Greece, Turkey, Syria, Lebanon, back across a little bit of Syria into Jordan. He's there doing construction work on the hospital the rest of the semester, hauling cement and doing that sort of thing, sleeping in a sleeping bag with the Bedouin. I think this is perhaps a terrific experience for a 19-year-old; I rather envy him! But we hope he'll go back to school.

*Christian Life*—And the youngest?

*Mrs. Graham*—He's 13, Nelson Edman. He was named for my father and Dr. (V. Raymond) Edman of Wheaton College. We call him Ned. He goes to a Christian day school in Asheville.

*Christian Life*—What is a typical day?

*Mrs. Graham*—Well, I try to work on letters in the morning. But every day is full of interruptions and I have to play this by ear. I think one thing that a busy housewife and mother has to learn is to accept interruptions as from the Lord. And the sooner she learns it, the happier she'll be. When you do, then you roll with the punches, and each interruption is an opportunity. In other words, if I tried to keep to a rigid schedule, every interruption would make me frustrated and irritated. But when I accept each interruption as from the Lord, life becomes much more interesting—and much more relaxed.

I try to handle my correspondence half a day each day. Most people write in about problems, and I am not at all sure that they couldn't be handled better by, say, some minister in the person's home town. All I know is what they write. There may be another side. The only thing I can do is try to point them to the Lord. If they are in a right relationship with Jesus Christ and will take their problem to Him and try to learn all He has to teach them through that problem, that's all they need. It's not that the problem is going to be solved; some problems are unsolvable.

*Christian Life*—Have letters asking for your advice increased since your talk at the Minneapolis Congress on Evangelism in 1969?

*Mrs. Graham*—I don't know whether they've increased—they're just piling up! (laughter) That's my big hang-up, the letters that don't get answered. It's not easy to sit down and answer a letter from someone who's facing a tragedy. You just can't send a form letter. Sometimes it takes a whole morning on one letter, with time out to answer the telephone and things like that. So they pile up.

*Christian Life*—For the rest of your day, have you tried to spend so much time with each of your children, like Mrs. Wesley did?

*Mrs. Graham*—I wish I had more of Mrs. Wesley's . . . of course, Mrs. Wesley didn't have telephones or television to deal with. I think modern civilization, with all of its short cuts, also creates certain problems.

*Christian Life*—How would you describe your philosophy in raising children?

*Mrs. Graham*—I think the very first thing, and this is where I have fallen so far short, is to be the woman that God wants me to be. Now, this verse came to me this summer after Franklin had taken off for London. When you send a 19-year-old boy to pick up a Land Rover in London and drive it to Jordan, well, I was praying! And I was reading John 17, which I had read on other occasions, as my prayer for the children. This was our Lord's prayer before He died, as He was leaving His disciples behind. Only in this case, the child was leaving me, not the other way around. Still, the prayer was very appropriate. Any mother could read it for her children. The verse that really hit me between the eyes was the 19th where Jesus says, "For their sake I consecrate myself that they also may be truly consecrated."

If our Lord needed to pray that prayer, how more do we parents for our children's sake. We can't expect them to be truly committed if we aren't. This is where so many of us fall flat on our faces. We're great at preaching, but we're terribly weak on the practicing part. I think how often I have failed my kids on this. I expected more of them spiritually than I was willing to give myself. The important thing is to be what God wants us to be. If I were the type of person God wanted me to be, 90 percent of the problems in the family would be solved.

*Christian Life*—In executing this day to day, in terms of the telephone, the car, the TV, do these things come off permissively?

*Mrs. Graham*—I'm afraid,—and this is a confession—I'm not a good disciplinarian, to the children's detriment. A good disciplinarian is someone who disciplines consistently, no matter how he or she feels. If I'm real tired, I usually just give in on a point if the children press it. Or, if I get really upset, I'm likely to be too strict with them when I shouldn't have been. I think a good disciplinarian is much more objective and consistent than that. Because Bill has been gone much of the time, I have loved the children not wisely but too well. I get emotionally involved, and sometimes I'm inclined to be more lenient with them, thinking I have to make up for the fact their father is not here, when really they would like me to be a little tougher with them. One day last summer, when we were out in California our 13-year old was getting out of hand, and I was chewing him out.

"Now listen," I said, "you've got to realize that I've been pretty lenient with you on this trip."

"That's the trouble, Mom," he said. "You should have been more strict."

I don't think this is unusual. Kids appreciate discipline. So when I say that I have been too lenient, I wish I hadn't been. I wish I had been stricter.

*Christian Life*—How about your husband?

*Mrs. Graham*—If he had been home consistently he would have been a tremendous disciplinarian. This is the ideal in a family, I think, when the father can be the disciplinarian, and the mother can relax and just be sweet and loving. But when the father is gone most of the time, the mother has to be disciplinarian as well.

*Christian Life*—Would this give a distorted view to the children, though, if the father is always the one who is strict and the mother is the one who is gentle?

*Mrs. Graham*—I don't think so, not if they blend. The father would also have periods of play and what have you. I may be wrong on this point. But we didn't want Bill to come home and have all the children's misdeeds piled up for him to sort through and mete out the punishments. Many things went wrong at home that we never told him. I tried to settle it with the kids, but Bill wasn't informed of it. The children have tremendous respect and great love for their father. If there has been a lack of having the father figure be the disciplinarian in the family, God has so far very graciously overruled it. I'm counting on this. Our family isn't a normal family, because the husband is gone most of the time, and also because he is fairly well known. This puts an additional strain on the children.

*Christian Life*—A fish bowl existence?

*Mrs. Graham*—Well, we've tried to keep them out of the fish bowl, but there are people, unthinking people, who expect too much of them. It's like the average preacher's kids who are told, "You can't do thus and so." It's so easy for a child to say, "Well, I'll prove to them that I can." I have banked on the fact that, since God called Bill to be in the ministry, He would make up to the children and the family what they otherwise would have had in his being home. I am banking heavily on God overruling my mistakes and supplementing my shortcomings, which up to now He has very graciously done. The kids have taught me a great deal.

*Christian Life*—How much is Dr. Graham home?

*Mrs. Graham*—We've never actually sat down and figured out how much he is home. I would guess between a third and a fourth of the time.

*Christian Life*—It's common knowledge that you're an exemplary wife. Do you gear what you do to the times when he comes, or do you try to live your own life? Do you try to arrange things so that, when he's home, there's no particular crises; so that you can pretty much give yourself to whatever his need happens to be at the moment?

*Mrs. Graham*—That's what I try to do. I think it's very important when a busy, tired man comes home that his needs be catered to. In other words, home can be a place where he recharges his battery. How you handle this depends entirely on the temperament of the man. Some husbands relax better with company and people to talk to; others relax better working out in the yard; others relax better with television. So when Bill comes home, he calls the shots. We only have company when he wants to have company, unless it is really an exceptional case. He does what he feels he needs to do. He has an awful lot of work piled up when he comes home—correspondence and so forth.

*Christian Life*—How does he unwind?

*Mrs. Graham*—On the golf course is his best way. But he also has taken up running—to keep his blood pressure down as much as anything. He runs a mile to two miles a day.

*Christian Life*—Is he a putterer or a tinker?

*Mrs. Graham*—No, he's not. I wish he were!! Boy, I've got a lot of things piled up that somebody's going to have to putter with! In the evening my relaxation is reading, but that's been Bill's work all day in preparing messages, so he relaxes better watching television or something, which bores me to death—either that, or I get so involved that I can't quit it and it's a waste of time.

*Christian Life*—What have you been reading lately?

*Mrs. Graham*—Let me see! I was counting up the other day the books that I am reading, none of which I have finished. For spiritual stimulation, I adore C. S. Lewis and George McDonald. For refreshment, and just plain old blessings, Amy Carmichael. I have a friend who when things get tough says, "This calls for Amy!" A good cross-section of secular and spiritual. Having all these unfinished books around bothered me until I realized that when I go into the pantry, I don't eat all the peas before I start on the asparagus, and I don't eat all the peaches before I start on the **apricots, and not all the Vienna sausage before I start on the tuna fish. In other words, I don't always need the same book the same day. So there is a whole row of them that I can read, depending on the** circumstances and the way I feel.

*Christian Life*—How have you handled the spiritual development of your own children? Do you have devotions each morning?

*Mrs. Graham*—We try to keep devotions free, but we try to be consistent. The ideal is in the morning at the breakfast table just after breakfast. We arrange to have either a few verses, or one verse even, and a brief prayer before they're off to school. If they don't remember anything else, they'll remember that we bowed in the presence of God to ask His blessing on the day. At night, just before they go to bed, we like to gather as a family. Sometimes this is difficult because so many interruptions come in the evening. The children were taught to pray. I prayed with them when I tucked them in bed at night.

*Christian Life*—Individually?

*Mrs. Graham*—Individually, yes, when they were small. And when they reached a certain age,—usually around 12—they took over and would rather pray alone.

*Christian Life*—Did you make it a point to talk to each one about committing his life to Christ, or did you just let your teaching accumulate through the years?

*Mrs. Graham*—We spoke to each one when they were small. Gigi, our oldest, was about 3½ when she made her commitment to Christ. She remembers it, too. I was very strong on hellfire and brimstone at that point. You know, "If you die tonight you will go to hell and we will miss you." This is really a dreadful approach to a child. I'm afraid that you can get most any child to go along with you unless he's terribly stubborn and strong-willed. I'm not sure how much of this is because they want to please you and they're scared to death of not being together with the family in eternity, and how much is true repentance and turning by faith to Jesus Christ. We have to be led by the Holy Spirit.

I read where one godly person who said that her approach to the children was that Christ had died for them and loved them so much we must not reject such love.

A mother has to pray very earnestly and be led of the Spirit of God as to just when and where to present the claims of Christ to a child. But still it's a miracle of grace. All we can do is to explain it simply enough for them to understand, and trust the Holy Spirit to perform the miracle.

*Christian Life*—Then you try to point your conversations with them to this specific end?

*Mrs. Graham*—Yes, as soon as they're old enough to understand, which would be 3 or 4. It's amazing how much a child can grasp spiritually. We think that they have to be grown, but our Lord said, "except ye become as little children." I think they're perhaps more able to grasp deep spiritual truths than older people. But sometimes God has to wait and use an outsider to break through.

*Christian Life*—What do you see, now that your children are about raised, for your future?

*Mrs. Graham*—I think to be more available to Bill, to help him in any way he might need. And to enjoy my hobbies.

*Christian Life*—Will you travel more with him?

*Mrs. Graham*—Probably. I think I would love it. I could get addicted to traveling.

*Christian Life*—What are some of your hobbies?

*Mrs. Graham*—I like sewing. I love anything to do with fixing up a home. I really like reading. I think writing could become a hobby if it were not so full of interruptions.

*Christian Life*—And speaking?

*Mrs. Graham*—I don't plan to do any more

speaking. I just don't feel called to speak. If I had to take a choice between speaking and writing I would put everything I had to say in a book and let people read it, and I wouldn't have to get up and say it. And in the spring, gardening. That's my therapy—to get out in the flowers and work. I just love it! There are so many things I'd like to do. I love to cook...

*Christian Life*—Let me ask you about your early years. Did you have a feeling that you were going to marry a man who would be an evangelist of note?

*Mrs. Graham*—I don't think we can ever see into the future. I did know when I first met Bill that God had His hand on him in a very special way. I don't really call it a premonition—I couldn't possibly have visualized what lay ahead. I'm glad I couldn't—I wouldn't have had courage to marry him!

*Christian Life*—Where did you first get the feeling that evangelism would be what he would be doing and that he would be blessed so greatly in this field?

*Mrs. Graham*—It's something that grew, fortunately. It's like when you have a baby. You don't start carrying a 35-pound baby around. It starts off at 7 pounds and you adapt to the weight as it grows older. This is something that just sort of grew, and we adapted to the responsibilities as they came along. I knew when I married him that God had called him to be an evangelist, which was just fine with me. He did take a church for two years (in Western Springs, Ill.) but he never was completely at home in the church. However, I think this was in the providence of God because it gave him a sympathy for, and an understanding of, ministers and their problems. And when he goes into a town or a city he couldn't possibly put on his crusades without the help and support of the local ministers. He knows better than anybody else that they've done the sowing and all he does is come in and do the reaping. The two years he had in the ministry gave him this appreciation.

*Christian Life*—Tell me something about your childhood. You were born in China and raised there, were you not?

*Mrs. Graham*—Yes. I came over here when I was 17. Actually I was born in China and spoke Chinese before I spoke English. I'm sorry I've forgotten most of it. We were tutored through the eighth grade, then we were sent to North Korea to Pyingyang where the Pueblo crew was incarcerated, and then to college at Wheaton. They were very happy years. The recent book about my father (Dr. Nelson Bell), *A Foreign Devil in China*, tells about them. Many missionaries are so good and dedicated that you couldn't possibly even approach them, but my parents were very "human." If I had thought when I left China that I would not get back, I would have been crushed.

*Christian Life*—Maybe you will get back!

*Mrs. Graham*—I can take up ping pong! (laughter)

*Christian Life*—Can you pick out two or three things in your childhood that were formative on your later years?

*Mrs. Graham*—I think the quality of the Christian home in which I was raised is important. There was strict love, but a lot of love and a lot of play—I mean fun and games, along with the discipline and the Christian training.

*Christian Life*—Did your parents spend a lot of time with you?

*Mrs. Graham*—They did, every evening. Of course, we had our school work and what have you in the morning. In the afternoon mother was in charge of the women's clinic. But after supper, after Daddy had made his hospital rounds—he was head of the surgical work in this large mission hospital—the evening was devoted to the family. The men took turns reading aloud. We went through the old classics, Scott, Dickinson, all of them, while the women did handwork. We were taught to sew, crochet, braid rugs, and that sort of thing. So it was a very warm family atmosphere. We were not distracted by television, no picture shows to go to, no outside amusements. Occasionally we met with other missionaries in the homes for an evening of relaxation. Prayer meeting was on Thursday. Sunday afternoons we had foreign church. But home on the mission field is what home should be—an oasis in the desert. I think it was this warm spiritual atmosphere—seeing Mother and Daddy live their Christian faith, seeing their love for the Lord and their love for people, seeing the thrill they got when they heard that someone had received Christ—that made a tremendous impression on us children.

*Christian Life*—Do you think your own home life set the standard for the way you raised your children?

*Mrs. Graham*—I never came up to the pattern Mother and Daddy set for me, due partly to the kind of life we've had to lead. We've had more distractions. And television, although I think it's a tremendous boon in many ways, is a great handicap in others. We haven't played as many games together in the evening, for example. My family was a great one for games. I think this is good.

*Christian Life*—The TV screen is always there, always easy to switch on.

*Mrs. Graham*—I can't say it's altogether bad. There are some good programs on television. If you can teach the children to select—it's like reading or anything else, music, or movies. They've got to be taught selection. It's the same with food. In everything there is trash and there are things that are nourishing. If you can watch some TV programs together, you can help children face life, can help them see what's wrong and what's right, whereas if they are completely sheltered from all of this, and suddenly leave a Christian home and are thrust into the world, it can be a tremendous shock. So you're sitting in your home, you're looking on the world as though it were through a window, watching it go past, and you can comment, "This is wrong," and "This is unwise," and "This person is not behaving the way that he should," and why.

*Christian Life*—Is there anything you would have changed through the years in the handling of your children or in your own spiritual life?

*Mrs. Graham*—Yes, I think so. I remember years ago, when I had only one or two children, someone asked me to write an article on mothers. At the time, I wanted to emphasize the danger of being diverted from the main task of being a mother. I used the illustration of the Grahams' old cow dog down on the farm. He was a tremendous cow dog unless a rabbit or a butterfly went across his path. Then he was off like a streak of lightening, tail wagging, ears up, barking madly, going through all the motions of being a good cow dog. But after what? A rabbit or a butterfly!

It's so easy for us just to go through the motions of being a mother. This is why we must be liberated from outside commitments. I really mean this. Mothers of young children don't even need to teach Sunday School or get involved in organizations if it's going to take time away from the rest of the family or time that should be spent with the children. Even worthwhile projects can be diversions.

If I could do anything over, this is where I'd like to change things. Even sewing, or making curtains, or reading—things that I enjoy—I would put aside when the children are home. They need our full attention. That, and a consistent walk with God. It's mighty easy to get sloppy or careless because we're too tired. It's not a duty. It's a glorious thing. And I would urge everyone, everywhere, to concentrate on this.

# Sooner or Later You'll Meet Marabel Morgan

ADON TAFT

I'm certainly not the total woman," smiled Marabel Morgan, author of one of the most controversial and best read books on the role of women in marriage. "And I hasten to add that I do not have a perfect marriage because we (she and husband Charles O. Morgan, Jr.) are two imperfect people. Life is a struggle all the way, a challenge."

Nevertheless, the trim, 38-year-old blond mother of two girls has had such success in her own marriage and in helping others through *The Total Woman* and the self-improvement courses based on it that she has written a sequel entitled *Total Joy*. (published in 1977 by Fleming H. Revell). It's basically a recounting of marriage success stories reported to the Miami housewife in letters from thousands of readers of her first book which outsold its nearest rival *(Centennial,* by famed novelist James Michener) by nearly 40,000 volumes in its initial full year of publication. Well over 600,000 hard cover copies and nearly 2.5 million paperback versions now have been sold.

*Total Joy* also reiterates the basic principle of the wife adapting to her husband which, when set forth in *Total Woman,* drew strong criticism from women's liberation groups both outside and within churches. In addition, it continues to emphasize the sexual pleasures of marriage—an emphasis which brought denunciations of *Total Woman* from many pulpits.

"I don't try to answer my critics," said the blue-eyed "Miss Congeniality" of the 1958 "Miss Ohio" segment of the "Miss America" contest. "There are an awful lot of opinions in the world and I never planned to push my opinions on anyone. I just share what has happened in my own life."

What happened in her life was that she got her priorities mixed up, confessed the woman who is a member of the Key Biscayne Presbyterian Church. "I have four priorities for my life. First, I'm a person responsible to God. Since I'm married, my second priority is my partner. My third priority is that of a parent. Fourth is my professional or public life.

"When your priorities are in order, there is enough of yourself to go around. But I used to be guilty of having number four first. A lot of women are like that. And when your priorities are upside down, you are in trouble."

Marabel found herself in trouble nearly seven years ago. Her life was filled with such good works as teaching a course on Christian beauty and ethics at the Florida Bible College, teaching Bible study courses in churches and homes, and even teaching her *Total Woman* courses out of which her book grew.

"But I was not practicing what I was teaching," she said. "I had kidded myself for years that we had a marvelous marriage. I told myself that our marriage was better than most others I knew. The fact that Charles and I never talked much about vital issues bothered me some, but I put that aside. Finally there were a couple of incidents in the same week that made me realize that if we kept it up, in 10 years we would hate each other.

"The climax came one night when he announced at the table that we were going out for dinner the next evening with some business associates. The announcement ruined my plans for the night, and I protested," said the attractive woman who found it hard to let someone else schedule her life after running it for herself for 27 years.

" 'Why do you challenge me on every decision I make' Charlie snarled in anger. 'Challenge you?' I shouted back. 'I don't challenge you!'

"Boiling mad, I ran from the dining room

to our bedroom. I threw myself on the bed and sobbed. I kept thinking, 'How could Charlie be so insensitive? Why isn't he more considerate? What is wrong with our marriage?' "

The marriage had begun as a good one six years earlier. Charles Morgan was the son of a music store proprietor who was one of the leading evangelical laymen in south Florida. Marabel saw the young lawyer as a strong, intelligent, good-looking, spiritually sensitive, ambitious and lovable man with a charming personality marked by wise and witty conversation.

On her part, Marabel had brought to the marriage the good looks of an Ohio State University beauty queen, the practicality of a girl who had worked several years as a beautician and had studied home economics, and the spiritual commitment growing out of an encounter with a beautiful older woman who had been a regular client in her beauty salon.

Marabel's father, a policeman, had died while she was in junior high school. She had gone to church all her life and had taught Sunday School, but had not found the inner peace for which she had been searching. At Ohio State she studied the principal religions of the world, hoping to find something. But she was disappointed. So she saved her money and took a tour of Europe, thinking that travel would satisfy her yearning. She was disappointed again.

Back in the beauty shop, she kept hearing the lovely customer talk about the Lord.

"She glowed," recalled Marabel. "She had an inner beauty because she had a personal relationsip with Jesus. And she told me I could have that same relationship with Him.

"I thought it was too simple. But I had tried everything else, so I said, 'Why not try this?' I prayed, thanked God for dying for my sins, and was saved.

"I had always believed about Jesus, but I had never really received Him personally into my life," Mrs. Morgan said. When she did, her life changed and she began witnessing to others about what Christ could do for their lives. She enrolled in a Bible college in Miami and went to the campus of the University of Miami to witness. And that's where she met Charles, then a senior law student.

"At first, things went as I dreamed," said Marabel. "Ours was a marriage seemingly made in heaven. But as the months passed, our lives became more complicated and we gradually changed. I was amazed to realize that Charlie and I had stopped communicating. Barriers had grown up between us, and, as the years wore on, things got worse.

"Drying my eyes in our bedroom that night, I made a decision to find out what had gone wrong in our marriage and to change it. I bought all the books on marriage I could find. I studied books on psychology. And I began searching the Bible for principles to apply to our marriage.

"For six years I had been trying to change Charlie, and that wasn't working. So I decided to change myself. I made up my mind that no matter how Charlie acted, I was going to be the best wife and mother I could be. I was determined to be the kind of woman that God wanted me to be regardless of his response.

"The nice part about it is that he did respond," declared Mrs. Morgan with the enthusiasm that has made her a popular guest on such national television programs as "The Today Show," "60 Minutes," "The Phil Donahue Show," "The Merv Griffin Show," "To Tell the Truth," and "Good Morning, America."

Marabel began sharing what had happened in her life with such friends as Anita Bryant and the wives of such sports figures as Jack Nicklaus, Alvin Dark, Joe Frazier, Tom Landry, Bob Griese, Norm Evans, and Karl Noonon. Many of them became teachers when the demand for Mrs. Morgan's marital advice grew into a course. She has taught in churches; classes of wives of West Point officers and corporation wives; and other groups. Out of all that grew her book—and both national acclaim and denunciation.

The criticisms of her book don't bother her much, said Mrs. Morgan, who insists, "I did it that way because the Lord led me to do it."

But Marabel doesn't really see any real justification for the criticism, whether it comes from the side of the women's liberation movement (whose members have picketed her courses) or from fundamentalist churchmen.

A letter in *Newsweek* magazine described the Total Woman as a "plastic wind-up toy." Another said she "obviously feels her husband is too insecure to accept criticism, so impotent that he needs constant sexual stimulation, and too selfish to take care of anyone's needs but his own."

"If I'm married to a wind-up toy, that's the first I've known about it," declared Charles, who has been named "president of the marriage corporation" by his wife who serves as "executive vice president."

The United Methodist magazine *Response* and the unofficial Lutheran magazine *The Wittenburg Door* have criticized *Total Woman* as being "riddled with advice that eliminates self-respect from a woman. . . . The morality is anti-human and anti-Christian." The Methodist magazine went on to say that the book "almost adds credence to that belief expressed by some radical feminists and others that there is no difference between being a prostitute and being a wife. A prostitute exchanges her services to a man for a material reward. So does a Total Woman, as expressed in this book."

But Marabel does not see her book at odds with women's liberation just because she refers to such Scripture passages as, "Wives, submit yourselves unto your own husbands, as unto the Lord . . . "

"The women's movement has opened up opportunities to women and that's super. We have a choice and the freedom to do our own thing. That's what I'm doing, and I love it! Of course I am liberated! Jesus sets you free, and I am free."

She is convinced that "a man wants an intelligent, spunky, opinionated woman. He wants her to know who she is and where she's going. He wants her to have goals and to reach them. He wants her to be a person in her own right."

That does not conflict with the Biblical concept of submission, as Mrs. Morgan views it. She has her input, but when the chips are down, Charles makes the decision. However, if she has been fulfilling her role as a loving wife, she and her views get real consideration when that decision is made, insists Marabel, who finds it a little hard to understand some of the criticism of the book. She wants 11-year-old Laura and six-year-old Michelle to read it before they go off to college. (*Total Woman* talks a lot about stimulating and fulfilling a husband sexually.)

"I've tried to tell them about the facts of life at their level as we go along," she said of her daughters. "I want them to be better prepared than I was. I had no idea what marriage was all about. I had no idea what was required. It was work, work, work.

"Maybe it's not as deeply theological as some would like," she said of *The Total Woman*. "But that was not the purpose of the book. It was never written to the Christian at all. It was written to non-Christians as a secular marriage enrichment course. It was designed to catch the eye of the non-believer and, hopefully, make her a believer. It's geared for those who have never heard the Gospel. When I tell them how to have happiness in the kitchen and in the bedroom, they try it and find that it works. So then when I tell them how to have true happiness in their hearts, they believe that too."

Mrs. Morgan has the satisfaction of knowing that many women—and men, too— have had just such a life-changing experience from reading the book or taking her course. She cited this example.

"There was a beautiful young girl who was shaking because she was so mad after the first class session," Marabel recalled. "I had given the class a homework assignment on how to treat their husbands. She said, 'I can't do it. My husband and I are not speaking.'

"I said, 'Well, why don't you go home and make a nice supper, put on something comfortable, and that's all you have to do tonight. That's your assignment.'

"She was still real huffy but she said, 'Well, okay,' and spun around and left. I began praying for her. The next morning, she was there an hour early. She wanted to tell me that she went home and prepared supper, bathed, and did all the things to get ready for her husband to be home at six. But he was not there. By seven he still was not there and she was about to call it quits, but she stuck it out. He got home at nine and had no excuse.

"He had dinner and said, 'What's the matter? How come you're not clawing at me as usual?' And she said, 'I love you. I want to be a good wife.'

"He was stunned. He came around the table to her and cried. After that, she said, it was the best night in their whole married life.

"Then at the end of the course, I gave the Gospel," continued Mrs. Morgan. "And this girl came up crying. She said, 'Please help me get Jesus in my life. I don't know how.' Then I led her to the Lord. She believed me because what I had told her before had worked. It's typical of what happens. Many women find a brand new life."

In fact, so many thousands of women—and men—have written to tell her about their new lives that "I felt guilty keeping their stories to myself, they were so tremendous," Marabel said. "So I just jotted them down and they became the heart of *Total Joy*. It just gives you hope!"

# 39

# On using humor

LESLIE B. FLYNN
Pastor, Conservative Baptist Church,
Nanuet, NY

Humor in religious writings?

Why not? The Bible contains lots of humor. Dr. A. T. Pierson said that almost every type of humor was used by prophets, apostles and even by our Lord Himself to expose error and reflect truth. God made us so we can recognize the incongruities of life and laugh at them. A sense of humor, sanctified by the Spirit, buttresses man in his struggles with the frustrations, tensions and depressions of life. Just try to get through twenty-four hours without making or hearing a joke! How unbearable the day!

A Christian musician doesn't give up the use of note C. Nor does a Christian poet refrain from using the letter M, or the mathematician stop employing the number five. Why should a Christian journalist surrender the faculty of humor?

**Interject humorous anecdotes**

Interjection of humorous anecdotes into your writing can help rescue readers from pressure and untie emotional knots. The editorial guide-sheet of a Sunday school paper for youth suggested that readers who laugh at the problems of others can learn to laugh at themselves and their own problems. Abraham Lincoln once said, "If I didn't laugh with the strain that is on me night and day, I should go mad." In our hectic age few prescriptions are as inexpensive and as potent as the wonder drug of laughter. Your flashes of wit may make life more bearable for readers who labor under great anxiety.

**Humor can teach**

Humor can be a teaching device, clarifying, illustrating, objectifying. A farmer whose barns were full of corn used to pray that the poor be supplied, but when anyone in need asked for corn he said he had none to spare. One day after hearing his father pray for the needy, his little son said, "Father, I wish I had your corn."

"What would you do with it?" asked the father.

The child replied, "I would answer your prayer."

This story gets its point across quickly that often we ourselves possess the resources to answer our own prayers. Humor wrapped in the barb of an anecdote not only makes truth plainer but obviates the need of a laborious explanation. It likewise makes deep subjects more easily understood. Erasmus pointed out that the greatest minds of classical antiquity wrote humorously on subjects because they knew that many readers would reap more advantages from such treatment. Humor is like the sugared coating of a healthful pill. Many a truth is spoken in jest. Someone has said, "In proper place nonsense may be sense."

The mind which naturally flags after brief concentration on any subject can be recaptured by humorous material at well-chosen spots. If the subject is deeply emotional, humor can give much-needed relief from sustained tension. In the old-fashioned melodrama the overwrought feelings of the spectators were relaxed by the entrance of the comic man. Ready for tears, the audience burst into the respite of laughter. The relaxing power of humor was tacitly recognized in *The Case History of the October 1959 Holiday* magazine which was made available to journalism students to show how the editors planned and created this issue. It was related that in early editorial meetings where article-subject possibilities were listed the feeling was repeatedly expressed that the contents badly needed humor and light articles.

**Humor can soften**

Humor can soften up unpleasant truth. One editor in accepting a manuscript on a different theme wrote, "You have a saving grace of humor in this article which makes it palatable." One writer began an article on the not always acceptable subject of money with this lead, "The most sensitive nerve in the human body is the one that leads to the pocket-book." Humor can blunt the sharpness of rebuke or conquer situations that resist frontal attacks.

**Five musts in humor**

Humor must be limited to proper times and topics. It should be clean, never suggestive.

It should be mild, never injurious. Pleasantries are all right; "meaneries" all wrong. Kindliness, an element of genuine humor, keeps writers from capitalizing on others' handicaps, appearances or misfortunes. Mercy, not malice, must manipulate the scalpel of ridicule.

Humor should not be announced in advance. Don't inform your readers that you are about to tell a humorous story. Let them decide if it's funny.

As in all your writing, be brief. Don't give too much detail—just enough to get your story across.

Humor must be purposeful, not pointless. Never write anything funny just for the sake of being funny. If it's not your nature to be humorous, use it sparingly. If you are of mischievous makeup, don't overdo it.

Humor must be reverent, never sacrilegious. Serious truths should not be joked about, such as hell, the Spirit or "Peter at the pearly gates." By so doing we dull the serious edge of these truths for those who read our flippant treatment.

Humor is to be used, not abused. Since humor is a gift of God for which He provides opportunities for exercise, some day we may be called to account for this happy faculty, just as we shall have to answer for our talents. Let us not bury our sense of humor, but invest it wisely in our writing.

# 40

# Basics of trade writing

JAN LOKAY
Editor, *Christian Bookseller*

Why write for trade magazines?

Simply because they provide a viable market for your articles. In fact, you may be surprised at how easy it is to become a successful trade magazine writer.

To write for a trade magazine or paper, you first must *know* your audience. Ask yourself, "Who are they? What are their needs? How can I help them better their business?"

Familiarize yourself with the trade by visiting various business establishments. Note their methods of merchandising, advertising and sales. Talk to key people in the industry. Be alert to trends and breakthroughs in marketing and sales. The trade writer not only notices details, but also has a panoramic view of the industry.

**Ten pointers on trade writing**

Here are some pointers paramount to trade writing:

1. *Attract the reader's eye with a catchy headline.* For example, "Bridgebuilders: Avoid that U-Turn in your Stores"; "The Musical: An Experience with a Message:" "Dear Christian Bookseller: I Love You in Spite of the Wart on Your Nose." Remember, the purpose of a headline is two-fold: to attract attention to the story and to tell the story as completely as possible in a phrase.

2. *Induce the person to read on with a striking lead.* For example, an

*Though mostly a secular field, there are some religious trade magazines.* Christian Bookseller *offers help to Christian bookstores. Photographs, such as this one showing a display, should accompany your article. (Visual Concepts)*

article on Bible sales reads: "The Bible business has gone up," reports president and founder Earl Fitz of Riverside Book and Bible House. "Our twelve incoming WATS lines never stop ringing for Bibles."

3. *Develop an opinion to fit the facts you have found.* Ideally, an opinion is the result of a process of investigation. Avoid ideas that are typical. For example, the majority of Christian booksellers have had more sales success with their Bible department at the front of the store, rather than at the rear. You would relate the example of the majority.

**Substantiate ideas**

4. *Always substantiate ideas with striking concrete examples.* Here is a paragraph from an article on student sales. "Key not only the display window, but also inside displays to student interests. Current events and popular issues offer ideas for windows. For example, St. Benet in Chicago, next door to DePaul University, did a Cesar Chavez window during the farm workers' election last spring and a 'Right to Life' window showing fetal development from conception to birth."

5. *Guide your selection of detail.* Decide what is distinctive about what you want to describe and the overall effect you want to produce.

6. *Get immediately to the point!* A busy executive or manager does not have time to wade through your eloquence and irrelevant detail. You'll be wasting his time and your own. In other words, cut the verbiage down to the essentials.

7. *Develop a style all your own.* What your writing sounds like and feels like is determined in part by how formal or informal you make it. To be readable, your writing must have personality. Keep the reader from saying to himself, "But I have read twenty articles just like this one!"

8. *Find the appropriate word. Be specific in your diction.* Instead of using the word "thing" or "contraption," use "lid," "lever," "valve," "tube," or "coil."

9. *Vary sentence beginnings.* Avoid continual subject, verb, object order. Begin with a verb or prepositional, adjectival or adverbial phrase. For example, "Is there a science to a sale?" or "Conversing with many store managers..."

So now you're ready to give trade writing a go. Remember, know your audience, write simply and specifically, develop a "nose" for trends and get the facts.

# 41

# How to turn what you know into cash

ALMA GILLEO

Free-lance writer; Instructor, Christian Writers Institute

One of the most overlooked areas for potential sales is the how-to-do-it article or book. This is surprising because there is an insatiable market for this type of material, including local newspapers, national magazines, and book publishers.

A quick search through a local library is likely to reveal an array of how-to-do-it books that would boggle the mind. These include such diverse subjects as: how to insulate your house, 365 ways to cook hamburger, how to play winning tennis, how to build a swimming pool, how to make bobbin lace, how to collect antiques, how to improve your personality, how to make soft toys, how to do oil painting, how to be a better parent, how to earn money in your spare time, and even how to write articles that sell.

The local magazine stand features scores of magazines devoted to subjects ranging from coin collecting to decorating the home.

**Everyone knows how to do something well**

Many writers don't consider how-to-do-it articles because they feel they are not experts in any area. One doesn't have to be. Everyone knows how to do something well. That something may be what other people would like to do if they knew how.

For example, a third-floor apartment dweller amazes his friends by serving lettuce, tomatoes, radishes, and green beans which he raises on

*Some of the most popular how-to-do-it writing concerns leisure time activities. (Biola College)*

his balcony. A local newspaper or a magazine might buy an article telling other apartment dwellers how to raise vegetables on a balcony.

A woman's auxiliary of a local hospital puts on an annual Christmas bazaar to raise funds for expensive equipment for the hospital. A member of the committee may find a quick sale for an article on how to plan a successful bazaar to raise money for a worthy cause.

**Constantly alert**

Ideas for how-to-do-it articles are abundant. To spot them, one must be constantly alert to the possibilities. For example, consider a mundane activity like shopping for groceries. Shoppers may not have noticed the nutrition labels which appear on many food packages. Or, if they noticed the labels, they may not be using them to plan more nutritious meals. Recently I sold a manuscript on eating better for less money by using the nutrition labels on packaged foods.

Other how-to-do-it ideas are born when problems are solved or needs met. Most people seem to feel pressured by work and necessary duties and cannot find time for hobbies and other personal activities. An individual who has learned how to set priorities and schedule activities to accomplish both might easily find a market for a how-to-do-it article.

Religious publications need how-to-do-it helps, too. Ideas for such articles may come from experience or observation. A few years ago I used my hobby of stamp collecting to interest junior-age students in missions. The idea was the basis for a how-to-do-it article which made a quick sale.

When I was superintendent of a junior department in Sunday school, I noticed that eight of the classes usually reported one or more absentees weekly. New students were enrolled only when new families began attending the church. But one class seldom reported absentees and new students were enrolled each month. An article on how the teacher kept attendance high and brought in new members was an easy sale.

**Three basic questions**

A how-to-do-it article is easy to write. After selecting a timely and significant subject, the writer answers three basic questions: what? why? and how?

Depending on the subject, the article may be written in narrative form with high human interest. Or it may follow a straight news format. Whichever format is used, anecdotes are needed to get and hold readers' attention. Both facts and anecdotes must relate to the main theme. Peripheral ideas must be subordinated or deleted. Steps showing how to accomplish the activity must be clear and precise.

If a how-to-do-it article is timely, significant, and well-written, there is little doubt that it can be marketed.

# 42

# How a book is born

BERNICE CARLSON FLYNN
Free-lance writer

Over a period of nearly half a century, few people have known as many writers of Christian books as Wilbur H. Davies, retired chairman of the executive committee and member of the board of directors of Fleming H. Revell Co., a publishing house founded by the brother-in-law of the famous 19th century evangelist, Dwight L. Moody. Fewer still have played so important a part in discovering and encouraging the kind of persons who are willing to pay the price of becoming successful authors.

An elfin-faced, stocky man with a jutting jaw, Davies will talk for hours about books and authors. According to Davies, almost every person has dreamed of one day writing a book. Most never do. His stories of those whom he has helped are laced with laughter and tears. And most of the accounts Davies comes up with have a twist to them—like the one about the Methodist minister.

In one of the southern states, a bookstore placed an order with Davies' company. The size of the order—1,000 copies—required Davies' approval. Four weeks later, four telegrams from four other booksellers asked for 250 copies each of the same book.

Davies immediately got on the telephone. "What's happening?" he asked the bookstore manager.

"A preacher has a column in the local newspaper and he has been talking about Christian books," he explained. "We've had a run on them ever since."

Davies was convinced that if anyone could do so well selling someone else's books he ought to be able to write one himself. He contacted the man, Dr. Charles L. Allen, and urged him to put his thoughts on paper. To date, Revell has published 22 books by him.

Davies, president of his company from 1962 to 1968 and for years known as one of the top salesmen of religious books in the U.S., has never written a book himself. "It's more fun for me to get other people to write them," he says. He also takes pride in being able to anticipate the public's response to a book.

One day the Hollywood entertainers, Dale and Roy Rogers, were traveling east by train from California. At a newsstand in Chicago, Dale bought a copy of Norman Vincent Peale's *The Power of Positive Thinking.* The book inspired her to write the story of Robin, her Mongoloid baby, who had brought both joy and tears to the Rogers family before her death while still a toddler. When she later showed the manuscript to the noted minister of Marble Collegiate Church in New York City he suggested that Dale take the manuscript to his publisher. It was turned down there because it was too short. She then went to another publisher who also turned it down. Finally Peale suggested she try Revell.

**An important subject**

Because the book dealt with an important subject by an author with a genuine Christian experience, Davies sensed it would have appeal. He published it under the title *Angel Unaware.* It has sold more than a million copies.

Often a book was suggested to him by a friend, Davies says. One day he received a phone call from a small-town Connecticut banker who coupled a warning with his recommendation of a manuscript.

"I think I should tell you it was declined by Revell at one time and also by the publisher you formerly worked for," he said.

"Send it in anyway," Davies replied.

The author, an older man, evidently didn't trust the mails, but delivered the manuscript in person.

"It's been rejected by 28 publishers," he explained apologetically. "But I keep trying. The book deals with proofs for the existence of God. Even though it sticks to theism and doesn't go beyond that into Christianity, I think it is important."

When he read it, Davies agreed. When the book was published it caught the eye of *Reader's Digest* editors and appeared in *RD* as a book condensation. It also was used as a supplementary text at Wheaton College. No other Revell book has been translated into so many foreign languages. It sells today in condensed form under the title *Seven Reasons Why a Scientist Believes in God* by Cressy A. Morrison. In unabridged form it sells as *Man Does Not Stand Alone.*

One day Davies visited the Biola Book Room in Los Angeles to interest the buyer in stocking up on his company's titles.

"We could sell a lot of this new panorama Bible study book—if we could get it," said the bookseller.

He held up a paperback on Bible prophecy titled *New Panorama Bible Study Course.* Loaded with diagrams, it was selling for $2. The author, Dr. Alfred Thompson Eade, had been publishing it privately but was giving it up for health reasons.

As a result of a phone call to Eade, who was in the hospital, Davies was able to publish this, plus three other books by the same author. Eade became one of Revell's bestselling authors.

**Bookstore managers are good leads**

Bookstore managers often provided good leads for books. Some years ago, the manager of the Baptist Bookstore in Kansas City, Mo., was the catalyst for a string of books.

"There's a group called Fellowship of Christian Athletes out here who are thinking of doing a story about the witness of some of their young athletes," he told a Revell salesman. "You ought to get in touch with them."

The information was relayed to Davies. With his characteristic enthusiasm he went to work. He talked to the athletes and eventually persuaded them to sit still long enough to put several books together.

On a trip to Florida, Davies happened to pass a drive-in church in St. Petersburg pastored by Dr. J. Wallace Hamilton. When he saw 2,500 cars parked outside he immediately thought of a book. "Anybody who has an audience also has the potential of a reading public," is Davies' philosophy. Unable to find Hamilton, Davies chatted with his wife.

"If Dr. Hamilton has any manuscripts, we would be interested," he told her.

"I'm sorry," she replied. "He's just sent one to another publisher."

As Davies left, he said, "Well, if the book isn't accepted there, we'd like to consider it." As it turned out, the first publisher wanted to make so many changes that Hamilton sent the manuscript to Davies who published it as it was and had another best seller on his hands.

Somewhat by chance, David Wilkerson, director of Teen Challenge in New York City, became a Revell author. His first book, *The Cross and the Switchblade,* published by a secular company, Bernard Geis, was secured for Revell's paperback series. When Revell's advertising manager set up a lunch with Wilkerson to discuss the promotion of the new edition, Davies went along. At lunch, Davies said casually, "You're probably giving your next book to Geis." Wilkerson replied that he was not committed, since he had scratched out the option clause in the contract. As a result, Davies got *Twelve Angels from Hell* for his publishing house.

Old line houses once took the position that if another publisher was issuing all the books of an author, they wouldn't try to get that author. Now, if an author publishes with two publishers, he is open game for anybody.

One day Davies received a phone call from a member of the Billy Graham organization.

"Wilbur, you ought to get in touch with Mildred Johnson," the man said. "She has a story which she shares with all kinds of groups, businessmen and chambers of commerce."

A follow-up on the call resulted in *The Smiles, The Tears,* a book recounting how Mrs. Johnson faced widowhood victoriously.

**Hard work and persistence**

In addition to intuition, Davies credits hard work and persistence for the successes he has had. Walking down the hall one day in his office building, Davies stopped at the desk of the managing editor who asked if Davies thought they would be interested in the managing editor's report—especially Vonda Kay's statement that her Bible was no good luck charm but a book by which she lived.

Knowing that anyone named "Miss America" would be under contract for a year, Davies advised the editor to contact Vonda's father. After checking every hotel in New York City, he reached Dr. Van Dyke. Through him arrangements were made for a book with the understanding that Vonda would sign a contract at the year's end. During the year, Vonda Kay taped material for an editor assigned to help her. As soon as she resigned the Miss America title, she signed a contract. Her first book, *The Girl in Your Mirror,* was followed by a second.

On another occasion, while in a Cincinnati bookstore, Davies

*Selecting manuscripts which will end up in a best-seller display requires intuition, knowledge, experience and the grace of God.*

happened to remark to a lady that he was trying to locate Helen Steiner Rice. To his amazement, the lady said she had a friend who had been with Mrs. Rice the previous evening.

"I'll call this friend and ask her where Helen can be reached," she volunteered. But Mrs. Rice was going to have her hair done and had no time to talk to Davies. When he finally was able to contact her, she gave him the poetry book, *Heart Gifts from Helen Steiner Rice,* which sold out immediately. A second printing of 50,000 soon followed.

Sometimes a publisher works to get a book and loses it.

"You can't get them all," he says. "One book we missed was *All the Women of the Bible* by Edith Deen. On a trip to Texas I heard that Edith Deen was working on a book on Bible characters. I called her, but the manuscript wasn't completed, so I didn't bother to see her. I told her that I would keep in touch, but somehow I failed to do so. Some years later, I picked up a new book just published by Harper & Row. The title was *All the Women of the Bible* by Edith Deen. And it has been a good seller for them."

At other times, a publisher *almost* misses a book.

Davies read somewhere that Bud Collyer, of TV fame, was an elder and taught a young people's class in the Presbyterian Church in Greenwich, Conn. Davies checked on Collyer's home address in *Who's Who* and wrote a letter. No reply came. Six months later, Davies wrote again. This time Collyer telephoned, explaining that he thought he had answered the first letter.

Revell didn't get a book about Collyer, but later did publish two books by him: *Thou Shalt Not Fear* and *With the Whole Heart.*

**Professional writers**

Often, Davies found that some of the books he wants are by people who are not writers. He has to get professional writers to make them readable. An exception is Dale Evans Rogers who writes all her own books.

"She writes them on envelopes, on pieces of brown paper, on anything that happens to be nearby when she gets the urge to write—and sends it all in to us," Davies says. "We have an editor who correlates the material, organizes it and puts it into shape. But it is Dale Evans' material, in her words.

"David Wilkerson gives us a great deal of material in his own handwriting. He also gives us pamphlets that he writes, and he puts some material on a tape recorder. We usually provide a writer who then puts everything together for a manuscript.

"You have to get an editor who is congenial to the author," Davies explains.

Davies wanted to do a book on a man who built his business into a billion dollar concern. The man insisted on writing every word of the book, but when it was completed it wasn't publishable.

"I got that book—and we've got to go with it," Davies said. He prayed about it, then went to see the man.

"Mr. X, you're one of America's leading businessmen," Davies said, "I'm just a squirt who's a bit embarrassed to say this. Your manuscript shows you have many important things to say—but it needs the touch of a professional writer. I have somebody in mind who could re-do it. Each chapter would be sent for your approval." The businessman agreed, and the book which resulted became one of the choices of the Christian Herald Family Book Club.

Although most of the books Revell publishes within a year are written without help, a stable of writers is on tap who help authors with their manuscripts.

"If these writers have attained a status, they can demand that their name appear on the book, asking a share of the royalty which might be as high as 50 per cent. If they haven't attained that status, they may be willing to do it for a lesser share of the royalty, or they may be willing to do it for a fee," Davies explains.

Most publishers have a hard time getting the books they want. "Out of fifty books published, forty-five may be our idea," says Davies. But as an encouragement to writers, Davies says, one of their ten best sellers—*None of These Diseases*—was sent in by the author, S.I. McMillen, M.D.

"Ideas for new books often were the result of Wednesday morning meetings. We met in our conference room around a big table. Three times a year we brought all our staff together from Los Angeles, Texas, Philadelphia, Toronto and Chicago to pick their minds for ideas. Sales and promotion people sat in with the editorial and sales staff," Davies says.

**Manuscripts carefully examined**

New writers always are encouraged. Every manuscript is examined carefully.

"You can tell quickly those you can't use, or those that are out of your field. If a book looks like a possibility, we send it to various readers. Sometimes it takes weeks before we can decide. Often a publisher must turn a book down because he's just published another book on the subject. It isn't right to pit authors against each other."

Final say on whether or not a book will be published comes from a staff meeting. Many years ago Davies wanted to do a book by Pat Boone. Only one staff member would agree with him. As a result, Prentice-Hall published Boone's book *Twixt Twelve and Twenty* which became the best-selling nonfiction book in the U.S. that particular year.

Knowledge of a subject and ability to foresee the sales potential of a book are two different things. Cass Canfield of Harper & Row tells how he sent a manuscript on history to one of the top professors in the country for his expert advice.

"Best book on history I've seen in my life," he wrote back. "It's just too good. It wouldn't sell."

Harper & Row turned it down. It was Spengler's *Decline of the West* which became a best seller for Random House.

Often sure-selling authors, even of religious books, receive an advance royalty of as much as $10,000. At no time has Revell given an advance on a book that did not materialize, although a few books did not do well enough to offset the payment. Royalty rates can be 10 per cent on the first 5,000, 12½ per cent on the next 5,000 or 10,000 copies.

**To be a bestseller**

To be a best seller, a book needs to sell at least 50,000 copies," says Davies. "A publisher begins to show a profit at 10,000 copies. Sixty per cent of the books published in the U.S. lose money. Thirty-six per cent break even, and only four per cent make money. Some publishers find themselves dependent on other rights—book clubs, magazines, newspapers, translations—to go over the break-even point."

Wilbur Davies believes book publishing is an exciting business and religious publishing more so.

What sort of book does Davies believe will have the greatest sale today? "I have always believed that books which encourage the reader, books that help him discover all God can mean to him in overcoming the problems of life will always be good sellers," he said.

Publishers are pleased when they score with a good book. They enjoy past successes. But they look to the future, anticipating the birth of another book. "Perhaps yours," says Davies.

(Reprinted from *Christian Life* magazine)

# 43

# How to write a tract

NATHANAEL OLSON
Director, Familytime Ministries, Inc.

A vital ingredient in the tract-writing recipe is *attitude.* A person should be "sold" on tracts if he wishes to succeed as a tract writer.

An assurance that God's Word, even in tract form, will "not return unto Him void" is vital.

Once you are confident that tract distribution is not a waste of time, but rather one of the most economical and effective means of spreading the good news, your manuscript will have the ring of I-must-tell-you this. "Woe unto me if I write not the Gospel."

So much for attitude. Now for some practical pointers learned from thirteen years of experience.

1. Get a new slant on an old subject.

**Get a new slant**

Tell "the old, old story" in a new, refreshing way. For example, we all agree that people do not get to heaven by taking any way except Christ. But how can we say this in a catchy, memorable manner? One of my tracts bears the title, "You *Can* Miss It!" Here is a twist on an age-old premise that the man on a street is familar with. And from it I go to show him that a person *can* miss heaven.

Another of my tracts declares, "What You Don't Know *Does* Hurt You." Here is a fresh approach to the fundamental truth that eternity gained or eternity lost hinges on faith or rejection of Jesus Christ.

"The Kite That Wanted to Be a Jet" appeals to the imagination of children and yet gets across the truth that it takes real power, Christ's power, to be a successful Christian.

Other titles of some of my seventy-five tracts may throw more light on this point. The following will illustrate:

"The Crowd May Be Wrong"; "Is Life Worth Living?"; "Do Things Just Happen?"; "The Pig from China"; "How Is Your Disposition?"; "Where to Find Happiness"; "Dare to Be Different."

**Study published tracts**

2. Study published tracts.

When you read a tract that you enjoy, look to see the name of the publisher. Remember that he has invested a lot of money to get this title. Therefore it represents what he likes to publish. If you can think up something similar in style, yet on a different subject, you can be quite sure that this publisher will be interested in your manuscript.

There are many fine publishers of Gospel tracts. However, the two that follow are perhaps the largest and offer you a varied market.

American Tract Society, Oradell, New Jersey 07649.

Good News Publishers, Westchester, Illinois 60153.

**Develop your own style**

3. Develop your own style.

Sound individualistic, not merely an echo. Sprinkle your manuscript with words, expressions, or illustrations that sound like you, not somebody else. For example, my style has developed as a fast-flowing, epigrammatic one, with flashes of pointed humor, such as: "Two things ruin a church—loose living and tight giving."

Style is something you will develop as you write and rewrite. Always seek to improve it for it is vital to writing success, especially in the tract field.

Perhaps you will want to begin by following the tried-and-true formula of AIDA:

A-attention

I-interest

D-desire

A-action

Use any formula that you like but begin now to "Preach by Print" for the tract market is wide open. So come on in!

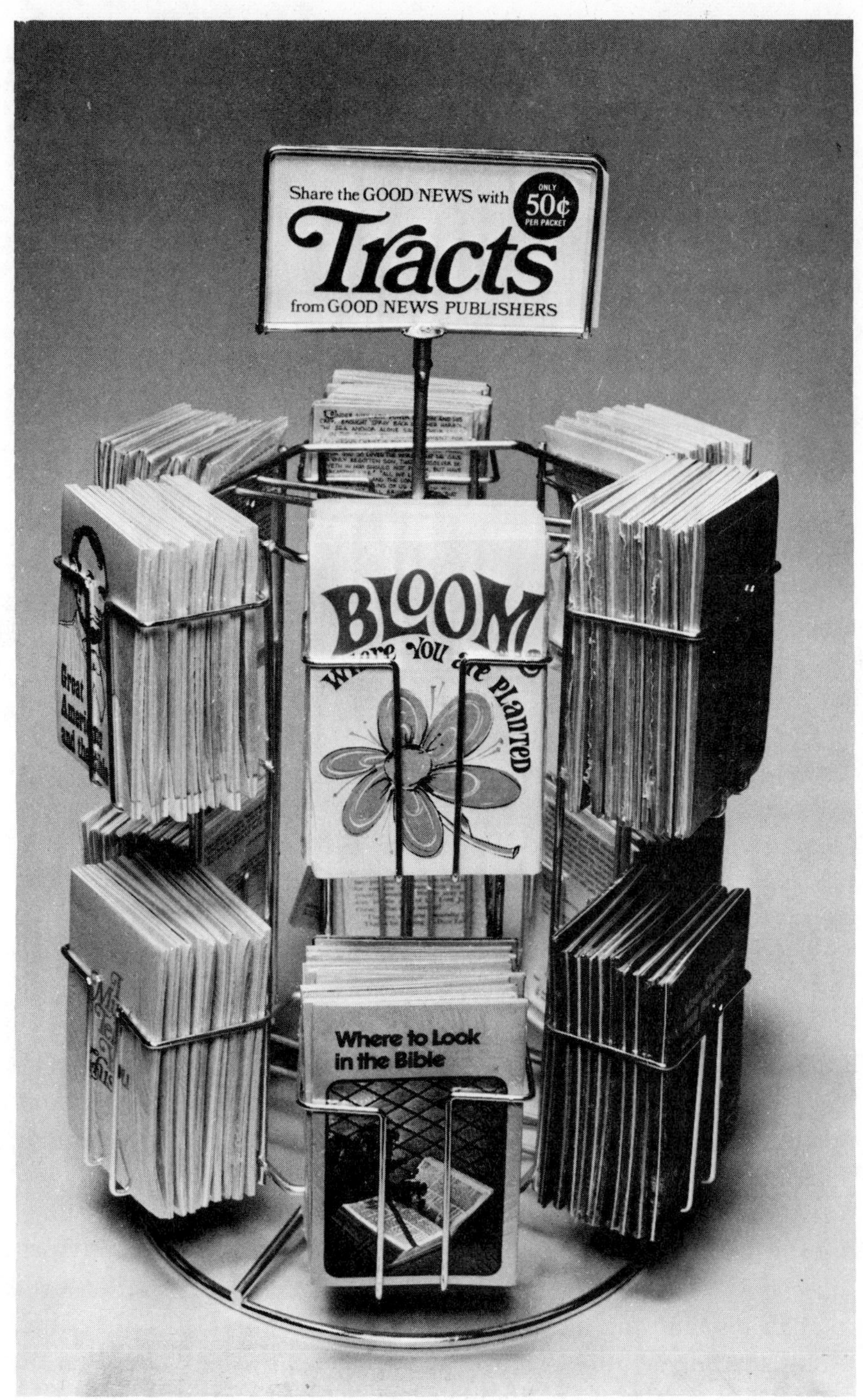


*A writer needs the guidance of the Holy Spirit in order to write a good tract.*

# 44

# Try different types of writing

MARY POWELL
Instructor,
Christian Writers Institute

Has your writing been getting stale lately? Perhaps you've collected a fistful of rejection slips and you don't have a fresh idea in your mind. Although that's a sad state to be in, it doesn't have to be fatal to you. Maybe you just need a change of pace. Any writer can go stale doing one type of writing. If you're in a "void" now, try doing some fillers, puzzles or quizzes and see if they can't spark you again.

Nearly every publication buys some filler material from free-lance writers. And it's a pleasant, fast way of adding a few dollars to your bank account. Fillers, for you just starting out, are those capsule anecdotes that magazines use to fill up a short column. But wait a minute before dashing to your typewriter to pound out a dozen 100 or 200-word stories. You may have a file folder fill of intriguing human interest stories you've collected from many sources. But most of them may be unsuitable for fillers because they have been told so many times they're shopworn. Ask yourself these questions before writing up a filler; is it fresh and original? Does it say something worthwhile? (Even though it's amusing it's best if it's not *just* a joke). Is it interesting? Study the publications you usually write for, or read, to see what the editors like. Some take quotations, some amusing little stories of what famous people have said or done, some like stories about children,

**Definition of a filler**

**Important questions**

some publish scientific facts. And if you keep a sharp lookout you might find one suitable for *Reader's Digest* and that would add a number of dollars to your postage fund!

Some adult publications take puzzles; most children's magazines do. If you enjoy the daily crossword, this is a natural type of writing. It will take time but the fun of making up a puzzle can take you out of the doldrums fast. When you send puzzles to an editor they should be done on light cardboard or heavy white paper with india ink, ready to be photographed if the editor wants to do that. Put the answers on a separate sheet.

**Types of quizzes**

Almost every publication you pick up contains some sort of quiz: How to choose a mate; Are you a good driver? What's your word score? etc., etc. Everyone, adult or child, likes to test himself to see how he rates with other people. Quizzes can be multiple choice, complete-a-line, fill-in-a-blank or anything else you can think of. And they can be on any subject the readers would be interested in. Just look through a few magazines and Sunday school papers and the ideas will begin to come. Do try to be original. Copying a quiz you like by using the same subject and style of questioning is out, of course. But there are enough

*Levi Keidel (right) has written many adventure and feature articles, usually with a missionary theme.*

things in the world to keep you going for a long time and still be different.

If you work your puzzles, quizzes and fillers out carefully you'll usually find that you receive more acceptances and fewer rejection slips from this type of writing than from any other. That's exhilarating, especially if you've been in a slump. So try it for a pepper-upper. You may find you enjoy it so much that you'll make it an everyday part of your writing schedule.

But don't get stuck just writing fillers either. There are still other types of articles that can be written. Some major types of articles used in publishing today are the trend article, the feature article and the true adventure article.

We've given some good examples of each type of article rather than tell you how to do it. Read the article and the editorial comments and pick out your own principles of writing these types of articles. Then try a different kind of writing!

## EXAMPLES: FILLER, TRUE ADVENTURE, FEATURE, TREND

**True adventure articles—those exciting narratives which use fiction techniques—are perhaps the most fun to write. Fillers are perhaps the easiest. They're short, to the point. Trend articles involve research; point up what is happening in the world today. Features take many forms, but usually are about people or organizations.**

# Is the New Christian Music Too "Worldly"?

PAUL JOHNSON

Whether we like to admit it or not, contemporary trends in sacred music are influenced by the secular culture in which we live. Christians always have had trouble with this; having felt that in order for something to be truly sacred it must be divorced from the world.

There are a number of ways the church has tried to divorce music from the world and thus make it sacred:

*By venerating church music of the past.* This position intimates that the older something is, the more sacred it is. Therefore, the music of Handel, Bach and others is more sacred than the music of John W. Peterson or Ralph Carmichael.

However, in Handel's day the Gregorian chant was a great deal more sacred than the "worldly" theatrical works Handel was creating. To make matters even worse,

Handel's secular compositions did not sound a bit different than his sacred compositions. Handel, Bach, Wesley and Luther all made bold, "blasphemous," innovative steps in the evolution of sacred music. However, what was questionable in their day has been made to be a measuring stick for today. Somehow the church has allowed time to change the definition of "sacred."

*By making tonal, harmonic and rhythmic distinctions between sacred and secular music.* This position intimates that life has two categories—that which pertains to God and that which pertains to man—and that the two cannot mix. Therefore, life is compartmentalized into spiritual (prayer, church attendance, good works) and non-spiritual (entertainment, vocation, recreation) activities.

It is difficult to understand how the church ever fell into the trap of this kind of thinking since Christianity's most basic teaching, the doctrine of the incarnation, so beautifully shows how God intended the sacred and the secular to be blended together. The "Word becoming flesh" is what Christianity is all about.

*By placing restrictions on music dynamics.* In other words, by presupposing that harmony and rhythm can be graphed on a linear, horizontal scale increasing in intensity and complexity from left to right. The presupposition is that music becomes more secular the further one moves to the right of the scale.

The best way to explain why Christians fall for this kind of thinking, I think, is related to the fact that Christians generally believe spiritual perception comes through the soul and body (intellect, emotion and the five physical senses). However, this kind of thinking makes for better Gnosticism than it does Christianity. The Bible never teaches that matter is evil and spirit is good, but that matter divorced from spirit is incomplete . . . that spirit, soul and body are interrelated and that the Gospel of Jesus Christ relates to all levels and dimensions of life.

Therefore, if music is perceived through the senses, and/or the intellect, and/or the emotions, as well as by the spirit, and if the music dynamics incorporated make you snap your fingers or tap your toe, it should not diminish its sacred value any more than smelling a fragrant rose or savoring the taste of a crisp delicious apple. If any of the above mentioned levels of perception are out of relationship with each other (i.e. the emotions and the intellect) the problem is one of aesthetics . . . not of spirituality.

So far we have seen that the church has tried to confine sacred music within certain limitations which are neither scriptural nor conducive to a correct world view . . . all of which goes to prove that God certainly does achieve His will in spite of us, not because of us. Just the same, it's time for all of us to quit being "old wine skins" and become expandable for the "new wine" which Jesus wants to channel through us to today's culture. If in our defense of tradition we actually hinder the flow of the Holy Spirit through us, what have we accomplished other than to "teach for doctrine the commandments of men"?

Today the church faces a world that is not the least bit interested in hearing us defend our sacred cows. It is interested, however, in hearing a solution to the crises it faces in the realm of personal identity, economy, ecology, ethics, guilt, and hope for the world's future, all of which have profound solutions in the Person of Jesus Christ.

As a Christian musician I find these crises and solutions worthy of musical composition. Indeed, I have discovered that music is one of the most profound methods of communicating what I believe on these issues. I do find, however, that the limitations and restrictions which Christians have placed on sacred music in the past make my task as a Christian musician in today's world quite difficult. If I must limit my method of communication to robed choirs and pipe organs in order to retain a sacred label for my work as a communicator of the good news, then my job is defeated before it begins.

It is true the Church has embraced a lot of musical change in the last ten years. It has been forced to because the results have been good. I would dare say that more people have been drawn to Jesus by Bill Gaither's music in the last few years than through the sacred music of the Reformation period. This would not strike a responsive chord in the hearts of legitimately trained musicians; however, all are nonetheless forced to confess that the Holy Spirit anoints that which is offered as a sacrifice of praise . . . whether it is sophisticated or not. It is good for us all to recognize this fact. The "foolish" still confound the "wise" in God's economy.

Though it is important for the Church to see that results of contemporary Gospel music are healthy, I think it is also important that the church understands why this is true. Contemporary trends in Gospel music are healthy for a number of important reasons:

**1. Today's gospel music opens up a channel of communication to today's world, meeting the challenges and crises that are current and immediate. The Word becomes flesh and dwells among us and we find that the good news is indeed tailored for today and not for the reformation period alone. We find that time has nothing to do with what makes something "sacred" or "secular," but the presence of God in that situation.**

**2. Today's gospel music does not make distinctions between secular and sacred harmonies, rhythms and tonal relationships. It does not see these as being inherently good or evil but as relationships which can be used for either good or evil.**

**3. Today's gospel music does not, for the most part, try to bypass the body and soul in order to minister to the spirit, but speaks to the individual on all levels and situations of life without extreme compartmentalization. (There may be exceptions here in certain charismatic gatherings; however, most Pentecostals would acknowledge music which is generated by the Spirit and that which is with understanding as being equally valid.**

**4. Today's gospel music is neither afraid of nor ashamed to participate in today's technology and culture. It is willing to be involved "in it" while being aware of the dangers of being "of it," or manipulated by it.**

**I've listed a number of healthy things about today's trends in sacred music which may sound as though the trends have no faults. This is not true. Let me just say that composers of today's music can just as easily make the same mistakes as previous generations. The musicians can be and often are arrogant ("my variation of interpretation is less worldly and more spiritual than yours"), the music can be and often is shallow (utilizing lyrics that validate salvation through experiences and feelings rather than by the Word of God), and composers can be and often are resistant to change (feeling more comfortable with what is familiar than to be threatened by something new).**

**The most important thing that every Christian must remind himself of is that music is not the end, it is a means toward the end, which is Jesus Christ Himself. Music is like the law of Galatians 3—it is a vehicle to deliver us to the ultimate source. Once it has done that it has achieved its purpose. If we see music as being equal with the source then we have pantheistically established an idol which must be defended by traditions and restrictions. Idols are always under our control by such limitations and music can indeed be an idol . . . even sacred music.**

**What we do need to see is that music is not something immaterial or metaphysical. Music is basically a mathematical relationship of vibrations and a combination of such relationships. Melody, harmony and rhythm are all mathematical, which may come as a surprise. To say that some relationships of vibrations are secular and some are sacred is as absurd as insisting that there is a distinction between good and evil mathematics. It's what one does with mathematics that makes it either good or evil.**

**No one will deny that there is power in rhythm and volume, but power is not intrinsically good or evil. Atomic energy is not good or evil but it certainly can and has been used for both. There is power in the rhythm of a march, but did Hitler's use of it make it unacceptable for "Onward Christian Soldiers"? Did Jimmy Hendrix's use of rhythm and amplified electric instruments make them intrinsically evil? It's time for our Christian mentality to**

mature beyond the pre-Renaissance superstitious caverns we're often hidden in. Truth is on our side. We need not be afraid of it. It will always validate our faith, not destroy it.

We also need to learn to love what God loves: "For God so loved the world." We have not loved the world sufficiently and therefore hold contempt for it. As a result, our values (as we have seen with sacred music) become perverted and we presuppose things about Scripture that do not in fact exist. We then turn around and superimpose such values on the world in the name of Christianity and thus misrepresent the truth of the gospel.

It is the world system (that system which profits at another's expense) not the world (the cosmos) which we are to despise as Christians. Matter is not our enemy but our friend when we are in right relationship to it. If we hold contempt for what God has created (including all varieties of tonal vibrations and combinations thereof) then we cannot properly respect and worship the One who created such possibilities. We must learn to love what God loves, and everything He loves is sacred.

Let us then not be afraid of discovering new varieties of tonal and rhythmical relationships in music, and let us not be reticent to recognize what is sacred to God. And if the secular world discovers something new, we need not be alarmed. The world has the right to uncover a new dimension of the cosmos that our Father has created.

The sun was created to "shine on the just and the unjust." Mathematics may be calculated by criminal and saint alike. God never said that the children of His Kingdom would have a monopoly on the world. He promised only that we would someday inherit it. And if along the way we find that the secular culture has discovered something we can benefit from as musicians and communicators, may we not be too arrogant to stop and listen and, with Christian gratitude, say, "Thank you." We have been done a favor.



# The Jelly Roll Caper

## FERN WRIGHT SCHMIDT

You are an accessory to a crime!" My father's words chilled me to the bone. "Your sister is also an accessory to a crime! But she is younger than you, so I hold you responsible."

I am sure Father would not have been as angry if he had not been minister of our church. That made the situation worse.

I was nine years old. My sister Ruth was only six. She was my tag-along sister. I didn't mind most of the time because she was pretty and giggled a lot. Ruth thought I was very funny and very smart.

"Father, Ruth and I didn't steal anything. How can we be an accessory to—to a crime if we didn't take anything?"

"You girls were with your friend who did the stealing. You didn't say anything. You are just as guilty as Dora Mae."

"We didn't share any of the loot," Ruth spoke up. Until now she had been standing on one foot and then the other, twisting the hem of her dress into a knot.

"Loot!" Father fairly shouted the word. We both jumped. Being a minister, and a very good preacher, Father knew when to shout a word or when to use one softly. Looking into his face now, I could see neither his expression nor his words were going to be soft.

"Loot!" he shouted again. "Where have you picked up such language?"

Big tears spilled over and ran down Ruth's apple-pink cheeks. "I heard the word l-o-o-t" (she spelled it in a whisper) "at the movie last Saturday. Father, it was a keen cowboy movie. You should have gone with us."

When Father was a very young man, he had worked as a cowboy on some large ranches in the Texas Panhandle. He knew real cowboys, not just movie ones. He loved to read true Western stories, and even wrote some himself.

Ruth had the *smart* this time. She hoped she could get Father's mind off our crime and maybe into a less severe mood.

It didn't work though, so I thought I would try some *smart*. Smart meant using your brain. "We came to tell you, Father. We were trying to be honest like George Washington, and like Jesus. Jesus even forgave the worst sinner."

Father thought this over for a minute. I was hoping that faith (and crossing my fingers behind my back) would get us no more than an extra chore in the kitchen. Father rubbed his chin. Ruth stopped twisting the knot in her dress hem. Maybe some color was returning to my cheeks; I felt kind of warm. For awhile I had felt cold and shivery, though it was a blistering day.

"H-u-m." Father made a soft noise this time. We felt better. "Jesus also said, before you come to the altar go and ask forgiveness of anyone you have wronged. Make restitution. Then come to my house with a pure heart and I will hear your prayers."

I knew the Bible passage Father referred to, though he didn't quote it word for word. At the moment I didn't think my *smart* would really be *smart* to quote it back to him correctly.

"Now," he said, "tell me exactly what happened. We will then decide what is to be done."

"Well," Ruth smoothed out the hem of her dress. "It has been such a hot day, we were thirsty."

"What has that to do with stealing?" Father was hot and thirsty too. We could tell he would like to get the crime and punishment over with so he could get some ice water and read on the porch where it was cool.

"Mama sent us to the bakery shop for a loaf of bread and some sweet rolls. She said it was too hot to start the oven. Dora Mae was here, and her mama let her go with us. The road was hot on our bare feet. On the way home we got so thirsty we couldn't even spit."

"Fern," Father frowned. "Don't say 'spit.' Young ladies do not use such language."

"All right," I told him. "We all had cotton mouth. Is that all right to say?"

Father sighed and nodded his head.

"When we got to the cafe on the highway it just seemed natural to go in and ask for a glass of water. There wasn't anyone in the cafe, Father, and Mr. Ed said he didn't mind giving us a glass of water." The very worst part was coming, so I kind of dropped my voice to a whisper.

"Speak up, girl." Father was stern-looking again. My heart began to beat hard.

"Mr. Ed put our water glasses on the counter—with ice in them, too. It sure was good water. About then a man came in and ordered a hamburger. Ruth and me had taken our bonnets off when we came into the cafe. The bonnet strings were too hot . . . . Dora Mae has a new straw hat. It sure is a keen hat."

"Father, can we have a straw hat?" Ruth interrupted. "Hardly anybody wears bonnets anymore." Ruth wanted a straw hat so badly she would even let Dora Mae rock her favorite doll sometimes, just to get to wear Dora Mae's straw hat for a little while.

"Don't change the subject," Father told Ruth.

"Anyway, Dora Mae was sitting on the stool between Ruth and me. She didn't take off her straw hat. Right in front of Dora Mae on the counter was a big platter of fresh made jelly rolls. Boy, they smelled good."

**R**uth began to cry. Father lifted her onto his knee. Being nine years old, of course I was too big to cry or sit on knees. Besides, I was too tall and gangly to fit on anyone's knees very well. I sure felt like crying, though.

"The man waiting for his hamburger was reading a paper and paying us no mind. Mr. Ed had his back to us, frying the meat." I tried to go on, but when I opened my mouth the words just stuck in my throat. I guess all that compassion Father speaks about in his sermons came to him at the right time. He put his arm around me and pulled me close to the chair.

"Dora Mae reached out and took the jelly roll. She took off her straw hat and put the jelly roll on her head then put her hat over the jelly roll.

"Anyone should know a straw hat didn't fit like that," I decided in retrospect.

"Mr. Ed looked at Dora Mae real funny like. Then he looked at the jelly roll plate.

" 'Well,' he said, 'one of my fresh rolls seems to be missing. Did either of you girls take one?'

"Ruth said, 'No,' and ran out the door. I said, 'No, Mr. Ed, and thank you for the water.'

"Dora Mae said, 'No, who would steal a twenty-cent jelly roll?' She put her hand on top of her straw hat, jumped off the stool and ran all the way home."

"You know, Mr. Ed is very sure who took that jelly roll." Father spoke gently now. "Think of this, girls. Does Mr. Ed know you were not part of the plan to take the jelly roll? You should have told Mr. Ed that Dora Mae took the roll. By just going away, you look guilty, too."

"But, Father," I protested. "Dora Mae is our friend."

"Isn't Mr. Ed your friend, too? He sometimes gives you jelly rolls before they go stale. Mr. Ed is honest, and he expects you to be honest. By not speaking up, you have done him a disservice and placed yourselves in a very doubtful position. The question is, what will you do to set things right?"

**F**ather paused for suggestions. None forthcoming, he continued. "A jelly roll costs only twenty cents. But some days when things are slow—and money is scarce these days—twenty cents may be all Mr. Ed makes in a whole day. Mr. Ed is a very old man. He shouldn't even be working in that hot little building."

Ruth brightened. "Father, give us twenty cents. We can give it to Mr. Ed and tell him we are sorry, and really didn't have anything to do with taking the jelly roll."

"That is a good solution," Father agreed, "but I can't do it. That would make me part of the wrong doing. If I give you twenty cents, then you haven't honestly made restitution. You will have to get the money yourselves."

"How in the world can we get twenty cents? Can we take five cents a week out of our Sunday School money?" I really thought that was using my *smart.*

"Oh, no." Father was stern again. "You can't take from the Lord to pay your part of a wrong doing. You girls will have to find some other way to pay Mr. Ed."

The subject was closed. Father went for water and his books.

Our law breaking occurred on a Wednesday. Friday the perfect opportunity presented itself. My older brother, Bill, was church custodian. He also was on the high school debating team. He was to be out of town attending a debating meet on Friday. You see, Fridays were always church cleaning days because all day Saturday Bill worked in the chili joint down by the railroad station. He also shined shoes. My brother would have managed somehow, rather than give up extra money to have someone else do the chore, except this Friday was the day Grandma Haines' funeral was to be at the church. Straightening up couldn't be left to the last minute.

There are emergencies, you know, even in a church. One time we had a hurry-up midnight wedding. I never did understand that.

Bill told Ruth and me he would give us twenty-five cents if we would straighten up the auditorium after the funeral. We made the deal with joy. Besides wiping out our debt to society, we had two whole days to decide how we would spend the extra five cents.

**R**uth, Bill and I were not the only children in our family. There also were Brooks, Robert, Calvin and Betty. We were poor, but didn't know it. We kept a cow in a little pasture at the edge of town. Bill milked, but it was my chore to boil the bottles, separate the cream, churn the butter, then deliver the milk. The money we received for the butter and milk bought feed for the cow. We always had fresh butter and milk for our own table. We made jams and jellies in season, canned vegetables, and had a root cellar. We were never hungry. Our big problem was shoes. Come fall we went to the cotton fields with Mama and picked cotton. So as long as the farmers made a cotton crop, we had shoes.

All of this doesn't seem to have too much to do with "The Jelly Roll Caper," as Bill had named our crime. But in a way, it does. Today kids have allowances, do odd jobs for pay, baby sit, and have full-time jobs during the summer. When I was nine years old, we were too busy helping one another, friends and people down on their luck, to have jobs. We never asked pay for helping or sharing. Like the time a lady asked Mama if one of the older girls could keep her baby while she took her son to a specialist in the city. My older sister went.

Later the lady came by the parsonage. "Mrs. Wright, I know its time for you to be sewing the girls underthings for school. You cut them out. I have plenty of time, what with just two children, to sew all the panties together and put in the elastic."

That was the way everyone helped each other. The only trouble was that, this time, the lady sewed all of the panty fronts to the fronts, and all the backs to the backs. She did a neat job of sewing, but we couldn't sit down. We had to take 24 pairs of panties apart and resew the fronts to backs and do the elastic again. It took so long, with our other chores to do, we never did get the lace whipped on the legs.

Brother Bill got the worst part of it although he didn't wear panties, but wore undershorts. Mama bleached sugar sacks to make his shorts. That year the sugar company began using a new dye on the cotton sugar sacks. Try as Mama would, she never completely bleached all the printing out of the cotton. Across Bill's seat that year appeared the words "Sweetest Sugar" in dull green letters.

How he hated those undershorts. But I was glad, really glad, he had to wear them. I called him "Sweetest Sugar" all winter, and he was mad all winter.

So Bill decided to get even. When he hired Ruth and me to clean the auditorium after the funeral, he told my oldest sister Brooks to get a sheet and hide in the choir loft. She was not to make any noise until we had finished cleaning, then put on the sheet, raise up and make a moaning sound.

When the funeral service had ended and the people had left the church, Ruth and I went to the auditorium to do the cleaning. Ruth gathered the song books and put them in the racks on back of the pews. It was late in the afternoon; dusk was coming on. The smell of flowers still hung in the church. The aroma seemed strongest when I swept up fallen petals and leaves in front of the pulpit. I imagined the casket had been about there, so I swept as fast as I could. The stained-glass windows of the church were shadowy. There was a quiet loneliness everywhere.

Ruth came to hold the dust-pan for me. "Did you ever see anybody dead?" She looked as though she might faint.

"No, and I don't want to talk about it." I was getting up the last of the dust and leaves.

"I guess Grandma Haines is dressed all in white and ready to be raised up to heaven as soon as the Lord calls her, don't you?" Ruth was making us both nervous. She looked around the church. The shadows were heavy now. "Lets go home. Aren't we through yet?"

"Nearly," I said. "Let me dust Father's pulpit and the three chairs." I already had the dust cloth in my apron pocket. While Ruth gathered the broom, dustpan, and the sack of dirt and flower petals, I dusted the pulpit, straightened Father's big Bible, and did the three chairs. We had almost reached the broom closet by the swinging doors as you go from the auditorium to the vestibule when my sister stood up in the choir loft, covered with a sheet, swaying and moaning.

Ruth froze. I froze. Then we both screamed and hit the swinging doors at the same time. I beat Ruth to the big double outside doors, but before I could open one, she had gotten in front of me and had hold of the handle of the opposite door. I yanked the door open, with her in front of me and her arm in the big long handle of the other door. One door flew open and hit her right between the eyes. The impact threw me sideways; the other door flew open, and hit me right between the eyes.

You have never seen four blacker eyes or two more swollen noses in your life.

My sister was not allowed to have a date for a whole month, or even play her phonograph. Brother Bill had to pay us twenty-five cents every Saturday for a whole month for punishment for his part in the frightful affair.

Ruth and I went to Mr. Ed and told him the whole truth, then paid the twenty cents for Dora Mae's jelly roll. I don't think Mr. Ed really wanted to take the money, but somehow felt it was important to us.

Father went with us to the church on Sunday afternoon so we could kneel at the altar and ask God's forgiveness. That way we wouldn't have to turn around to face the congregation with our black, purple, blue and yellow puffed-up faces.

We put the money Bill had to give us in the mission fund. We felt good all over, having paid a debt to a friend and to society; and received God's forgiveness. Our Father forgave us too.

The only thing that hurt was when we had to blow our noses!



# Death and Dying

## JAMES HEFLEY

In a Denville, N.J. hospital, a pretty young girl lay curled in fetal position, her ravaged body shrunken to half her normal 120 lbs. Eyes open, but unseeing, 21-year-old Karen Quinlan was unaware of the court battle swirling around the continuance of her life.

On one side were her parents and spiritual advisers, on the other her doctors and the state of New Jersey.

John and Julia Quinlan, parents of three, argued that their daughter, who had been in a coma for seven months, should be taken off the respirator that had kept her existing in what her doctors admitted was "a chronic vegetative state." They were supported by two outside neurologists and their parish priest.

"It is beyond the competency of physicians to deal with the quality of life themselves—that is what this trial is all about," said one of the neurologists, Dr. Sidney Diamond. Dr. Julius Korein, the other neurologist, declared that the purpose of the trial was to end a medical hypocrisy. He said doctors say publicly they must keep trying to save people beyond hope, but in practice obey an "unwritten law" that allows terminally ill patients to die through "judicious neglect."

The doctors and state authorities who opposed "pulling the plug" noted that the girl's heart was still beating, that she could breathe irregularly without the respirator, that her permanently damaged brain was continuing to emit steady, though slight signals on an electroencephalogram (EEG).

Disputes over the fate of Karen Quinlan continue to spread around the world. In Rome, Catholic theologians disagree among themselves. Father Domenico Grasso, a Jesuit professor at Rome's pontifical Gregorian University, argues that no one has the moral responsibility to keep alive a person who has no hope of recovery, and that nature should be allowed to "take its course." But Father Gino Conetti, writing in the Vatican newspaper *L'Osservators Romano,* maintains that the right to life of a human being must be protected to the "maximum possibility. The case of Karen Ann Quinlan is certainly heart-rending, but with all the compassion that we may have for the parents—traumatized and anguished by the situation—we do not feel we can accept their thesis." He said that every human being must be respected to the final limit of life, adding, "this duty is that much greater when the life is threatened or endangered."

While testimony was being given in the Quinlan trial, a similar court case was being heard in nearby Newark, N.J. Donna Powell, 39, and refused to sign an authorization for feeding tubes and bone marrow tests for leukemia, saying she wanted to die. Doctors were asking Superior Court Judge William J. Camarata to appoint and authorize a guardian to act for her.

Both the Quinlan and Powell cases were drug related. Karen Quinlan collapsed into a coma after a combination of tranquilizers and alcohol. Miss Powell, depressed over her own drug addiction and rejection by a boyfriend, took 140 tranquilizers and tried to drive her car into a stone wall.

The Powell case was quickly decided. Judge Camarata cited a New Jersey Supreme Court decision which had held that a Jehovah's Witness did not have the constitutional right to refuse a blood transfusion on religious grounds. "There is no constitutional right to die," he said.

The Quinlan case developed into a bitter court battle. Finally, a State Supreme Court decision gave Miss Quinlan's stepfather the right to obtain doctors who were willing to abandon extraordinary medical measures to keep her alive. She was taken off a mechanical respirator in June, but left on intravenous feedings and antibiotics.

The case is called a landmark. Never before was a judge asked to approve the ending of life support and thus, in the view of many, authorize euthanasia (Greek: *eu*-*"good," Thanatos*-"death") or mercy killing.

The dust has not settled. Thanks to wide press interest in the Quinlan case, what has been suspected all along is now known to be true. Doctors in cases where the death processes seem irreversible often halt life-support measures. A machine is unhooked, a drug discontinued, or surgery rejected. Now, because of rising concern for patient rights and doctors fear of malpractice suits, the dispute over what to do about gravely ill or injured patients has opened the age of bioethics.

Medical experts, psychologists, legal scholars, philosophers, theologians and other recognized authorities are participating in ethical "think tanks" such as the Institute of Society, Ethics, and the Life Sciences at Hastings-on-Hudson, N.Y. Medical schools are adding ethics courses to their curricula. Medical societies and some church groups are sponsoring lectures and seminars on bioethical topics. An *Encyclopedia of Bioethics* will be published next year.

Evangelicals are just beginning to get involved. The subject has been discussed at meetings of the Christian Medical Society and the evangelical American Scientific Affiliation. The Southern Baptist Christian Life Commission is promoting dialogue between the medical profession and church leaders. A few seminary ethic courses broach the problem in class. Beyond this, evangelicals have tended to shy clear of the knotty questions which have been raised: When is a person dead? When should life support be withdrawn in seemingly hopeless cases? Is mercy killing ever permissible? And who should decide these issues?

It is time that we begin speaking from Scripture and our value system about these matters. We cannot afford to leave the field to liberal theologians and secularists who hold only a this-life perspective. To paraphrase Christian philosopher Edmund Burke's comment at the time of the American Revolution: "All that remains for atheism, materialism, and Big Brotherism to triumph, is for God's people to do nothing."

*What/When is Death?*

Let us begin by facing up to the reality of what our youth-obsessed culture tries to deny—death.

Our health industry helps us stave off the inevitability of death by expensive last-ditch treatments. According to a recent study by Dr. Selma Mushkin of Georgetown University, an estimated 20 percent of our national health dollar goes to support the dying. And when the hospital gives up, our funeral industry helps us make one last expensive effort to disguise death's grim reality.

Nevertheless death is real. It is a divine appointment, a judgment for sin that apart from the return of Christ everyone must keep.

Scripture speaks frankly and frequently of death. It is the dissolving, the taking down of the earthly tabernacle (II Corinthians 5:1). It is the departure of the soul-person that has inhabited the biological temple called the body (II Timothy 4:6). For unbelievers it is the entrance to everlasting punishment; for believers the door to eternal bliss (Daniel 12:2).

We look in vain for a medical definition of death which approaches the knowledge of our time. This is because the Bible was inspired to speak first to the knowledge and culture of the period. It is not that God did not have all wisdom. It is that in His wisdom He spoke truth with which that age could relate.

Dying in Scripture is simply giving up breath (translated "ghost" in King James). This definition was sufficient until recent times. A doctor used a feather or mirror to check on a dying patient's exhalation. The absence of breath spelled death. A little later the cessation of heartbeat was added, then the absence of reflex action.

Death is not so quickly pronounced in a modern hospital today. When breathing becomes difficult or ceases a patient may be hooked up to a respirator that breathes for him. If his heart suddenly ceases to beat, the nurse may sound a Code Alert that will bring a cardio-pulmonary resuscitation team on the run. Businessman Ben Strong of Alexandria, La. was "brought back" 29 times in one day by ventricular respiration and lived to tell about it!

A flat brain wave—"brain death"—for a certain period of time is now the legal moment of truth in eight states, but not in New Jersey where death can be certified upon the cessation of breathing and heartbeat. Even if New Jersey had required brain death, Karen Quinlan would still have been considered alive since some cerebral activity was registering on her EEG.

The trend in medicine is to follow criteria presented by Harvard University researchers in 1968: no spontaneous respiration, no reflexive response to external stimuli or to pain; no brain activity showing on an EEG, checked by two observers 24 hours apart. The latter is also recommended by the American EEG Society, "provided that coma is not due to overdose of depressant drugs." Among 2,650 patients whose brains were declared dead, three later gained some recovery of cerebral functions. They suffered from massive overdose of nervous system depressants.

Modern diagnostic equipment and knowledge makes it impossible to pinpoint an exact moment of death. Every part of the body does not die all at once. In actuality the process of death begins at birth. The body ages much like an automobile until it begins falling apart and reaches a point where a vital function cannot be restored. The process can never be reversed, only slowed. Despite sensational predictions of cryogenic "resurrections" (being frozen and then warmed up when a cure is found) and unlimited organ transplants, science offers no real hope of defeating physical death.

"What we actually record [on the death certificate]," says Dr. Christopher M. Reilly, a former president of the Christian Medical Society, "is the time at which the individual is pronounced dead."

This time can be extremely important in determining heirship when a husband and wife die from a common disaster. It also can be crucial where the death of a transplant donor is in later dispute. Two instances of the latter are on record.

In August, 1963, David Potter was admitted to an English hospital suffering multiple skull fractures and extensive brain damage from a beating. After he stopped breathing, a respirator was hooked up and in two operations, 24 hours apart, his kidneys were removed and transplanted. At the trial of the victim's assailant, the defense attorney blamed the removal of the vital organs for the victim's death. The examining pathologist and a neurologist disagreed, contending that the respirator had been hooked up *after* death occurred and only for the removal of the kidneys. The jury agreed with the doctors and convicted the assailant of manslaughter.

Five years later a more bizarre case almost went to trial in Houston after the heart of a beating victim—whose brain showed no sign of life—was transplanted. The attorney for the assailants argued that he had not really been murdered because his heart was still beating in another body. However, the plea was rendered irrelevant when the recipient died and those arrested were indicted for murder.

In states where cessation of brain activity is not the legal definition of death, doctors are understandably hesitant about performing transplants. The result is that hundreds of needy persons have died, who might otherwise have lived many more active years. A single minute's delay in removing an organ can be crucial.

*When Is It Right To Die?*

The transplant enigma is only part of the larger question faced by doctors who wonder if they are sustaining life or merely prolonging death.

According to Dr. Reilly, a physician has three options in treating the supposedly incurable patient: (1) active treatment for maximum lengthening of life; (2) passive management to shorten the dying process; (3) active intervention to end life (euthanasia).

The attending physician must weigh these options against a variety of factors in consultation with colleagues, the family, and the patient if rational:

A. The remote possibility of recovery and/or remission and the likelihood that a cure might be found if vital functions are prolonged.

B. The level of pain. The doctor is often caught on the horns of a Hippocratic dilemma when he cannot relieve pain without shortening life.

C. The financial effect on the family of further doubtful treatment. (Bills of over $50,000 for prolonging the life of a terminal patient are not unusual.)

D. The medical care and equipment which might otherwise be provided for a patient with a better prognosis.

E. Legalities involved where a patient or parent/guardian may have requested that support be maintained even where there is a flat EEG.

F. The quality of life. When does life reach the point where it is not worth preserving?

The first two options, whether to try and lengthen life or allow death to take its course, offer the greatest latitude for decision. There are obviously no absolute answers because no human has absolute wisdom. Nor does a doctor necessarily "play God" in deciding to give or not to give additional treatment. He can only do what seems best for all concerned.

The decision will test the value system of a patient and/or his family to the core. Which is better: A few more months of suffering in this life or to depart and be with Christ? To use savings for expensive life support or for college tuition? To keep one person alive for a brief time or to give a memorial that will save the lives of 50 children in a land stricken by famine?

Difficult considerations? Yes. But fortunately, Christians are promised special resources. When we need guidance, He promises to give wisdom "liberally" (James 1:5). When we are uncertain about the rightness and consequences of a decision, Scripture assures, "Entertain no worry, but under all circumstances let your petitions be made known before God by prayer and pleading along with thanksgiving. So will the peace of God, that surpasses all understanding, keep guard over your hearts and your thoughts in Christ Jesus" (Philippians 4:6,7, *Berkeley*).

The third option, active intervention to end life, is fraught with the most danger and the greatest possibility of wrongdoing. This may involve the introduction of a death-dealing agent or the removing of a life support. The first is always suicide or homicide, except in cases of insanity. The second is in moral dispute.

Dr. Robert N. Butler, a Washington psychiatrist, recalls an older man who came requesting a mental competency exam. He was facing an illness that would leave him helpless and his family in debt. He had decided to kill himself and wanted certification of his sanity so there would be no legal complications with his will. If the doctor were to take him before the mental health commission for involuntary commitment to a psychiatric hospital, he would deny it all. The doctor could not dissuade him and later he did commit suicide.

Dr. Nathan Schanaper, a Baltimore psychiatrist, tells of a terminally ill young man bargaining with him for a sizable amount of barbiturates "when the time comes." The doctor told a *Washington Post* reporter, "I might end up handing him 50 Seconal, and say, 'One a night; it's to help you sleep.' But he knows what to do with Seconal . . . . Morally," Dr. Schanaper asked, "is it more difficult to let somebody die an obscene, undignified, miserable, painful death? Or to help him, in some way, to die quickly when you know he has to die?"

Defendants have been tried in court for taking direct measures to end the life of the dying. Juries have tended to be lenient. Up to 1968, according to medico-legal expert Joseph P. Fletcher, no Anglo-American doctor had ever been convicted of murder or manslaughter for having opted to end the suffering of his patient. Nor had any layman or doctor been convicted of failing to take steps that could have averted death.

However, no court of law or of human opinion can absolve one from the overt taking of life, even the life of the dying. If such practices should continue to be condoned and authority given to government the next step might be murder of deformed, handicapped, and other socially undesirable people. It happened in Nazi Germany. It could happen again.

The removal of life support is somewhat different. The relevant question here is: When?

We may say when the death process cannot be stayed, when the injury or disease is incurable, when the coma is too deep for recovery. But all of these points require human judgment, and all doctors have seen exceptions. "I have seen people in comas who have survived after many days on machines," plastic surgeon McCarthy DeMere conceded in *Time* (Oct. 27, 1975).

Or when the continuance of life support becomes untenable. The reason may be finances (insurance policies have limitations), status (prominent persons are usually kept breathing longer: Mexico's comatose former president Adolfo Lopez Mateos was kept "alive" for over two years before he succumbed to a brain disease), or other demands for the machines (there is not enough support equipment to go around).

Or when the quality of life seems not worth preserving. Dr. Julius Korein, one of the neurologists who supported the Quinlan parents, declared that their daughter's response to sound, light and pain did "not mean she is either aware or is consciously directing those movements." He said these were patterned reactions built into the nervous system, unrelated to active brain functioning. "I and many of my colleagues are not interested in saving a life that will lie as a vegetable for 10 years," he added.

"In the old days," another physician told science writer Arthur J. Snider of the *Chicago Daily News,* "when things we identified with a human being disappeared —his capacity to reason, to think, to sense, to communicate—when these were destroyed, he stopped breathing, his heart stopped and he died. But now medical science has allowed us to disturb this congruity between personhood and living matter. Now we can keep the pump going and either keep a person in a state of what should not be called life or keep alive something that should not be called a person."

This raises some profound theological questions. What and where is the soul, and when does the soul or eternal person leave the body?

Dr. John D. Freeman, a Southern Baptist scholar, defines the soul (Hebrew, *nephesh*; Greek, *psyche*) as the "non-material ego" and "self." Soul is further represented, he adds, by a number of "psychological nouns . . . . each in a different functional relationship: 'mind' *(nous)* is the self in its rational functions; 'mind' *(phronema)* the self as deeply contemplating; 'heart' *(kardia)* the self as manifesting a complex of attitudes; 'will' *(thelesis)* the self as choosing or deciding; 'spirit' *(pneuma)* the self when thought of apart from earthly connections."

Where is the soul or the eternal self? Is it in the heart? Does it depart when the respiratory and circulatory systems fail and then return when a patient is brought back to life through resuscitation? Dr. Elizabeth Kubler-Ross, a world renowned psychiatric authority on dying, says resuscitated patients commonly recall an experience of "floating out of the physical body and hovering over it." Her investigations have convinced her that there is an after-life. But could not this sense of "floating" be a mind trick?

"Heart" is used more than 900 times in Scripture and almost always refers not to the fleshly organ, but the seat or center of the intellect, the feelings, the will. In some tribal cultures, the liver and stomach take on this connotation.

Evangelical theologians tend to *associate* the soul with the brain and its functions. They do not locate the soul in any part of the brain. A portion can be destroyed and consciousness remain.

When is the soul's association with the brain severed? What about patients whose brains continue to give off weak signals long after medical authorities say they are in effect dead? How much brain activity is required to maintain soul consciousness?

What about the deep freeze technique used in cryosurgery? Does the soul leave the body while the brain tissues are inert and then return when the cells show life again?

What of the resurrections recorded in the Bible? Lazarus was in the grave four days. Wrapped in burial clothes and decaying he certainly was dead. What was the state of his soul during that time? And what of the man who Paul said "was caught up into Paradise, and heard inexpressible words . . ." (II Corinthians 12:2-4)?

Such questions can continue ad infinitum. They may not ever be answered on this side of eternity. In this life we are bound to time and spatial thinking, seeing only "through a glass darkly." When we come into perfect knowledge we shall understand fully (I Corinthians 13:12). Meanwhile, we can be comforted with God's promise of eternal life to all who trust in Christ for salvation and have been redeemed.

Still the crucial question remains: Who shall decide the critical questions which medical science has raised about the dying?

In the past these decisions have been made by doctors. Let us give them the benefit of doubt and say that most have decided conscientiously, and with the good of all concerned. But there is disagreement over whether this practice should continue.

Many believe that every hospital should have a committee of representatives from the community, which would include a theologian and/or an experienced pastor, available to advise doctors on difficult cases.

If so, shouldn't evangelical physicians and other church leaders take the lead? At the very least, evangelicals in a community should insist on representation.

Additionally, there is something every evangelical adult can do to provide for his own future and to save his family from possible agony. He can make a "living" will. While it might not be legally binding, it would be seriously considered by those responsible for his care when he cannot act for himself.

A proposed form:
TO MY FAMILY, MY CLERGYMAN, MY PHYSICIAN, MY LAWYER:

If and when the time comes when I am incapable of deciding my own future, I wish the following statement to stand as the testament of my wishes: If there is no reasonable expectation of my recovering from an illness or injury, I request that I be allowed to die in dignity and not be kept alive by heroic measures.

Specifically, I ask that, in such an illness, drugs be administered to me only for the relief of pain and not to prolong my earthly life, even if these pain-killing drugs may hasten my release from this life. This is because I believe that for me "to be absent from the body is to be present with the Lord" and also because I wish to avoid placing an undue burden on my loved ones and my nurses and doctors. I would also much prefer that money that might be spent to keep me partly alive a few days longer be used for the relief of others whose futures can be more assured.

This request is made after careful and prayerful consideration. I trust that those who love me will feel morally bound to follow its mandate without feeling any guilt for their actions.

Date: ______________________

Signed: ______________________

Witnessed by: ______________________

As one who believes that matter is not all that matters, it seems to me that we who have eternal life should be permitted to die from that perspective.



*FOR FURTHER REFERENCE: II Samuel 12:19-23; Psalms 23; 49:15; 116:15; Proverbs 14:32; Ecclesiastes 7:1; Luke 23:39-43; John 11:23-24; Romans 5:12-14; I Corinthians 15:21, 22, 26, 55-57; II Corinthians 5:1: II Timothy 4:6-8; Hebrews 2:14, 15; Revelation 21:4.*

# St. Francis, Here We Come

## HARALD BREDESEN

If you happen to be walking in a shopping center in your community one of these days you shouldn't be surprised if a bright-looking young man or woman asks you, "Do you know that Jesus loves you?"

That's because Christ Is the Answer, a team of 150 young people led by founder Bill Lowery, has decided that shopping centers are "where it's at" in the average city in the U.S. today. As a result, this team of itinerant evangelists heads for the shopping centers when they move into a community.

"Usually we have no problem," explains Lowery. "We don't pass out literature. We don't stand on soapboxes and preach. And we don't harrass people."

Their technique, developed over a period of five years' experience in the major cities across the U.S. and in many major metropolitan centers of Europe, has proved successful.

"When we ask a person, 'Do you know Jesus loves you?' and he replies 'Who me?' we open our Bibles and show him how to accept God's gift of His Son," explains Lowery.

"But if he says, 'Go to hell,' we just smile and walk on."

Despite this soft sell, however, members of the Christ Is the Answer team do have problems on occasion. Some shopping centers are privately owned. And occasionally the owners object to the presence of team members on their property. (Actually a case has been brought by a labor union to the U.S. Supreme Court which claims that all shopping centers are public property and therefore open to freedom of speech on the part of anyone.) Some team members have been arrested for so-called "trespass" and actually jailed. The response of the remaining members is simply to send additional personnel into the shopping center. When they too are arrested, another group takes their place.

Eventually the shopping center owner,

the police and city officials are so embarrassed by the resulting adverse publicity that team members are released, although sometimes it takes a minor concession on the latter's part.

Another interesting aspect of the Christ Is the Answer program is their ability to operate by faith. They move from community to community in a huge caravan of motor vehicles—50 or 60 in all with a half dozen semitrailers. They carry a huge tent seating several thousand which they pitch on a campsite acquired by an advance team of scouts who visit the community weeks ahead. Mobile trailers house the family units, and single men and women sleep on cots in separate tents.

"While we concentrate on the shopping centers because this is where we find great numbers of people," says Lowery, "we also try to saturate the community with the Good News of Jesus Christ."

This means that there is a singing and preaching service in the big tent each night in addition to the personal evangelism which goes on in the shopping centers and elsewhere throughout the community. Sometimes the team sponsors special events—which also are dramatic demonstrations of their faith operation.

One fall, for instance, the team was located in a community where they noticed that many people were complaining about the high cost of food. Accordingly they determined that they should serve a Thanksgiving dinner for all those who would attend. They printed up 500 tickets and throughout the week preceding distributed them to people they thought would benefit most.

"Up until 10 o'clock Thanksgiving morning we had no idea where the food would come from," says Lowery. "But we believed that God had led us to meet the physical as well as the spiritual needs of the people. So we just trusted Him."

At 10 o'clock a man arrived with a dozen precooked turkeys. From 10 o'clock to 12 there was a steady parade of people coming to the big tent with food of all kinds.

"It was an unbelievable sight," says Lowery. "It was just like Jesus' feeding of the 5,000. Because after we had fed the 500 people who came with their tickets plus our own families there was food left over."

I had known Bill Lowery for some time and had been greatly impressed by his ministry. But I was somewhat taken aback one day a number of months ago when he said, "Harald, how about you and your family joining us on a team crusade across Europe this summer?"

That's how I happened to be talking with a Croatian professor at the Jesuit Theological Seminary in Zagreb, Yugoslavia one evening.

"This morning I read about you in St. Francis of Assisi's vision, and tonight you are here in Zagreb. He prophesied you would come in the latter days, but he didn't tell us you would arrive with guitars and conga drums," the professor said in his Oxford accent.

Throughout the evening as our Jesus folk singers had sung and witnessed, I had kept stealing sideways glances at his suave, inscrutable face, trying to gauge his reactions.

I could almost hear him saying, "These young Americans with their simplistic Gospel and corny music are not my cup of tea!"

But I had been wrong. He had just been telling me he wanted us to come back for a concert in Zagreb's biggest Catholic auditorium. Now he was saying that St. Francis, the 12th-century monk, had prophesied of our coming to Yugoslavia.

"Yes, in his *Little Flowers,* he describes you to a T. In the latter days, he said, the Holy Spirit will choose uneducated youths and simple plain persons who are looked down upon . . . . The Spirit of Christ will select and fill them with a pure love of Christ. They, like he, will forsake all to follow Jesus. They will go outside the church into the highways and byways to share Christ as he and his followers had done . . . as you are doing."

**So God had done it again. As He had so often since our arrival in Southern Europe, He had gone ahead of us to open doors where there were none, and used a Catholic to do it.**

**Ten days earlier, we had arrived in Vienna. We had come 37 strong in our wheezy old diesel bus—my wife, Gen, and myself, our two teenage daughters, DeDe and Meg, and 33 Jesus people, led by Bill**

Lowery, their laughing-eyed, fiery-haired, fiery-hearted founder, and with him, his wife, Sara, and their baby boy, Ace. Huge letters on both sides of the bus proclaimed our name and our message, CHRIST IS THE ANSWER. On top of the bus, under the seats, and in our accompanying van, we carried the instruments and electronic gear of our "Last Generation" folk singers and our "Joyful Noise" rock band.

With the exception of a three-day stint in Holland, we had traveled almost non-stop from Sweden and had arrived bone weary, bedraggled and expectant. After all, the Christians of Sweden had received us with open arms and had packed their stately old Lutheran churches to hear us. Why shouldn't the Viennese?

Not only had the Swedes received us, they had taken generous offerings to back our mission. In the Iron Curtain countries where we were headed, there would be no offerings.

At the end of our four-week Swedish tour, we had a "war chest" of nearly $2,200. That should take care of everything with a tidy sum left over to help defray the $10,000 our round trip fare to Europe had cost. But there was one thing we hadn't reckoned on—the bill our "volunteer" manager was to present to us our last night in Sweden. It was $2,000! And we had thought his was a labor of love! That's why we had had to drive almost non-stop to Vienna, subsisting on bread and cheese and what little sleep we could catch between jolts.

It was rough. But one thought sustained us—the warm welcome we would receive from the Christians in Vienna. An evangelical mission there was expecting us, we assumed. But when at 10:30 p.m. we finally found the mission, the bespectacled man who peered out at us through the barely-opened door looked anything but warmly welcoming.

Yes, he was the pastor. No, he was not expecting us.

Could we spread our sleeping bags on the floor of the mission and give him a service the following night? we asked.

He did not answer. He just stood looking us over . . . up and down, back and forth. From the expression on his face, we could see that scraggly beards and granny gowns were not his bag.

Finally he spoke, "You may sleep on the floor tonight. You may sing at our service tomorrow night, and you, Pastor, can speak. Then we will tell you what we think."

The next night at the end of the service, he said, "Now I will tell you what I think. You must know that the Viennese are a very cultured and refined people. They will not appreciate your appearance or your music any more than we do. Neither has any place in the church. Please, will you vacate within 24 hours."

So there we were, in a strange city, with 37 hungry mouths to feed, weary bodies to house, practically no money, and no open door. But that night, as we prayed about it, the Lord gave us a verse. "When my father and mother forsake me (ie, my own spiritual family, those to whom I would be most apt to look for comfort and support) the Lord will take me up."

We knew that God was going to open a door, and meanwhile, there were the city streets. Somewhere out there must be someone who would want to hear what we had come all the way from America to share. Quite incongruously, we stationed ourselves just outside the Stadt Opera House and began to sing. Almost immediately, a crowd of 90 to 100 gathered.

Some stayed long enough to satisfy their curiosity and went on, only to be replaced by others. The crowd continued to grow. Then up walked a young man of about 6′4″, as slim and straight as he was tall. There was something so very British about him you looked twice for the monocle. For ten minutes he stood listening and making smiling asides to his camera-toting companion.

BJ, one of our most personable "disciples," went up to him. "Sir, are you saved?" he asked.

"No, I'm not saved," he replied, "but I do love God."

He didn't seem embarrassed by the question, just amused. Amused, he told us later, that that question should be asked him just then, coming as he had, from the Moulin Rouge Nightclub, where he and his friend had been photographing strip tease dancers for publicity purposes. He extended his hand.

"I'm Werner Groher, president of the Vienna Arts Club. We are out to encourage fresh young talent. I also happen to be PR man for the leading discotheques and nightclubs of our city. How would you like for me to put you tonight in Vienna's newest and second largest discotheque, the Voom Voom?"

That night, just as we were to open, I nearly blew everything. Ten minutes before our first number, I mused to Werner, "Isn't it amazing? Last night in a church, and tonight in a discotheque!"

"You were in a what?" exclaimed Werner.

Realizing I'd said the wrong thing, I replied, "Why . . . why . . . in a church."

"You mean, your group sings only spiritual music?"

The tautness in his voice and face told me that if I said "yes" everything was off. But what else could I say? That was all we did sing. *Lord, help me!* I prayed under my breath.

"Well, they kicked us out," I said. "They said our music had no place in the church."

He beamed his relief. "Yes, that's the way with the church. They're out of touch with this generation. Anything this generation is for, the church is against. On with the show!"

Now that we'd survived that crisis, I braced myself for the next. That would be when the "Joyful Noise" belted out their first gospel number in this ungospelish setting. I knew better than to hope that they would start off easy, with something calculated to win their audience before they gave them the "hard sell." So I wasn't surprised when they started out with our theme song, "I don't know why Jesus loves me, I don't know why He cares, I don't know why He sacrificed His life, Oh, but I'm glad, so glad He did!"

Through the smoky haze I watched Werner's face to see his reaction. He was smiling and swaying, tapping his long narrow foot to the beat!

Then I noticed a young man in a long white leather coat trimmed with black dog fur pushing toward him. His red hair fell to his shoulders. His red walrus mustache, bright blue eyes, and noble forehead reminded me of the artist's conception in my boyhood history book of Vercingetorix, the Germanic chieftain who fought Julius Caesar. He was the co-manager and leaned over to speak to Werner.

"What did he say?" I asked.

"Fantastic!" chortled Werner.

Judging from their excited expressions, the young people who thronged the place appeared to agree.

Now Werner took my arm and was propelling me toward a private office. There his girlfriend joined us. He closed the door so that we could talk without shouting to be heard above the din (you must shout to be heard in a discotheque).

"If I'd only known the talent in your group, I would have booked you in the largest concert halls of Vienna. But it's not too late. I'm going to get on the phone immediately!"

When he stepped out of the room, his girlfriend said, "I'm so glad you've come! I am a practicing Catholic, and so concerned for Werner's soul. I'm afraid he's going to die and go to hell."

In a moment Werner was back. "I just called the Camera Club," he said. "They'll give you 2,000 schillings if you'll come there a week from tonight. Now I'll call our largest nightclub, the Chattanooga."

Meanwhile, our team was at work amongst the customers. While one group was performing, the other was going out one-by-one or two-by-two to the patrons who were either crowding around the performers or sitting in their cubicles, taking it all in. Before the long evening was over, 16 persons had accepted Jesus Christ as Savior—among them "Vercingetorix" who, from that point on, followed us around like a puppy dog.

Driving home in the van at 1:00 that morning, we praised God for what He had done. We thanked Him that the language barrier had not proved to be insurmountable, since in Austrian schools English is required; that the Swedish evangelical pastor had unexpectedly turned up and was so impressed by what he saw he had rescinded his 24-hour expulsion notice; that Werner was now so sold on us we would not lack for open doors to discotheques, nightclubs, and folk masses as long as we were in Vienna; that one of the people who had come to Christ that night was the daughter of the Canadian ambassador and that she had invited the "Joyful Noise" to the Embassy for her birthday party to sing and testify.

Gen put the capstone on our thanksgiving. "Thank You, Lord, that You slammed the door to the mission. If You hadn't, we would have spent the week ministering to convinced church people—and missed what you really had for us."

The next morning we talked about our next move. Bill turned to me. "Things are going so famously here, why don't you and the 'Last Generation' push on to Yugoslavia?"

Two nights later, our bus pulled up in front of a large beautiful new Jesuit monastery and theological seminary, overlooking Ljubljana's ancient Catholic cathedral. Slovenia, it turned out, had a 1,600,000 Catholic population, and this was the Jesuit center for the entire Republic.

We had stopped first at a Pentecostal evangelical mission, but the pastor had told us, "You cannot stay here. We are under especially close surveillance. Right now someone is probably taking down your license plate."

"You speak in whispers," I said to him. "Is this room bugged?"

"Very possibly," he replied. From the guarded manner in which he spoke, he obviously was assuming that it was.

So now we were at the Jesuit Center, and Father Edmond, the society's superior general, was making us warmly welcome, and in no time at all was getting out the word to the Catholic students of the nearby university, summoning them to a special meeting in our honor.

To our delight, they came toting guitars and, to our amazement, under the direction of the young chaplain of the monastery, Brother Tom, sang us one Negro spiritual after another, alternating with us.

Then I was invited to speak. What to say? I prayed. Once I started, the Lord gave the words. I recalled Pope John's prayer for another Pentecost and how God was answering with a tremendous outpouring of the Spirit, with the result that not only were hundreds of thousands of Catholics being born again and filled with the Holy Spirit, but the walls between Catholics and Protestants were dissolving and we were realizing our oneness in Christ. The warm glow that already suffused the audience seemed to deepen with each passing moment. When I finished the radiant-faced old superior general came up to me and, giving me a double *abrazzo*, kissed me on both cheeks.

"My father, my father, it is the grace of God that has brought you here tonight. Do you know what our great prayer has been? Come, Holy Spirit. And tonight He has come," he said.

He was soon joined by Brother Tom, who asked me to come to his room. He explained that he was the head of all nonvarsity Catholic youths between the ages of 16 and 21 for the entire Republic of Slovenia. Then he pulled out a copy of the manuscript which he had just sent to a Catholic magazine and translated a passage from its pages. "We hold the Holy Spirit captive within our hearts. We must set it free, but how?"

Then he added, "Tonight you have told us how. I must carry this message to all the Catholic youths of the Republic."

By the time of our final meal together, every monk, priest, professor, and student who had been there that evening had been filled with the Holy Spirit, including Father Edmond and Brother Tom.

But this trip back in 1973 was only the beginning of Christ Is the Answer's outreach beyond the U.S.

The next year Christian Broadcasting Network put up $10,000 to help construct and transport a tent seating 3,000 to Europe for evangelistic meetings across the continent.

In northern European countries the team was welcomed in city after city. Great crowds filled the tent. Then the team decided that Italy should be the next target of their evangelistic outreach.

"Everyone told us it would be impossible to get into the country, especially Rome. But we were confident that God would specialize in impossibilities," says Lowery.

A Communist in a high government position befriended the team, made over 100 phone calls in one day, and secured all the necessary permits to allow them to erect their tent and set up camp on a choice piece of ground that normally rented for $300 a week. They got it for $3 a month.

So great was the impact in Rome that the team received a letter of invitation from the mayor and the city fathers of Palermo, Sicily.

The city cleared a beautiful lot and gave it to the team at no cost. Meetings from the first night were capacity crowds. Because of the effect on the hundreds of children and teenagers, Catholic churches throughout the island began to support and announce the meetings from the pulpits in their masses.

So many young people responded that a separate tent was purchased. Two meetings were conducted: one in the afternoon and one running concurrently with the evening meetings for adults.

Astonishingly, local financial support in Sicily far surpassed the support given the team in the average community in the U.S.

Christ Is the Answer founder, Bill Lowery, is a lanky 33-year-old who was born on a farm in Weldon, Ill. After a stint in the army he went into selling mobile homes. But his marriage soon was in trouble and boozing jeopardized his business career.

A dramatic conversion in a Methodist church brought an end to his confusion.

"I felt as though 2,000 pounds were lifted off my shoulders—I felt new," Lowery says. His conversion to Christ was followed by a great desire to share his faith with others. During a short stint in Bible school he fell into a conversation with a minister one day.

"Whatever became of the old tent revivals?" he asked him, recalling his boyhood days in southern Illinois.

"You want a tent?" his friend asked. "I just happen to have one."

So for $800 Lowery had a tent, a beat-up truck, 300 chairs and some lighting equipment. He was in business.

"I began evangelizing at Fairfield, Ill.," says Lowery. "Sara and I lived in a truck, and our food and clothing came from donations.

That was 1969. The next year Lowery made his first evangelistic tour of Europe. He returned more determined than ever to become totally involved in evangelism.

"Jesus' commandment to take no thought for your life and to pray for daily bread became an overwhelming desire," he says.

Soon other young people began to share his feeling for living one day at a time and trusting God to meet every need. Lowery smiles as he admits that some of the followers were ex-drug addicts, hippies and college drop-outs. But they all had one thing in common: a born-again experience and a desire to follow Jesus at any cost.

Although some college and seminary graduates, as well as ordained ministers, have joined the team, most of the preaching is not done from church platforms.

"Personal evangelism in the marketplaces is our bag," says Lowery. "There is no room in camp for individualism. Our Christian community has 'all things in common' as in Acts 2:44. This common purse is just an expression of our desire that we all might be one."

Today, Christ Is the Answer has more than 400 members in the U.S. and Europe. The U.S. base is located in the modest central Illinois community of Weldon. There 32-year-old Jim DeKuyzer, ex-construction foreman from Moline, heads the 10-member U.S. headquarters team which lives and works in a renovated grade school building. The team's monthly street publication, *New Manna,* also is mailed from there.

Another permanent house ministry was launched last year in Washington, D.C. It is headed by DeLon Thompson, former manager of a large department store in Peoria. Forty disciples work out from there into the nation's çapital.

European headquarters are in Goteborg, Sweden, where Jerry Romprey, a former assistant pastor in the large Baptist church in Denver, is now heading up the 15-member team consisting of both Europeans and Americans.

The 150-member tent team traveling Europe, composed of Americans, Swedes, Fins, Italians, Africans and Germans, frequently exchanges disciples with the 200-member American tent team.

"Presenting Jesus Christ to people is an experience of confrontation," says Lowery. "We don't have a martyr complex and we're not looking for trouble. We simply want to give people the opportunity of accepting Christ as their Savior."

Curiously enough, however, the team's experience in its five years of activity indicates that wherever the Gospel of Jesus Christ is presented, sooner or later opposition comes. That it should come in the freedom-loving land of America, and particularly in its suburban shopping centers, is all the more astonishing.

In their efforts to exercise freedom of religion, Christ Is the Answer has found many supporters. Last year Skeeter Davis, Nashville singer, and her band were in one city when K-Mart officials began insisting that police jail team members. Her support and that of several ministers eventually led to a compromise on the part of K-Mart officials.

But whether it's Decatur, Costa Mesa or Jacksonville, Christ Is the Answer team members continue their witnessing in shopping centers, on street corners and nightly in their camp meeting tent. And regardless of harrassment by local hoodlums, or jailing by the police, they are convinced that indeed Christ is the answer.



# Won Without a Word

## SUZANNE ATWELL

Did God intend a woman to obey a husband like *mine?* Certainly *not,* I concluded. Bill had made a promise, and now was keeping me from doing what he had given me permission to do.

Bill was being unreasonable, and there was nothing in my Bible that said I had to submit to such a brute. Or, was there? Slowly the words from I Peter 3:1 (RSV) filtered through me: "Likewise you wives . . ." (and I knew, sadly, that the "likewise" referred to the way bad masters treated their servants) ". . . be submissive to your husbands, so that some, though they do not obey the word, may be won without a word by the behavior of their wives."

I was a Christian of about two months, with a depressing history of psychiatrists, pep pills and a violently stormy marriage. I was trying to let God have a turn at my life. But His way seemed unfair.

I had checked with Bill from work to make sure it was all right for me to attend my weekly prayer meeting that night. It was my only source of fellowship—an oasis in the desert—and I trusted the Lord to work things out so that I could go. Bill gave his okay, but because of past resentments, I bent over backwards to avoid anything that could possibly cause him problems. I prepared an exceptionally good dinner. I had the four children bathed and ready for bed. And I wore my sweetest face during the dinner hour. Bill seemed pleasant, and it looked as though everything was working as I had planned.

*The Lord is good,* I thought.

But just as I was ready to leave the house, Bill casually said, "How about making me a pot of coffee before you go?"

That's no big thing—except that the extent of Bill's coffee drinking is one cup of instant coffee in the morning. Furthermore, I am notorious for my horrid perked coffee, and he is my number-one critic. It was absurd for him to ask for a pot of coffee.

I marched dutifully to the kitchen and made the coffee. I felt smug and self-righteous in my obedience, but I tried to be pleasant. I was reasonably victorious—if there are degrees of victory.

I pushed the screen door open a second

time, ready to breathe my sigh of relief, when Bill rather callously said, "Some of your good ol' Baker's chocolate brownies sure would taste good."

That's no two-eggs-and-water concoction! He obviously was trying me. At that point, a Women's-Lib debate began in my mind. I turned from him to keep him from reading my face while I made my decision. That's when God slipped the little verse from I Peter into my brain, and I knew in my spirit I *had* to make those brownies.

". . . so that they might be won without a word." My face flushed and my anger burned, but I went into the kitchen and started putting the brownies together. It was difficult to sing "Praise God" through clenched teeth. But by the time I popped the brownies into the oven, I was belting out the praises; and I felt as though all the choirs in heaven were singing with me.

God did not magically remove me from making those brownies. I even was late for my meeting. But I was totally victorious emotionally. I knew that to disobey Bill would be to disobey God. Bill might fail me again and again, but I knew that God would never fail me.

Today Bill walks in obedience, too—to Jesus Christ—and he is learning to love me as Jesus loved the church and gave Himself for it. The days of unreasonable demands are long past, but he says that the "brownie incident" played a large role in his conversion. After living with me for 12 years, he knew I couldn't have kept my mouth shut if I had wanted to. He saw Someone living inside me that made me behave differently.

Today, Bill often reads that Scripture from I Peter and adds that he was "won without a word."



## GENERAL MAGAZINE PUBLISHER'S MARKETS

ALIVE NOW! (The Upper Room), 1908 Grand Ave., Nashville, TN 37215. Mary Ruth Coffman, editor. (B). Devotional material: poetry, prose, parables, music, cartoons, photos. 300 wds max. Pays $15-$25.

BOOKSTORE JOURNAL (Christian Booksellers Association, Inc.), 2031 W. Cheyenne Road, Colorado Springs, CO 80906. Julie Cove, editor. (10 issues/yr). Open to receiving articles but preference is to personally assign specific articles to selected writers.

CALL TO PRAYER (World Gospel Mission), 3783 S.R. East (Box 948), Marion, IN 46952. Hollis F. Abbott, editor. (10 issues/yr). Missions oriented.

THE CHRISTIAN ATHLETE (Fellowship of Christian Athletes), Traders Bank Building, 1125 Grand Ave., Suite 812, Kansas City, MO 64106. Gary Warner, editor. (9 issues/yr.). Bridges the worlds of sports and faith. Aimed at high school, college and pro athletes and coaches. Uses personal profiles, articles, and features pertaining to sports; especially likes testimony and personal profiles of known and unknown athletes and coaches. Articles should have spiritual thrust. Query is good but not necessary. Good pictures a selling point for a mss. Length preferred: 1000 to 2500 wds.

CHRISTIAN BOOKSELLER (Christian Life, Inc.), Gundersen Dr. & Schmale Rd., Wheaton, IL 60187. Jan Lokay, editor. (M). This trade magazine, serving religious bookstores and general bookstores with religious book departments, needs articles which develop, in depth, business techniques for Christian bookstores. Reports on industry trends and unusual bookstores also needed. Feature articles are 1000-1500 wds in length. Pays 4¢-5¢/wd on publ. Also uses personal training and managerial and administration how-to articles.

THE CHRISTIAN CENTURY, 407 S. Dearborn St., Chicago, IL 60605. James M. Wall, editor. (B). Interested in articles for clergy on the small church, informational, how-to, personal experience, interviews, think pieces. 1800 wds max. Pays $10/page on publ. Query first. Use SASE.

CHRISTIAN HERALD (Christian Herald Assc., Inc.), 40 Overlook Dr., Chappaqua, NY 10514. Kenneth L. Wilson, editor. (M with Ju-Au comb). Personal Christian living for individuals and families; first-person approach often useful. Also uses articles that offer challenge and/or information about social or religious issues of concern to the Christian. Prefers query before seeing major articles. Top length 2500 wds. Pays $100+ for full-length piece; $10+ for short stories and poetry. No fiction.

CHRISTIAN HERITAGE (Christ's Mission, Inc.), 275 State St. (Box 176), Hackensack, NJ 07602. (M except Ju & Au). Articles of about 2500 wds should be related to the theme which *Christian Heritage* provides through its articles, international press reports, critical assessments of person-centered relations and its Christ-centered evangelical message of hope for a world convulsed by unprecedented revolutionary changes. Protestant-Roman Catholic topics.

CHRISTIAN LIFE (Christian Life, Inc.), Gundersen Dr. & Schmale Rd., Wheaton, IL 60187. Jan Franzen, exec. editor. (M). Slanted for alert Christians, this magazine is looking for articles which show how God is working in the world today—through the lives of individual Christians, organizations, missions. Uses trend articles (2500-3000 wds) which provide evidence of significance and development of an idea, event, or person's impact on society and the meaning of that impact for the reader; inspirational and devotional articles (1500-2500 wds); true adventure articles (2000-2500 wds) which use short story techniques; short stories up to 2500 wds; personality profiles up to 2500 wds and general features. Photos should accompany articles when possible. Pays up to $175 on publ.

THE CHRISTIAN MINISTRY, 407 S. Dearborn St., Chicago, IL 60605. (B). There is a theme for each issue; material on the themes stand the best chance of acceptance. Best to first write the editor about the idea or subject you want to submit.

CHRISTIAN STANDARD (Standard Publishing), 8121 Hamilton Ave., Cincinnati, OH 45231. Edwin V. Hayden, editor. (W). Uses articles of about 1600 wds on Biblical doctrine, applied Bible exegesis, evangelism and stories of accomplishment in Christian life and service. Pays according to length and quality.

CHRISTIANITY TODAY, 1014 Washington Bldg., Washington, D.C. 20005. Harold Lindsell, editor. (Bi-W). Suggest query.

CHURCH ADMINISTRATION, 127 Ninth Ave. N., Nashville, TN 37234. George Clark, editor. (M). How-to-do-it articles dealing with church administration, including church programming, organizing and staffing, administrative skills, church financing. 750-1200 wds. Pays 2½¢/wd on acceptance. Use SASE.

CHURCH GROWTH: AMERICA (Institute for American Church Growth), 333 E. Foothill Blvd., Arcadia, CA 91006. Winfield C. Arn, Jr., editor. (B). Audience is pastors and laymen concerned with church outreach and evangelism. Articles should be on related areas of "Church Growth" in America. Research, current thinking and theorization, case studies of growing churches and analyses, book reviews in church growth, interviews with leading authorities, articles related to church growth based on personal experience. Pymt determined on basis of article ($10-$50). Length 500-2000 wds.

COMMUNICATE (Evangelistic Enterprises Society), Box 600, Beaverlodge, Alberta, Canada TOK OCO. Rev. K. Neill Foster, editor. (M except Au). News accounts of Christian events, especially in Canada, news format, not too long. Photos if possible, current. Pymt if accepted.

DAILY BLESSING (Oral Roberts Evangelistic Assc., Inc.), P.O. Box 2187, Tulsa, OK 74102. Oral Roberts, editor; Billye Morris, managing editor. (Q). Uses meditations that are positive and uplifting in tone. Length: 50 characters/line, 27 lines including title and Scripture verse. Pays $5-$15, depending upon editorial work involved. Suggest close study of magazine before writing meditation.

DAILY MEDITATION P.O. Box 2710, San Antonio, TX 78299. Ruth S. Paterson, editor. Uses inspirational, self-improvement, nonsectarian religious articles showing the way to greater spiritual growth; experiences of God's mysterious ways; archaeological discoveries pertaining or related to the ancient Maya; some poetry and fillers. No fiction. Length: articles: approx 300, 750, 1200, 1650 wds.; fillers: up to 350 wds; poetry: 4 to 12 lines most usable, none over 20 lines. Be sure to give exact wd count on each mss. Pays ½¢-1¢/wd for articles and fillers with 14¢/line for poetry on acceptance. Reports within 60 days. Two checking copies of the issue using mss. sent to author on publ.

DECISION (Billy Graham Evangelistic Assc.), 1300 Harmon Place, Minneapolis, MN 55403. Roger C. Palms, editor. (M). Uses nonfiction articles, preferably personal testimonies or "as told to" accounts which convey what Christ has done. They encourage the writer to study the publication and notice the types of testimonies they use. Length approx 1800 wds. Uses devotional thoughts and short poems in "The Quiet Heart" column; 8-50 line poems (free verse preferred); fresh, brief narratives (400-800 wds) as short features; fresh, original statements (1-3 sentences) as fillers. Pymt is at discretion of editor

DEEPER LIFE (Morris Cerullo/World Evangelism), P.O. Box 700, San Diego, CA 92138. George Ekeroth, editor. (M). All material is currently being written by the staff.

DOORWAYS (International Students, Inc.), P.O. Box C, Star Ranch, Colorado Springs, CO 80901. Hal Guffey, editor; Linda Twedt, asst. editor. (Q). First person stories of internationals and their conversion experiences. Prefers 1500 wds. Urgently needs photography: internationals in Bible study, conferences, close-ups, at meals, showers, parties and picnics with Americans. B & w. Also publishes books concerning experiences of converted Hindus, Muslims and Buddhists. Buys full rights but will consider other rights. Pymt varies according to use. Book rate is standard.

ETERNITY (Evangelical Foundation), 1716 Spruce St., Philadelphia, PA 19103. William J. Peterson, editor. (M). Researched articles on issues in Christian living and thinking such as politics, psychology, archaeology and relationships.

FAITH AT WORK, 11065 Little Patuxent Parkway, Columbia, MD 21044. Walden Howard, editor. (Eight issues/yr). Personal experience articles dealing with conversion, growth and ministry. Must reflect commitment to Christ. 1200-2000 wds. Pays $25-$50 on publ.

FELLOWSHIP (Fellowship of Reconciliation), Box 271, Nyack, NY 10960. Jim Forest, editor. (M). Nonfiction principally but some fiction if related to central theme: creative self-giving love in all situations, particularly of conflict and war. Wants articles on nonviolence, ecology, minorities, civil rights, capital punishment, etc. Also reviews of books on subjects listed above. Prefers 500-1000 wds with limit of 2000 wds. Real-life incidents of nonviolence in action especially desired; also analytical articles with religion implicit rather than explicit. No pay.

FLOODTIDE (Christian Literature Crusade), P.O. Box C, Fort Washington, PA 19034. John and Kathleen Whittle, editors. (B). Published for adults and for college-age young people. Uses articles featuring the power of the printed Gospel in lives; challenges to young people for full-time service; articles showing literature workers on the job in bookstores, bookmobiles, publishing; missionary news and views; other Christian literature-related activities. Articles up to 750 wds. Does not pay.

GOSPEL CALL (Eastern Europe Mission), 232 N. Lake Ave., Pasadena, CA 91101. Paul B. Peterson, editor. (B). Missions.

GOOD NEWS BROADCASTER (Back to the Bible Broadcast), Box 82808, Lincoln, NB 68501. Thomas S. Piper, managing editor. (M with Ju-Au comb). Articles on various ministries of the local church. Mainly for adults, but includes articles for ages 16-21. True stories on salvation, how to live Christian life. 1500 wds. Up to 4¢/wd.

THE GUIDE (Christian Labor Assc. of Canada), 1036 Weston Road, Toronto, Ont. M6N 3S2. Edward Vanderkloet, editor. (10 issues/yr). Labor, economics and related issues.

GUIDEPOSTS, 747 Third Ave., NY 10017. Ruth Stafford Peale and Norman Vincent Peale, publishers. Arthur Gordon, editor. (M). An inspiration magazine written by and for people of all faiths. Uses short features up to 250 wds as well as longer articles up to 1500 wds, all first-person, true experiences with spiritual emphasis. Very few poems used. Pays up to $300 on acceptance.

THE HERALD (Asbury Theological Seminary), 204 N. Lexington Ave., Wilmore, KY 40390. Frank Bateman Stanger, editor. (M). Inspirational anecdotes, the Christian life, informational, personal experience. All of our material is Bible-centered or has to do with religion and the work of the church. Length open. Pays $20-$30. Wesleyan-Arminian publication.

THE HORN BOOK MAGAZINE (The Horn Book, Inc.), 585 Boylston St., Boston, MA 02116. Ethel Heins, editor. (B). Articles on children's books, authors and illustrators. 3000 wds max. $20 a page. Some poetry.

INDIAN HOPE (American Ministries International), Rt. 3, Box 444, Rapid City, SD 57701. Rev. R. L. Gowan, editor. (B). Uses very little free lance material unless specifically Indian in nature. Does not pay.

INTERLIT (David C. Cook Foundation), Cook Square, Elgin, IL 60120. Gladys J. Peterson, editor. (Q). Articles are mostly assigned as each issue is thematic. Purpose of periodical is to inform and serve as a forum for expression. Communication and media ministry mostly involving missions.

LIBERTY (Review & Herald Publishing Assc.), 6840 Eastern Ave. NW, Washington, D.C. 20012. Roland R. Hegstad, editor. (B). Uses nonfiction, current events and historical (primarily former) dealing only with religious freedom and church-state separation. Pays approx $60-$100/article. Pictures accepted also; pays $7 b & w, more for color if used as color. Up to $150 for photo used on front cover.

LISTEN MAGAZINE (Pacific Press Publishers Assc.), 6830 Laurel St., Washington, D.C. 20012. Francis A. Super, editor. (M). Copyright by Narcotics Education, Inc. Material and stories on positive alternatives to a drug way of life. 1500-2000 wds. Pays 3¢-5¢/wd.

LOGOS JOURNAL (Logos International Fellowship, Inc.), 201 Church St., Plainfield, NJ 07060. William Carey Moore, managing editor. (B). Interdenominational in scope and deals primarily with the move of the Holy Spirit in today's world. Although main emphasis is charismatic, articles dealing with the move of God among evangelicals, Catholics or main-line denominational churches are also accepted. Material may be first person, reportive, humorous, newsy or educational in format. Subjects not likely to receive consideration are poetry, Bible exposition and fiction. Also tends to reject material that attacks or berates other Christians, which is inherently negative, self-serving or has political overtones. Max length 2500 wds with 2000 wds being preferred. Pays 5¢-7¢/published wd upon publ.

THE LOOKOUT (Seamen's Church Institute of New York), 15 State St., New York, NY 10004. Carlyle Windley, editor. (10 issues/yr).

Basic purpose of the publ is to engender and sustain interest in the work of the Institute and to encourage monetary gifts in support of its philanthropic work among seamen. Emphasis is on the merchant marine, NOT navy, pleasure yachting, power boats, commercial or pleasure fishing or passenger vessels. Buys free-lance marine-oriented articles (on the old and new, oddities, adventure, factual accounts, unexplained phenomena) of approx 200-1000 wds (together with art) for up to $40, depending on quality, length, etc. Does not use fiction. Buys small amount of short verse paying $5. Does not use technical pieces. Buys vertical format b & w (no color) cover photos on sea-related subjects paying $20. Pays on publ. Prefers queries. Sample issues provided on request.

MATURE YEARS (United Methodist Publishing House), 201 Eighth, Nashville, TN 37202. Mrs. Daisy Warren, editor. (M). Stories and articles of 1500-2000 wds.

MESSAGE OF THE CROSS (Bethany Fellowship Inc.), 6820 Auto Club Road, Minneapolis, MN 55438. Rev. A. T. Hegre, editor. (B).

MISSION JOURNAL (Mission Journal, Inc.), Box 15024, Austin, TX 78761. Ron Durham, editor. (M). Substantive but popularly written articles on theology, ministry, and religion in life. Primary readership from noninstrumental Church of Christ. Length: 2500-3000 wds. Does not pay.

MOODY MONTHLY (Moody Bible Institute), 820 N. LaSalle St., Chicago, IL 60610. Jerry B. Jenkins, editor. (M). Conservative, evangelical, family magazine. Pays up to 10¢/wd. Needs short profiles on people (not superstars), science articles, family features. Free sample magazine and writers' tips. No unsoliciteds. Query first.

NATIONAL CHRISTIAN JOURNAL (United Ministerial Assc., Inc.), P.O. Box 2022, Oakland, CA 94604. Rev. Max A. X. Clark, D.D., editor. (B and special issues). Articles on Christian living, patriotism, Bible history, theology, homiletics and politics to some extent. Prefers short articles, two pages typewritten, double-spaced. No stories. Does not pay but will give free copies.

NAVLOG (International magazine of The Navigators), P.O. Box 20, Colorado Springs, CO 80901. Monte C. Unger, editor. (B). Does not read or accept unsolicited mss since they have their own in-house editorial staff.

NEW WINE (Christian Growth Ministries), P.O. Box 22888, Fort Lauderdale, FL 33335. (M). Articles ranging from 10-15 pages typed double-spaced, on themes basic to Christian living and Spirit-filled life. Pymt varies with length and quality of article.

OMS OUTREACH (OMS International, Inc.), Box A, Greenwood, IN 46142. Eleanor L. Burr, editor. (M except Au). Does not use freelance material unless free. Is not a subscription magazine but sends copies to all donors of $3+/yr to the work of OMS.

THE OTHER SIDE, Box 12236, Philadelphia, PA 19144. John F. Alexander, editor. (B). Articles and poems which stress justice and radical discipleship. Pays $15 on acceptance.

THE PENTECOSTAL TESTIMONY (The Pentecostal Assemblies of Canada), 10 Overlea Blvd., Toronto, Onto, Canada M4H 1A5. Joy E. Hansell, editor. (M). Needs 1000 wd, salvation message article with strong evangelistic appeal. Can use articles on Pentecostal doctrine. Should be of general interest, clear, sound and scriptural. True stories of soul-winning, outstanding conversions and answers to prayer written in first person. Authentic pictures illustrating feature articles welcome (pymt $2.50+). Pays 1¢/wd for mss upon publ.

POWER FOR LIVING (Scripture Press Publications), 1825 College Ave., Wheaton, IL 60187. Don Crawford, exec. editor. (W). Sunday school paper for adults. Wants a variety of nonfiction that will help the reader realize that it is Christ who supplies the power for joyous living: profiles of colorful Christians whose achievements make them article material; first-person stories of how God has helped individuals to triumph in different circumstances; adventures-missionary and otherwise. Wants adult fiction that's true to life, has unpreachy Christian impact. 1500 wds. Pays up to 7¢/wd. Ask for "Tips to the Writer" packet.

POWER FOR TODAY, 2809 Granny White Pike, Nashville, TN 37204. Dr. Joe R. Barnett, editor. (B). Daily devotional guide. Does not pay.

PSYCHOLOGY FOR LIVING (Narramore Christian Foundation), Box 5000, Rosemead, CA 91770. Jeanette Lockerbie, editor. (M). Material is either staff written or guest writers in the same field. They receive much unsolicited material and although some is quite good, it is not geared for them.

PURPOSE (Mennonite Publishing House), 616 Walnut Ave., Scottdale, PA 15683. David E. Hostetler, editor. (M in W parts). Although published by Mennonite Publishing House, they are trying to be nonsectarian in approach and are aiming at a broader audience. Uses a limited amount of poetry. Sweet or artificially rhymed stuff is out. Poetry under 12 lines has a better chance. Pays from $5-$10 depending on substance. *Purpose* is a story paper communicating Christian truth whether fact or fiction. Stories should deal with hard decisions and events in life but should end upbeat even though the outcome is not always positive. Focus is on showing discipleship or faith at work. Max length: 1200 wds. Pays up to 3¢/wd. Material with illustrations has best chance of selling. Pays from $5-$35 for pictures with usual pymt of about $15 for good b & w.

RELIGIOUS BROADCASTING (National Religious Broadcasters, Inc.), Box 2254R, Morristown, NJ 07960. (B). Needs articles on communications.

THE ST. CROIX REVIEW (Religion and Society), Box 2AA, Stillwater, MN 55082. Angus MacDonald, editor. (B). Articles must focus on a contemporary problem in such a way that the message is timeless. Must be with the background of academic knowledge but must also be directed to laymen. Needs good literature that is historically informed. Not interested in "love" articles or mental health. Interested in classical economics as a basis of social reform. Advances the limitations of government rather than the efficacy of government. Pays in additional copies of journal in which article appears.

SIGNS OF THE TIMES (Pacific Press Publishing Assc.), 1350 Villa St., Mountain View, CA 94042. Lawrence Maxwell, editor. (M). Uses short devotional articles, approx 1800 wds, showing the meaning of the Gospel in personal and family life. Freshness of style and relevance to today's living are important. Pays up to $90.

SUNDAY DIGEST (David C. Cook Publ), 850 N. Grove Ave., Elgin, IL 60126. Darlene McRoberts, editor. (W). Personal experience, personality profile, devotional, self-improvement, fiction, missionary, church and Bible history. Interested in top reprints. Up to 1500 wds. Pays up to 5¢/wd on acceptance.

THESE TIMES (Southern Publishing Assc.), Box 59, Nashville, TN 37202. Kenneth J. Holland, editor. (M). Nonfiction: how-to's, personal experience and interviews, 1500-1800 wds. Pays 6¢-10¢/wd. Fiction: parables. Poetry: blank verse, free verse and traditional forms. Photos: b & w $15-$20; color $50-$75. Write for guidelines and sample copy.

THOUGHT (Fordham University Press), 441 E. Fordham Road, New York, NY 10458. Joseph E. Grennen, editor. (Q). Scholarly articles, not excessively technical, in any field of learning or on any aspect of culture, dealing with questions of permanent value and contemporary interest. Length: 5000-10,000 wds. Pymt is 25 offprints of the article. Some poetry. Scholarly review.

20th CENTURY CHRISTIAN, 2809 Granny White Pike, Nashville, TN 37204. Dr. Joe R. Barnett, editor. (M). Narratives of Christianity at work in the present age. All materials scrutinized in view of Bible teachings.

UNITED EVANGELICAL ACTION (National Association of Evangelicals), Box 28, Wheaton, IL 60187. Tom Johnston, editor. (Q). 1800-2500 wd articles on issues and answers related to evangelical thought and action. Pays approx. 3¢/wd on publ. Query essential.

THE UPPER ROOM, 1908 Grand Ave., Nashville, TN 37203. Maxie D. Dunnam, editor. (B). Meditations are purely devotional. They must be world-wide and non-sectarian, presenting in positive terms the merits of the Gospel of Christ in all its fulness and power. A meditation should include a good pointed story. It should not be so familiar that it is threadbare. The meditation should develop one idea only. Max 250 wds includes Bible text, body, prayer and thought for the day which must not be poetry. Meditations should be received at least 10 months in advance of publ date. If quoting a scientific fact or statistic, give source. Pays $7. Leaflet on writing meditations and topics free on request.

VANGUARD (Wedge Publishing Foundation), 229 College St., Toronto, Ont., Canada M5T 1R4. Bonnie M. Greene, editor. (10 issues/yr). Feature articles on third world concerns, struggles for justice, effort among Christians to put their faith into concrete forms that meet the needs of poor and oppressed peoples. Other issues related to a radically Christian lifestyle are acceptable provided authors query first. Length: 650-1800 wds. Pays $50 for full-length article by author earning $6000 or less/yr. Other authors are paid in copies.

WITTENBURG DOOR (Youth Specialties), 861 Sixth Ave., Suite 411, San Diego, CA 92101. Denny Rydberg, editor. (B). Articles that touch on church renewal. Preferably humorous. Prefer articles not more than 1500 wds. Pymt ranges from $15-$40.

WORLD VISION MAGAZINE (World Vision), 919 Huntington Dr., Monrovia, CA 91016. (11 issues/yr. Ju & Au comb). Portrays Christian missionary fields, projects, ministries around the world. Most articles assigned or staff written. Free-lancers should query before submitting, enclosing SASE. No fiction or poetry.

WORLDWIDE CHALLENGE (Campus Crusade for Christ), Arrowhead Springs, San Bernadino, CA 92414. Judy Downs Douglass, editor. (M). Needs only small amount of free-lance material. Audience is the Christian lay person generally acquainted with Campus Crusade. Purpose is to expose reader to God at work, challenge him to be available to God to personally help fulfill Great Commission, build reader in faith. Nonfiction stories about people, groups, events God is using, unusual strategies of evangelism; motivational, informational, educational articles on various aspects of Christian life. Needs some good (not contrived) fiction stories. Needs good thought-provoking poetry, preferably free verse. Article length 1000-2000 wds. Pymt $25-$75.

## GENERAL BOOK PUBLISHER'S MARKETS

ABINGDON PRESS, 201 Eighth Ave. S., Nashville, TN 37203. Paul M. Pettit, religious book editor. Wants 200 page books on general subjects: biography, philosophy, art, music, religion, the family, social concerns. Standard royalty. Query first.

ACTON HOUSE, INC., 1888 Century Park East, Suite 216, Los Angeles, CA 90067. Nancy Bundy, editor.

ADDISON-WESLEY, Reading, MA 01867. Kathleen Leverich, editor. 20 books/yr. Book mss for children, ages 1-17. No specific length. Advances vary. Standard royalty.

ARLINGTON HOUSE, 165 Huguenot St., New Rochelle, NY 10801. Richard Band, editor. Send sample chapter.

ASSOCIATION PRESS, 291 Broadway, New York, NY 10007. Robert Ray Wright, managing editor. Religion (nondenominational), education, family living, how-to, social and behavioral sciences, recreation, sports; quality paperbacks; general nonfiction.

BAKER BOOK HOUSE, 1019 Wealthy St., SE, Grand Rapids, MI 49506. Dan Van't Kerkhoff, editor. Wants nonfiction mss from 30,000 to 60,000 wds: Theology, Bible puzzles and games, quote books, religious reference works, family living, personal living, counseling, sermon outlines, Bible study, discussion guides on issues. Publishes for ages 9 and up.

BETHANY FELLOWSHIP INC., 6820 Auto Club Road, Minneapolis, MN 55438.

THE BETHANY PRESS, P.O. Box 179, St. Louis, MO 63166. Looks for publishable book mss. Wants nonfiction. Essay type treatment of religious, educational, philosophical, and humanitarian themes. Query before submitting mss. Publishes hymnals as well.

BIBLE VOICE, INC., P.O. Box 7491, Van Nuys, CA 91409. Dan O'Neill, editor.

CHOSEN BOOKS, Evergreen Farm, Lincoln, VA 22078. Richard Schneider, editor. Seeks to publish excellent first person, narrative style books by Christians whose experience will be helpful to others. Examples: *Born Again, The Hiding Place, Adventures in Prayer, Deliver Us From Evil.*

CHRISTIAN HERALD HOUSE, 40 Overlook Dr., Chappaqua, NY 10514. Gary A. Sledge, editor-in-chief. Publishes family fiction, nature stories, animal stories, poetry. 250 mss pages min. Nostalgic and inspirational nonfiction. Evangelical Christian books of wider perspective. Query first with outline and sample chapters. Standard royalty.

WILLIAM COLLINS-WORLD PUBLISHING CO., INC., 2080 West 117th St., Cleveland, OH 44111.

COMMUNICATION FOUNDATION PUBLISHERS, Box 386, Lindale, TX 75771. C. E. "Buddy" Hicks, editor. Looking for good writers that have "Christian growth books" or challenging biographies.

CONCORDIA PUBLISHING HOUSE (Lutheran Church-Missouri Synod), 3558 South Jefferson Ave., St. Louis, MO 63118.

CREATION HOUSE, 499 Gundersen, Wheaton, IL 60187. Lila Bishop, editor. Publish exclusively evangelical Christian literature. Accept a few mss dealing with contemporary issues or subjects of interest to a wide spectrum of Christian readers, but special interest is church growth and renewal. Attempt to be in the forefront in reporting God at work in the world today. Religious fiction and poetry have only a slim chance. Most books written in popular, rather than scholarly, style. Varied lengths. Standard royalty.

DIMENSION BOOKS, P.O. Box 811, Denville, NJ 07834. Thomas P. Coffey, editor. Publishes nonfiction books of about 15,000 wds by established writers only. Current and traditional items.

DOUBLEDAY, 245 Park Ave., New York, NY 10017. Alex Liepa, religion editor. Both fiction and nonfiction at 50,000 wds+. Do not send mss, which will be returned unopened. Send letters of query describing your project and include autobiographical material.

EVANGELISTIC ENTERPRISES SOCIETY, Box 600, Beaverlodge, Alta, Canada TOH OCO. Rev. K. Neill Foster, editor. Prefer mss of Christian personal experience written to appeal to general public. Approx. 30,000 wds or less in length. Royalty basis.

EXPOSITION PRESS, INC., 900 S. Oyster Bay Road, Hicksville, NY 11801.

FIDES PUBLISHERS, INC., Box F, Notre Dame, IN 46556. Theological, scriptural, devotional and liturgical books in the high-popular level; religious and related field, such as early childhood and value education. From 30,000 to 70,000 wds.

FRIENDSHIP PRESS, 475 Riverside Drive, New York, NY 10027. Rev. Ward L. Kaiser, editor; Linda Ferm, associate editor. No unsolicited mss. Specialists in education for Christian life and mission. Interdenominational. All programs projected by Interchurch Representatives from U.S. and Canada.

GUARDIAN PRESS, P.O. Box 9351, Grand Rapids, MI 49509. Donald R. White, general editor. No definite needs at present. Use free lance editors and proofreaders.

HARPER & ROW, 10 E. 53rd St., New York, NY 10022.

HAWTHORN BOOKS, INC., 260 Madison Ave., New York, NY 10016. William H. Gentz, editor of religious and inspirational books. Interested in a wide variety of books on religious and inspirational themes, primarily nonfiction. 30,000 to 60,000 wds most desirable length. Report in one month. Royalty basis. New department for Hawthorn Books.

HERALD PRESS BOOKS (Mennonite Publishing House), 616 Walnut Ave., Scottdale, PA 15683. Paul M. Schrock, editor. Releases one new book every other week. Paperbacks and hard cover, popular and scholarly, juvenile and adult books in the areas of inspiration, Bible study, self-helps, church history, fiction, devotionals, peace studies, current issues, missions and evangelism, personal experiences, family life, and Christian ethics.

A. J. HOLMAN (Division of J. B. Lippincott Company), East Washington Square, Philadelphia, PA 19105. Religious nonfiction slanted to the evangelical market.

HOUGHTON MIFFLIN COMPANY, 2 Park St., Boston, MA 02107. Austin G. Olney, editor-in-chief. Approx 150 titles/yr. Book-length fiction or nonfiction mss for publ on a royalty contract basis.

HUNTER MINISTRIES PUBLISHING COMPANY, 1600 Townhurst, Houston, TX 77043. Charles and Frances Hunter, editors. Largely charismatic books.

INTERVARSITY, Box F, Downers Grove, IL 60515. James W. Sire, editor. Wants books which present biblical Christianity to an intelligent Christian or non-Christian audience. These books may range from expositions of Scripture, presentations of theological scholarship, analysis of society and culture from a Biblical perspective and help in living the Christian life for Christians of all spiritual ages. Length 5000 wds+. Pymt is flat fee or royalty on the retail price.

THE JUDSON PRESS, Valley Forge, PA 19481. Harold L. Twiss, editor. About 35 books/yr. Book mss of inspiration, Bible study, educational methods for Christian education, Christian experience. Between 22,500 and 50,000 wds. Pays by royalty.

JOHN KNOX PRESS, 341 Ponce De Leon Ave. NE, Atlanta, GA 30308. Dr. Richard A. Ray, editor. Rarely buys fiction. Types of religious books wanted: books dealing with prayer and personal faith; family and interpersonal relationships; Biblical and theological scholarship and the relation of religion to social, cultural, ethical, or aesthetic concerns; inspirations. It would be helpful if the author's covering letter includes a brief description of the book's potential market and its uniqueness in the field.

KREGEL PUBLICATIONS, 525 Eastern Ave. SE, P.O. Box 2607, Grand Rapids, MI 49501. Paul W. Bennehoff, editor. Very few new mss are accepted. Our primary interest is in the reprinting of the older, more classic religious and theological books which have gone through numerous editions during past years and for which there is a present demand.

LIBRA PUBLISHERS, INC., P.O. Box 165, 391 Willets Road, Roslyn Heights, L.I., NY 11577. Wants both fiction and nonfiction with 20,000 wds. min. Some poetry.

LOGOS INTERNATIONAL, 201 Church St., Plainfield, NJ 07060. Viola Malachuk, editor. Interested in popular treatments of Biblical prophecy, serious trends in discipleship, teaching for children, and biographies. 15,000-500,000 wds. Standard royalty.

MASTER'S PRESS, 20 Mills St., Kalamazoo, MI 49001. Earl Roe, editor. Accepts both fiction and non-fiction. Two book lines: small book using approx 15,000 wd mss and trade size line requiring 30,000-40,000 wd mss. Biography, devotional, inspirational material, Bible studies, basic Christian truths, practical Christian living, contemporary issues, books for juveniles. Query first. Send outline and sample chapters. Pymt is standard royalty. Publishes accessory products as well.

MOODY PRESS, 820 N. LaSalle St., Chicago, IL 60610. Leslie H. Stobbe, editor. General publisher, so both fiction and nonfiction should contain a distinctly Christian message. For fiction, they prefer the complete mss. For nonfiction, particularly textbook level material, they prefer query containing outline and sample chapters.

MOTT MEDIA, Box 236, Milford, MI 48042. George Mott, exec. editor. Biographies of contemporary personalities who have found answers to their problems in their faith and practice of Biblical Christianity. Royalty varies.

MULTNOMAH PRESS, 10209 SE Division, Portland, OR 97215. Larry R. Libby, editor. Approx. 6 titles/yr. Editorial committee reviews book mss which are typed, double-spaced and mailed with return postage. Looking for material which is original and reflects on evangelical, Biblical perspective. Contracts with authors are negotiated on an individual basis. Uses photography and some poetry.

NAZARENE PUBLISHING HOUSE, Box 527, Kansas City, MO 64141. J. Fred Parker, editor. Inspirational, devotional, Bible study, beliefs. Evangelical, Wesleyan viewpoint. 10,000-30,000 wds. Query first. Standard royalty.

THOMAS NELSON, INC., 407 Seventh Ave. South, Nashville, TN 37203. Peter E. Gillquist, editor. Seeking out mss which deal with areas of the Christian life which are of interest in today's world. Nelson authors must be orthodox, honest, speaking to a specific need of readers and must have quality scholarship and communication. Prefers initial letters of query as opposed to finished mss to begin our relationship with an author. Write editor at above address.

OXFORD UNIVERSITY PRESS, 200 Madison Ave., New York, NY 10016. E. Allen Kelley, editor. Editorial news, reference and religious books for undergraduates and adult religious education. Book length. Pays in royalties.

PRENTICE HALL INC., Englewood Cliffs, NJ 07632. Full book length mss in all fields except poetry, westerns and mysteries. Especially interested in biography, popular history, self-help, inspirational and how-to-do-it books.

RAND MCNALLY & COMPANY, P.O. Box 7600, Chicago, IL 60680. Stephen Sutton, adult editor. Dorothy Haas, children's book editor. Paul Tiddens, senior map editor. Publishes no adult religious books and a limited number of religious children's books.

REGAL BOOKS, Box 1591, Glendale, CA 91209. Fritz Ridenour, editor. Does not accept mss for review. Query first with thorough outline. Does not publish fiction or poetry and only limited amount of children's books.

FLEMING H. REVELL COMPANY, Old Tappan, NJ 07675. Dr. Frank S. Mead, editor. Nonfiction at about 30,000 wds.

SWEET PUBLISHING COMPANY (Church of Christ), Box 4055, Austin, TX 78765. Charles Kip Jordon, editor.

TYNDALE HOUSE PUBLISHERS, INC., P.O. Box 80, Wheaton, IL 60187. Dr. Victor L. Oliver, editor-in-chief. Virginia J. Muir, Isabel Erickson, book editors. Book mss only in general Christian field. Standard royalty contract. Query preferred.

VICTOR BOOKS, P.O. Box 1825, Wheaton, IL 60187. Wightman Weese, editor. Junior fiction, approx 25,000 wds. Mss or queries to be addressed to Miss Grace Fox, Children's book editor.

VISION HOUSE PUBLISHERS, 1507 E. McFadden Ave., Santa Ana, CA 92705. Jack Hanslik, Jr. editor.

WHITAKER HOUSE, Pittsburgh and Colfax Sts., Springdale, PA 15144. Victoria L. Botta, editor. Approx 12 books/yr. As a publisher of mass paperback books, we are looking for teaching and testimony mss of approx 200 pages. The author's royalties are based upon a percentage of the cover price of the book.

WORD BOOKS, PUBLISHERS, P.O. Box 1790, Waco, TX 76703. Floyd Thatcher, exec. editor. Adult nonfiction mss of book length.

ZONDERVAN, 1415 Lake Dr. SE, Grand Rapids, MI 49506. T. A. Bryant, mgr. editor. Inspirational; personal stories; the humanities and social sciences; personal development and interpersonal relationships; Biblical studies; marriage and family; contemporary social problems.

# Section IX
# The Writer Specializes

45

# Writing for children, ages 1-6

BARBARA CURIE
Primary Editor, Standard Publishing

Children are a special kind of people. So the writer for children must be a special kind of person, attuned to their interests and needs, aware of their limitations. Someone has said that a creative teacher is one who mediates between a child and his world. What an apt description of a creative writer for children!

**Specialize in children**

A writer for children must possess the same basic skills needed by any other writer. In addition, this writer must specialize in children. Keen observation is a skill needed by successful writers. The writer for children will use his powers of observation to learn about the children. He will observe children at play, at home, at Sunday school, in a toy store. He will find himself sitting on a park bench to watch children play. He will listen for children's voices wherever he goes. His observations will fill to overflowing his treasury of story ideas.

The writer for children will do more than observe children; she will talk to them. She will learn to feel comfortable in a conversation with a three-year-old, for her writing will be just another way of talking to children.

**Learn and act**

The writer will learn and act upon his knowledge. Because he knows that children want to be grown up and like to feel big, the writer will create stories about helping and cooperating. Because he knows

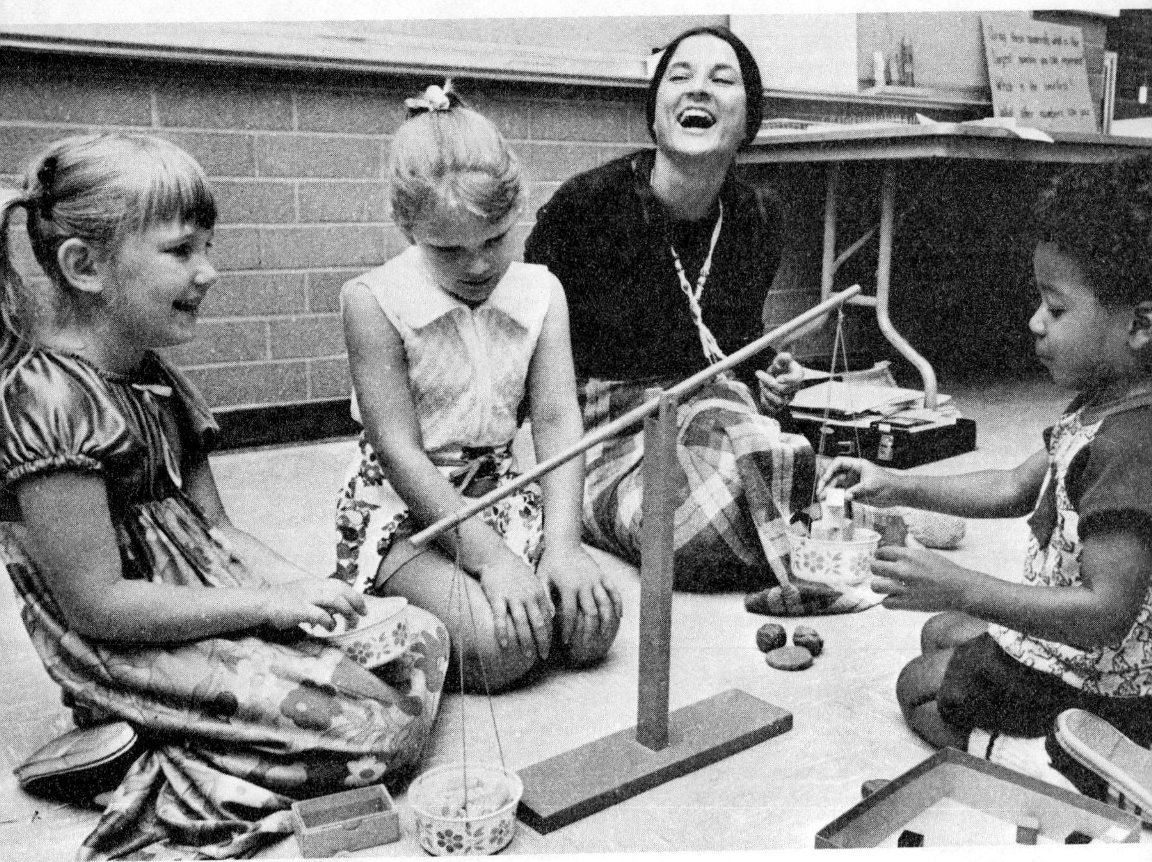

*A writer for children will observe children at play, at home, at Sunday school, everywhere. He should both listen and be able to talk to children. (La Verne College)*

children have fears, he will write stories that help children deal with fears. (He may combine this with children's love of animals and write about a puppy who overcame a fear.)

The writer for children will recognize their love of new words and will incorporate such words in stories. She will use "sayable" words, words and phrases that sound like what they mean, and she will use repetition. For example, she may say, "Old Nell went clippity-clopping down the road. Old Nell was tired. Clip-ity, clop; clip-ity clop. Then Old Nell's owner flicked her with the reins and told her to hurry. And Old Nell hurried. Clippity-clop! Clippity-clop! Clippity, clippity, clippity, clop!" The writer has painted a word picture.

Rhythm enhances children's literature and makes it more readable, whether it be rhythmic phrases like the ones above or an actual rhyme.

Sylvia Martin in *God Is Everywhere* (Standard) has used rhyme and repetition to good advantage. One recurring phrase is, "God is here, God is there, above, before, behind me; Be it high or be it low, there is nowhere I could go that God could never find me."

**Capitalize on the imagination**

Imagination is a part of childhood and the writer will capitalize on this as did Merle Prince in *I Might Have Been a Mountain* (Standard). From the opening phrase, "I might have been a mountain with my head up in the sky. . ." to, "I might have been a cactus. . . .a pony. . . .a pup," etc., the author utilizes a child's imagination and concludes, "I might have been so many things, but still I'm not, you see? And so I know God must have wanted me to be—just me."

To know children is to know what to write for them. A person who combines this knowledge with his writing skills and his desire to communicate truth from God's Word can perform a special and much-needed ministry.

## MARKETS FOR CHILDREN, AGES 1-6

HAPPY TIMES (Concordia Publishing House), 3558 S. Jefferson Ave., St. Louis, MO 63118. Linda Schroeder, editor. (M). Wants material that strengthens and supports Christian home training by providing home activity suggestions, stories with Christian themes, poems. There is a pre-primary picture story. Ages 1-8. Buys all rights. Pays \$3-\$7.50/double-spaced page on publ.

HIGHLIGHTS FOR CHILDREN, 803 Church St., Honesdale, PA 18431. Walter B. Barbe, editor. (M with Jn-Ju comb & Au-Se comb.; S in De). For children 3-12 years, this nondenominational publ. wants stories which the preschool child will listen to eagerly and the older child will also enjoy reading. Avoid references to crime or violence. Should be moral but not necessarily religious; never Sunday-schoolish. Also wants novel things to make and do. Pymt min 5¢/wd for stories on acceptance. Stocked with verse.

NURSERY DAYS (Graded Press), 201 Eighth Ave. South, Nashville, TN 37205. Doris Willis, editor. (M). Written for 2-4 year olds. Designed to give child first religious concepts in terms of life experiences. Relates closely to curriculum material. Areas include child's relationship to and experience in the fellowship of the church; child's understanding of God's basic plan for growth and the importance of being accepted; God's plan for persons to depend on one another; beginning understandings of the Bible as an important book; some Bible stories, ideas and verses that are understandable to the child. Max of 250 wds. Poems and prayers about 4-8 lines. Pymt on acceptance. 2¢/wd for stories; 50¢/line for poems. Buys all rights. Permission given for book rights. No query necessary. Work will not appear for at least one year.

WEEKLY BIBLE READER (Standard Publishing), 8121 Hamilton Ave., Cincinnati, OH 45231. Barbara Curie, editor. (W). Currently buying a limited amount of material. Poems, puzzles, things to make and do are the only needs. Materials need to correlate with our curriculum themes, so request a list of up-coming themes before submitting. Materials should be aimed at 6 and 7 year olds. Pays $1-$5 for poems and puzzles. Will consider glossy photos of animals, nature study, children of the world. Photos pay up to $10.

WOW(American Baptist Churches in the USA), Valley Forge, PA 19481. Gracie McCoy, editor. (W). Fiction 300-400 wds in simple vocabulary. Also puzzles, articles, short poetry, projects, prayers and art writings by children. Pays up to 3¢/wd on acceptance. Use SASE. Ages 6, 7.

46

# Let's stop kidding the kids

DON BOOTH
Free-lance writer

Have you ever had a story take the bit in its teeth and go running off in a direction that you hadn't anticipated when you started it? It is this kind of story that keeps Christian writing from becoming a humdrum, pigeonholing production line for "religious" copy.

**Defy trite pieties**

Perhaps a minor character, created to introduce the antagonism which the hero will confront and conquer, asks a question that defies answering with any of the trite old pieties. Sometimes a character becomes so alive that he refuses to be walked through a contrived plot designed to illustrate a preconceived theme. A verse of the Bible may be introduced into an everyday situation that gives it a depth and meaning it never had for you before.

Writing a profound truth of the Bible or getting across a challenge in 1,000 words is difficult because there is little room for building a plot or characterization. So, in order to save words, I've used two boys, Tom and Jeep, as main characters in my stories. Jeep, who only recently decided to live for Jesus Christ, is not experienced in explaining Christian doctrines. Tom is Jeep's next-door buddy. There has been no Sunday School, Bible or time for God in Tom's background, and he's not familiar with a lot of the words and phrases that Jeep is learning. As Tom and Jeep get involved in the kind of things that all healthy boys get into: kite-flying, swimming, playing with their dogs, building clubhouses, watching ants going in and out of their anthills, Jeep endeavors to tell Tom about Jesus and to answer Tom's skeptical questions.

**Find adequate words**

Sometimes, however, Tom's honest questions, which are perfectly normal from a boy who is hearing about the joys of being a Christian, leave Jeep and me trying desperately to find words that are adequate for the job.

And that, fellow Christian writers, is how I got into trouble.

It was to be a simple story. Tom and Jeep were up in Jeep's tree house on a slow summer afternoon reading some old Sunday school papers. Tom had never read Sunday school papers before—you know, the kind of stories that you and I write.

Jeep was surprised when Tom wadded up the paper he was reading and threw it against the wall. "Christians are selfish! They think they can order God around and He'll give them everything they ask for. That's stupid! Phooey!"

"Take that back," Jeep said, grabbing Tom in a bear hug.

"I won't," Tom gasped.

They rolled around on the floor and wrestled and banged until they tired themselves out. Leaning back against the wall, fingering their bumps, lumps and bruises, the two boys looked at each other and began to laugh.

"Boy! That's the first time we've had a good go-round since you became a Christian," Tom said. "I've sorta missed it."

"M-m-hm," Jeep agreed. "But you're wrong. Christians aren't selfish."

"Sure they are, and I can prove it." Tom pointed with his toe at one of the papers he'd read. "Did you read that?"

"Sure. It was about a girl who wanted a part in a school play. She prayed and asked God for the part. But in the tryouts, the teacher gave the part to another girl. But just before opening night, the girl who had the leading part got sick and the girl who had prayed was asked to do the part. What's wrong with that? God answered her prayer."

"Okay," Tom said. "How about that one?" He pointed to another story.

"Well, that's about a boy who wanted a big red bicycle in the store window but he didn't have the forty dollars for it. He found a wallet with enough money in it to buy the bicycle but he returned the money

*Christian books for children should prepare readers to face the real world.*

and the owner bought him the bicycle as a reward. That's still God answering prayer."

"Okay, how about this story?" Tom smoothed out the paper he'd wadded up.

"Well, that's a story about a boy who accepts Christ as his Savior and when he tells his father, who's been a drunkard all his life, about it, the father begins to cry and wants to become a Christian. That's still..."

"God answering prayer," Tom mimicked what Jeep had said before.

"Well, sure," Jeep said uncomfortably. He didn't quite know what Tom was driving at. The stories all seemed pretty much like the Sunday school stories that he'd been reading all of his life. "You do believe in prayer, don't you?"

"Sure, I do. But you're telling me that if I were to become a Christian, I could pray for anything I want, and God would serve it up on a silver platter."

"Well, not exactly," Jeep said, realizing for the first time how the stories could look to Tom. "These people prayed and God worked it out so they got what they asked for. But a Christian can't pray for just anything and get it. That'd be crazy."

"Why? If I prayed for a new bicycle like this boy did in the story, wouldn't God work it out for me, too? Haven't you ever prayed for something and you didn't get it?"

Jeep thought for a long time. "Yes, I have," he admitted. "But that's different. With these stories, it's make believe. With you and me . . . that's real life."

And there was my predicament. My theme of "The Value of Prayer" had gone right out the window. I began to read through my files of Sunday school papers published by the different denominations, as well as those from non-denominational publishing houses. I found that, read through the eyes of the "Tom's" of the world, they did look pretty false, often offering something as an inducement to becoming a Christian that no one could really hope to receive.

**Reward for virtue**

There is usually reward for virtue; almost always an ending where the hero, a Christian, gets what he prays for while the poor sinner gets by-passed. There is the idea that the hero's being a Christian is accepted and popular, that there is little cause for real sacrifice or service without seeing a reward, that all parents of good Christian boys are understanding of their new faith and soon become Christians in response to their witnessing to them.

There is seldom a story where a boy reports his acceptance of Christ and faces being thrown out of the house, where a drunken father refuses to let a boy go back to that bunch of "Holy Rollers" and pulls him out of the church with only the thread of a new salvation experience to hang onto, where a boy won't play in a sport because of the knowledge that God is expecting him to spend his time at home helping with the chores.

# 47

# Juveniles have problems too

MARY POWELL
Instructor,
Christian Writers Institute

You've decided you'd like to write fiction for children. You feel that winning a child to the Lord or helping one grow into a strong Christian has more lasting worth than the same done for an adult because you don't know what a blessing to the world the child may become.

Only the best is good enough. A child, like an adult, will not read a story that doesn't hold his interest.

Years ago some writers felt that anyone could "write a sweet little story for children." But children have changed—or maybe they haven't—and they don't like "sweet little stories—yeech."

Preschoolers learn math and reading; third graders learn about the planets and can discuss the problems of space travel; sixth graders are starting on algebra. So it's easy to understand why they don't like a story that talks down to them.

**A real problem in every story**

*Probably the most important thing to remember in writing for children is that there should be a problem in every story—and it should be a real one.*

Even young children have problems. What do they do when older kids gang up on them? How do they know the Bible is true? That God really can help?

A youngster, under two years of age, overheard his mother dis-

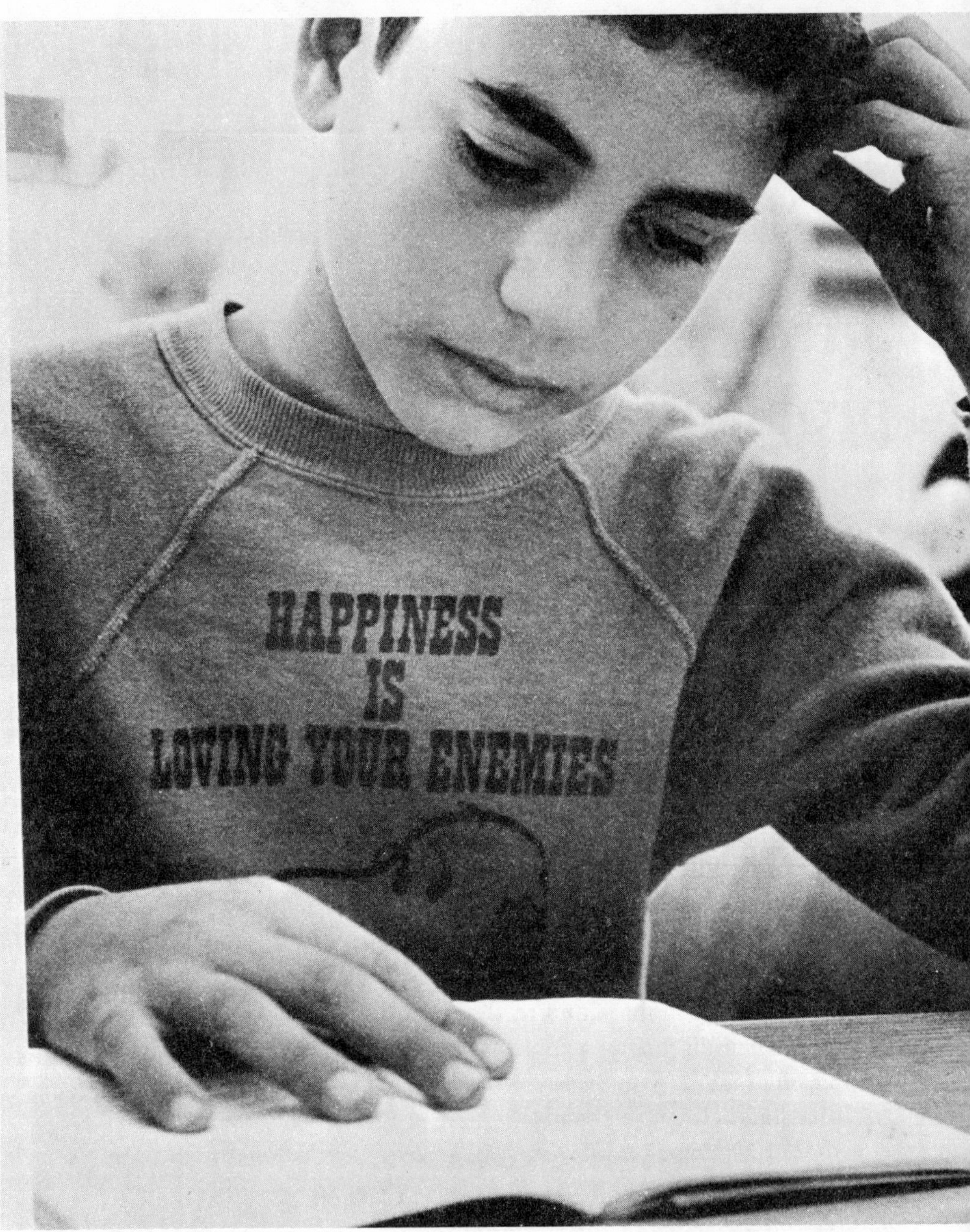


*A child who likes your work will read everything you write and believe everything you say. (Religious News Service)*

cussing Christ's crucifixion with an older child. A couple of days later she said something about Jesus helping people. This "baby" said,

"How can He help anybody? He's just a dead man." Of course, it was explained to him that Jesus rose from the dead but this same youngster, several years older now, said recently, "I know the Bible says it's true and you say that God can do anything, but it's still hard to believe." And in how many other children's hearts is this same doubt?

What about such a simple thing as accepting Christ? A child knows a person can't actually get inside his beating heart even though people tell him to let Jesus come into his heart. What do these grownups really mean? And kids learn in school that their heart stays the same color so how can it turn from black to white? Even though they may want to love God will they grow spiritually if they don't quite understand or believe what they've been told?

What about the older child? The eleven or twelve-year-old. The one in Junior Hi. He may be a Christian but he probably has times of wondering if God really knows he's around—does God really order his life? Or what about witnessing? How can he be a witness? The results usually are discouraging. One eighth grader said, "Mom, all the articles and stories in the Sunday school papers make it sound like kids are hungry for the Gospel. But in real life it doesn't work out that way. You talk about God and they either shrug or change the subject. It's rough."

Of course, every problem doesn't have to be *big*. Making friends in a new school or even getting money for something special can be a problem. After you have a real problem, *be sure the solution is believable.* Very seldom, in real life, does the memory of a Scripture verse solve a problem for a youngster.So think hard before you have it work that way for a story youngster. The work in writing for children is to come up with a fresh, believable, helpful solution.

**Believable solutions**

Sometimes your climax won't be happy. Maybe nobody, no way, is interested in the Lord from the witness of the young person. But he might somehow realize that he's grown spiritually from trying to put into words what he believes. Just because a witness doesn't see results doesn't mean that he hasn't accomplished anything.

This kind of writing takes time—and thought. Every part must dovetail into every other part. It's rewarding though—if a youngster likes your work, he'll notice who wrote it. He'll read everything you write and he'll believe the things you say.

Adults may read your writing because of the intriguing way you express yourself without thinking much about your message. Kids are most interested in what you say.

# 48

# How to plot a juvenile

BERNARD PALMER
Author

Ask a dozen juvenile writers how to go about plotting a new book and the chances are you would get a dozen answers. Paul Hutchens starts with an interesting situation and lets much of the plot develop as it goes along; my wife and I are at the opposite pole. Everything we write has to be set down in some detail before we begin.

Our notebooks, our research file and our travels have provided the bulk of our ideas for a decade. My wife and I have been squirreling away books and clipping magazine and newspaper accounts on subjects that appear to have possibilities for more years than we care to remember. Skin diving, pioneers, mountain climbing, wilderness adventures and a host of other filing topics provide a sharp goad to the imagination and adequate authentic information to use as background material.

An idea may come from the chance remark of a friend, the recitation of some personal problem, or a random thought jotted down in our ever-present notebook. Wherever it comes from we again go to the file and read the material we have on the subject.

We have found, except in very rare cases, that it is not profitable to decide upon a topic and then research it. The process takes too long. A good up-to-date file, on the other hand, will likely contain all the authentic information you will need for a juvenile.

Authenticity, of course, is one of the chief yardsticks sharp young readers will use as a measure for any work. Accuracy is a must which underscores the importance of an adequate filing system. **Authenticity**

Once we have a germinal idea and have boned up on the setting and special skills or situations involved we are ready to plot. Many authorities say one should never talk out his story with anyone until after it is written. My wife and I do our plotting while on a drive in the country. It seems that we have to get away from the telephone and

*Bernard Palmer poses beside the books he has written, most of them for young people.*

numerous household interruptions in order to get the story framework.

We choose our characters and start talking about them as the real people they must become before we have finished the book, accepting and discarding possibilities until we have a short paragraph or two which tells in very broad terms what the book is going to be about. Certain plot complications are considered.

At this time we also develop the Christian problems we plan to stress, taking special care to weave them into the plot.

With that in hand we work out a chapter by chapter synopsis. Usually we break each chapter into four scenes and number them. That helps to make for a highly dramatized story. It has been easier for us to grasp and dramatize one scene at a time than it has been to dramatize continually a long, and perhaps somewhat involved, story. Breaking each chapter into scenes helps us develop a minor climax in each chapter.

We have found such an outline to be most helpful in pacing the story so the length falls into that most desired by the publisher. Once we start to write we often telescope two or more chapters into one and expand others, as our sense of pacing seems to indicate is wise. But we find a tendency to ramble unless we have a detailed outline to use as a guide.

When the plot is fully developed, the characters so well thought out that we think of them as persons we know intimately, and the spiritual thread is firmly implanted in the outline we are ready to go to work.

**First draft**

We do the first draft on a dictating machine, as rapidly as possible to preserve the vitality and life of the story. Little regard is given to sentence structure, grammar or the best choice of words. Our rough drafts are only for the purpose of expanding the story and building a portion of the dialogue. The real writing comes later.

The tedious, painstaking work of outlining your new juvenile may seem a waste of time when you are so eager to get into the story. If so, we won't quarrel with you. The important thing is to have a system that works.

We feel, however, that the preparation of a detailed chapter-by-chapter plot helps us to turn out a juvenile in less time, and with a minimum of re-write.

Thinking back over the work of the last three or four years, it occurred to me that the books we have had the most difficulty in writing, the books that took the most time and with the most wasted copy were the books with which we tried to short-cut the early preparation.

49

# Writing for juveniles

RUTH TILTON

Free-lance writer

One of the most profitable fields in religious journalism is that of the juveniles. It is profitable for two reasons: first, because you have the opportunity to reach young people who have all of their lives before them in which to serve the Lord, and secondly, because it is a steady, wide-open market where beginning writers are welcomed and often make their first sales. Editors of Sunday school weeklies keep a steady lookout for material, and Christian book publishers have a ready market for the longer manuscript.

**A profitable market**

Craft is necessary here as well as in adult publications. Editors today are looking for quality material. Fiction must be plotted and have the dramatic qualities that make for good writing. The Gospel teaching should be an intrinsic part of the story plot, not a tacked-on moral. However, because the stories are necessarily short, the plot can be simplified, with a lessening of complication, and the number of story characters should be kept to a minimum. In nonfiction, organization is important and anecdotal material desirable. The wise author will also slant for a certain publication.

**Taboos for any children's writing**

There are a number of taboos for any children's writing, but especially in the Sunday school field. These vary for publications, but Christian personalities in fiction or real-life must act in accordance with evangelical standards. Use of slang which can be interpreted as swearing and other slang, unless characterization makes it a must, is generally avoided. Dances, movie attendance, extreme make-up, the wearing of shorts or slacks by girls, "necking" among the teen-agers are avoided unless presented in an unfavorable way.

For the child of primary age or younger, stories of death, tragic accidents or gruesome physical handicaps or disease are frowned upon by most editors. Also, it is better to teach a positive lesson to this age, such as "It pleases Jesus when you share with others" rather than "It makes Jesus unhappy when you don't share."

**Broad subject matter**

The subject matter for children's writing is very broad, especially for those of junior age (from 9 years) into the teens. Children are eager to learn, and the world around them is wonderfully intriguing. Science, other people, nature, sports, animals and travel but touch on the things they are interested in. One should have a happy outlook to write for these so-impressionable young people, looking at the world through their fascinated eyes, writing to challenge and inspire and instruct and encourage them.

## MARKETS FOR CHILDREN, AGES 7-12

THE BEEHIVE (United Methodist), 201 Eighth Ave. South, Nashville, TN 37203. Martha Wagner, editor. (W). Church history and Biblical stories; modern-day stories; science and nature articles; travel stories or stories of other countries; puzzles, cartoons, how-to-do-it crafts. 500-700 wds. B & w photos or color transparencies used. For 9-11 year olds. Pymt on acceptance. Min 3¢/wd plus additional pymt for art work or photos. Poetry, 50¢/line. Buys all rights.

CLIMB (Warner Press), 1200 E. Fifth St., Anderson, IN 46011. William A. White, editor. 250-1000 wd articles for 10 and 11 year olds that deal with current situations this age group might face. Use lots of dialog. Pays $10/1000 wds on publ. Adventure stories should be 800-1200 wds. Same pay as nonfiction.

COUNSELOR (Scripture Press Publications), P.O. Box 513, Glen Ellyn, IL 60137. Grace Fox, editor. (Q in W parts). Ages 9-11. Special-

*Subjects for children's writing are everywhere. To them the world is wonderfully intriguing. (Family Films)*

izes in true stories that demonstrate the thrill of walking with Christ. Wants interesting true stories with good photos. 600-1200 wds. Query first. Free "Tips to Writer" packet gives more information. Pymt 5¢-7¢/wd.

DASH (Christian Service Brigade), Box 150, Wheaton, IL 60187. Paul Heidebrecht, editor. (8 issues/yr). Stories, articles, projects, puzzles of interest to boys aged 8-11. 500-1200 wds. Pymt 1¢-4¢/wd. Topics such as history, outdoor adventure, science, nature, sports and television are popular. Photos on similar subjects also purchased. Pays $7.50-$15.

DISCOVERY (Light and Life Press), 999 College Ave., Winona Lake, IN 46590. Vera Bethel, editor. (W). Needs fiction for children age 9-11, that is full of action; boy's viewpoint needed most; seasonal fiction always needed; 1500-2000 wds. Needs interview articles about kids' pets, hobbies, vacations; craft articles with photos or sketches. B & w photos enhance the salability of any article. Articles 200-1000 wds. Uses 4-16 line poetry. Pays 2¢/wd for prose and 25¢/line for poetry on acceptance.

THE GOOD DEEDER (Your Story Hour radio program), Berrien Springs, MI 49103. Colleen S. Garber, editor. (10 issues/yr). Character building, not moralizing stories. Must be true to life. Needs materials on anti-smoking, drinking, drugs. Also uses short stories (up to 1000 wds) adapted from the Bible for youngsters 9-13 years. Other stories 1000-1500 wds. Pymt 1¢/wd on publ. Buys one-time rights; likes second rights material. Sample copies and writers' guidelines available for 10¢.

JET CADET (Standard Publishing), 8121 Hamilton Ave., Cincinnati, OH 45231. Dana Eynon, editor. (Q in W parts). Fiction stories, 1000-1200 wds, that correlate with curriculum lesson themes. List of themes and Scriptures available on request. Pymt up to 1½¢/wd. Stories must appeal to children 8-11 years old and contain Christian character-building elements.

JUNIOR DISCOVERIES (Nazarene Publishing House), 6401 The Paseo, Kansas City, MO 64131. Ruth Henck, editor. (W). Fiction, 1200 wds; serials of 3 or 4 parts, 5000 wds; feature articles, 500-750 wds. Photos or illustrative material welcome. Photos should be glossy, 5 x 7 or 8 x 10. Pymt 2¢/wd on acceptance; $1-$10 for photos; poetry, 4-16 lines, 25¢+/line.

JUNIOR TRAILS (Gospel Publishing House), 1445 Boonville Ave., Springfield, MO 65802. Berneda Warner, editor. (Q). Fiction, 1500-1800 wds, presenting Christianity in action. Biography, missionary material using fiction technique. Historical, scientific or nature material with a spiritual lesson, 500-1000 wds. Fillers, up to 200 wds, containing an anecdote and with strong evangelical slant. Special day material should be sent 10-12 months in advance. Pays 1¢/wd upon acceptance.

MY PLEASURE (Union Gospel Press), P.O. Box 6059, Cleveland, OH 44101. (Q in W parts). Ages 9-12. Uses fiction with a strong emphasis on Christian living; biographies about Christians whom children can admire and follow; how-to articles; some short fillers (devotionals, illustrations, short stories, short articles); poems, puzzles and quizzes. Articles 900-1500 wds; fillers 200-900 wds. Pymt 3¢/wd, 35¢/line for poems, up to $7.50 for puzzles and quizzes.

ON THE LINE (Mennonite Publishing House), 616 Walnut Ave., Scottdale, PA 15683. Helen Alderfer, editor. (M in W parts). Needs articles for the 9-14 child, 800-1200 wds designed to increase the child's interest in Christianity; his understanding of the Bible; his identification with church; nature and hobbies. Needs wholesome stories 1000-1200 wds encouraging Christian attitudes toward himself and others and the situations in which he finds himself. Serials to five parts. Pays about 2¢/wd (1¢/wd for second rights mss). Also uses verse, 4-16 lines; often semihumorous with unexpected twist; puzzles and quizzes. "When You Write" brochure and sample copies free on request.

RAINBOW (American Baptist Churches in the USA), Valley Forge, PA 19481. Grace McCoy, editor. (M). Fiction 800-1500 wds. Also biographies, articles, projects, poetry, puzzles, prayers, Bible stories, cartoons and art writings by children. Pays up to 3¢/wd on acceptance. Use SASE. Ages 8-11.

STORY FRIENDS (Mennonite Publishing House), Scottdale, PA 15683. Alice Hershberger, editor. (M in W parts). Stories up to 900 wds which reinforce scriptural principles; provide patterns of forgiveness, respect, responsibility; present variety of ethnic and economic backgrounds with authenticity; develop appreciation for Christian heritage; offer workable suggestions for the child's involvement in caring-sharing life of the Christian community; portray families or churches celebrating Christian holidays. Pymt up to 3¢/wd. Also uses activities, poems, puzzles, quizzes, riddles—pymt usually $4-$5. Photo stories paid on basis of number of photos. Ages 4-9.

TOUCH (Calvinettes), Box 7244, Grand Rapids, MI 49510. Joanne Ilbring, editor. (M). Stories, 1500 wds; general articles, 1000 wds; craft articles, 500 wds. Pymt 2¢/wd up to $35. Ages 9-13.

TRAILS (Pioneer Girls), Box 788, Wheaton, IL 60187. Sara Robertson, editor. (B). Ages 9-13. Articles and fiction consistent with Christian principles. Historical and geographical articles, crafts, puzzles, jokes, and nature material. Pays $20-$40 for articles and fiction; $5-$20 for puzzles and crafts. 500-1500 wds. Usually buys first rights material.

THE VINE (United Methodist Church), 201 Eighth Ave. South, Nashville, TN 37215. Betty M. Buerki, editor. (M in W parts). Published for ages 8-10. Contains stories, articles, light or religious verse, puzzles, quizzes, matching games, worship resources, photo and special occasion features. Buys all rights. Stories, 500-800 wds, must be in harmony with best Christian standards of thought, feeling and action. Pays 3¢/wd; articles 500 wds or less, 3¢/wd; poetry 50¢-$1/line.

WONDER TIME (Nazarene Publishing House), 6401 The Paseo, Kansas City, MO 64131. Elizabeth B. Jones, editor. (W). Needs stories, 750 wds or less, based on Christian principles and relevant to the experiences of today's child. These should help to give a child hope, courage, and incentive to do right. Pays 2¢/wd. Ages 6-8.

# 50

# Writing for teens, ages 13-18

ROY LYNN
*Editor, Teens Today,*
Nazarene Publishing House

Keep in mind several "key words" when preparing a manuscript for today's teens. Realism and believability, story line and climax, vantage point, and editorial criteria are the ones this writer wishes to deal with briefly in this article. **Key words**

Today's teens are as idealistic as those of previous generations, but their idealism has been tempered by a dose of realism. Younger teen-agers are studying subjects in school that ten years ago were reserved for those in high school.

As a result, the older teens are studying some of these subjects in-depth and moving on to material previously reserved for early college studies. This increased knowledge has brought more realism into teen-agers' lives.

It has not had a significant effect on the emotional maturity, however. Teens still have a tendency to be idealistic. It is the kind of idealism which says, "Don't bother me with the facts—my mind is already made up." A story or article for young people must be realistic enough to convince the reader that the story could in fact have happened, or did happen. At the same time there must be enough idealism to keep the reader emotionally involved and to challenge or inspire him or her.

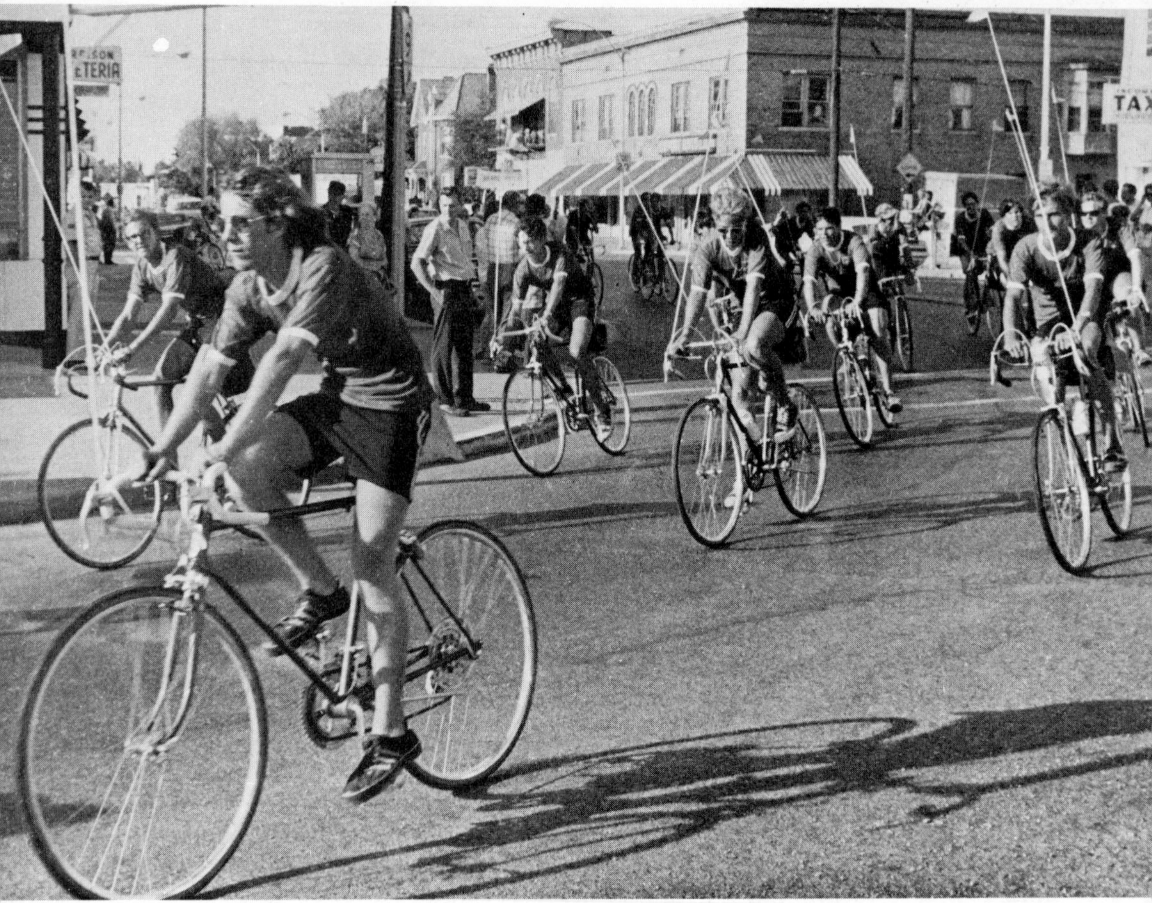


*If your teen story deals with some interest of this age group, it will have readers. (Bette Lux)*

Two distinct story line philosophies appear in the manuscripts that cross my desk. Some manuscripts simply tell a story; there is no apparent climax, except the moral—which is understood when the final lines are read. Others have the characters falling in and out of predicaments as quickly as a page is turned. A story should be more than a mere narration of current events in the lives of a group of teens. On the other hand, teens' lives are not really a sequence of crises, even though some of them would have us think so. Two very important facts need to be remembered. Not all problems of teens are solved in the "malt shop," which went out with the '50s. Not all situations are resolved with a happy ending in the view of the characters.

**More than mere narration**

**Identify with a personality**

A reader needs a personality with which to identify if he is to enjoy and complete a story or article. While some young readers can and will identify with someone significantly older, few, if any, will identify with a character significantly younger. This being the case, a story for teens should revolve around the concerns of that age group. Readers need to identify in the story either their perceived self or idealized self. The story or article should be related from the perspective of teen-agers.

**Specific criteria of editor**

Probably the most baffling of all considerations are the specific criteria of a particular editor. Some criteria which an editor uses are undefinable, but some criteria are commonly held. Manuscripts should be clearly typed, double-spaced, on 8½ x 11 inch clean white paper. When an article has poor grammar or misspelled words on the first two or last two pages, it is certain to be rejected. Most editors must be captured in the first two pages and must be satisfied with the conclusion or they will probably not read the meat in the middle. Most stories could be as well told if 20 percent of the words were eliminated. When a manuscript is cold (you have almost forgotten parts of it), become an editor and eliminate all extraneous material yourself. The result will be a sellable piece instead of wordy wall paper.

Television is getting more attention than magazines or books. Paper and ink prices have inflated as much or more than other consumables. More persons today are attempting to write for the teen market than ever before. So the stories and articles which sell are believable, explicitly written for the age group, realistically ideal and prepared in a professional manner.

## MARKETS FOR AGES 13-18

ACCENT ON YOUTH (United Methodist Publ. House), 201 Eighth Ave. S., Nashville, TN 37203. (M). Articles, 800-1200 wds, 3¢+/wd. Short stories, 1500-2200 wds, $75+. Photo features, cartoons, photographs (8 x 10, b & w, color transparencies). Teen activities, self-guidance, health, personality, behavior, etiquette, etc. Faith and ethics. Especially slanted to junior high understanding and experience. Fine and popular arts. Public affairs and social issues, sciences, and the natural world, Biblical and theological issues.

ALIVE! FOR YOUNG TEENS, P.O. Box 179, St. Louis, MO 63166. Darrell Faires, editor. (M). Needs articles about youth, youth-related concerns. They get lots of fiction, poetry and fillers. 1200-1500 wds with b & w glossy photos if available. Pays 2¢/wd on acceptance.

BREAD (Church of the Nazarene), 6401 The Paseo, Kansas City, MO 64131. Dan Ketchum, editor. (M). Short stories up to 2500 wds. Infrequent use of fiction. No sermons or sermonettes. Slanted to high school level, ages 14-17. Pays 2¢+/wd for prose; 15¢/line min for poetry; approx $10 for photos.

CAMPUS LIFE (Youth for Christ), Box 419, Wheaton, IL 60187. Philip Yancey, editor. (M). Wants practical material dealing with the problems of modern Christian teenagers. No sermons. Articles must be constructive and show understanding of adolescent minds and problems. Uses almost no free-lance material. Pays $100+, depending on quality. Ages 14-25.

CHRISTIAN ADVENTURER (Pentecostal Church of God of America), P.O. Box 850, Joplin, MO 64801. Mrs. Marthel Wilson, editor. (Q in W parts). Needs 1500 wd fiction or true-to-life stories illustrating some facet of Christian experience. Can also use 800-1000 wd stories of well-known Christians or interesting incidents from the life of the writer, or a discussion of some topic of interest to teens. Also uses puzzles or quizzes. Must be Bible-based, suitable for teens from 13-19 and require no art. Pays quarterly ½¢/wd.

CHRISTIAN LIVING (David C. Cook Publishing Co.), 850 N. Grove Ave., Elgin, IL 60120. Marlene D. LeFever, editor. (Q). Well researched, contemporary, interesting articles on topics of interest to senior highs; features on teens working in their communities and churches, doing special service projects; teens doing unusual things which may serve as idea starters for readers; young people who have unusual experiences or accomplishments which would be an encouragement to other readers; fiction. Articles should be approx 1200 wds. Pays 3¢-5¢ on acceptance. Ages 15-17.

FREEWAY (Scripture Press Publications), Box 513, Glen Ellyn, IL 60137. Anne Harrington, editor. (Q in W parts). Needs personal experience stories showing how God has worked in a young person's life. First person account of how God has blessed through exciting or trying circumstances. Profiles of contemporary Christians who would be of interest to older teens and whose lives demonstrate that Christianity works. Real-life stories should be supported with good action photos. Stories of sports figures also needed. Pays up to 7¢/wd. Ask for "Tips to the Writer" packet. Ages 14-25.

GLAD (Standard Publishing), 8121 Hamilton Ave., Cincinnati, OH 45231. Judy Trotter, editor. (Q in W parts). Need mature material for older teens. Short, humorous fiction, 700-1000 wds dealing with dating, college life, getting a job, etc. Serious, mature fiction where perhaps everything doesn't turn out OK in the end—challenging, thought-provoking, geared to encourage Christian values and life-style, 1000-1200 wds. Also articles giving mature treatment and analysis of current issues such as TM, cults, drugs, politics, music, movies, and the Christian's response to such. No preaching or moralizing. Pymt determined by length and quality. Made on acceptance. Also needs b & w photos and cartoons. $10-$15. No queries. Age 16-19.

GUIDE (Review and Herald Publishing Assc.), 6856 Eastern Ave., Washington, D.C. 20012. Lowell Litten, editor. (W). Needs true stories, biographical sketches, nature articles. Should have positive approach, be dramatically written, inspiring 10-15 year olds to honesty, faithfulness, reverence, etc. 2000 wds. Pays 2¢-3¢/wd on acceptance.

HIGH SCHOOL TEACHER (Scripture Press Publications, Inc.), 1825 College Ave., Wheaton, IL 60187. Ardith Hooten, editor. Already has large volume of material but does consider free-lancers who have a definite "burden" for communicating to teachers and students through curriculum materials. Teaching tip articles and poetry (200 line max). Writers must have practical experience in working with and relating to teens. Brief biographical sketch and statement of personal faith, plus reference to previously published works (if any). Ages 14-17.

INSIGHT (The Young Calvinist Federation), Box 7244, Grand Rapids, MI 49510. Rev. James C. Lont, editor. (M except Jn & Au). Fiction and poetry with a Christian emphasis meaningful to youth ages 15-20. Length up to 2500 wds. Pays up to $35. No more than 25 lines for poetry.

LOOKING AHEAD (David C. Cook Publishing Co.), 850 N. Grove Ave., Elgin, IL 60120. Marlene D. LeFever, editor. (Q). Well researched, contemporary, interesting articles on topics of interest to junior highs; features on teens working in their communities and churches, doing special service projects; teens doing unusual things which may serve as idea starters for readers; young people who have unusual experiences or accomplishments which would be an encouragement to other readers; fiction. Articles should be approx 1200 wds. Pays 3¢-5¢/wd on acceptance. Ages 12-14.

MY DELIGHT (Union Gospel Press), P.O. Box 6059, Cleveland, OH 44101. (Q in W parts). Uses fiction with strong emphasis on Christian living; biographies about Christians whom young people can admire and follow; how-to articles; some short fillers (devotionals, illustrations, short stories; short articles); poems, puzzles and quizzes. Sound Biblical emphasis. Fiction, biographies, and how-to articles 900-1500 wds; fillers 200-900 wds. Pays 3¢/wd for articles and stories; 35¢/line for poems; up to $7.50 for puzzles and quizzes. Ages 13-17.

NOW (Standard Publishing Company), 8121 Hamilton Ave., Cincinnati, OH 45231. Sherry Morris, editor. (Q in W parts). Fiction and nonfiction but not preachy. Center on problems teens face today. 1500 wds max. Pays 2¢/wd. Also uses teen poetry, cartoons, b & w photos, good fillers. Submit seasonal materials at least 2 months in advance. Ages 12-15.

PROTEEN (Light and Life Press), 999 College Ave., Winona Lake, IN 46590. Carolyn Dingus, editor. (W). Especially in need of humor: jokes, cartoons, humorous poems, funny incidents written by young teens about themselves. Also needs puzzles for young teens, short articles about true-life experiences and general topics. How-to articles (approx 1500 wds), poems about nature or life experiences may or may not have a spiritual emphasis. Pymt for prose 2¢/wd. Poetry pays 25¢/line. Ages 12-15.

REACHOUT (Light and Life Press), 999 College Ave., Winona Lake, IN 46590. Carolyn Dingus, editor. (W). Wants good fiction, aimed at teens in grades 7-9, of 1300-1800 wds. Serials should not be more than 8 chapters with each chapter about 1500 wds. Uses biographical articles (subjects should be deceased) and personality articles of 200-1000 wds. Good b & w photos enhance the salability of articles. Short devotional or Christian living articles are needed, appealing to young teens. 400-800 wds. Uses 4-16 line poetry. Pays 2¢/wd for prose, 25¢/line for poetry on acceptance.

REFLECTION (Pioneer Girls), Box 788, Wheaton, IL 60187. Sara Robertson, editor. (B). Articles and fiction consistent with Christian principles and illustrating God's relationship to contemporary youth problems. Historical and geographical articles of unique interest, crafts, puzzles and jokes, and how-to ideas are also purchased. Pays $20-$40 for articles and fiction; $5-$20 for puzzles and crafts. Usually buys first rights material. Ages 14-17.

TEEN POWER (Scripture Press), Box 513, Glen Ellyn, IL 60137. Allison Hale, editor. (W). For specifics, send for "Tips to Writers" packet. Ages 14-17.

TEENS TODAY (Nazarene Publishing House), 6401 The Paseo, Kansas City, MO 64131. Roy F. Lynn, editor. (W). Stories showing senior highs solving true-to-life situations through the application of Christian principles. Stories should portray definite Christian emphasis, but not be preachy. Setting, plot and action should be realistic. Write for free folder, "Suggestions to Contributors," for greater detail and denominational taboos. Article length 800-1200 wds; fiction to 2500 wds. Pays 2¢/wd on acceptance. Ages 15-18.

VENTURE (Christian Service Brigade), Box 150, Wheaton, IL 60187. Paul Heidebrecht, editor. (8 issues/yr). Stories, articles, cartoon features and humor for boys aged 12-18. Teenage problems must be dealt with from Biblical perspective. 500-1200 wds. 1¢-4¢/wd.

WIND (Wesley Press), Box 2000, Marion, IN 46952. David L. Keith, editor. (M). The official paper of The Wesleyan Youth organization. Wants articles on careers, devotional, inspirational, biographical, seasonal, sports, historical, poetic, humorous—anything youth-related. Uses short stories. Pays 2¢/wd; pymt for poetry varies. Ages 14-15.

WOW (Standard Publishing), 8121 Hamilton Ave., Cincinnati, OH 45231. Sherry Morris, editor. (Q in W parts). Needs fiction and nonfiction suitable for ages 12-15, between 1000-1500 wds. Should not be preachy but deal with life-as-a-teenager problems such as parents, school, first dates. Pays 2¢/wd for first rights. Also needs teen-written fiction, articles and poetry. Pays approx 1¢/wd for stories and articles; 3¢/wd for poetry. Aim is to make religion practical and meaningful in the lives of teen readers.

YOUNG AMBASSADOR (Back to the Bible Broadcast), Box 82808, Lincoln, NB 68501. Melvin A. Jones, editor. (M). Articles about teenage activities. Simple Bible study articles. 2000 wds max. 3¢/wd. Extra pymt for accepted photos. Ages 12-15.

YOUTH ALIVE! (General Council of the Assemblies of God), 1445 Boonville Ave., Springfield, MO 65802. Carol A. Ball, editor. (M). Uses biographical, fictional, some how-to-do-it motivational and seasonal articles. Also use some poetry and cartoons. Interested in second rights, multiple submissions, and other reprints. 300-1600 wds. Pays 1¢-5¢/wd. Rate determined by creativity, amount of research, type of rights offered, amount of editorial work required. Extra pymt for photos. Color transparencies and b & w glossies.

YOUTH ILLUSTRATED (Scripture Press Publications, Inc.), 1825 College Ave., Wheaton, IL 60187. Ardith Hooten, editor. Needs cartoons, puzzles, topical (Christian living/doctrinal), seasonal articles and poetry are considered. Actual writing of curriculum Bible study lessons is highly specialized and anyone who is interested in this type of writing is carefully screened and tested.

YOUTH IN ACTION (Free Methodist), 901 College Ave., Winona Lake, IN 46590. Alice Wallace, editor. (M). Official youth publication for the Free Methodist Church. Style of writing should be appropriate for young people at approx the 9th to 10th grade level. Uses nonfiction and fiction, cartoons, poetry, photography. Fiction should be from 500-1500 wds. Nonfiction 250-1000 wds. Pays 1½¢/wd, $7-$15 for b & w photos. $20 for color.

# 51

# Writing for the young adult

MARK TAYLOR
Editor, *The Lookout,* Standard Publishing

If you are between the ages of eighteen and twenty-five, you're experiencing what may be the most exciting period of your life. If you're older than this, try to remember what it was like when you were in that age group.

Young adults are wrapped up in finding themselves and in making the great decisions of life. They are testing their abilities, determining their skills, choosing marriage partners, establishing a life-style, finalizing values and charting their careers. They are independent at last (although often still comparatively close to home) and finding their place in the world.

**A transition time**

Young adulthood is a transition time. Those who write for young adults are helping them through their last and often most crucial stages of preparation for life. It can be an exciting and important ministry.

It's sometimes difficult too. Although most young adults have the above points in common, don't ever think young adults are all alike. Their interests and their needs vary widely.

Some of these people are in college or have just graduated. Others of this age went straight to work out of high school. They may have several years of experience at work, at marriage, and at *living* life in general. Their college counterparts, on the other hand, may not have

*Singer Anita Bryant's books appeal especially to young married people. Anita poses here with her family.*

done more than *study* about life—life on an independent basis.

**Observe young adults**

How do these different backgrounds make the two groups different? Observe the young adults you know, and you'll see several ways. (By the way, if you don't know any young adults, vow right now that you'll get to know some. You should feel close to many. Then write as though you were writing directly to them. This is an obvious but often overlooked point, and I can think of no more important advice.)

**Philosophical and abstract**

The young adult in college tends to be philosophical and abstract. He's interested in the reasoning, the logic, the thinking behind what you're saying. The young working-man tends to be more practical and down to earth. He wants to know whether your ideas work and what they'll do for him. The college student is interested in great ideas. The young adult at work thinks more about daily needs.

**Interested in great ideas**

Because of this, the young adult at school tends to be more open-minded and ready to consider change. In fact, he may be campaigning for change as he looks at a troubled world he's eager to improve. The young working-man, by contrast, will often be more set in his ways. He has settled into the routine of going to work or maintaining a family. He is often quite wrapped up in improving his home, bettering himself at work, or pursuing hobbies and leisure-time activities.

**Great faith or severe doubt**

Young adults in college often experience great faith or severe doubt. The doubters need convincing of the basic apologetic questions surrounding any issue you may be considering. The believers will want to have this information too, to help them defend their faith to the many doubters surrounding them. The noncollege young adult may be (although not always) rather indifferent. His faith may not be very well defined. He will often have vague ideas about *what* he believes, but he may not have wrestled with *why* he believes.

Like all generalizations, these don't always apply. But an awareness of these prevailing tendencies will put you well on your way to reaching the young adult market.

## MARKETS FOR AGES 19-25

GLAD (Standard Publishing Company), 8121 Hamilton Ave., Cincinnati, OH 45231. Judy Trotter, editor. (Q in W parts). Needs short, humorous items (700 wds max) on funny aspects of teen life. Also serious fiction (1000-1200 wds max) dealing with the heavy problems of teen life—drugs, dating, sex, parents, friends, school, etc. Should point up Christian principles in decision-making without being "preachy" or dogmatic. Would like Christian stories that let teens make conclusions—where main character doesn't always do the right and glowing thing—and teens learn by nonexample. Ages 16-19.

HIS MAGAZINE (Inter-Varsity Christian Fellowship), 5206 Main St., Downers Grove, IL 60515. Linda Doll, editor. (M-Oc-Jn). Devotional, biographical, missionary, expository, theological articles; Christian evidences, carefully documented; poetry; college how-to-do-it in witnessing, etc; other items of interest to college and university students. Pays 1¢/wd prior to publ.

THE LOOKOUT (Standard Publishing), 8121 Hamilton Ave., Cincinnati, OH 45231. Mark Taylor, editor. (W). Needs short stories of 1000-1200 wds. Also articles of 1000-1200 wds. Chiefly methods or news type articles on phases of educational work of the local non-denominational church or dealing with personal or family problems of Christian life or work. Will buy glossy photos, 8x10, human interest or scenic. Pays up to $35 for short stories and articles; up to $15 for photos.

REACH (Advocate Press), P.O. Box 12609, Oklahoma City, OK 73112. Alfreda Flowen, editor. 500-1200 wd articles related to youth and women. Ages 15-20.

SEEK (Standard Publishing), 8121 Hamilton Ave., Cincinnati, OH 45231. J. David Lang, editor. (W). Needs articles of personal interest and inspiration, controversial subject matter and timely issues of religious, ethical or moral nature, 800-1200 wds. Pays approx 2¢/wd.

# 52

# Writing for the sunday school

MARJORIE MILLER
Editor, Primary Sunday School Curriculum,
*Weekly Bible Reader,* Standard Publishing

More children are touched by the love of Jesus Christ in the Sunday school than in any other setting. More teens find a solid foundation for making right decisions in the Sunday school than in any other group. Families who attend Sunday school together discover that life together can be beautiful and meaningful. And adults of all ages find in the Sunday school the fulfillment of their needs. *This makes the Sunday school a pretty important institution!*

Sunday schools—Sunday school teachers and leaders and pupils need all the help they can get! In some places, the Sunday school is dead. In others, attendance is down. And in far too many, the old Sunday school banner is flying at only half-mast, with minimal outreach and influence and enthusiasm. *It is high time good Christian writers address themselves to the needs of the Sunday school* for motivational articles, for contemporary curriculum materials, for appealing take-home papers.

**Motivational articles**

Christian education magazines (such as *KEY to Christian Education)* are read by teachers, superintendents, ministers, directors of Christian education, youth leaders, and Christian education professors. These leaders are looking for ideas, programs, methods, experiences that will help them and the people with whom they work become better, more effective servants for the Lord.

*Share success stories.* Tell how a record attendance was achieved, how new methods are bringing results, how facilities are being designed. Write about innovative church activities, successful projects, teacher improvement programs, helpful organizational procedures.

*Initiate (or adapt) ideas:* ideas for visuals, teaching tips, bulletin boards, classrooms, pupil involvement, field trips, crafts, puppets, music, special programs, witnessing, promotion.

*Speak to contemporary issues.* What are some trends in education? How can they work toward Sunday school improvement? What are the current problems in our society? How can they be solved? How can the Sunday school program relate to today's complicated life-styles?

**Curriculum materials**

If we were to define curriculum as it relates to Christian education, we might say it is a program of studies designed to guide and direct students toward maturity in the Lord Jesus Christ. The curriculum itself, the materials, and the format are usually determined by the publishing company. But there is a constant demand for good Christian writers to develop curriculum materials for all ages: writers who know and love the word of God, writers who will work with pupils of the age for which they write, writers who are familiar with and use good, up-to-date methods of teaching.

The same writer is usually assigned most of the materials that are designed to be used together for any given quarter (teacher's manual, pupil's activity book, and visuals packet, for example). New writers may be asked to prepare a complete sample lesson before an assignment is made.

**Take-home papers**

Perhaps the most diversified field of Christian writing is in the area of Sunday school papers. Articles for such publications may be written to help, to teach, to amuse, to move, or to inspire. They may be for young children or senior adults. They may be fiction or nonfiction. They may be as long as 1200 words (for adult papers) or as short as 100 words. They may be written from personal experience, from observation, from supposition. They may even be controversial.

Most editors will be happy to send a list of guidelines upon request. Study the publication. Observe the guidelines. And write something that will change somebody's life.

*More children are touched by the love of Jesus in Sunday school than in any other setting. Will your writing convey Jesus' love to a child?*

## CHRISTIAN EDUCATION MARKETS

ADULT BIBLE TEACHER (Church of the Nazarene), 6401 The Paseo, Kansas City, MO 64131. John B. Nielson, editor. (Q). Adult Christian education articles based on Uniform Sunday School lessons on methods, inspiration, lesson themes. 250-1000 wds. Pymt $20+/1000 wds for articles on acceptance; 10¢+/line for poetry. Send mss to Department of Church Schools.

THE BETHANY GUIDE (Disciples of Christ), Box 179, St. Louis, MO 63166. Arthur Syverson, editor. (M). Oriented toward education leaders in congregations of the Christian Church (Disciples of Christ). Almost all articles are written on contract; accept almost no freelance mss. Query first.

BRIGADE LEADER (Christian Service Brigade), Box 150, Wheaton, IL 60187. Don Dixon, editor. (Q). For men associated with Brigade clubs. Informational, personal experience, inspirational. 800-1200 wds. Pays 1¢+/wd on acceptance.

BUILDER (Mennonite Publishing House), 616 Walnut Ave., Scottdale, PA 15683. Levi Miller, editor. (M). Uses articles slanted to teachers and ministers in local congregations. Materials, for most part, are solicited by the editorial staff. Pymt up to 1½¢/wd.

CATECHIST, 2451 East River Road, Dayton, OH 45439. Patricia Fischer, editor. (8 issues—during school year). Articles directed to working teachers of religion, preschool through adult. Wd length is generally 1200-1500. Pymt $35-$75 on publ.

CHRISTIAN LIFE (Union Gospel Press), P.O. Box 6059, Cleveland, OH 44101. (Q in W parts). Uses fiction with a strong emphasis on Christian living; biographies and autobiographies of Christians that show the practical side of their faith; articles on the Holy Land and the history of Christianity that draw applications of faith in action; testimonies; short fillers (devotionals, illustrations, short articles); poetry. Articles should be 900-1500 wds. Pymt is 3¢/wd. Fillers should be 200-900 wds. Same pymt. 35¢/line for poems. Exclusive rights. Use SASE if return of mss is desired.

THE CHRISTIAN TEACHER (National Assc. of Christian Schools), P.O. Box 550, Wheaton, IL 60187. Dr. Billy A. Melvin, exec. editor. (5 issues annually—SE, NO, JA, MA, MY). Scholarly and/or practical articles slanted to Christian school teachers, administrators, board members and parents. Length 3-5 pages, double-spaced. Pymt negotiable.

CHURCH MANAGEMENT, 4119 Terrace Lane, Hopkins, MN 55343. Manfred Holck, Jr., editor. (M). Occasionally buys good articles on practical tried methods in finance, administration, psychology of leadership. Also buys articles of authority on modern church building. Slanted for Protestant clergymen. Pays from \$5-\$25/article.

CHURCH RECREATION MAGAZINE (Baptist Sunday School Board), 127 Ninth Ave. North, Nashville, TN 37234. Elgene Phillips, editor. (Q). 10% freelance. Wants articles of interest to all ages on drama, sports, crafts, camping, recreational leadership, retreats, hobbies, parties, banquets, fellowships, etc. Preferred length 700-1400 wds. Especially looks for a quality of personal experience, how the activity or program was organized and carried out and its results. Query suggested. In the area of fiction, skits and dramatic presentations suitable for presentation in churches are used. The latter are humorous and serious skits, dramatic productions with a Christian message. Same pymt as for nonfiction. Buys photos with mss, b & w only, 5 x 7 or 8 x 10. Pays \$2+/photo used. Buys first rights. Pays 2½¢/wd.

EVANGELIZING TODAY'S CHILD (Child Evangelism Fellowship), 23033 N. Turkey Creek, Morrison, CO 80465., B. Milton Bryan, editor. (B). Original how-to-do-it ideas for teachers of preschool through junior age children in Sunday School, children's church, clubs, camps, etc., 200-400 wds. Pays from \$5-\$15. Contemporary stories for children dealing with problems they are facing at home, school and play. Stories must have a scriptural solution worked into text practically and believably. State aim. 700-800 wds, \$20/story. Mss for a visualized lesson of 2000-2500 wds which clearly presents the Gospel and a step in Christian growth for children must first be submitted in outline form. Purchase of all rights; \$40-\$80;

most feature articles on Christian Education are solicited but outlines may be submitted for consideration.

JOURNAL OF CHRISTIAN CAMPING (Christian Camping International), Box 400, Somonauk, IL 60552. Edward Dulund, editor-in-chief; Samuel Johnson, managing editor. (B).

KEY TO CHRISTIAN EDUCATION (Standard Publishing), 8121 Hamilton Ave., Cincinnati, OH 45231. Marjorie Miller, editor. (Q). Written for all Christian education leaders. Needs practical ideas on every facet of Christian education. One-page articles, 750 wds, pays up to $20; two-page articles, 1500 wds, pays up to $35. Tested ideas, 150 wds, pays $5. Photos used $5 (more upon special arrangement with editor.) Not interested in Christian education theory. Strictly a "how-to" magazine for the Christian education worker.

LEADERSHIP LIBRARY (Success With Youth Publications, Inc.), P.O. Box 27028, Tempe, AZ 85282. (Every 4 months). Looking for articles relating to ministry with children and youth other than Sunday school. Needs features in categories of sponsor's workshops, relationships, how-to, bonus activities. 1000-3000 wds. Pays 2¢/wd.

PERSPECTIVE (Pioneer Girls), Box 788, Wheaton, IL 60187. Alyce Vantil, editor. (Q). Articles related to leadership skills or qualities, interpersonal relationships. 1000-3000 wds. Pays 1½¢-2¢/wd. Craft ideas, complete with step-by-step instructions and illustrations or b&w photo of completed project. Pays $5-$10/idea. For leaders of girls clubs.

SUCCESS (Baptist Publications), 12100 W. Sixth Ave., P.O. Box 15337, Denver, CO 80215. Mrs. Edith Quinlan, editor. (Q). Solicits nonfiction on subjects of general interest in the line of Christian education. The articles may fit specific departments such as preschool, elementary, youth or adult or may be slanted to all departments in general. 500-2000 wds. Pays 2¢-3¢/wd, based on value of article to publ and amount of editing required. No query necessary. Photos are welcome. Pymt for photos, $2-$10. Free sample copy and information sheet to writers upon request.

SUCCESS WITH YOUTH, INC., P.O. Box 27028, Tempe, AZ 85282. Publishes curriculum for expressional training groups on five age levels—preschool through senior high. Writing similar to Sunday school curriculum. Approx 2000 wds/program. Pymt ranges $40-$50/program depending on age level.

SUNDAY SCHOOL COUNSELOR (Assemblies of God), 1445 Boonville Ave., Springfield, MO 65802. Sylvia Lee, editor. (M). Addressed to Sunday school leaders, teachers and workers. Currently in need of articles which will inspire the teacher to excellence in the Christian education ministry. Also use first person experiences related to Sunday school teaching. Always in need of new ideas and information on classroom techniques, visual aids, pupil-teacher relationships. Occasionally use photo feature on an innovative Sunday school or Sunday school class. 800-1000 wds. Pays up to 2¢/wd on acceptance.

VISION (National Educators Fellowship Inc.), P.O. Box 243, South Pasadena, CA 91030. Benjamin S. Weiss, editor. (M). Articles on teacher witnessing in the classroom, Christian teacher service, religion in schools, teaching the Bible in school, teacher's experience with prayer. Approx 500 wds. Does not pay.

YOUR CHURCH, 198 Allendale, King of Prussia, PA 19406. Richard L. Critz, editor. (B). The major subjects covered are church architecture and design, audio-visual equipment and material, art symbolism and book reviews, church equipment and administration, church finances, worship, church school and special ministries. Mss should be 5-12 typewritten, double-spaced pages. Also, any illustration, b & w glossy photos, 4 x 5 color transparencies or artwork, will be considered to accompany publ of the mss. If a mss is accepted, the author will be contacted concerning honorarium payable on publ.

YOUTH LEADER (American Baptist Churches, USA), Valley Forge, PA 19481. Jeffrey D. Jones, editor. (M). Articles 750-1500 wds on teenage psychology from the Christian viewpoint; successful teenage church school classes and youth programs, guidance for adult counselors, teaching methods in youth classes, suggestions to leaders, philosophy of ministry with youth.

53

# Writing for today's woman

KATIE FORTUNE
Executive Editor, Aglow Publications

Writing for women is a unique ministry and the key to this ministry is found in the Word of God.

**Key to writing for women**

"Bid the older women similarly to be reverent and devout in their deportment, as becomes those engaged in sacred service, not slanderers or slaves to drink. They are to give good counsel and be teachers of what is right and noble, so that they will wisely train the young women to be sane and sober-minded, temperate, disciplined and to love (their) husbands and (their) children; to be self-controlled, chaste, homemakers, goodnatured (kindhearted), adapting and subordinating themselves to their husbands, that the word of God may not be exposed to reproach - blasphemed or discredited" (Titus 2:3-5 TAB).

Note that it is the older women that are to teach the younger women. This is not limited to chronological age but could also apply to women who are "older in the Lord" teaching women who are young Christians.

The same principles found here in Titus apply to women who wish to write for other women, for a ministry in writing is just as important as a ministry with the spoken word. In fact, I believe it may have a much broader impact since the written word reaches so many more individuals.

If you wish to have such a woman-to-woman ministry, you first of all need to examine your own relationship with the Lord to find out if you are equipped to reach other women through the written word. As a writer you need to have experienced something yourself before you can adequately communicate it to other women. Out of the riches of your own life you can share with others.

**Four qualifications**

Secondly, you need to take a look at the four qualifications indicated in Titus 2:3:

1. Are you "reverent and devout" in deportment?
Do you have a personal love for God and for the Lord Jesus Christ? If so, you have the greatest news to communicate to women everywhere! The degree of your own victorious living will be reflected in your words and style.

2. Are you a "slanderer"?
A slanderer is a gossip. For most women this is an occupational hazard. But as you let Christ become Lord of your tongue, both your verbal words and your written words will reflect your eagerness to edify others.

3. Are you a "slave to drink," or to any other habit?
As you mature in Christ, old habits will fall away. Like the Apostle Paul, you'll become only a "slave to Christ."

4. Are you able "to give good counsel"?
Have you studied the Word of God and learned how to share it effectively with other women? The measure of help you will be to others will depend upon your ability to communicate God's truth in palatable and relevant ways.

**Discover real needs**

Thirdly, you need to discover the real needs that women have and how you can minister to these needs most effectively through your writing. Note how practical the seven needs are in Titus 2:4, 5. Your ministry is to make the Gospel relevant to women's day-to-day lives:

1. Women need to be "sober-minded." Since a woman tends to be motivated by her heart, rather than her head, she needs to learn how to be disciplined mentally. She must grow in this. It will enrich her life. Women will benefit from good teaching on mental attitudes, moderation in actions, and the balanced life.

2. Women need to be taught how to "love their husbands and their children." The ability does not necessarily come naturally. The rising rate of divorce and child abuse bears this out. Most of a married

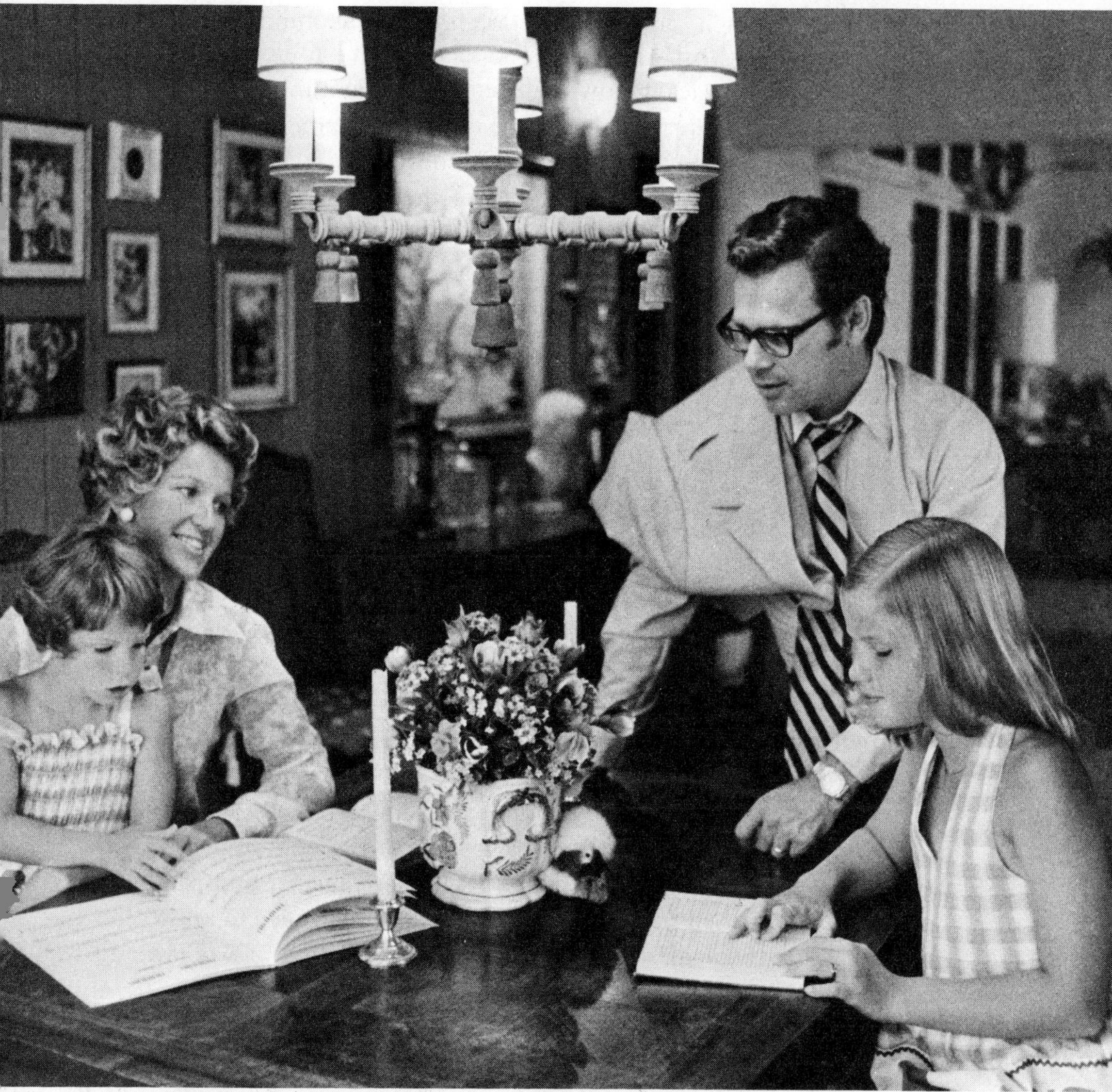

*Marabel Morgan's book for women,* The Total Woman, *became a best seller which started a controversy that hit the pages of the leading women's magazines.*

woman's success will be measured by her relationship to her husband and her children. Women are vitally interested in learning how to be truly successful in marriage and motherhood. Many desperately need to know not only how to love but also how to effectively express that love.

3. Women need to be "self-controlled." God created women with an

extensive capacity to express emotions. But the taming of a woman's emotional life brings her increased security and a sense of self-worth. Women need to learn how their temperaments can yield to the lordship of Jesus Christ by the power of the Holy Spirit.

4. Women need to be "chaste." Traditionally women have been responsible for the moral standards of their generation. God made a woman to be happy and fulfilled in her faithfulness to one man. When she violates this, she violates her basic nature. In a day when popular mores teach a liberation that is license, women need to be able to differentiate between facts and fancies.

5. Women need to discover the delights of being a "homemaker." A woman is like a thermostat; she sets the climate in her home. There is no other part of the world over which she will have more influence than her home. In addition to practical homemaking skills, women also need to learn skills in setting the spiritual and emotional temperature in their homes.

6. Women need to be "good-natured." A woman needs to be able to express kindness in her family, to her neighbors, in her work, and in community organizations and activities. Women were created to be givers. Women need to discover how Jesus Christ can increase their kindheartedness and provide them with opportunities for its expression.

7. Women need to develop in "adapting and subordinating themselves to their husbands." The women's liberation movement is causing untold damage to women's minds and emotions, leaving a wake of confused roles and scarred lives. Women need to know God's truth about women's roles and relationships and how a woman's submission (both in right attitudes and actions) to her husband truly liberates a woman to become all that God created her to be.

If you are growing in your own relationship with the Lord, and if you can share insights and incidents from your own experience on any or all of the seven subjects listed above, you are qualified to write for today's woman.

## WOMEN'S MARKETS

AGLOW, 7715-236th SW, Edmonds, WA 98020. Katie Fortune, editor. (Q). Looking for 1000-2000 wd, first-person articles written for women by women of all ages. Each article should be either a testimony of or teaching about Jesus as Savior, as baptizer in the Holy Spirit or as guide and strength in everyday circumstances. Also looking for 4800 wd teaching mss that can be published in booklet form. Themes can deal with any aspect of spiritual life. Query first including sample writing. Mss of 20,000-45,000 wds will be prayerfully considered. Query first including two chapters and an outline. Limited poetry. Pymt for magazine articles is made on publ. Royalties for other items are paid monthly. Use SASE when submitting a mss plus photo.

CO-LABORER (Women's National Auxiliary Convention of Free Will Baptists), P.O. Box 1088, Nashville, TN 37202. Cleo Pursell, editor. (Q). Uses articles on missions, Christian living, woman's life and problems and devotional or inspirational materials slanted for women. Length 1100 wds max. Does not pay.

CONCERN (United Presbyterian Women), 475 Riverside Drive, New York, NY 10027. Sarah Cunningham, editor. (10 issues/yr). Contributions come largely from solicited writers who interpret the program of United Presbyterian women—a program of the United Presbyterian Church, U.S. Does not pay.

FREE INDEED, 3624 Tilghman St., Allentown, PA 18104. Diane R. Jepsen, Jan Abramsen, editors. New magazine looking for biographies of spiritually active women, of autobiography sketches, fiction, poetry, news of interest to women, how-to articles involving skills in home management, relationships, Christian growth. Central focus is woman's identity in Christ being primary before any other chosen role. Length varies from 500-2000 wds. Devotional materials least needed. Does not pay at this time.

SCOPE (Augsburg Publishing House), 426 S. 5th St., Minneapolis, MN 55415. Dr. Lily M. Gyldenvand, editor. (M). Prefers brief, timely and relevant articles and illustrative stories with definite Christian orientation slanted for average church women. Glossy photos and filler material welcome. Pymt varies.

54

# Writing for the family

LOIS CURLEY
Manager, Education Resources Division,
Gospel Light Publications

Today I read a gripping article in the *San Francisco Examiner's* "Opinion" column titled "Disposable Husbands and Wives." The data in this column screamed for answers to the problem of divorce. One million couples obtained divorces in 1975. And more than one million children under eighteen were involved. This number of divorces is more than double the number of family breakups recorded in 1966, and three times that of 1950.

Marriage breakups continue to multiply.

Family decisions demand knowledge about everything from abortion to drugs to career counseling and where to go on vacation.

Parents are living with young people who are well-informed, restless, frightened and often directionless.

**More family authors today**

No wonder there are more authors today than at any other time in history writing on subjects related to marriage and family life. A quick review of books and articles for the family published just in the last few months reveals a wealth of secular and "religious" writings. Some authors give complicated explanations and equally complex answers. Others take a simplistic approach offering pat answers. But sales indicate that a good part of all that is written for the family is read.

People are looking for answers. They want to know what the Bible

*Couples want to know what has actually worked in someone else's life. They are not interested in theory. (Family Films)*

**People are looking for answers**

says about marriage and family living. They want to read and identify with authors who have personally experienced or have other firsthand understanding of what they write. The personal experience stories that offer an unusual, dramatic, but credible account involving well-knowns or unknowns continue to be the bread-and-butter material features for family oriented publications. More precisely, Christian magazine and book editors are looking for accounts written from a positive perspective in which God's hand is particularly evident in the circumstances and relationships. Readers want to know that the Lord can and does make a way through any and every marriage and family problem.

**Four recommendations**

Now, as a matter of very practical nature, here are some basic recommendations for those whose ministries in the family life area take written form:

1. Select a subject that is significant to you personally, either on the basis of experience or understanding, or both. Here are major subject areas to consider for periodical and/or book publications:

a . . .what families can do together to increase understanding and enjoyment of one another.

b . . .Christian marriage, with a heavy emphasis on how to be a better spouse including communication, premarital preparation, Biblical roles of husband and wife, finances, planning, decision making, sexual guidelines.

c . . .Christian parenting including discipline of children, teaching Christian values, building self-esteem, communication with children, sex education of children.

d . . .family human interest angles on actual couples and families —how they live, cope, worship, serve Christ.

e . . .areas of the family life cycle—single parents and their problems, the middle years (empty nest), retirement, aging.

f . . .reports on successful family life programs that are making a difference.

g . . .crises management in family situations—death, illness, accidents, emotional illnesses, divorce.

2. Do your homework. Become familiar with the books and articles being published currently in the area of your concern. Learn something about the publishers featuring family life titles. Attend marriage and family life seminars. Be aware of current community, state, and federal

influences and pressures on the family.

3. When you are familiar with the current literature in your subject area of interest, and you are convinced that someone else has not already recently published (within the past twelve-eighteen months) just what you had in mind, decide to what target audience and market you will aim your manuscript. In other words, have clearly in mind the needs and interests of those to whom you want to direct your thoughts.

4. This done, you are ready to outline your article or book manuscript and send off your manuscript proposal query to a publisher who is effectively reaching that audience.

**Be cautious!**

Publishers walk a cautious path between the writers who are preparing what *should* be read and the readers who are selecting articles and books to meet their needs. (Blessed are the writers and readers whose publishers understand and maintain the balance between supply and demand to the benefit of all.) Secular and Christian publishers who

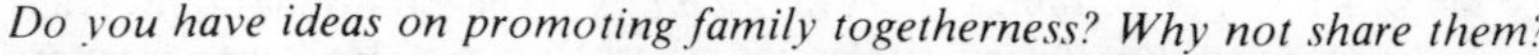

*Do you have ideas on promoting family togetherness? Why not share them?*

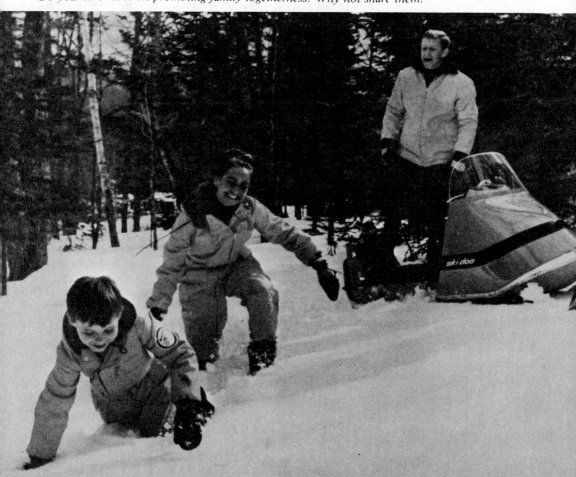

promote family life features are looking for able writers, like all other publishers. If, then, God has given you contacts, experiences and insights related to marriage and/or family, and you are motivated to share these for the help and encouragement of others, by all means investigate and seize the opportunities currently open in publications related to that field.

May God guide your pen!

## EXAMPLES OF FAMILY ARTICLES

# Pat and Shirley Boone: How We Raised Our Girls

ROBERT WALKER

*No other Christian family has appeared on national television during the last five years as often as Pat and Shirley Boone and their daughters. As professional entertainers themselves, Cherry, Lindy, Debby and Laury occasionally perform alone. Pat, of course, often appears singly and with Shirley. But clearly, the family combination of parents and daughters is evoking an ever-growing interest today.*

*One reason may be the phenomenon of a family involved in the entertainment profession in which each member claims a personal commitment to Jesus Christ as Savior and Lord.*

*Another may be the curious picture of a family in the entertainment profession in which four attractive daughters have openly espoused at least two old-fashioned principles of conduct. One is that they have willingly submitted to the discipline and guidance of their parents. The other, that they have frankly opted for virginity as a way of life before marriage in an environment where it is virtually unthinkable.*

*Late last year the two oldest Boone girls were married. In this interview Pat Boone opens the door to some of the intimate details leading to the weddings and to a lifestyle which many families miles away from Hollywood would like to emulate.*

*—The Editors*

*Christian Life*—The Pat Boone family is acclaimed—both in the Hollywood entertainment world and on the Christian scene—for its commitment to high standards of morality and personal faith in Christ. But what is little known by either public is the lifestyle of your closely knit family which has made it so exemplary. Will you give us some of the secrets of your success?

*Boone*—Well, I'll do the best I can to answer your questions. But really, the answer is this simple: we invited the Lord to live at our house, and in us—and He does.

*Christian Life*—Let's begin with the question, "How old are the Boone girls today?"

*Boone*—That's easy. Cherry is 21, Lindy 20, Debby, the blonde, is 19, and Laury just turned 18. They will be like that for another few months, then Cherry turns 22 in July.

*Christian Life*—Would you say that you and Shirley have brought up your daughters as average children, or have you prepared them for careers in the entertainment profession? In other words, have they had a normal childhood?

*Boone*—You are really asking two questions. I'd like to go into the first in more detail, but let me say at the beginning that we have considered our children as loaned to us by God. We are permitted to enjoy them during their childhood. But we have the responsibility to prepare them for a life of commitment and service for Him. Yes, we have tried to give them a normal childhood, so far as that has been possible with my involvement in the entertainment profession—but as a dedicated Christian, at least since I discovered the reality of the Holy Spirit seven years ago.

*Christian Life*—Then have you or probably Shirley—prepared them to handle the responsibility of running a home, caring for a husband, children, etc.? Or will they have domestic help?

*Boone*—No, no! In fact, McLean Stevenson on *The Tonight Show* said last year, "Both your girls getting married, eh?"

I said, "Yeah."

"Do you approve of the guys?"

I said, "Oh yeah."

"Do they both have jobs?"

I said, "Yes."

He said, "Praise the Lord!" (He must have thought that was what I was going to say.)

They do have jobs, but neither is in a high-paying job, and I'm sure it has not entered their minds that they could afford any kind of domestic help.

*Christian Life*—Your daughters obviously are very attractive. How have you handled the matter of dating?

*Boone*—Rigidly. In fact, we laid the law down a couple of years ago that there was just no point in dating anybody but Christians.

*Christian Life*—Wasn't that difficult?

*Boone*—Yes. We have been through some pretty touchy situations, where one or another of the girls was strongly attracted to somebody who was not a Christian. We felt apprehensive about it and very negative toward the idea. But what evolved out of this experimentation and taking each situation as it came up was sort of a set of ground rules. First of all, we as a family want to know the boy. We do not allow our girls to date guys that we don't know. And it has been understood that if any of our daughters wants to date a guy, first she makes sure that we get to know him. That means he comes over to the house. We are very happy for any of our girls to invite a guy over to dinner and to go to church with us and maybe go to places where we are appearing, to come along and be part of our family group. That way we get to know him and see if he fits into our family's kind of activity. He also finds if he is going to be comfortable with us and whether he wants to pursue it any further.

*Christian Life*—Can you give us a specific instance?

*Boone*—Well, there was one very rough situation where an older man wanted to date one of our girls. We met him when we were doing a television commercial. Number one, he was 10 years older than the girl he wanted to date. (I'm being a little nonspecific because I'm not sure my daughter wants this known or wants to be spotlighted in this situation.) The man was handsome and very debonair, a man-of-the-world type, and was very drawn to one of the daughters. At first he wouldn't say how old he was and so we really didn't know. It turned out he was older than he looked and older than we thought.

We were very leary of the situation but we said, "All right, bring him along to Magic Mountain," where we were appearing. We said, "Invite him to church and for dinner. If he is comfortable with our family activities, and once we know how old he is, then we can make a decision. It may be that we'll have to ask him to wait for a year or two until you're a little older."

Well, our daughter went along with it okay. He went to Magic Mountain, but never did go to church with us. He felt uncomfortable being part of our family situation, but was pressing hard to take our daughter out. Finally we had to have a meeting. I let my daughter have an hour with him first.

She asked, "Can we go over to the park, or can we drive around?"

I said, "No, you can just have your meeting right out there in the side yard if it is warm weather. It can be out of earshot, but not out of eyesight."

She understood without our having to explain. I let them sit there for an hour and I could tell that she was doing a good job of trying to convey our thinking and make him understand. But he was really putting on some hard sell. So I went out and sat down with the two of them and finally he had to accept—by now I knew how old he was—that the age made a great difference to us.

He said, "Well, why? They are just numbers. They don't mean anything."

I said, "They may not mean anything to you, but this girl is 17 at this point, and in a year or two or three the age span won't make as much difference. But she has not dated nearly as much, she hasn't had the kind of experience you have had, and we just don't feel it is wise for you to date. We like you, and you are welcome to go to church with us and be involved in our family activities, but as far as single dating is concerned, that's out for a couple of years."

He was exasperated and said, "I agree with the way you are bringing up the girls except for this age thing. I'll tell you frankly, I've already been through the sex and the drugs, all the trips, and I'm more settled now. I think I would be better for your daughter than some young kid who is still experimenting with those things."

I said, "We're not planning for our girls to date any guys who are experimenting with those things, and I don't think they want to."

It was hard to make him see our viewpoint because he had not been brought up with any kind of spiritual background at all. I told him the story of Jacob and Rachel and Leah, and how Jacob had to work 14 years for the one he wanted.

He said, "I'd never do that."

I said, "Well, few people would, but then because Jacob did it, because he was willing to wait and meet his future father-in-law's conditions, he became not only the ancestor of the 12 tribes, but of David and the Messiah—so there *are* advantages to waiting and doing things God's way. And the parents' way."

Well, he didn't really understand, but that did settle it and now our daughter has moved on to other relationships.

*Christian Life*—Do you handle all the girls the same way?

*Boone*—Obviously not. Each is a different personality. But we do try to be consistent. That was another thing I told the man I referred to. We had not allowed the other girls to date fellows that were older, and we were not going to allow this girl to. We believe we must be consistent. We couldn't make exceptions just because one man happened to be charming or there was a special set of circumstances. We had not allowed any of our girls to date until she was 16. We have been consistent in not allowing them to be out past midnight.

*Christian Life*—How do the girls react to this?

*Boone*—Our girls have found and are ready to say that discipline—a loving authority—has made a tremendous difference in our family life and in their own well-being and security.

Merv Griffin had them on his TV show recently. He asked them if we weren't very strict parents, especially by Hollywood standards, and they said, "Oh, yes."

He said, "What are they strictest about?"

Cherry said, "Respect." And the audience applauded.

We do demand respect, as parents. We consider ourselves as their friends —but more than that, we want them to know that we also are their mother and dad. We didn't let them forget that, although we are also their friends.

*Christian Life*—What was Merv Griffin's reaction?

*Boone*—He said to the girls, "Now, be honest with me, hasn't having strict parents caused you to miss out on some things?"

And one of the girls shot back, "Yes —trouble." Again the audience applauded.

Then the girls went on to amplify what they meant. Each of the girls, even Laury the youngest, has seen friends whose parents did allow them to date older men, who got into drugs and sex, nervous breakdowns, abortions, and bad emotional problems. That erases the glamor.

They said that they are grateful we have been this protective.

To show you how it works, I was out playing volleyball after dinner with Laury about a year ago. While we were doing that we talked.

"Daddy," she said, "my friend 'Lynn' and I were talking, and we've decided we're the only virgins left in our class."

It was hard for me to keep on playing volleyball, but I tried to act as nonchalant about it as she had. She was 15, almost 16 then.

I said, "How do you know that?"

She said, "Well, the girls all talk about it at school—about their experiences and who they go out with and who they go to bed with. Some of my friends at school live with just one parent or the other and don't get much supervision. A number of the girls go home in the afternoon with guys and a couple of girls have come home and found their mothers in bed with somebody other than their dad. We were going down the list of all of our classmates and we decided that we are the only two left."

I said, "How does that make you feel?"

She said, "Well, we feel very fortunate and sort of sorry for our friends because we know this hasn't made them happy. Some of them have really gotten messed up and it makes 'Lynn' and me feel sort of special."

I could have cried at that point because she is my youngest, and many times the youngest child feels he or she has to prove that she is different, and may go a different direction from the others. For her—a pretty girl who is almost 16—to feel special and a little bit sorry for her friends who had already given up their virginity made me feel awfully good.

In fact, Shirley shudders a little bit when I say this because she thinks maybe I'm "borrowing trouble." But I've said two or three times in small groups that I'm very grateful to identify with Philip in the 21st chapter of Acts, "who had four daughters, virgins, who prophesied." And when Shirley feels that I'm borrowing trouble I just remind her that, like Paul, we know the Lord is able to keep that which we have committed unto Him, and it is not we who have kept our girls pure. It is they and the Holy Spirit who have done it.

*Christian Life*—Two of your daughters were married last year. Can you tell us something about them and how they met their husbands?

*Boone*—Yes. Cherry and Lindy are two very, very special young ladies, and their husbands know it. Debby and Laury I am sure are going to be just the same. We're more grateful for that than we can put into words. I guess I wouldn't bring it up at all except that I want people to know that it is possible these days and that if it can happen in an entertainer's family in Hollywood with all the opportunities, all the peer pressure that our girls have been exposed to, then young people all over America can make those same choices and know the same joys and freedom from guilt that tends to cripple other young people.

I'm sure they are sold a bill of goods all the time—that it's just passe to be pure and chaste, that it doesn't work, that it is even harmful to them emotionally, that it stunts their psychological growth. Even the young teen magazines now are always reporting the episodes of infidelity of movie stars, even the young ones, and set up as examples those young singers, actors and actresses who jump from one bed to the next as though that were really the smart way to live.

I think it might be good to let people know—especially young people who are the age of our girls and maybe even younger—that you don't have to go that way and that there are advantages to not going that way. You're a whole lot more special these days—not weird but special—if you keep yourself for the one you are going to marry and bring that husband or wife the greatest wedding present of all—an unspoiled mate.

*Christian Life*—Who are the young men Cherry and Lindy married and what are their occupations?

*Boone*—Dan O'Neill married Cherry and was a trainer with Youth with a Mission.

He lived in about 20 foreign countries and finally settled in Israel on a kibbutz. He learned Hebrew and worked in the life of the kibbutz just as a young man who loved Israel. He returned on some Youth with a Mission business and was going back to pick up his life on a kibbutz when he met Cherry. George Otis, a friend of the family, introduced them. They fell in love, and now Dan works for Otis as an editorial assistant, graphic artist and sort of "right arm."

*Christian Life*—What about Lindy's husband?

*Boone*—Doug Corbin works for Mike Curb, a successful record producer who does our records—Shirley's and mine and the girls'. Doug works on the promotion of records. He got his degree from Pepperdine College and was going to be a coach and teacher. His first job was in an all-black school close to Watts in southwest LA. But he wound up being more of a military policeman than a teacher or coach. There was a pretty heavy gang life problem there. A lot of the kids came to school armed and weren't interested in the academic part of things and Doug became disillusioned about teaching. Mike Curb offered him a job and he went to work. So that worked out very well. But they are both fine young Christians, and Shirley and I feel that is the best part of all.

*Christian Life*—How will these marriages affect the other two girls—and how will it affect the Boone family act?

*Boone*—It is going to slow down our family activity, at least as far as traveling is concerned. I said the girls are finishing their first album and it is a winner.

The real adjustment I've had to make, is having to get the permission now of Dan and Doug before I can commit the girls to any family involvement in 1976. Several times now, even on Cherry's honeymoon with Dan, I had to ask how she and Dan felt about a commitment for the family to appear at the Florida State Fair. So I called her on the telephone.

Cherry said, "Here, I'll let you talk to Dan."

Dan got on and heard me out and said, "Yes, I think that will be okay." That was a different kind of experience for me, to have to ask somebody else if it were all right to commit my daughters to something.

*Christian Life*—Did the boys ask you and Shirley if they could marry your daughters?

*Boone*—Yes, they did. It was a beautiful thing. In both cases they came and said, "We believe the Lord has chosen us for each other, but now we want to submit it to you." And it was implicit as they asked that if we had said no, or wait, that they would have. In fact they each said, "This is your daughter, she is under your authority and therefore I place myself willingly under your authority."

This was a Jacob and Laban kind of situation where Jacob had to submit to his father-in-law's authority, before and after marriage. The boys have both done that. We are very grateful.

Lindy and Doug want to write a book eventually about their courtship and marriage because he was a guy who had been around a good bit, was not a Christian during his high school and early college days. He became a Christian and met Lindy after that and was soon filled with the Holy Spirit and then had to submit himself as an older fellow—older than this girl that he was in love with—to a kind of parental authority he had never known.

He did, and it has worked out beautifully for him and for her and has been a great experience for Shirley and me too. They feel that as young newlyweds they have something to share with other people. They asked and submitted themselves to our requirements about dating and about the engagement period. And even after they were engaged, they did not—either of the men—in any way demand rights or freedoms that we weren't prepared to give.

Imagine—here is a 27-year-old man, Dan, and Cherry turning 21, and we are regulating when they were to get in and where they could go. Even up to within a couple of weeks before their marriage they asked if Cherry could have dinner with Dan and what time they had to be in.

*Christian Life*—Will you be helping your married children financially? Do you believe parents have this responsibility?

*Boone*—No, I've never really felt that parents have a responsibility to help their children financially. Shirley and I for a long time lived out in Texas, where I was making $44.50 a week. We were really scrimping, but I didn't ask my folks for anything and I didn't ask her dad, Red Foley, for anything. I really felt that once we had accepted the freedoms of marriage, we also accepted the *responsibilities* of marriage.

*Christian Life*—Have you or Shirley counseled your daughters on how you believe a family should be arranged?

*Boone*—We really haven't except we have encouraged them to wait a year or two before they have children. We think that if a couple can have a year or two to get to know each other and have some freedom *before* they take on the responsibility of children, that is better. But we are not very good examples of that, and we don't know a thing about arranging a family because we didn't plan ours.

But there have been some wonderful advantages to having them grown and on their own while Shirley and I are still in our mid-forties. We think there are lots of things that we want to do, and that we will still be young enough to do after we have already done our major life's work, which is getting our family raised and successfully married.

We can't give them too much counsel on arranging their families, and we haven't even given them too much in the way of specific sexual advice because Shirley feels, I think pretty wisely, that they will work all this out on their own. Whatever the girls have wanted to know we have always told them. We have been quite frank and open and we have discussed things like contraception. Their response surprised our family doctor, who offered several times in the last few years discreetly and privately to provide the girls with a contraceptive if they wanted it, as most all of his girl patients did. Each of our girls told him, "Thanks, but no thanks."

This has been a tremendous testimony to our doctor who is Jewish, and who in the Hollywood area is exposed to the worst imaginable things among the kids of families he treats.

*Christian Life*—Assuming that two girls at home will require less of your time and attention than four, how do you believe God is leading you to employ your additional time?

*Boone*—Shirley and I do plan to do a book together on our more recent experiences as parents whose children are growing and starting to pair off. And also on the parallels we see between human marriage and spiritual marriage, in our relationship to Jesus as a bridegroom. Also we are going to be doing more speaking and sharing together.

I'm really up in the air about how I'm going to involve the family in my singing, unless we do a television series.

I don't see Shirley and me becoming a husband and wife singing team because she is too nervous about it. She can sing beautifully but unless it's with the family it's very difficult to get her to sing with me. So I have a feeling that we are going to wind up doing some television out of LA.

Shirley and I will be involved with the younger two girls, of course. But I'm going to try to carve out some time for Shirley and me to enjoy each other and catch up on some things we would have done earlier if we hadn't had the children so soon!



# One by One by One

## BERNARD PALMER

Ellen is getting a divorce from Albert and is dating his best friend," our oldest daughter, Bonnie, said during one of her frequent visits to our home. "God promised to save our family, Daddy. Does this apply to her, too?"

"Of course it does," I assured her—but with some misgiving. Only a miracle could free Albert from his dependence upon drugs and alcohol—and Ellen from all the problems that had piled up around her. And how could they be helped unless they got out of their current pleasure-seeking rut?

After Bonnie and her three boys left, my mind was flooded with thoughts of Ellen (not her real name). Although only a "distant relative," she had a special place in our hearts, and we had claimed her for God, according to the promise in Acts 16:31 (NASB), "Believe in the Lord Jesus. and you shall be saved, you and your household."

Ellen was born in a sleepy little Nebraska town where churches outnumbered taverns. But itching feet had taken her parents East. She grew up a typical child of affluent suburbia. Raised in a home where money and the pursuit of pleasure were everything, she had no interest in the Person of Jesus Christ.

She got to Sunday School once in awhile—if her parents hadn't been up too late the night before. And she usually made it at Christmas and Easter. For all of her 19 years, however, Ellen had been conditioned to walk her own selfish, Godless way. How could anyone expect her to change?

That was my first reaction. Then I got to thinking about our more immediate family and the miracles prayer had worked.

There had been a time when I was only a nominal Christian and had little interest in the spiritual condition of anyone else. Then my wife died after a brief illness, and I was awakened to the shortness of life. From then on Christ meant much more to me. By the time I married again I had a new awareness of the importance of a vital relationship with Jesus Christ.

Our Christian growth was steady. After several years I joined the Gideons, began to write for religious publishers and was active in Youth for Christ. Soon my Danny Orlis stories were being aired over Back to the Bible broadcasts, then published in books. Our relatives were somewhat disturbed by the change, and we stood virtually alone.

"Bernard and Marge would be all right," they would say condescendingly, "if they weren't so religious." In their eyes we were fanatics, early-day "Jesus Freaks," who weren't to be taken seriously.

But we prayed for them. How we prayed! And in our fumbling way we tried to tell them about Jesus Christ.

I will never forget the time I went out to coffee with one of our relatives and tried to get him to commit his life to Jesus Christ. He was a man who drank a lot but was proud of his accomplishments in the business world and his position in the community.

As I talked, his face flushed and he squirmed to get away.

"We're in church every Sunday....And there's something else I do. Every day at nine o'clock in the morning I say a little prayer even though I'm driving down the highway." He glanced at his watch and, face flushed with embarrassment, excused himself.

That was the last time he would go out to coffee with me alone.

At first we had difficulty in facing up to the fact that some of our closest relatives were not really Christians, and when our children asked about one of them, chances were we would try to excuse him by saying he just wasn't living the way he should. We didn't realize the harm in that approach, even when our oldest son, Barry (main character in my book, *My Son, My Son,* Moody Press) revealed his reaction at the age of 5.

"I want to be a Christian like — — —," he said. "He does anything he wants to."

When we recognized that our relatives were spiritually "lost," we became concerned enough to pray for them.

Barry was disturbed and confused by the fact that God permitted his mother to die when he was 2, and determined to go his own way.

Even before his waywardness drove us to our knees, we began to pray for the persons our kids would marry when they grew up. We couldn't take credit for thinking of that; we borrowed the idea from close friends.

Years passed, and Marge and I still stood alone, except for our three youngest children and my parents, who made their decisions for Christ. The scorn and ridicule continued. One cousin and his wife refused even to speak to us for ten years because of our witness to them. It looked as though there were going to be no other Christians in the entire Palmer clan.

Barry was the first of our children to marry. We never once suspected that his wife, Kathryn, wasn't a Christian. When I arranged for her to see Dr. Epp, founder and director of Back to the Bible Broadcast, I made it clear that she only needed encouragement. She was pregnant and more miserable than normal because of Barry's drinking and infidelity. Before she left Epp's office, however, she had made her decision for Christ.

"I knew you thought I was a Christian," she told us, "and I was too proud to let you know I wasn't."

Randy Oswald joined our family next by taking our foster daughter, Annie Philipsen, as his wife. Raised in a Christian home, Randy knew Christ as his Savior and enrolled at Grace Bible Institute in Omaha, where he met Annie. But a streak of rebellion ran through him. He chafed at the rules, and demerits piled up until both he and the staff began to think the school would be a better place without him.

He and Annie broke their engagement for a few months, and he was on his way to Omaha to enroll at Omaha University (now a division of the University of Nebraska) when he changed his mind and went back to Grace. He was now subdued and unrebellious. Annie graduated from GBI, visited her parental home in Holland for a few months, returned, and married Randy.

Judy Masters lived on a ranch in northwestern Nebraska. The closest town had no evangelical church and there seemed to be no way that she could be reached for Christ because of the problems of geography. But God was faithful. We hadn't even known her when we began to pray for the girl our younger son, Morrie, would some day marry, but God saw to it that an American Sunday School Union missionary found her and induced her to go to camp. There she committed her life to Jesus Christ. She and Morrie met at Grace Bible Institute and are now living with their two children in Petaling Jaya, a suburb of Kuala Lumpur, Malaysia. Morrie is the Evangelical Free Church missionary editor of the *Asian Beacon*, a magazine in English but slanted for the Oriental.

Doug Young started going with Bonnie, our daughter, when they were still in high school. He was always a good lad and regular in attendance at a gospel-preaching church in Holdrege. Nevertheless, he was not a Christian. She asked him to go to special meetings with her where he, too, acknowledged his sin and received Christ's forgiveness.

Ed Fowler, the husband of our youngest daughter, Jan, is the product of a Baptist minister's home. He had made a decision for Christ as a boy but found it difficult to live in the shadow of the pulpit. It wasn't until he had played his way through a year of college with indifferent grades and had gone into service that he began to face up to the realities of living the way he should.

Although all of our own family, with the exception of Barry who did not acknowledge his need of Christ until shortly before he died in 1967, were now Christians, there was still no break among the other members of the Palmer clan. At this point no one could have looked at the answers to our prayers and found encouragement regarding Ellen. Her situation was different. She had no contact with Christ, and was so pleasure-bent she listened to no one.

Then my brother, LaVern, gave his heart to Christ—but only after his drinking problem exploded upon us. Bewildered and helpless, we began to meet after prayer meeting each week with another Christian couple to pray, specifically, for our relatives. We had been praying only a couple of months when LaVern and his wife were transformed by Jesus Christ. Today their oldest son, Del, and his wife and two children are missionaries to Japan.

Shortly after that I wrote to my cousin who hadn't spoken to us for so long. The answer came by return mail—a warm, glowing testimony.

"Both Rog and I are saved," his wife wrote. Their sons, too, are living for Christ, and their daughter claims to be a Christian.

An uncle of mine came to Christ almost on his death bed when a converted drinking buddy stopped by to see him from Minnesota.

A cousin came to Holdrege to live and his son went to Canada with us to spend a month. Before he went home I had the thrill of taking him to my writing shack and leading him to Christ. Later his dad made a profession and gave some evidence of a changed life, but only for a time. If he is a believer, it isn't apparent by either his actions or his words.

Jim and Mary Jacobi, distant cousins, were probably the closest in attitude to Ellen and her parents. They were members of a liberal church and joined a small discussion group, but most of the sessions seemed to be aimed at finding fault with the Bible. They went home afterwards more confused than ever.

Then a blind man started holding Bible studies in their section of Omaha, and they began to attend. About that time they came across a copy of my first novel, *Parson John*, which was based on the life of my grandfather. Excited about the book, Jim called me. During the conversation I blurted out the question that was churning in my mind.

"Jim, are you a Christian?"

Later he told me it made him so mad he almost hung up, but I wasn't aware of that. All I knew was that he sputtered like a damp firecracker.

"Of course I'm a Christian."

Months later I learned that was the first time he had ever been asked, point-blank, if he was a follower of Jesus Christ. It proved to be a crisis-point in their lives, and it wasn't long until they both yielded their hearts to God. The spiritual growth they have experienced since has been steady and encouraging.

Yes, I told myself, there is hope for Ellen and her husband.

In the days that followed, we prayed for them. Not as much as we should have, I must admit. We were still claiming God's promise to save both of them, but I was sure it would be long in coming, that we would have to wait many years to see the answer to our prayers.

But God's ways are not our ways.

After a week or two, Albert came back and begged Ellen to drop the divorce action. When she did so, his best friend (and her new boyfriend) quit his job and left town. But he continued to write to her. It wasn't long until his letter told a thrilling story.

"I came home the other night and decided the drug scene is a living hell," he wrote. "Then I got to thinking that if this is what hell is like I don't want to go there.....Now I'm through with all of that. I'm a new person in Christ. I've been born again...."

"That sounds interesting," she answered. "Tell me more."

His next letter explained the way of salvation as best he could and set in motion a series of events that took her to a church where she, too, committed her life to Christ. Two or three days later she came back to Holdrege briefly.

"I've never been so happy," she told Bonnie.

Albert, however, was furious. He ridiculed her and continued to live the same as ever. He mortgaged their furniture to buy a car and took off. It was days before she heard from him. During that time her rent came due and she was given a few days to raise the money or be moved out into the street.

"I've been on tranquilizers for the last year or so," she wrote to Bonnie, "but I wasn't nervous about this at all. The day I had to have the money I got two checks in the mail that were enough to pay the rent so I didn't have to move."

Before that week was out, she heard from Albert. He called from Brownsville, Texas, where he had tried to cross the border from Mexico with marijuana in the car and had been caught. For three weeks he lay in jail before being placed on probation.

He came back home, thoroughly chastened, and told her he was going back to work and was through with drugs.

"Everything in his house, except aspirin, is going out of here," he informed her.

He got his old job back in spite of the sagging economy, and occasionally went to church with her. At this writing he has not made a decision for Christ, but those who have been in their home say it is happy in a way it has never been before. She is continuing to pray for him and for her family.

We were in Canada when we got Bonnie's letter telling us what had taken place in Ellen's home. As I sat there, tears filling my eyes, I thought back to the time when we were in Dr. Theodore Epp's office talking with him about Barry before he became a Christian.

"You may not live to see the day when God will bring your loved ones to Christ, but if you are faithful in living and witnessing and praying, you can be assured that He will!" Dr. Epp had said.

I took a sheet of paper and wrote down the names of family members who have become Christians since Marge and I first began to pray. Twenty eight— and the end is not yet. We look forward with confidence to the day when Albert and the other members of Ellen's family will join us in His service. Then will come our children's children...



## FAMILY MARKETS

AMERICAN BIBLE SOCIETY RECORD (American Bible Society), 1865 Broadway, New York, NY 10023. C. P. Macdonald, editor. (M - Jn & Ju comb. Au & Se comb.). Articles only on Scripture translations, publications and/or distributors. Not to exceed 1700 wds. Pymt on acceptance.

THE CHRISTIAN HOME (Graded Press), 201 Eighth Ave. South, Nashville, TN 37202. Florence Lund Williams, editor. (M). Short poetry, general articles for parents of children and youth.

CHRISTIAN LIVING (Mennonite Publishing House), 616 Walnut Ave., Scottdale, PA 15683. J. Lorne Peachy, editor. (M). Needs articles on marriage and family living that deal with one specific problem and how to solve it. These problems should be those that occur in relationships between a couple, between parents and children, between a family and the church, and between family and the local community. Length up to 2000 wds. Pays up to 3¢/wd. Poetry also accepted. Pays $10 to $15. Should be on same subjects.

FAMILY LIFE TODAY (Gospel Light Publications), 110 W. Broadway, Glendale, CA 91204. Lois Curley, editor. (M). Family night plans: by assignment only; articles on Christian marriage with heavy emphasis on being a better spouse: communications, premarital preparation, Biblical role of husband and wife, finances, planning, decision making, sexual guidelines; articles on being a Christian parent: discipline of children, teaching Christian values, building self-esteem, communication with children, sex education of children; features with human interest angles on actual couples and families: best free-lance opportunity; articles and features on other areas of family life: single parents and their problems, middle years, retirement, aging, etc.; articles and features on churches doing interesting and significant things in family programs. Pays 3¢-5¢/wd.

MARRIAGE AND FAMILY LIVING (Abbey Press), St. Meinrad, IN 47577. Ila M. Stabile, editor. (M). Informative and inspirational articles on all aspects of marriage, especially husband and wife relationships. 2000-2500 wds. Personal essays relating dramatic or amusing incidents that point up the human side of marriage. Up to 1500 wds. Profiles of outstanding couple(s) whose story will be of interest for some special reason and profiles of individuals who contribute to the betterment of marriage. 1500-2000 wds. Interviews with authorities in the field of marriage on current problems and new developments. Length up to 2000 wds. Pays 5¢/wd. Photos purchased with mss, b & w glossies or color transparencies. Pays $17.50/half page; $35/full page. Requires model releases.

THE SUNDAY SCHOOL TIMES AND GOSPEL HERALD (Union Gospel Press), P.O. Box 6059, Cleveland, OH 44101. (S). Uses articles concerning present day Christians and Christian groups, churches, and organizations. Material about current issues of interest to Christians, inspirational items, personal testimonies, articles on the Holy Land and the history of Christianity. Limited amount of poetry and fiction. 1800-2000 wds. Pays 3¢/wd for articles; 35¢/line for poems.

TODAY'S CHRISTIAN PARENT (Standard Publishing), 8121 Hamilton Ave., Cincinnati, OH 45231. Mrs. Wilma L. Shaffer, editor. (Q). Family life problems and pleasures. Family devotions. Usual article length 600-1200 wds.

WORKING FOR BOYS (American Northeastern Province of the Xaverian Brothers), Box A, Danvers, MA 01923. Brother Jerome, CFX, editor. (Q). Uses seasonal material, also factual and historical. Fiction, not necessarily religious. 1000 wds at 3¢/wd. Seasonal poetry not more than 12 lines at 25¢/line. Address all mss to Associate Editor, Brother Alois, CFX, St. Johns High, Main Street, Shrewsbury, MA 01545.

# 55

# Writing for a denominational publication

G. ROGER SCHOENHALS
Editorial Director,
Free Methodist Publishing House

What happens when your manuscript arrives at the editor's desk? How does the editor decide which article to reject and which one to publish?

1. *First Impression.*

**First impression**

Your article rarely arrives alone. It competes with others in the same pile. Therefore, first impressions are crucial. A dog-eared, handwritten piece already has two strikes against it.

Editors are busy with lots of articles to read and evaluate. They have learned that sloppy manuscripts are nearly always weak on content. Instead of diligently looking for the exception, they tend to pass these by with little more than a glance.

In contrast, articles neatly typed (good ribbon), double-spaced, with wide margins suggest quality. The editor is more likely to consider a manuscript that appears to have been carefully prepared.

2. *Subject Matter.*

**Subject matter**

What is the article about? The title or brief cover letter should make this clear. Obviously, editors will not waste time wading through material that is beyond the purpose of their periodical. A denominational magazine like *Light and Life* would hardly carry an article on "The Art of Hang-Gliding," or "How to Buy Real Estate in Walla Walla."

Before submitting an article, consider the purpose of the periodical, evaluate past issues, and consult (if available) a writer's guide prepared by the editor. A query letter suggesting a subject to the editor is a good idea.

Editors are not interested in subjects that are too heavy, too general, too shocking, or too common. Instead of an abstract article on the meaning of Christian love, they would be more interested in something concrete demonstrating love in action. Truth caught is more powerful than truth taught. (Consider the parables of Jesus.)

So select your subject carefully. Research it well. Make sure it is fresh, personal, positive, and practical.

**Holding power**

3. *Holding Power.*

Readers are easily bored. They live in a Madison Avenue world. From every direction clever attention getters bombard them. Except for a few who are motivated enough by the subject to plow through a listless article, most readers will simply flip the page.

So editors want grabby (not gabby) writing. The opening paragraph must reach out like a meat hook. The rest of the article must have holding power—right up to the last word. This means writing that is anecdotal and swift moving.

If the editor loses interest you can expect to find a rejected manuscript in your mailbox.

**Clear purpose**

4. *Clear Purpose.*

A manuscript may be attractive and may present appropriate subject matter in an interesting way and still be rejected. There must be purpose and direction. What is the reader supposed to do after reading the article? Why did you write it?

John likes to write. He is overcome with a fantastic idea. He hurriedly writes down the thoughts. Conscientiously he works the manuscript over, rewriting it once or twice before mailing it. A few weeks later the article is returned. Reason? John never took the time to think through his specific purpose. The article was clever and interesting, but pointless. Editors want material with purpose.

5. *Strong Impact.* **Strong impact**

Hitting the target is one thing, hitting it hard is something else. Editors ask: How well did the writer achieve his purpose? What is the impact of the article?

The difference between a good article and a great article is at the point of response. Is the impact strong enough to alter the reader's thinking and behavior?

Editors want articles that will change the lives of their readers.

6. *Simple Style.* **Simple style**

Readability is the name of the game. Our desire at Light and Life Press is to follow the example of Jesus and use clear, simple language. We want the "common people" to read us gladly (Mark 12:37).

The day of flowery mumbo jumbo writing is over. Readers are lazy. They would rather switch than consult a dictionary. Articles must be easy to read and understand. As the saying goes, "keep it simple, stupid" (KISS).

Editors usually won't fool around with manuscripts crawling with long complicated sentences and multisyllable abstractions.

7. *Editorial Needs.* **Editorial needs**

Every editor works with certain "givens." He is not free to take anything that comes along. Consequently, an article may pass all the above criteria and still be rejected. It must also meet the unique editorial needs of that particular publication. There are at least four.

a. *Slant*—An article must fit into the peculiar ideological context of the publication. For example, *Light and Life* magazine is evangelical, Wesleyan-Arminian and Free Methodist. We would not print an article extolling the virtues of Calvinism.

b. *Slot*—Is there a spot in the editorial layout of the periodical for your article? Most magazines have well-defined goals for the kind of article to appear on each page. A sixteen-page periodical like *Light and Life* must carefully apportion the space in order to achieve a balance of material.

c. *Size*—This relates both to reader involvement and available space. The longer the article the harder it is to maintain a high level of interest. Editors must cater to the hurried, interrupted life of the readers. A variety of shorter articles also makes editorial balance more easily achieved in each issue.

d. *Supply*—The editor may already have a file of the type of article you submit. Or maybe the subject has been covered adequately in recent issues.

Editors want the best they can get for their readers. They are as anxious about mail delivery as writers are. By following guidelines suggested above, you will not only make the editor happy, you will find something better in your mailbox than a rejection slip.

## DENOMINATIONAL MARKETS

ADVANCE (Assemblies of God), 1445 Boonville Ave., Springfield, MO 65802. Gwen Jones, editor. (M). Magazine for Assemblies of God ministers and church leaders. Uses sermon ideas (complete outlines, or brief thought-starters); sermon illustrations (original material); articles slanted to ministers on preaching, doctrine, practice, etc. (1000 to 1200 wds); how-to-do-it features of interest to ministers and church leaders. Pays 2¢/wd+ on acceptance.

ADVOCATE (Churches of Christ in Christian Union), P.O. Box 30, Circleville, OH 43113. Rev. P. Lewis Brevard, editor. (B).

THE AMERICAN BAPTIST (American Baptist Educational Ministries), Valley Forge, PA 18481. Philip E. Jenks, editor. (M). Would accept feature articles dealing with specifically American Baptist topics, or topics of universal interest to Christians (testimonies, devotionals, etc.). 1000 wds or less. May pay $25.

BAPTIST HERALD (North American Baptist Conference), 1 South 210 Summit Conference, Oakbrook Terrace, Villa Park, IL 60181. Dr. R. J. Kerstan, editor. (M). Inspirational articles or general religious news. Pays small honorarium.

CALVINIST CONTACT (Reformed Faith), Guardian Publishing Company, 99 Niagara St., St. Catherines, Ont, L2R 4L3. Keith Knight, editor. (W). Christian features, short stories concerning Christian living; length under 1000 wds. Pymt varies, usually $10 or $15/article.

CHRIST FOR ALL (Assemblies of God), Division of Home Missions, 1445 Boonville Ave., Springfield, MO 65802. Ruth A. Lyon, editor. (B). Very limited for free-lance writers. Must be about Assemblies of God chaplaincies or special ministries in cooperation with missionaries or chaplains. Also stories based on truth about the people with whom they work or stories about the missionaries. Queries are welcome. Pays on publ. Approx 800 wds.

CHURCH ADMINISTRATION (Southern Baptist Convention), 127 Ninth Ave. North, Nashville, TN 37234. George Clark, editor. (M). Wants articles, 850 to 1500 wds, dealing with church programming, organization and staffing, administrative skills, church financing, church facilities, food service, communication, pastoral ministries and community needs. Also, how-to-do-it articles for pastors and other church staff members. Interest in down-to-earth matters of pastoral ministry and church administration. Pays 2½¢/wd for all rights. Queries acceptable.

THE CHURCH HERALD (Reformed Church in America), 630 Myrtle N.W., Grand Rapids, MI 49504. Dr. John Stapert, editor. (Bi-W). Seeks feature articles that deal with problems and issues the Christian faces in present-day world; articles which show how Jesus Christ transforms individual lives and how Christian principles put to work in lives can transform family life, society and government; research articles on significant facts or events relating to the Bible or Christian history; personality or biographical articles on well-known Christians of today. All should have evangelical slant without being preachy. Articles can be from 500-2000 wds with 1500 preferred. "Guidelines for Writers" as well as copies of the magazine are available on request. Pays 2¢+/wd. Also can use children's stories on themes of present day interest with practical, moral and religious teaching; between 600-800 wds at 2¢+/wd.

CHURCH OF GOD EVANGEL, 1080 Montgomery Ave., Cleveland, TN 37311. Dr. O. W. Polen, editor. (S 2nd & 4th Mondays).

Nearly all material is provided through denominational sources.

CONTACT (National Assc. of Free Will Baptists), P.O. Box 1088, Nashville, TN 37202. Eugene Workman, administrative editor. (M). Articles illustrating victorious Christian living. How-to articles relating to any phase of church work. Average length is 1000 wds. Most features are commissioned. Unsolicited articles pay approx 2¢/wd on publ.

CONTACT (United Brethren Publications), 302 Lake St., Box 650, Huntington, IN 46750. Stanley Peters, editor. (W). Biographical sketches of noteworthy Christians, Christian fiction, how-to, inspirational, fillers. Major articles 1000-2000 wds max. Short articles 400-500 wds. Fillers 100-300 wds. Use SASE. Pays 1¢/wd for first rights, 3/4¢/wd for second rights. Poetry pays 7¢/line.

THE COVENANT COMPANION (Covenant Press of the Evangelical Covenant Church of America), 5101 N. Francisco Ave., Chicago, IL 60625. James R. Hawkinson, editor. (S). Most material solicited from their offices but does invite mss of approx 1000 wds. Pays $15 on publ. Looking for good humor. Use SASE.

THE DISCIPLE (Disciples of Christ), Christian Board of Publication, Box 179, St. Louis, MO 63166. James L. Merrell, editor. (S 1st & 3rd Sundays). Poems, 4-16 lines, $1-$5; meditations, about 150 wds, $5. Other devotional material, not exceeding 500 wds; prayers, litanies, Biblical meditations, paraphrases, personal experiences, $3-$10; sermons and articles (related to the general concerns of the Disciples of Christ), approx 750 wds, $3-$15; cartoons, $4-$5; photos, b&w glossies, for cover illustrations, $7½-$12½. Subject matter: religion, theology, home, church, school, business or social life, historical events, seasonal topics. Humorous material suitable to a church journal is welcome. Pymt ordinarily at end of month of publ.

THE EDGE (Church of the Nazarene), 6401 The Paseo, Kansas City, MO 64131. Melton Wienecke, editor. (Q). Informative and inspirational articles, 1000-2000 wds on all phases of Christian education in the local church. Methods, successful ideas, programs. Pays 2¢/wd on acceptance. Very little poetry is used in this publication.

EMPHASIS ON FAITH & LIVING (The Missionary Church), 336 Dumfries Ave., Kitchener, Ont., N1H2G1. Dr. Everk R. Storms, editor. (S). Short articles (500-800 wds) on practical Christianity with an "emphasis on faith and living." Pays $5. No poetry. Reply in one month.

ETCETERA (Nazarene Publishing House), 2923 Troost Ave., Kansas City, MO 64109. J. Paul Turner, editor. (M). First person articles from a Christian perspective receive first priority. Author's own spiritual pilgrimage, pressing spiritual needs and/or victories will be considered over other types of articles. No fiction, cartoons or quizzes. Poems with a distinct Christian message either stated or strongly implied will be considered. Poetic form is author's discretion. Sample copy of magazine on request. Articles should be 1200 wds or less. Pays 2¢/wd on acceptance.

EVANGEL (Light and Life Press), 999 College Ave., Winona Lake, IN 46590. Vera Bethel, editor. (W). 800 wd personal experience articles. Pays 2¢/wd on acceptance.

EVANGELICAL BEACON (Evangelical Free Church of America), 1515 E. 66th St., Minneapolis, MN 55423. George M. Keck, editor. (Bi-W). Occasionally buys material from free-lancers. Articles to be 500-1500 wds along devotional lines. Some photos, some poetry.

EVANGELICAL VISITOR (Brethren in Christ Publications), 301 N. Elm St., Nappanee, IN 46550. John E. Zercher, editor. (S). Articles on home, family, devotional, Christian education. 1000 wds max.

THE FREE METHODIST PASTOR (Free Methodist Church of North America), 901 College Ave., Winona Lake, IN 46590. G. Roger Schoenhals, editor. J. Arthur Howard, managing editor. (M except No & De). Publication by and for ministers of the Free Methodist Church. Offers opportunity to "break into print" and work on writing skills. 700 wds max. Does not pay.

THE FREE WILL BAPTIST (Free Will Baptist Press Foundation, Inc.), 811 North Lee St., Ayden NC 28513. Tommy Manning, editor. (W). Children's stories with moral (1000-2000 wds). No pymt but good exposure for writer. General interest articles of religious nature, personalities, or unusual incidents (2000-3000 wds). Poetry with Christian theme, 25 lines max.

FRIENDS JOURNAL (Friends Publishing Corp.), 152-A N. 15th St., Philadelphia, PA 19102. James D. Lenhart, editor. (S). Articles 1500 wds max related to the activities, concerns or beliefs of members of the religious society of friends. Does not pay.

GOSPEL CARRIER (Pentecostal Church of God of America), P.O. Box 850, Joplin, MO 64801. Mrs. Marthel Wilson, editor. (Q in W parts). Need fiction or true-to-life stories of about 1500 wds illustrating some facet of Christian experience. We can also use 800-1000 wd stories or articles which may be fiction or true-to-life. Well-known Christians, interesting incidents from the life of the writer, or discussion topics of interest to either men or women. Need short fillers of one paragraph to 300 wds—inspirational thoughts, stories in brief, devotional material. Particularly interested in material that will be of interest to men. Pays quarterly at ½¢/wd. No poetry.

GOSPEL HERALD, 616 Walnut Ave., Scottdale, PA 15683. Daniel Hertzler, editor. (W). Theological and practical Christian issues affecting Mennonite readers. 300-1500 wds. Pays 1½¢+/wd on acceptance. Use SASE.

HEARTBEAT (Free Will Baptist Foreign Missions Dept.), P.O. Box 1088, 1134 Murfreesboro Rd., Nashville, TN 37202. Don Robirds, editor. (M). 1200-1500 wd articles. Pays 3¢/wd on publ.

HERALD OF HOLINESS (Church of the Nazarene), 6401 The Paseo, Kansas City, MO 64131. Dr. John Allan Knight, Sr., editor. (B). Devotional articles from 600-800 wds dealing with practical problems of Christian living today. Pays $8/article on publ. Send SASE for return of unused mss.

HOME LIFE (Southern Baptist), 127 Ninth Ave. N., Nashville TN 37234. George W. Knight, editor. (M). General articles, 1st person preferred, 1000-1800 wds. Fiction, 1000-1800 wds. Poetry, 4-16 lines. Poetry pymt \$5-\$10 depending on length. All should focus on family life. Pays 2½¢/wd on acceptance.

INTERACTION (Lutheran), 3558 S. Jefferson Ave., St. Louis MO 63118. (M). Purpose is to bring before readers theological, psychological and educational insights applicable to teaching in the church school. Articles up to 2000 wds. Pays from \$10-\$50. Wants popular, readable style.

IMPACT (Conservative Baptist Foreign Mission Society), P.O. Box 5, Wheaton, IL 60187. H. Walter Fricke, editor. (B). Does not purchase mss, only as they are solicited.

LIGHT AND LIFE (Free Methodist Church of North America), 999 College Ave., Winona Lake, IN 46590. G. Roger Schoenhals, editor. (B). 1st person accounts of God's help in personal crisis, Christian growth articles, 1500 wds. Christian living articles, discipleship articles, 750 wds. Some poetry. Pays 2¢/wd upon publ.

LIGHTED PATHWAY (Church of God), 922 Montgomery Ave., Cleveland, TN 37311. Clyne W. Buxton, editor. (M). Articles (500-1200 wds) should be inspirational, didactic, how-to, fiction. All material must be religious, slanted for youth (14-17). Pays 1¢/wd.

LIVE (Gospel Publishing House), 1445 Boonville Ave., Springfield, MO 65802. Gary Leggett, editor. (W). Fiction presenting believable characters working out their problems according to Biblical principles, character building without being preachy, 1200-1800 wds. Articles with reader appeal presented realistically, up to 1000 wds. Biography or missionary material using fiction techniques. Historical, scientific or nature material with a spiritual lesson. Brief fillers, purposeful, usually containing an anecdote with strong evangelical emphasis, up to 500 wds. Pays 1¢-2¢/wd on acceptance. Seasonal material should be sent at least one year in advance.

THE LUTHERAN (Lutheran Church in America), 2900 Queen Lane, Philadelphia, PA 19129. Dr. Albert P. Stauderman, editor. (S). Uses articles, 1500 wds max, on church work, personal religious life, great Christian personalities. Photos always helpful. Address queries to Features Editor. Pays about 5¢/wd on acceptance.

LUTHERAN FORUM, 155 E. 22nd St., New York, NY 10010. Glenn C. Stone, editor. (Q). Articles about important issues and actions in the Church. Pymt varies. 1000-3000 wds. Informational, how-to, personal experience, interview, profile, think pieces. 500-3000 wds. Pays $15-$50.

THE LUTHERAN JOURNAL, 7317 Cahill Rd., Edina, MN 55435. Rev. Armin U. Deye, editor. (Q). Inspirational, how-to, personal experience articles. 1500 wds max. Pays 1¢-1½¢/wd on publ.

LUTHERAN STANDARD (American Lutheran Church), 426 S. 5th St., Minneapolis, MN 55415. George H. Muedeking, editor. (B). Uses articles relating faith to daily living and to social problems. Examples of people or congregations (especially Lutherans) who live out their faith. 600-1200 wds.

MENNONITE BRETHREN HERALD, 159 Henderson Hwy., Winnipeg, Man., Canada R2L 1L4. Harold Jantz, editor. (W). Published for the whole family. Idea articles, interpreting Biblical teaching on the Christian life into real life situations within the family and in the community. Best length 1500-2500 wds. Children (9-12) slanted stories and articles. Should make a strong appeal to witnessing and to living a truly changed life. Best length 1000-1500 wds. Pays $10-$30/article. Pictures with articles welcomed.

MISSIONARY BAPTIST SEARCHLIGHT (Seminary Publications), P.O. Box 4536, Little Rock, AR 72205. L. D. Capell, editor. (B). Religious newspaper. News compiled in editorial office. No rate of pay, but will use contributions if they are suitable.

THE NEW OVERCOMER (Open Bible Standard Churches), 2020 Bell Ave., Des Moines, IA 50315. C. Daniel LebaCheuv, editor. (Q).

Do most of their own writing. Low budget and mostly denominational items.

NEW WORLD OUTLOOK (United Methodist Church), Room 1328, 475 Riverside Dr., New York, NY 10027. Arthur J. Moore, editor. (M with Ju-Au comb). Articles on the involvement of the Church around the world, including USA. Focus on United Methodist Church not necessary but helpful. Outreach, social concerns, Christian witness and mission. 1000-2000 wds. Pays $50-$100 on publ.

PENTECOSTAL EVANGEL (Assemblies of God), 1445 Boonville Ave., Springfield, MO 65802. Robert C. Cunningham, editor. (W). Wants true stories of conversions, bodily healing through faith in Christ, any remarkable answer to prayer. Uses fiction for Mother's Day, Father's Day, Thanksgiving, Christmas. Also wants devotional articles, Bible studies, articles telling how to be saved, 650-750 words; articles on Christian living, 800-1000 wds; fillers, various lengths. Pays 1¢+/wd on publ for first rights. Uses second rights material also.

THE PENTECOSTAL MESSSENGER (Pentecostal Church of God of America), P.O. Box 850, Joplin, MO 64801. Idabeth McDole, editor. (M with Ju & Au comb). Bible-based sermons conforming to fundamental teaching and dealing with issues Christians face in today's world; human interest articles with spiritual relevance and inspirational articles with seasonal effect. Uses material primarily for adults and young people; material of interest to various departments of the church, etc. Articles should not exceed 1500-2000 wds. Some 750-1000 wd articles acceptable. Pymt varies according to quality, beginning with ½¢/wd on publ.

PENTECOSTAL YOUTH (Pentecostal Church of God of America), P.O. Box 850, Joplin, MO 64801. Bonnie Yarnell, editor. (M). Needs 1500 wd fiction or true-to-life stories illustrating some facet of Christian experience. Uses some articles of how-to for teens. Uses a limited amount of puzzles or quizzes. Also uses suggested ideas for Christian youth meeting and programs which do not require preparations or unusual settings. A few Christian youth parties are used. Pays 1/2¢/wd quarterly.

PRESBYTERIAN RECORD (The Presbyterian Church in Canada), 50 Wynford Dr., Don Mills, Ont., Canada M3C1J7. Dr. DeCourcey H. Rayner, editor. (M except Au). Uses nonfiction; inspirational, factual, informative, general interest to Canadian Presbyterians. Includes material for all ages. 1500 wds. Short features 400-800 wds. Pays $15-$40.

PRESBYTERIAN SURVEY (Presbyterian Church in the United States), 341 Ponce de Leon Ave. N.E., Atlanta, GA 30308 (M). Mss keyed to current church activities and issues. Religion-at-work type mss with b&w pictures. 1000 to 2000 wds, preferably 1500 wds. Pymt varies according to subject, how well done, how timely, and need for certain subjects at the time mss received. No fixed rules. All mss accepted on speculation unless ordered in advance. Mss are read by the staff, then channeled to specialists in the fields involved before purchase or rejection. Tries to respond within 30 days to 6 wks. Send SASE. Buys first rights.

QUAKER LIFE (Friends United Press), 101 Quaker Hill Drive, Richmond, IN 47374. Frederick E. Wood, editor. (11 issues/yr. with Ju & Au comb). Most articles written by Friends for Friends and are solicited by the *Quaker Life* staff. Occasionally an article is published which has not been assigned. Carries articles of inspiration and information. Does not pay.

REACH OUT (Assemblies of God), 1445 Boonville Ave., Springfield, MO 65802. Ruth A. Lyon, editor. (B). Stories or articles must be about Assemblies of God churches not over three years old in cooperation with the pastors. Queries welcome. Pays on publ. Approx 800 wds in length. Home Missions.

THE REFORMED JOURNAL (Wm. B. Eerdmans), 255 Jefferson, SE, Grand Rapids, MI 49503. Marlin J. Van Elderen, editor. (M except Jn & Au). Theologically grounded essays in the application of the Christian faith, particularly in its Reformed (Calvinist) expression, to the major contemporary issues. Length: 8-12 typewritten, doublespaced pages. Does not pay.

THE SABBATH RECORDER (Seventh Day Baptists), 510 Watchung Ave., Plainfield, NJ 07061. John D. Bevis, editor. (M). Missions, Christian education and women's department. Special issues in color 3 times/yr. Does not pay.

STANDARD (Church of the Nazarene), 6401 The Paseo, Kansas City, MO 64131. (W). Distributed free through the Sunday schools of the Church of the Nazarene. Uses stories which show young people (older college or above) and adults solving true-to-life situations through application of Christian principles. Prefers 2500 wds. Serials of not more than three parts, each part approx. 2500 wds. Avoid preachiness. Secure free folder, "Suggestions to Contributers" to learn taboos. Free sample copy. Pays up to 5¢/wd on acceptance.

THE TEXAS METHODIST/UNITED METHODIST REPORTER (United Methodist), P.O. Box 1076, Dallas, TX 75221. Spurgeon M. Dunnam, III, editor. (W). Considers feature articles of 750 wds and less on persons putting Christianity to work in their daily lives. Preference given to articles related to United Methodists. Pays 3¢/wd. Newspaper.

THRUST (Evangelical Fellowship of Canada), Graphic Guild Arts, Publisher. Box 8800, Station B, Willowdale, Ont. M2K2R6. Rev. J. A. Shantz, editor. (Q).

THE UNITED CHURCH OBSERVER, 85 St. Clair Ave. E., Toronto, Ont., Canada M4T 1M8. Dr. A. C. Forrest, editor. (M). Human interest stories of the church at work through organizations and/or individuals in Canada and overseas. Personal experience articles if they describe something exciting or of significance to Canadians. Articles no longer than 2000 wds. Photo illustrations. Pymt according to merit.

UNITED EVANGELICAL (Evangelical Congregational Church), 100 W. Park Ave., Myerstown, PA 17067. Rev. Ronald B. Kuntz, editor. (Bi-W). Needs short stories and articles suitable for home reading, evangelical, devotional articles and how-to-do-its for the average church, Sunday School and other church organizations. Does not pay.

THE WAR CRY, (Salvation Army), 546 Ave. of the Americas, New York, NY 10011. Lt. Col William Burrows, editor. (W). Inspirational and informational articles with strong evangelical slant but not preachy. 1000-1800 wds. Pays $15-$35 on acceptance. Use SASE.

WESLEYAN ADVOCATE (The Wesley Press), Box 2000, Marion, IN 46952. Dr. George E. Failing, editor. (Bi-W). 1000-2000 wd articles of inspirational nature, Bible studies, personal experience, practical Christian experience, doctrinal, etc. Solicited material receives modest honorarium. Good quality unsolicited articles sometimes paid $5-$10.

WESLEYAN WORLD (The Wesleyan Church), P.O. Box 2000, Marion, IN 46952. Paul L. Swauger, Sr., editor. (M). Exclusively editorial, especially of factual reports from overseas denominational activity. 800 wd missionary features of promotional nature will also be considered. Pays 2¢/wd.

WORLD MISSION JOURNAL (Southern Baptist Convention), 1548 Poplar Ave., Memphis, TN 38104. Jim Newton, editor. (Q). Human interest features about interesting Baptist laymen; roles men play in making contributions of service to the Christian cause; features on Baptist missionaries in the USA and overseas; in-depth articles on issues affecting Christian missions. No fiction. Pays 3¢/wd, edited. Uses many photos. Tabloid format.

56

# Writing for roman catholics

RICHARD SCHEIBER
Editor, *Our Sunday Visitor*

Writing for Roman Catholics is not the same as it was ten years ago. While that audience today is not fragmented by any means, it does not have the same unity it once had. This is not to say there is no unity among Roman Catholics; it is simply a different kind of unity, a oneness in a diversity that was not always recognized prior to the Second Vatican Council.

**Oneness in diversity**

I doubt if one can legitimately speak today of "a Roman Catholic audience." There is a plurality of audiences under the umbrella of the Catholic Church. Interests vary widely, as do publications. Yet, strangely, the market has narrowed. The number of devotional magazines, once fertile fields for authors of devotional articles, has drastically diminished, partly because of a lessening of interest in that type of magazine, mostly because of economic conditions. The high price of publishing has simply driven many small circulation magazines to the wall. Only the best of the general interest magazines with large circulations remain. And these are hard to crack, since they rely heavily on staff-written and assigned articles.

This two-fold phenomena, the demise of small circulation magazines and the more careful attention editors are giving to the successful large circulation magazines, has dried up the market for marginal articles directed to a Catholic audience.

**The key word is quality**

Yet, for quality articles, the market has broadened because of the broadened interests of the Catholic audience. The key word is quality. There is hardly any place in the Catholic market for a writer who is not well-informed on both Catholic tradition and current Catholic thought. Writing for the Catholic audience requires infinitely more preparation, more research than it ever did before. But the rewards are greater, too. Most major Catholic publications, *Sign, St. Anthony's Messenger, Catholic Digest, Our Sunday Visitor,* and many others pay fairly well. And once a writer has established that he knows what he is writing about and can present his topic in a clear and interesting manner, he is likely to make multiple sales to these publications.

The list of topics and approaches to these topics is almost inexhaustible: marriage and family life, the liturgy, instruction of youth, the elderly, religious vocations, the Church in action, Catholic people in action, new approaches in every phase of the Catholic Church, all are topics which interest editors. But like the magazines, editors are getting better too, and can quickly spot—and reject—articles which do not thoroughly and fairly cover the topic.

**Critical audience**

To sum up, the Catholic audience today is an audience of widely varied interests, but it is a critical audience, demanding high quality writing, researching and thinking. It demands, too, lively writing, heavily laced with examples, personal experience, writing that moves. It's a tough assignment. But it can be a rewarding one.

## ROMAN CATHOLIC MAGAZINE MARKETS

AMERICA, 106 West 56th St., New York, NY 10019. Joseph A. O'Hare, S.J., editor. (W). Uses articles that report and comment on or interpret events and trends in the areas of politics, social and economic problems, letters and culture, as well as religion. Readership is well above average in education. Interests are in weekly events of the world and domestic scene with special interest in religious affairs. 1500 wds. Pays on acceptance.

COMMONWEAL, 232 Madison Ave., New York, NY 10016. James O'Gara, editor. (Bi-W). Uses timely and thoughtful articles on issues of the day—political, socio-economic, cultural and/or religious. 1000-3000 wds. Pays on acceptance.

THE COMPANION OF SAINT FRANCIS AND SAINT ANTHONY (Conventional Franciscan Friars), 15 Chestnut Park Road, Toronto, Ont, Canada M4W 1W5. Wants articles about live, modern topics. They should be of fairly wide interest to Canadians as well as to U.S. citizens. 1200-1500 wds. Uses wholesome, not preachy fiction of 1200-1500 wds. Photos should be b & w, 5 x 7 if possible. Pays 2¢/wd, extra for photos used.

FRANCISCAN HERALD (Franciscan Herald Press), 1434 W. 51st St., Chicago, IL 60609. Rev. Mark Hegener, O.F.M., editor. (M). Mostly staff written although they accept occasional articles as submitted. All articles for the magazine must reflect some aspect of Franciscan spirituality, outlook, history, etc.

MARIAN HELPERS BULLETIN (Marian Fathers and Brothers), Eden Hill, Stockbridge, MA 01262. Brother Robert Doyle, editor. (Q). Articles and photos of general interest. 400-1100 wds on devotional, spiritual, moral and social topics with a positive and practical emphasis may be submitted for consideration. Pymt varies. Made on acceptance. Use SASE.

MARRIAGE & FAMILY LIVING (Abbey Press), St. Meinrad, IN 47577. Ila M. Stabile, editor. (M). Pays 5¢/wd for articles 1500-2000 wds. Nonfiction articles dealing with husband and wife or parent and child relationships of a supportive or self-help nature. Also accept free-lance photography and poetry.

MARYKNOLL (Catholic Foreign Mission Society), Maryknoll, NY 10545. Miguel d'Escote, editor. (M). Foreign mission articles and photos. Pays on acceptance. Query first.

MESSENGER OF THE SACRED HEART (Apostleship of Prayer), 833 Broadview Ave., Toronto, Ont., Canada M4K 2P9. Rev. F. J. Power, S. J., editor. (M). Needs articles and short stories to 2000 wds which reflect the problems North American Catholics meet in their daily lives. Pays 2¢+/wd.

NEW CATHOLIC WORLD (Paulist Press), 1865 Broadway, New York, NY 11023. Robert J. Heyer, editor. (B). Uses fiction, nonfiction and poetry based on the themes of each issue. Should be 2000 wds, 10 pages double-spaced. Pymt depends on length of article or poem.

OUR FAMILY (Oblate Fathers of St. Mary's Province), Box 249, Dept. E., Battleford, Sask, Canada SOM OEO. A.J. Reb Materi, O.M.I., editor. (M). Wants articles, 1000-3000 wds, that deal with practical topics that concern people in their everyday lives—problems of home, youth, marriage, church, community, national and international affairs. Fiction, 1000-3000 wds, that reflects the lives, problems and preoccupations of the reading audience. When possible, photos should be submitted with articles (or their availability noted). Pymt is min of 3¢/wd for original articles on acceptance. Pymt for photos depends on quality and number of photos. Sample copy available for 25¢.

OUR SUNDAY VISITOR (Our Sunday Visitor, Inc.), Noll Plaza, Huntington, IN 46750. Richard B. Scheiber, editor. (W). Articles and features of interest to a Roman Catholic audience. Color photo stories and features. Doctrinal pieces, personality sketches. No fiction, no poetry. 1000-1200 wds. Pays $75-$150/feature, depending on length, photographic support, quality.

PACE 7 (St. Mary's College Press), Also entitled "Professional Approaches for Christian Educators," St. Mary's College Press, Winona, MN 55987. Mary Perkins Ryan, editor. (M). Trends on theological, doctrinal, moral and liturgical themes; teaching models and ideas about the what and how of religious education; raising and discussing controversial topics; approaches in programs and program planning; community aspects of Christian education. 800-1600 wds/article. Can be longer if divided for installments. $100 for articles written specifically for PACE, previously unpublished, and selected for publication in PACE by the editors.

PASTORAL LIFE (Society of St. Paul), Rt. 224, Canfield, OH 44406. Rev. Victor L. Viberti, editor. (M with Ju & Au comb). A professional review, designed to focus attention on current problems, needs, issues and activities related to all phases of pastoral work and life. Avoids merely academic treatment on abstract and too controversial subjects. 3500 wds max. Use SASE. Queries appreciated. Pays 3¢+/wd on acceptance.

QUEEN OF ALL HEARTS (Montfort Missionaries), 40 S. Saxon Ave., Bay Shore, NY 11706. Rev. James McMillan, S.M.M., editor. (B).

REVIEW FOR RELIGIOUS, 612 Humboldt Bldg; 539 N. Grand Ave., St. Louis, MO 63103. Daniel F. X. Meenan, S. J., editor. (B). Published for priests and religious sisters and brothers of the Roman Catholic Church. Articles on subjects related to Christian spirituality geared to this group are from 1000 to 10,000 wds in length. Pays $6/printed page. Poetry occasionally accepted, 50¢/line.

ST. ANTHONY MESSENGER, 1615 Republic St., Cincinnati, OH 45210. Rev. Jeremy Harrington, editor. (M). Modern society, family, religious, psychological and moral problems with positive suggestions for solution. 2500-3500 wds. Pays 6¢+/wd on acceptance.

SANDAL PRINTS (Capuchin Province of St. Joseph), 1820 Mt. Elliott Ave., Detroit, MI 48207. Rev. Allen Gruenke, O.F.M. Cap., editor. (B). Accept queries about articles built around the work of Capuchins in any apostolic field. The preference is for the work of the mid-west Capuchins. Pictures must accompany the article (unless something can be worked out). 2000-4000 wds. Pymt varies—on acceptance.

SIGN (Passionist Missions, Inc.), Monastery Place, Union City, NJ 07087. Arthur McNally, C.P., editor. (10 issues/yr). Needs articles focusing primarily on renewal within the church; profiles on people who dramatically exemplify what it means to be a Christian; fiction, articles emphasizing positive values in contemporary art and literature, politics and economics, science and technology. Pays $150-$400.

SISTERS TODAY (The Liturgical Press), Collegeville, MN 56321. Rev. Daniel Durken, O.S.B., editor. (M for 10 months). Uses in-depth studies of religious life in the Catholic Church today; the role of women; religion in the Church and in the world; the theology and practice of the evangelical vows of poverty, chastity and obedience; religious community life today, its promises and problems; pertinent Biblical commentaries; the analysis of spiritual and psychological growth; development and deepening of personal and communal prayer life. 3000-5000 wds. Pays $5/printed page on publ. Free-lance writers who have not had solid theological preparation and background as well as those who have had little or no experience of organized religious life today are not encouraged to submit mss.

SPIRITUAL LIFE (Washington Province of Discalced Carmelite Fathers), 2131 Lincoln Road, N.E., Washington, D.C. 20002. Rev. Christopher Latimer, O.C.D., editor. (Q). Serious articles about man's encounter with God in the 20th century. Language of articles should be college level. Technical terminology, if used, should be clearly explained. Material should be presented in a positive manner. Sentimental articles or those dealing with specific devotional practices not accepted. Articles should avoid the "popular" sentimental approach to religion and concentrate on a more intellectual approach. Sample copy of the magazine is sent upon request. Length 4000 wds. Pays $50+, depending on quality and length.

U.S. CATHOLIC (Claretian Fathers), 221 W. Madison, Chicago, IL 60606. Father Mark J. Brummel, editor. (M). Does not solicit free-lance material.

## ROMAN CATHOLIC BOOK MARKETS

ABBEY PRESS, St. Meinrad, IN 47577. John J. McHale, editor. Books of general religious nature. Royalty varies. Send query with outline and sample chapter. Use SASE.

ALBA HOUSE (Society of St. Paul), 2187 Victory Blvd., Staten Island, NY 10314. Rev. Anthony Chenevey, editor. Book length mss (55,000 wds) dealing with theological, liturgical, scriptural, moral and social gospel concerns. Occasionally, they do philosophical works. Normally offers 10% royalties.

THE CATHOLIC UNIVERSITY OF AMERICA PRESS, INC., 620 Michigan Ave., N.E., Washington, D.C. 20064. Wants works of original scholarship in Catholic theology, philosophy, history, language and letters from 100,000 to 120,000 wds. Two-page abstract of mss and curriculum viate listing previous publications must be submitted before actual mss. Complete mss will be considered only if it is submitted in response to the invitation of the Press Editorial Committee.

FRANCISCAN HERALD PRESS, 1434 W. 51st St., Chicago, IL 60609. Wants books having to do with any aspect of Franciscanism, history, spirituality, literature. Also books on general Christian spirituality, history and life. Send letter of inquiry first before sending mss. Also be prepared to send chapter heads and sample chapter. 25,000-30,000 wds.

OUR SUNDAY VISITOR, INC., Noll Plaza, Huntington, IN 46750. Accepts both nonfiction and textbooks on basic Roman Catholic religious topics. Texts on grade school, high school and adult education levels. From 50,000 to 100,000 wds. Royalties paid according to contract.

PAULIST PRESS, 1865 Broadway, New York, NY 10023. Both popular and scholarly Catholic and Protestant religious works. 30,000 wds min. Standard contract.

THE REGINA PRESS, 7 Midland Ave., Hicksville, NY 11801. George Malhame, editor. Bible-oriented, educational and inspirational books.

ST. ANTHONY MESSENGER PRESS, 1615 Republic St., Cincinnati, OH 45210. Rev. Jeremy Harrington, O.F.M., editor-in-chief. Insightful and inspirational topics for the ordinary Catholic. 25,000-40,000 wds. Royalty varies.

ST. MARY'S COLLEGE PRESS, Winona, MN 55987. Primary objective is the development and publication of religious education materials for high school students and adults. Require detailed outline of proposed book (extended 4 pg outline) and sample chapter. Books are preferred which can be used for high school quarter-length courses but can easily be expanded by the creative teacher into a semester of work. Often require authors to develop an accompanying teacher's guidebook. Pymt is negotiated by contract and differs as circumstances vary. Requests for information should be addressed to Sister Maureen Murray, SSND, Director of Development in Religious Education.

57

# Writing for the charismatic market

VIOLA MALACHUK
Executive Editor,
Logos International Book Publishers

Every week at *Logos* I face a formidable pile of unsolicited manuscripts. Most are accompanied by a letter urging us to publish the piece with the fewest possible alterations. Many claim some kind of divine inspiration and virtually demand that we acknowledge an infallibility in what has been written. How is one to judge such things?

As I read the covering letter there is one thing I am looking for: does it reflect a broken spirit in the author, or is it an ultimatum? The chronic problem of Pentecost is the assumption that revelation and spiritual gifts indicate personal merit in the receiver. The primary qualification for good writing aimed at the charismatic market is a contrite heart—emerging from a realization of one's own wickedness and uncleanness before God. In short, the message is not, "I speak in tongues," but "Jesus is Lord."

**Primary qualification**

I'm also looking for freshness and readability. If you are going to explain the meaning of some passage of Scripture to me, it would help to have a story from your own life or another's that will clearly illustrate your point. And if you do have such a story, is it original or am I likely to have already heard it? Is your writing clear, direct and simple? The ability to write well usually does not come automatically with the baptism of the Holy Spirit; it must be learned.

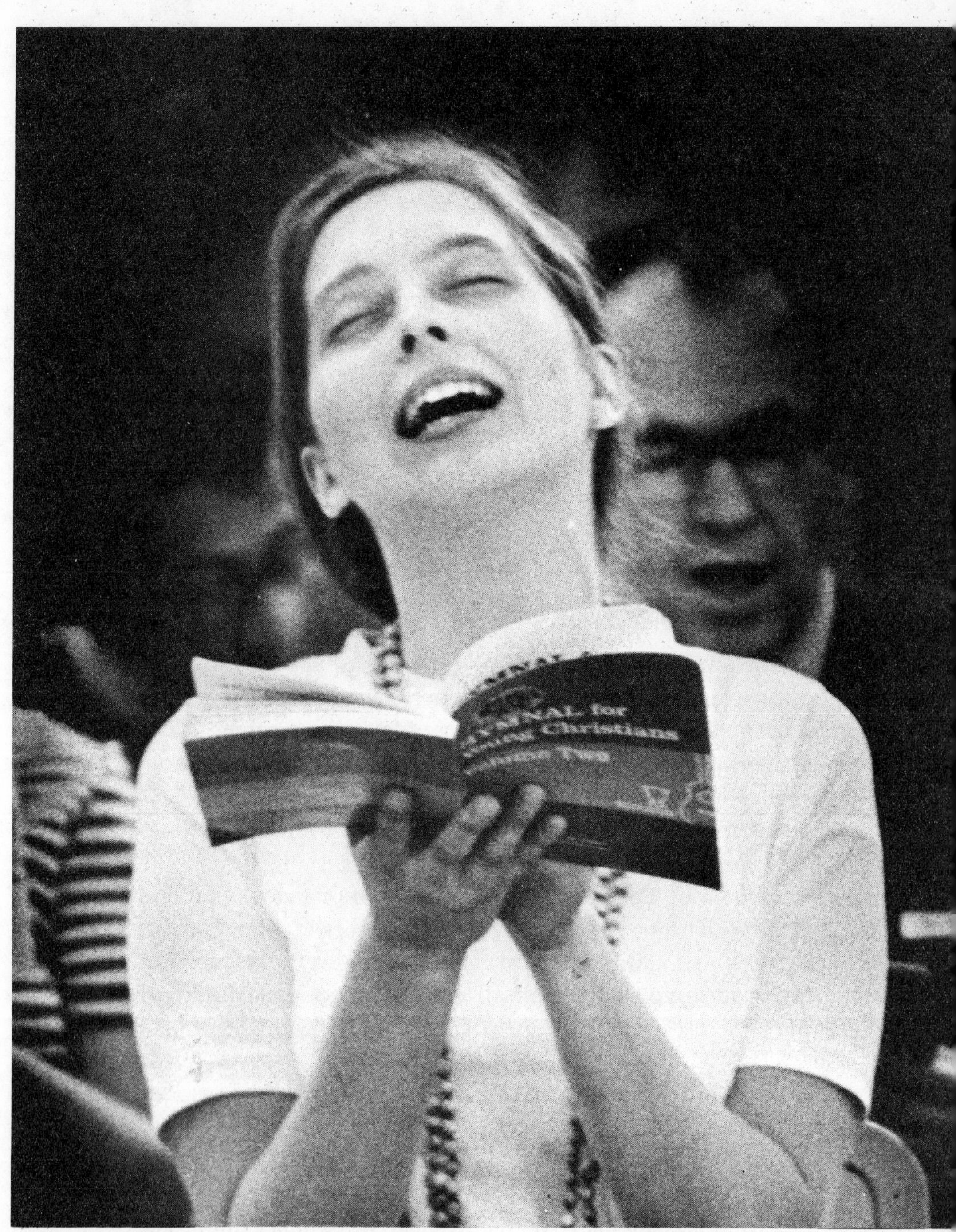


*Charismatics are often avid readers. More and more, publishers are opening their doors to charismatic books.* (Rockford Register Republic)

The majority of our bestsellers are autobiographical testimonies that, although they report miracles of healing, financial supply and the like, basically tell how the author came to experience brokenness before God. Their own stories contain fresh data that dramatically illustrate and, at the same time, revive a specific truth of Scripture that the Holy Spirit wants to bring to the attention of the Church.

**What every charismatic writer needs**

What every charismatic writer needs is a friend who will be friend enough to give serious critical appraisal of his or her work. Nothing is so valuable in producing good writing or, for that matter, good Christian character. Pray for such a friend—and don't overlook the obvious answer to that prayer—it could be the one from whom you least want to hear the truth, like your husband or wife.

**Seven questions to answer**

Here are some questions that your friend will help you answer:

1. Why are your writing this?
2. Have you done your research so that you are thoroughly acquainted with your subject?
3. Does what you have written meet specific current needs in the body of Christ and the world?
4. Has someone already covered the subject better than you can?
5. Will what you have written create understanding or cause confusion?
6. What purpose do the sensational aspects of your story serve?
7. Finally, and most importantly, who will be exalted by your writing? (There is a thin line, as Charles Simpson puts it, between bragging and testifying.)

**Combine the technical and the professional**

It is easy to see that writing for the charismatic market is not a task one lightly undertakes. To be a charismatic writer, one must combine technical and professional competence with a willingness to write what the Lord wants written. This can be costly. True, there will be miracles to report, and heart-lifting stories of the Lord's mighty works among His people. But there will also be the story of God's chastisement in one's own life—and it is never pleasant to tell of *that.*In short, if one is called to be a charismatic writer, there can be no room for pride or self-seeking. But that means that there will be plenty of room for the joy that always follows when one is doing the perfect will of the Lord.

# 58

# Selling your church

WINFIELD C. ARN, JR.
Managing Editor,
*Church Growth: America*

Tom Carlson will be in church next Sunday for the first time in twelve years, because of an ad in the morning newspaper. He will see a beautiful woman and a new Mercedes Benz. The copy reads . . .

> When two out of three are not enough . . .
>
> □ Rich
> □ Beautiful
> □ Happy
>
> There are a lot of people who are wealthy,
> but their lives are empty . . .
>
> There are people with beautiful faces,
> but their lives have no meaning . . .
>
> Jesus Christ did not come to make life easy . . .
> but he did come to make you strong.
>
> Join us for church next Sunday.
>
> **FIRST CHURCH OF KERNVILLE**

Advertisers spent hundreds of millions of dollars last year selling relief. Relief to people's hurts . . . needs . . . emptiness. Relief . . . but not solutions.

**Key to growth and vitality**

The key to the growth and vitality of your church . . . is its *unique* ability to meet people's needs with a real and lasting solution—Jesus Christ. This capacity of a church is mandatory to its growth and outreach. Without it, the church's existence is not worthwhile and it will satisfy real human needs and hurts only as well as Winston, McDonalds, or a new Corvette.

But, given the ability to provide meaning and fulfillment in a lonesome world, the church has "the best product in the marketplace." And the difference between selling a bottle of Alka Seltzer and selling your church is not so much in the technique as in the solution. Donald McGavran, founder of the modern church growth movement, says in the film *Reach Out and Grow,* "We constantly persuade people. We persuade people to play a game of tennis or to read a book. Persuasion is just an essential part of life. And evangelism simply extends that normal, beautiful act into the spiritual realm."

Likewise, we are faced with the task of persuading, or selling, people in the community on the fact that Jesus Christ and our church can meet needs in a way unique to the rest of the world (of course, once they are at church, there must be something worth returning for).

There are a myriad of techniques for selling your church. Here are some basic quidelines. . .

**What doesn't work**

First, what doesn't work? Pick up your paper next Saturday and turn to the church section. You may not be surprised to learn that absolutely no correlation exists between the little box with a smiling pastor or list of Sunday sermon topics and growing congregations. Last year over $20 million was spent on these ads with miniscule returns. Prudent advertisers would look elsewhere to spend their dollars.

Mass mailings to random samplings of people do not bring cost/effective returns. If people open the letter or flyer at all, they read it cursorily and seldom respond. Most of these mailings show little perception of people's needs and lack appeal.

**Remember your strength**

So what does work? Remember your strength: genuinely meeting people's needs and emptiness with practical solutions. Communicate your message in a way that speaks to these needs. The ad of a person seeking fulfillment . . . the promotion of a confidential telephone or personal counseling service . . . an article in the local newspaper on church activities that relate to the community (day-care, junior debs, taxi service, camping program, etc.) . . . the personally headed letter to responsive people in your community inviting them to a series of seminars on "Problems in marriage—divorce, drinking, child-raising; knowing yourself; the meaning of being a Christian; is the Bible infallible? . . ."

The church that finds a need, fills that need and sells itself as a viable answer to that need, will be the church that experiences exciting new growth and ministry to its own people and to the people in the community it will reach for Jesus Christ.

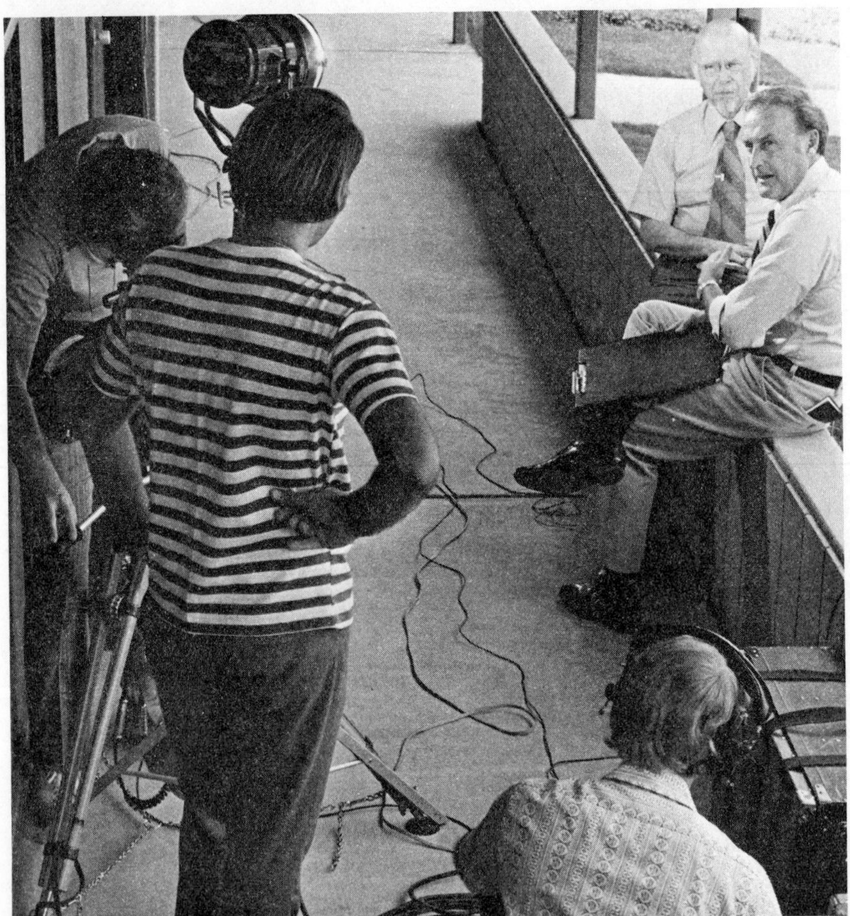

*Dr. Winfield Arn (left) and Dr. Donald McGavran face camera during the filming of* How to Grow a Church. *This film has helped many churches sell their programs to the community. (Christian Communication)*

59

# Writing for radio and television

BEN ARMSTRONG
Executive Secretary,
National Religious Broadcasters

Can you write for radio and television? If you can write and are willing to learn a few new things and develop your ability, you should be able to move into this area. This article is not meant to be a complete how-to course in writing, but it is a brief overview of what the writer does when writing for radio and television.

This type of writing need not be greatly different from any other writing, although one must keep in mind things that do set radio and television apart. In radio there is no visual component, but sound effects and music can be used to help the listener form a picture in his mind. In television there are visual and aural components, and the writer should make them work together for the maximum effect. In either case, it's not just a matter of writing words but of putting all the available means for conveying information together.

**First considerations**

Before actually starting to write a particular script, it is important to keep in mind what I'll call "first considerations" and to work from these. First (this is true in any type of writing), the writer must know the central idea to be communicated: what is to be said? Then, one must take his audience into consideration and write for them. Think of the age of the audience, their interests, what they want to hear, when they will be listening, etc. To be most effective, the writer must write for his

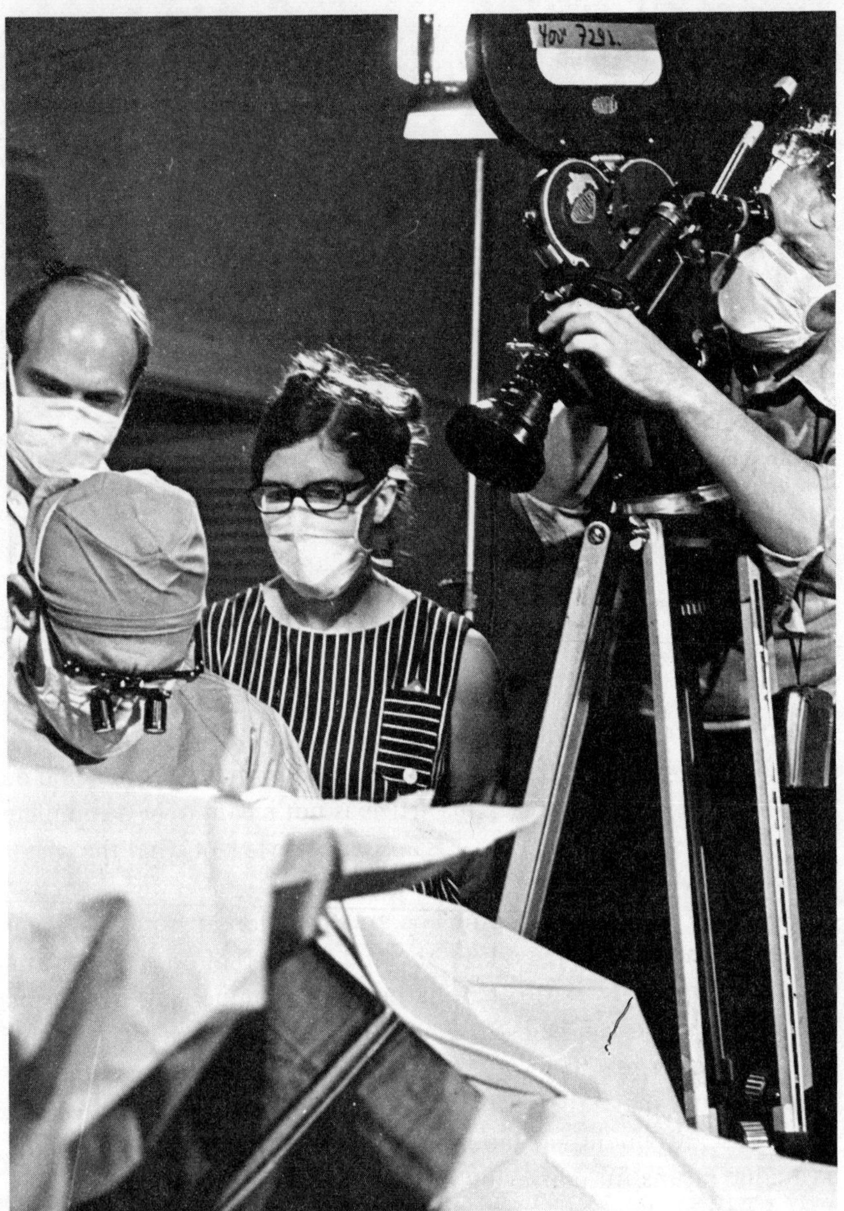

*Christian television is coming into its own today. Networks are beating the bushes for quality programs. (Radio and Television Commission of the Southern Baptist Convention)*

listeners. He cannot just write to please himself.

Other primary points must be considered before writing. How much time is allowed for the script? The writer must plan to say the most in the given time without getting too complicated. Also, the writer must know how the program is to be presented, i.e., lecture, discussion, drama, etc. This may have been determined already by someone else, or the writer himself may decide how the material would best be presented.

**Pull ideas together**

Having given some thought to these considerations, the writer can begin to pull ideas together. An outline of main points can be helpful, especially in a longer program. When writing, it is important to be interesting, imaginative and natural. Words should be chosen carefully so that they are understandable to the target audience, yet at the same time, vivid and interesting. Avoid stale cliches. The script should be brief and direct—not full of extraneous words. Finally, the writer should be truthful and avoid exaggeration when telling something to the listeners.

**Check your work**

After the material has been written, check on whether the work has lived up to the first considerations: the idea to be communicated, the audience, time, and manner of presentation. Any reworking should better fit the work to these prior specifications.

Writing for radio and television is a skill that is developed. The writer must know how to write and, also, how to combine the spoken word with other ways of putting an idea across to the audience. There is much room for innovation and creativity, and there may be room for you.

## BIBLIOGRAPHY

Anderson, Lois J., editor. *How You Can Broadcast Religion.* New York: National Council of Churches of Christ in the United States of America, 1957, pp. 56-69.

Parker, Everett C. *Religious Television, What to Do and How.* New York: Harper and Brothers, 1961, pp. 96-129.

Peck, William A. *Anatomy of Local Radio-TV Copy.* Blue Ridge Summit, Pa.: Tab Books, 1976.

Sheldon, LaVay. "Writing Principles for Religious Broadcasters," *Religious Broadcasting Sourcebook.* Morristown, New Jersey: National Religious Broadcasters, 1976, pp. J-1 to J-5.

Van Horne, Marion. "The Word at Work," *Religious Broadcasting Sourcebook,* pp. J-5 to J-11.

# 60

# The christian radio writer

JOE MUSSER
Free-lance writer

Many of the qualifications and requirements of radio writing are similar to those of other literary media. But there are other considerations which we'll discuss here.

**An elastic mind**

First of all, I think the Christian writer must be a person with intelligence, imagination, perception, and sympathy. He must have an elastic mind, a sensitive and varied viewpoint, and a wealth of experience from which to draw ideas. This person must be a man or woman with broad interests, acquainted equally with the mechanics of thinking and observation of human nature. But, he must be first and foremost a person of divine purpose, sincere, and completely dependent upon God, the Holy Spirit. I believe that the Holy Spirit makes up what he lacks of the other qualifications.

**Goals, ideals, motivation**

The writer must have goals, ideals, and motivation. These are the factors which distinguish Christian writing. A lack or neglect of these will mean an *occupation* in writing, but a realization and grasp of them will promote his writing to the level of ministry.

**Distinctions in radio writing**

Some distinctions, now, that apply to Christian *radio* writing. Compared with other writing there are certain likes and unlikes. Radio writing observes the same rules of rhetoric and composition. There must be unity, proportionate values (good structure, balance, and order). Likewise, there must be logical and chronological coherence. It must also have continuity of thought, provided chiefly by good transitions.

**Four technical principles**

The unlikes include the restriction of writing to an aural style and a high degree of intimacy. A radio writer is a composer in sound. Because of this, there are technical principles to remember.

1. The writer must strive for fluency, avoiding sibilants and tongue-twisting phrases. Spoken language differs from written language.

2. Writing for radio involves choosing words for simplicity, clarity, and accuracy. Sentences will be shorter, containing just one thought or idea.

3. Words having a homonym which could alter meaning will need substitutes.

4. Sentence structure will have more "looseness." Essentially, he will be writing "conversationally."

Good radio writing, as any other writing, can be helped by studying and capitalizing on the techniques of other successful writers.

These, then, are the basic considerations.

How about markets?

**Four market categories**

Some of the categories are:

1. *The noncommercial Christian radio station*—a station operated by a Christian organization or denomination for ministry of the Gospel

*Ever consider missionary radio? Writer prepares script for HCJB, Quito, Ecuador.*

and promotional purposes. This station will generally employ full or part-time *continuity* writers, a *copy* or *commercial* writer, and several freelance *dramatic script* writers. The commercial writer at the noncommercial station writes copy for public service and promotional spot announcements. He usually has other assignments as a *continuity writer*. The greatest potential for the Christian writer is found in this field, for it is probably the only market for *free-lance* or *contract* scripts.

2. A *Christian commercial station* is one owned by Christians, but designed to be a moneymaking enterprise. The amount of Christian programming will be less than the noncommercial "religious" station; therefore, the Christian writing needs will be fewer. These stations are smaller ones, generally speaking, so the writer will usually have other related responsibilities. Seldom is more than one full time writer on the staff of a smaller station.

3. *The Christian broadcaster* is someone who has a single program aired daily or weekly on one or more stations. The writer usually has other responsibilities in addition to his regular work. This category includes programs put out by a denomination as well as those written for a local church or organization.

4. *Missionary Radio*—ranging from single programs put out by mission boards to complete missionary radio stations. Small staffs, precipitated by low budgets, necessitates doubling-up of responsibilities here also.

**Disadvantages to be considered**

There are disadvantages that must be considered before thinking of a career in radio. Probably the greatest handicaps stem from the very nature of radio itself. Radio is immediacy. There are deadlines—constant deadlines—forcing a writer to work under pressure. Coupled with this problem of immediacy is that of volume, which contributes to a lack of new ideas. Another disadvantage is that of limited markets. Also, the radio writer must write to certain specifications and meet established standards. Occasionally, he must write about something in which he isn't even remotely interested. Radio writing is an anonymous profession for the most part and the free-lancer faces the prospect of "feast or famine" economically.

Well, that's the negative side. The fact is that radio writing is probably the most satisfying and spiritually rewarding of all Christian writing. The income is fairly good as compared to writing for other

Christian media. There's room for a variety of expression. A writer receives the satisfaction of hearing his writing presented by talented performers. Radio writing is probably the most flexible tool for making use of writing talent. And, although it's "feast or famine" for the free-lancer, remember—he's his own boss and sets his own hours.

**Four basic ways to get started**

How does one get started? There are four basic ways, three of them involve starting at the bottom.

1. One can go to work for a station. Learn radio through experience. Likewise, learn writing through experience. Most smaller stations have announcer-writers, salesman-writers, etc. Experience will be broad and radio background likewise will be broad.

2. Or a writer can start his own program. I did. Research and study in the field of radio, followed by a survey of local churches, CBMC or club groups, denominations and other Christian organizations will show what is currently being done in radio. It will also show where there is a *need* for a program.

3. Another approach is through advertising agencies. They write commercial copy for radio, so here's one way of getting in.

4. Free-lance or contract writing. The need here is for someone who has had previous experience, in both radio *and* writing, and preferably in *radio writing.* The market for the free-lancer is an extremely small one. Radio drama is not too common right now. (It used to be, and I think it will stage a come-back, but for the moment, the demand is limited.) Also, radio drama is a highly specialized field involving problems of plot, characterization, dialog, production and special radio techniques. It's definitely not a field for the beginning writer.

The Christian radio writer must face the temptations of "hack" writing and procrastination. He must do it while facing deadlines and lack of ideas. There are limitations, to be sure but the product must always be his best.

*Good radio writers are needed.*

Our responsibility as writers is to change thought, to cause reformation—of ideas and ideals. Radio is one of the most potent and influencial forces in the world. Radio can help the Christian writer fulfill this responsibility. There are almost 23,000,000 people living within the sound of the seven Moody radio stations. What I write has the potential to affect the lives of 23,000,000 people. And, with the help of the Holy Spirit, this is our purpose and goal.

# 61

# Writing for christian radio

JERRY RICE
Assistant Manager and Program Director, WMBI AM & FM

If you were to walk down the street and ask the next ten passers-by to describe Christian radio, their answers would probably range from, "What's Christian radio?" to, "Oh yeah, that's the station with the preachin' and the sacred music."

However, true Christian radio is more than exhortations by Brother Zeke or the endless repetition of great hymns of the church. The ministry of Christian radio is a precious, valuable means of proclaiming the Good News of Jesus Christ to a listening world.

It would be unfair as well as untrue to stereotype this ministry as one of only preaching and singing. For available to the Christian broadcaster today is a variety of ways to communicate a vital scriptural message.

One of these ways is dramatic programming. Once the backbone of secular radio's golden days, the radio drama has truly found a lasting home in Christian broadcasting. Its uses are unending . . . and so is its popularity.

Radio drama is the vehicle by which R. G. LeTourneau's life is portrayed in serial form . . . or it's an exciting 15-minute babysitter as children linger on every word of an adaptation of the popular Sugar Creek Gang series.

To many, the polished, well-paced dialog of quality radio drama often sounds spontaneous, requiring little or no preparation. But there is indeed preparation . . . a great deal of it going into the central object of all radio drama—the script.

**A script's importance**

Just how important is a script in producing a dramatic radio program? Let's examine . . . .

To deliver his goods, a truck driver would need a road map to guide him through new and unfamiliar territory. In much the same way, the radio actor depends upon his script for direction in delivering his message. In both cases there are signals to obey, obstacles to avoid, and even speed limits to abide by.

If you have aspirations to become a script writer, you may want to consider the following questions and suggestions.

**Script must meet objectives**

What makes a good dramatic script for Christian radio? Well, first and most important, the script's content must meet the objectives of the station or organization for which it was written. For example, the script objectives of the Moody Radio Network are fourfold: (1) to encourage believers; (2) to promote reliance on God in every area of human experience; (3) to promote positive action in Christian experience; and (4) to evangelize. As is true with many Christian stations, the majority of the audience of the seven-station Moody Radio Network consists of born-again believers. Therefore, the greater portion of dramatic thrust is on the first three points. However, all scripts should, at least indirectly, contain some evangelistic purpose. On some occasions, such as special seasonal programs, evangelism could play the major part in the objective.

**Communicate positive action**

It is particularly important in Christian radio that scripts do not end on a negative note. The script writer should strive to communicate positive action to the listener, offering spiritual approaches to life's problems. Never forget that people are looking for answers. It is the writer's job to supply those answers, using his creative efforts as a definite ministry.

**Keep a specific goal in mind**

Whether the script is original or an adaptation, the writer should always keep a specific goal clearly in mind, and then gear all his efforts towards attaining that goal.

A conscientious scriptwriter asks himself questions on every line he has written and then answers them. Questions such as: Does the script contain a discernible theme or message? What is it? . . . Is the plot

*Many secular stations, including the Voice of America (control room shown here), do some religious programming.*

realistic? . . . Are characterizations strong? . . . And are the motivations of the characters made clear and convincing?

**Checklist for examining script**

Now, as to the mechanics of scriptwriting, the same basic requirements would apply to Christian and secular stations alike. Again, use the self-questioning approach. Try this check list in examining your script:

(1) How is the opening? Is it fast? Is interest aroused at once?

(2) Are the time, place, and characters clearly delineated in the opening scene?

(3) Is the overall structure of the script good? Does it proceed swiftly

and surely from inciting action, through well-planned minor climaxes, to a major climax?

(4) Are all characters in the script well-drawn and properly identified at all times? Are any of the characters unnecessary?

(5) Are there any unproducible spots? Have you written in sound effects which are too complicated to produce? Do they add reality or confusion to the program?

(6) Are the sound effects and music called for in the script adequate? Is the script cluttered with unnecessary sound?

(7) Are all the scenes necessary?

(8) Are the scene transitions of the sort you want? Do they depict a change in location, attitude, or a short or long length of time?

(9) Are the scenes properly blocked so that it's clear at all times where the audience is in the scene, and where the characters are in relation to the audience?

(10) Are all entrances and exits covered with lines or sound? (A character cannot fade out unless he has either a line or a sound effect to fade on.)

(11) Is the action (both dramatic and physical) properly motivated?

(12) Are there lines which contain unconscious double meanings?

(13) Are there lines that are difficult for the actors to say? Is the dialog realistic and consistent with the character image being created?

(14) Are some of the speeches too long?

(15) Is the script approximately the right length? If it's too long, what can be cut out? If it's too short, where can it be stretched most effectively?

**Use of sound effects**

Be especially selective in using sound effects in your script. Don't include every sound that might occur in a real life situation, but use only those sounds that will actually stimulate the listener into visualizing the scene. Determine if the sound serves a real purpose. Use it only if it helps to make something clear, adds realism or dramatic impact, or if the audience expects to hear it. Examine each sound in the light of these criteria. If it satisfies none of them, eliminate it. If there are omissions in the light of these needs, create a sound to fulfill the need.

So you see, there actually is a great deal of preparation in making a radio script and its resulting drama sound spontaneous. Writing for Christian radio is unique, and by no means an easy task. But it is an exciting and challenging ministry—one that bears its rewards in the changed lives of faithful listeners.

62

# Combining the visual arts with the written word

MARIE CHAPIAN
Free-lance writer


Have you ever thought of coupling your writing talents with artistic expression?

We are in an age of visual communication, and we are accustomed to receiving visual artistic impressions every day. Advertising art in its myriad forms confronts us from all directions, and the major visual influence on our lives is the television screen. This has a serious effect on the writer and his work, unless he is an advertising copy writer or a television script writer.

A visually oriented culture such as ours can be of great benefit to the Christian author in his ministry of reaching souls for the Lord. It is this idea I want to explore with you.

Your writing might adapt perfectly with visual expression, and if it does, you will want to examine the many possibilities there are available for you to choose from.

**Two forms of visual expression**

Let's narrow these artistic possibilities down to two forms: *photography* and *art*.

For the most part, the writer does not do the job of an art director, but he must understand certain principles necessary for producing a literary product utilizing both visual art and the written word.

How do you begin? First, look over the manuscript and discover where there is pictorial emphasis in the writing. Look for visual identification. Writing has a point of view, and so must the art which accompanies it. If you're beginning the work, use the same tactic. Scrutinize.

Does the written message need to have visual expression? How can you decide whether or not a work stands well enough alone, or whether it might meet with deeper response if visuals are added? In discovering the answers to these questions, it is necessary to investigate the following principles of communication: *the technique, the aesthetics* and *the message.*

**The technique**

Let's begin by looking at *the technique.* This is the skill, or command, of the fundamentals of your art. It is knowing what is good and what is bad; what works well and what doesn't work well. Blake has said, "No man can embrace true art until he has explored and cast out false art."

To throw in a few paragraphs to make a book contemporary, or to create a picture-book with the idea of producing a good seller ought not to be your intention. Your intention hopefully, is nothing less than obeying the will of the Lord and producing what the Holy Spirit guides you to do.

You can't make a book any better written or improve the message by adding artwork. If it isn't in the words, it isn't there. You can take the most brilliant painting and reproduce it alongside an inferior piece of writing and the painting won't help it. In fact, both expressions will suffer.

**Acquiring photographs**

Let's assume your unsubmitted manuscript or idea is in order and you have chosen to combine it visually with photography. You can acquire photographs by: a) taking them yourself, b) hiring a photographer to take them for you, or c) buying photos from one of the many studios that have stock photographs on file for one-time use at specified rates.

You may also leave the entire matter in the hands of your publisher who will handle layout as well as the choice of photography. Your suggestions will be valuable, however, and here is where your forethought and preparation will show.

Technique, or skill, is necessary in selecting art. When you are examining a photograph or artwork, your question should not be, "Is it good?" Instead, ask, "What reaction does it evoke?" If the visual art makes a statement that is complete, it is usually superfluous to use any written material with it. Let the art stand alone.

Here is an example of what I mean. In my book, *City Psalms,* published by Moody Press, there is a poem entitled *Loneliness.* Printed on grey paper, it faces a photograph my husband took of a pigeon sitting on the ledge of the roof of our apartment building in New York City. The photograph has a lonely, desolate quality and I identified with it and wrote the words,

*I knew loneliness*
*before.*
*Barren, scalding*
*loneliness . . .*

which began the poem hidden in that arrested moment captured by the camera.

We could have selected a hundred other photographs for a poem about loneliness, but we used the one of the pigeon. It is a subtle, and yet compelling photograph that was not complete until a poem was added to it. Then it became complete. This is how you must choose your photographs and art. The photograph of the pigeon was in need of a story. Are your visuals obvious statements in themselves or are they pictures in need of a story?

If you are writing for magazines, you naturally study the magazine for its style and format, and you must do the same with visuals. There are certain styles and formats that each publication requires, and you must carefully observe these.

The publications using visuals as an integral means of expressing the message are: tracts, collections of verse, devotional books and, of course, children's books. The publisher's art department usually adds the artwork and the writer is involved only in the writing, except with children's books where artist and writer may work closely together.

**The aesthetics**

Technique is not enough, however, in combining the written word and visual art. There are *the aesthetics* to consider.

There are certain principles of aesthetics and values that must not be violated.

If you are considering using illustrations with your writing, you must ask yourself more than once why visual experience is necessary in the work. When you have your illustrations in order, look for comparison and contrast of expression. Does the writing confront, whereas the illustrations merely encounter, or vice versa? What are you reflecting in the art and in the writing? Finally, does the message remain clear and precise throughout?

Because a photograph or picture is great, it doesn't mean it would arouse attention or move readers to action if combined with the written word. Often it detracts instead of adds to.

A picture isolates a mood or a feeling as words press into a mood or feeling. In Marshall McLuhan and Harley Parker's book, *Through the Vanishing Point,* they write, "The advantage of using poetry and art simultaneously is that one permits a journey inward, the other a journey outward to the appearance of things."

**The message**

Now, let's look at the last and most important component of your work: *the message.*

The technique and the aesthetics are valuable, but without the message they have nothing to express.

The Christian author differs from the secular author in that his only motive is to convey the message of the Gospel of Christ. With this motive in the forefront of every word skittered across a page, the mes-

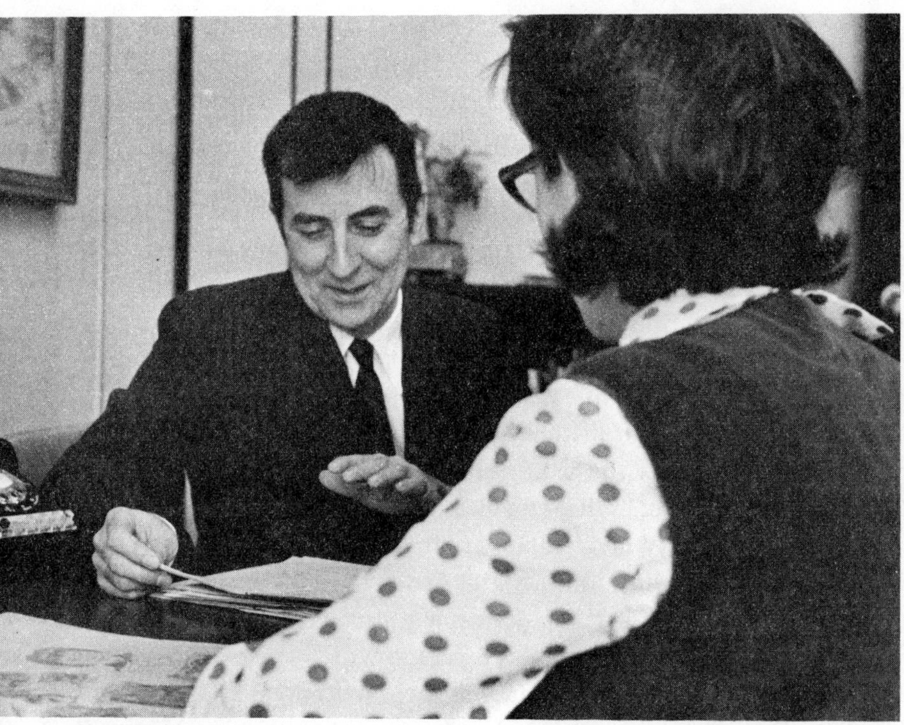

*Artist Bert Tiedemann talks over some cartoons he has done for Grace Fox,* Counselor *editor. (Scripture Press)*

sage is all important and more valuable than the writing and the art.

Examine the writing from the aspect of the message and ask: 1) Is the message clear as it stands? 2) Would visuals add an increased awareness of the message? 3) Would the addition of visuals heighten the perception of the reader and direct his mind toward God?

I recently bought a book filled with drawings, paintings, photographs, graphics with the written message in various quotes from the Bible and contemporary people in short paragraphs of pithy sayings. The book is striking, but the message is overpowered by the abundance of art. After reading the book, I am still not quite sure what was said.

The Christian writer and artist cannot forget that it is not the writing nor the art we wish to show off, but the *message.*

Photographs can be poetry in themselves, as they can be social commentaries in themselves. The idea of using art and writing together is not to overstate or demonstrate talent, but to make the message more dynamic and meaningful to the reader. The idea is to bring the reader closer to Jesus.

This does not mean that artistically we have any right to be shoddy, or less than the best. Far from it! We ought to be the finest craftsmen who ever put books together! We ought to be producing the finest literature and the most exciting art *because we have the most exciting message!*

**Knowledge of visuals**

To combine visual arts with written art you do not need to be an art director, nor do you need expert skill at the drawing board or in the darkroom. A good knowledge of visuals is valuable, however, and if you don't have it, find someone who does and collaborate.

If you have no training in art, your worst enemy is your own taste. One would hesitate to employ the services of a doctor who exclaims, "I don't know much about medicine, but I know what I like." The same applies to the writer with the attitude, "I don't know much about art, but I know what I like." What you like might not inspire anybody else.

With the necessary elements of technique, aesthetics and message formed to present a harmonious unit of words and art, we experience an expression which our visually-trained minds can receive gladly.

The Christian writer or artist is a person with a sense of active God expression, and one always finding in life something new and fresh to bring to others in the name of the Lord. Combining the visual arts with the written word is one idea. We need to explore every possibility.

# 63

# Photojournalism

WENDELL MATHEWS
Art Director, Carthage College,
*Christian Life* Magazine

You have heard it and read it a thousand times—starving people throughout the world are in need of your help. Then you see a photograph of a starving mother holding her hungry child. You are affected in a way that words, spoken or written, cannot always communicate.

The type of journalistic writing that depicts an event most graphically is the photo-story. Traditional journalism uses the photograph to illustrate copy. Emphasis is on the text. There are certain events, however, that are best communicated by a photograph—or a set of photographs— plus brief descriptive copy. In such cases the old proverb applies: a picture is worth a thousand words.

The photo story approach to journalistic communication with emphasis on photographs and succinct copy is called photojournalism.*

**The best photojournalism**

The best photojournalism involves the talents of an editorial trio—the photographer, the editor/writer, and the art director. The first two talents are often combined in one person. The photojournalist, in the real sense of the word, is equally at home with both camera

*Related material is often indexed under photo-feature, photo-essay, photo-reporting, photo-communication, press photography, and picture story.

and typewriter, able to produce a well-balanced editorial package.

It is beyond the scope of this chapter to discuss techniques for producing good photographs and well-written copy. Such technical knowledge must be developed before full concentration can be devoted to telling the story, but this knowledge is not enough. It is not the camera that makes the photo-story a universal language; it is the man behind the camera. The photojournalist must have experience with life. He is a generalist who sees news and feature stories in all sorts of events. This level of understanding and sensitivity ultimately distinguishes the mediocre photographer/writer from the photojournalist who produces photographs that penetrate into the essence of the event in such a way that little copy is necessary.

**Characteristics of the photojournalist**

Copy often takes the form of a caption that briefly describes the event. In his book, *The Business of Photojournalism* (Amphoto, Inc.; New York: 1971), A. E. Loosley suggests nine rules for writing photo captions:

**Nine rules for writing photo captions**

1. State your point in the first line in simple language.
2. Be sure the traditional who, what, where, why, when and how are answered.
3. Always double space when typing your captions.
4. Do not type on both sides of the sheet.
5. If the caption is long, put it on a separate sheet with instructions to the editor as to where it fits in.
6. Make sure every piece of paper (photograph, caption, covering letter, etc.) has your name on it.
7. Always date your captions and photographs.
8. Always keep a copy of your captions.
9. Attach captions firmly to the back of the photograph.

**A challenge to editors**

I wish to challenge editors to do their own photojournalism. Some articles can be made more interesting by adding a photo-box that gives background and human interest to the article (see example J).

The following examples illustrate some of the basic principles of photojournalism.

Unlike most summer mission enterprises, this one enthusiastically enlists young people aged 13-19. The results? Phenomenal. BY GARY HARDAWAY

## TEEN MISSIONS: GET DIRTY FOR GOD

The scene is an aerial panorama of a great American metropolis. Suddenly the skyscrapers partially fade from view as an attractive young woman materializes from thin air . . . with a noose around her neck! After dangling a moment above the crowds and the concrete she moans, "Man, have I got hang-ups." As millions of TV viewers chuckle, a voice says, "If you've got hang-ups, Dial-A-Teen." A telephone number fills the screen, and the serious business of a Dial-A-Teen campaign has begun. In a matter of a few weeks thousands have responded to Dial-A-Teen to receive sound Biblical advice and, in most cases, a clear presentation of the Gospel. As the name implies, the majority of the counselors are teenagers.

Meanwhile in the high Andes of Bolivia, another gang of teens is hard at work laying the foundation for a new camp dining hall. After a full day of hauling large rocks from a nearby creek bed, shoveling sand and mixing cement, they're tired, sweaty and blistered . . . but happy. They came to work, and when they go they intend to leave a job well done.

And in the Appalachians, seven more Christian teenagers, who have brought the first Vacation Bible School in years to one isolated mountain community, dismiss their flock of bright-eyed youngsters with the challenge, "Bring more tomorrow." The youngsters scamper off on the missionary errand, and their teachers count the handicraft kits, wondering if there will be enough. It's exactly the kind of problem they had hoped for.

Sounds like one of Snoopy's novels, doesn't it? The one in which he introduces a bunch of seemingly unrelated plots in the first chapter and then promises, "I'll tie it all together in Chapter Two."

In this case the tying it all together is being done by an embryo mission organization called Teen Missions Inc., whose emphasis obviously is on youth.

In its first summer of operation (1971), Teen Missions deployed 63 young people on various work projects in Mexico, Guatemala and Colombia. An additional 30 conducted the first Dial-A-Teen campaign at the Ohio State Fair in Columbus. In 30 days, 10,000 callers rang up. Inquirers were urged to drop by the Dial-A-Teen booth at the fair. Hundreds did and more than 380 recorded their decision for Christ.

From this not-so-humble beginning the mission launched a more ambitious program in 1972. Work teams tackled highly demanding projects in the Dominican Republic, Peru and Nicaragua, and two Dial-A-Teen squads ministered in Dallas and Fort Worth, Texas. The 38-member Nicaraguan team, which constructed a girls' dormitory at the Central American Mission's Bible Institute in Managua, later received word that the building was one of the few to withstand the devastating shock of the city's worst earthquake in history. During the crisis the dorm was converted into a shelter for many homeless families.

In addition to the lasting achievement of the structure itself, the team donated $3,800 to the Bible Institute. Teen Missions sets the support figure of each worker to include a $100 gift to the inviting mission organization. Often the total sum covers the expense of all the building materials, plumbing and fixtures of the new building.

As invitations multiply, the mission's scope of operation rapidly expands. The 1973 summer thrust mobilized 189 young *(continued on page 67)*



A

*Large photographs tell the story visually and create interest. These photographs were provided from outside sources. Gary Hardaway obtained his (top) from Teen Missions, Inc. As baseball writer for the Chicago Tribune, George Langford had numerous photographs available in the newspaper files. Photographs similar to this (bottom) can be obtained from United Press International (UPI) photo service and the publicity office of the ball club.*

## I ought to bite your head off

"We went into New York to play the Mets and we had a 2 1/2-game lead but our momentum was dipping," recalled Chicago Cub catcher Randy Hundley of that Monday night last September 8. He had been lounging in a chair at the end of a huge conference table in an insurance company office, legs extended and crossed at the ankles, thighs barely holding to the front edge of the chair, and shoulders resting on the top of the chair back. Then he straightened.

"The score is tied, 2 to 2, in the sixth inning and Tommie Agee bounces a ball to left field and when the ball slows down in the heavy grass he races into second base and I'm thinking, even before the next play develops, that there's no way we're going to get Agee out if this next fellow (Rookie Wayne Garrett) gets a base hit.

"But Garrett hits a line drive to right field, one hop to (Jim) Hickman. Hickman comes up and makes a perfect throw home and I catch the ball in one motion and tag Agee right up the side.

"Well, I turned, looked at first to make sure the runner wasn't going to second base. Then I'm looking for (Bill) Hands (the Cubs' pitcher) and I'm going to give him the ball and we're going to work on the next hitter."

A long, deep breath escaped, then he returned.

"All of a sudden I hear this big roar go up and I turn around and here's the umpire with his hands down saying Agee is safe. Well, Agee had almost knocked the ball out of my mitt. So there's no doubt I tagged him before he got to the plate. Here I'm thinking Hickman made a great throw, I've made a great play to get the ball, tagging Agee in one motion and holding onto the ball. The ball hit in the front of my glove pocket and jumped out and was hanging like on the tip of my fingers.

"I didn't know what to do so I just jumped straight up and down and argued with him for five minutes because this particular game was one that all of us

Randy Hundley, baseball catcher known for his competitive spirit, chews out umpires, rattles opposing batters, and predicts pennant for Chicago team.

BY GEORGE LANGFORD
Baseball Writer, Chicago Tribune

Christian Life MAY, 1970



B

C

Shirley Boone, wife of entertainer Pat Boone, and mother of four teenage daughters, explains what her "one woman's liberation" is all about in this excerpt from her new book, One *Woman's Liberation*, just published by Creation House.

THE SHIRLEY BOONE STORY:

FREE AS A BIRD

At 6 A.M. on February 9, 1971, I awoke up in an earthquake! The very ground upon which we'd built our physical and material foundations had become our foe. Like a horse trying to throw its rider, the earth heaved and tossed as though to rid itself of man and his works. To see the walls of our home waving like sheets on the clothesline, and to find the once-solid floor no longer solid, was upsetting—literally!

Yet, when I was awakened in my pitching, sliding bed, I didn't fall to my knees in terrified prayer. My spontaneous reaction as my feet hit the floor was to lift my hands and cry, "*Praise You, Jesus.*"

Wild? You bet! But not in the way you're probably thinking.

My reaction was wild only because I had been a dedicated coward most of my life. Yet now I felt calm, full of peace, in the midst of physical danger which frightened many people so much they later sold their houses and moved from the state.

Fear, however, never entered my mind, even though my husband Pat was out of town on a singing engagement. Thrown by the shaking from wall to wall as I tried to run down the hall to the girls' room, I repeated again—still instinctively—"*Praise You, Jesus.*"

Then I called, "It's all right, girls. It's an earthquake."

All right? An earthquake? I still find it hard to believe that I spoke so cheerfully and encouragingly without any trace of alarm. For, before the Holy Spirit filled my life, I was a mass of fears.

For example, I'd been a white-knuckled flier. Whenever I'd been on a plane, my heart had sunk in direct proportion to its rate of climb until, by the time it had reached cruising altitude, I'd become a package of pure panic.

I'd been afraid of public speaking, strangers, interviews, criticism, guilt and failure, and these had been only a *few* of my hang-ups. Psychologically, I'd been a mess, in bondage to dozens of terrors.

However, after my baptism with the Holy Spirit, I'd gradually discovered as various situations arose that I'd been freed from first one phobia and then another. I was no longer afraid of crowds or strangers or even failure, for I'd come to know that what might be failure in men's eyes is a triumph if it's ordained by God.

In short, as a Spirit-filled follower of Jesus, I'd been so freed from fear that *in an earthquake* I sincerely cried, "Praise You, Jesus."

Lindy and Cherry had been sleeping together with their door open, so the minute they awakened they saw the night light in the hall and could find their way to me.

Laury, too, could find her way, because she had a night light in her room. But Debby had been sleeping alone, in the dark with her door to the hall closed, because she had a bad cough.

But, as the Bible teaches us, the Lord prepares our way, for the only lamp knocked off a dresser by the quake fell in Debby's room and hit the floor in such a way that *the jolt turned it on!* So Debby, too, had light to guide her to the rest of us.

Because I'd awakened praising God, there was literally no place for fear in our house. The Bible says that perfect love casts out fear. And what is perfect love? God is love. Jesus is love. And surrounded by God's presence, the girls and I couldn't be afraid. Many California children were in psychiatric clinics for weeks after the quake. I heard news reports that said the major problem was not the fear of the quakes, but the children's reactions to *the fear they saw in their parents*. The Lord had taken care of that problem for us.

Crawling onto my bed, we joined hands and sang, "Praise God from whom all blessings flow." Then we began praying in the Spirit. Meanwhile, still shaking along with our whole house, we could hear water in the swimming pool just below my bedroom window sloshing like water in a giant bathtub!

I think the *sounds* of the earthquake

*Photos: Pat and Shirley's bedroom (left) often is the meeting place for prayer. The Boone family at home (this page, from left): Laury, Lindy, Shirley, Pat, Debby, Cherry.*

20 CHRISTIAN LIFE

JULY 1972 21

D

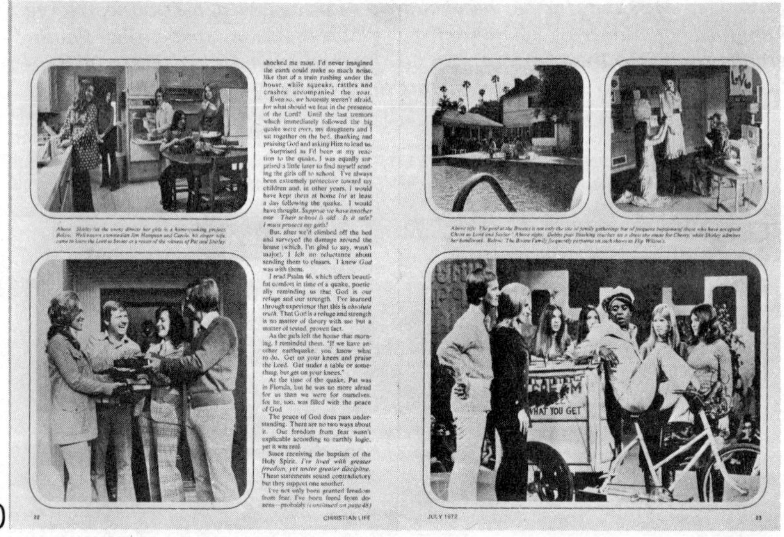

shocked me most. I'd never imagined the earth could make so much noise, like that of a train rushing under the house, while squeaks, rattles and crashes accompanied the roar.

Even so, we honestly weren't afraid, for what should we fear in the presence of the Lord? Until the last tremors which immediately followed the big quake were over, my daughters and I sat together on the bed, thanking and praising God and asking Him to lead us.

Surprised as I'd been at my reaction to the quake, I was equally surprised a little later to find myself sending the girls off to school. I've always been extremely protective toward my children and, in other years, I would have kept them at home for at least a day following the quake. I would have thought, *Suppose we have another one. Their school is old. Is it safe? I must protect my girls!*

But, after we'd climbed off the bed and surveyed the damage around the house (which, I'm glad to say, wasn't major), I felt no reluctance about sending them to classes. I knew *God* was with them.

I read Psalm 46, which offers beautiful comfort in time of a quake, poetically reminding us that God is our refuge and our strength. I've learned through experience that this is *absolute truth*. That God is a refuge and strength is no matter of theory with me but a matter of tested, proven fact.

As the girls left the house that morning, I reminded them, "If we have another earthquake, you know what to do. Get on your knees and praise the Lord. Get under a table or something, but get on your knees."

At the time of the quake, Pat was in Florida, but he was no more afraid for us than we were for ourselves, for he, too, was filled with the peace of God.

The peace of God does pass understanding. There are no two ways about it. Our freedom from fear wasn't explicable according to earthly logic, yet it was real.

Since receiving the baptism of the Holy Spirit, *I've lived with greater freedom, yet under greater discipline.* These statements sound contradictory but they support one another.

I've not only been granted freedom from fear. I've been freed from dozens—probably *(continued on page 48)*

22 CHRISTIAN LIFE

JULY 1972 23

*This excerpt from Shirley Boone's* One Women's Liberation *creates interest through numerous photographs which originally appeared in a photo-section of the book. Readers look at photographs and read captions before they start the article. In this case, they catch a glimpse of the life of a Hollywood family. When printing excerpts, editors should ask for recent photographs which update the material or make the article unique.*

# TO ALL THE NATIONS
## ...beginning at Dallas

By this fall, many observers believe, high school and college campuses, business offices and military bases will know that EXPLO '72 happened in Dallas as participants take the knowledge and inspiration of this most significant meeting with them.
BY BOB HILL

Something historical happened in Dallas last month! More than 100,000 high schoolers, college students, military personnel, pastors, business and professional men from every state and 70 foreign countries invaded the north Texas city for a spiritual rendezvous that is destined to be felt around the world.

A huge electric sign atop the Blue Cross building, bus placards and downtown window displays reminded residents that "Something historic is happening here—EXPLO '72," and the signs were right!

"This is not so much a time of inspiration, but a time of challenge," said Dr. Bill Bright, president of the sponsoring Campus Crusade for Christ. "We mean to initiate a great spiritual awakening throughout the U.S. and the world."

During the week, the orderly group of young people, described by police captain John Squier as the "best behaved group ever to assemble in Dallas," attended 63 organized training conferences scattered through the Dallas-Fort Worth area each morning for strategy meetings to share their faith. Ranging in attendance from 800 to as many as 12,000, the groups were challenged by more than 100 leading evangelical speakers and professional athletes. The afternoons were spent on the streets and in neighborhood door-to-door sharing of the "Four Spiritual Laws," with several thousand reportedly praying to receive Christ.

Executive conferences were held (continued on page 48)

20 CHRISTIAN LIFE AUGUST 1972

FOR MORE PHOTOS, TURN PAGE ▶

E

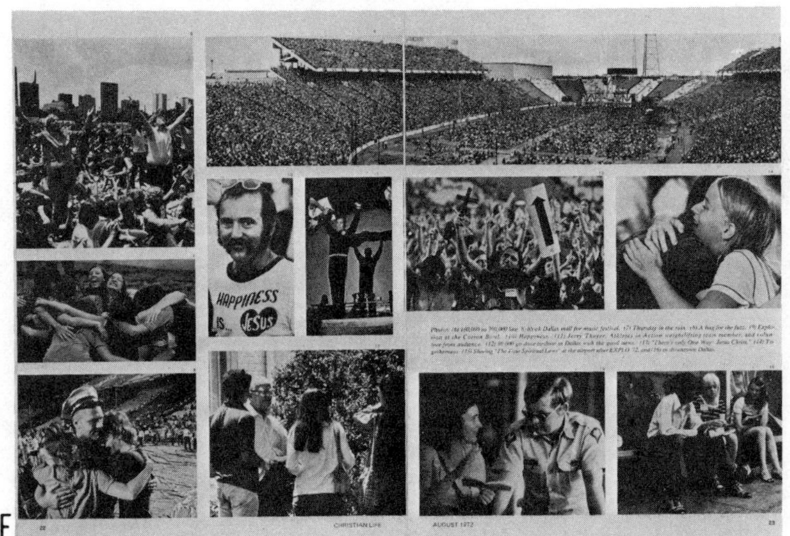

22 CHRISTIAN LIFE AUGUST 1972 23

F

*Here is a good example of photo-journalism techniques. Little copy is needed. A free-lance photographer provided numerous "sets." The editor and art director made selections that tell the complete story—key-note speakers, large gatherings, small groups, personal moments. Editors often want photo coverage of major conventions and conferences. It is best, however, to make arrangements with the editor in advance.*

G

Exciting sports programs—for both men and women—can be found on Christian college campuses from coast to coast. And participants are surprisingly professional. BY PAM PLASEK

AMATEURS - BUT, WOW!

CHRISTIAN LIFE SEPTEMBER 1974

H

Almost a billion people in some 40 developing nations face the possibility of starvation this year. You can help alleviate their suffering. BY JANICE JOHNSTON

HOW MUCH DO YOU REALLY CARE?

CHRISTIAN LIFE JULY 1974

*Opportunities abound for the photo-journalist in covering areas such as missions, colleges, films, music and Sunday schools. The editor or writer can obtain photographs from various professional and institutional sources. Example G focuses on the athletic programs of various Christian colleges. The material was compiled and written by the editorial staff. Example H presents the needs of people throughout the world. Photographs were provided by many Christian organizations working to meet such needs.*

*The current news section of a magazine usually relies on a photo-journalism treatment. The individual photograph with a short caption tells the story. Such photographs are usually provided by national news organizations.*

NEWS IN PICTURES

Billy Graham promises to pray harder for Indian evangelists as he speaks with general director of the American Indian Crusade Tom Claus and his wife during the recent Albuquerque crusade.

More than 10,000 jam "PraiSing 75" to hear Dean Wilder and Robert Hale, accompanied by the Nashville Symphony Orchestra. The occasion: debut of the 1975 edition of the Baptist Hymnal.

Men as well as women are being liberated from their stereotyped roles, says the Rev. Edward Chandler of Cincinnati, and proves it by demonstrating his prizewinning needlework.

Vaughan Booker (right), 32, while serving a life sentence for murder, is ordained an Episcopal deacon in the chapel of a Pennsylvania state prison.

MAY 1975 19

I

*Free-lance writers and editors can create reader interest by means of "boxed" materials. These boxes may form a complete page as seen in this example. Smaller boxes of a photograph and captions can be used to give breadth to a larger article.*

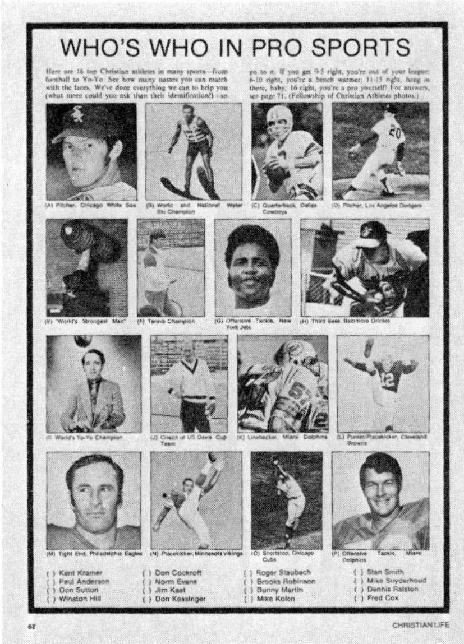

WHO'S WHO IN PRO SPORTS

Here are 16 top Christian athletes in many sports—from football to Yo-Yo. See how many names you can match with the faces. We've done everything we can to help you (what more could you ask than their identification?)—so go to it. If you get 0-5 right, you're out of your league; 6-10 right, you're a bench warmer; 11-15 right, hang in there, baby; 16 right, you're a pro yourself! For answers, see page 71. (Fellowship of Christian Athletes photos.)

(A) Pitcher, Chicago White Sox

(B) World and National Water Ski Champion

(C) Quarterback, Dallas Cowboys

(D) Pitcher, Los Angeles Dodgers

(E) "World's Strongest Man"

(F) Tennis Champion

(G) Offensive Tackle, New York Jets

(H) Third Base, Baltimore Orioles

(I) World's Yo-Yo Champion

(J) Coach of US Davis Cup Team

(K) Linebacker, Miami Dolphins

(L) Punter/Placekicker, Cleveland Browns

(M) Tight End, Philadelphia Eagles

(N) Placekicker, Minnesota Vikings

(O) Shortstop, Chicago Cubs

(P) Offensive Tackle, Miami Dolpnins

( ) Kent Kramer
( ) Paul Anderson
( ) Don Sutton
( ) Winston Hill
( ) Don Cockroft
( ) Norm Evans
( ) Jim Kaat
( ) Don Kessinger
( ) Roger Staubach
( ) Brooks Robinson
( ) Bunny Martin
( ) Mike Kolen
( ) Stan Smith
( ) Mike Suyderhoud
( ) Dennis Ralston
( ) Fred Cox

62 CHRISTIAN LIFE

J

## PHOTOGRAPHY MARKETS

HACKETT, GABRIEL D. (ASMP.ISP.) affiliated with GENERAL PRESS FEATURES, 130 West 57th St., New York, NY 10019. Creative photography. Also large, modern stocks. Subjects: history, music, arts, USA social problems, youth, behavior, counterculture, New York in depth, World Wars I and II, Nazism, persecutions, camps: American Indians (old and new); "Americana," both nostalgic and documentary. Fine pictorials of the West, Rockies, Switzerland, France. Special "Iron Curtain" file; occupied states and USSR, 1916-1976; portraits of famous people, US and Europe. Serving publishers mainly. Write for detailed lists. Stock picture code of the ASMP observed.

EUROPEAN ART COLOR SLIDES, Peter Adelberg, Inc., 120 W. 70th St. New York, NY 10023. 6000 items: original color transparencies featuring an outstanding collection of transparencies to illustrate the great ideas found in religion. Paintings, frescoes, mosaics, stained glass windows, illuminated mss, sculpture, architecture, churches, views, tapestries, etc. From prehistoric to contemporary art. All photographed ON THE SPOT in Europe, including Greece, Guatemala, Egypt, Israel, Mexico, Morocco, Yucatan. Print and reproduction fees charged. Price upon request. Detailed information available as to subject, artist and his work. Catalog $3.60 prepaid.

64

# You as a poet

PAUL BECHTEL
Chairman, Department of English,
Wheaton College

Robert Frost once observed that to be seriously interested in literature is no more than to be seriously interested in life. Literature and life fuse in all the significant work of the writer. From this fusion comes often a luminous vision of what it truly means to be a man.

From the writer many people have received their first stirring of moral sensitivity, their first concept of sacrificial love, their earliest knowledge of the everlasting mercy of God. You need, therefore, apologize to no one for a serious interest in writing. The writer has always been one of mankind's greatest teachers and benefactors.

**Benefactor to mankind**

If you are seriously committed to writing poetry, remember that yours is an ancient and noble craft. Remember, too, that the poet's art requires rigorously disciplined effort.

Sir Philip Sidney, in his classic "In Defense of Poetry," pointed out that all societies have honored the poet. David, who sang of "the inconceivable excellencies of God," was highly esteemed in ancient Israel. The Romans called the poet a prophet or seer. Wordsworth, with Sidney's same high vision, saw the making of verse as a public trust. For the poet, more than other writers, has the art to make man intensely aware of his own nature and of his responsibilities toward society. Often the poet has been the moral conscience of his age—as in

*Ann Kiemel uses a poetic form to express her bouyant faith and its application to her world.*

some respects T. S. Eliot has been to the 20th century.

The poet has been a benefactor to mankind because he takes his position at the center of things. Out of the chaos of experience he brings edifying order. He sees wholeness in the master plan of the universe. From the ebb and flow of life he extracts the tragic, the sublime, the ineffable to make a purposeful pattern of man's adventure in the world. The poet is an interpreter (and therefore a philosopher) as well as a maker of images.

**A master of the craft**

The poet, like the carpenter, must first master the elements of his craft. He must have thorough understanding of meter, rhyme, stanza structure, metaphor, connotation, and tone. Lacking this kind of competence, he will produce work without meaningful form; it will lack the power to bring through memorably an illuminating idea.

**Knowledge of history of poetry**

You as a poet ought also to have a good knowledge of the history of poetry in English. Such insight will help you avoid mere imitation of the great poets of the past. You will learn that no good modern poet uses words like "ere," "ne'er," "o'er"; that mechanical rhythms and obvious rhymes quickly struck off are no poetry at all; that a pious sentiment is not a substitute for poetic competence. You will note also that the free verse vogue of the twenties has run its course and the movement now is back to a tighter regularity of form. There is no substitute for historical perspective.

Rather than thinking of yourself as a Christian poet, call yourself a poet who is a Christian. This attitude puts the emphasis at first on your art. If you have only Christian sentiments to offer, without art, you ought to use prose. The idea in a poem is intensely important, but the form shapes it, gives it significance and clarity.

If you do not know the substance and sound of great Christian poetry, read the masters of this form—Donne, Herbert, Vaughan, Cowper, Hopkins, Eliot. Do not imitate them, but let their work become a touchstone by which you can recognize your own successes and failures.

Finally, remember that you are living in the 20th century. The world is grappling with issues more urgent than moonlight and roses, lovely as these are. War and peace, science, space, freedom, the reality of God in the age of the bomb, and concerns like these—this is your subject matter. Even in these desperate times perhaps your verse can bring healing to Everyman and his posterity.

# 65

# Poetry

LESLIE H. STOBBE
Editor, Moody Press

Poetry provides the Christian with one of the most satisfying and exciting forms of self-expression. He can run the gamut of contemplative introspection, sharing of innermost thoughts, expressions of love, outrage, concern, awe and worship.

The rising tide of poetry flowing across the typical editor's desk confirms that Christians are utilizing such poetic expression as never before. God may have one of several purposes in mind for this expression.

**Poetry forms**

Poetry may be a form of diary—a recording of life's experiences and the writer's reactions to them. Such poetic expression helps formalize our innermost feelings and provides an outlet for introspective reflection on the great purposes of life. We get to see who we really are.

On the other hand, poetry may be a commentary on life around us. This will reflect our sense of values and Christian convictions, while helping us to focus our response to life. Such commentary is a frequent feature of the Psalms.

Finally, poetry may be an expression of worship directed to our Creator and Redeemer. Instead of merely expressing our feelings and reactions, it expands on who God is—and His self-expression through

Jesus Christ. The focus remains on the great God, rather than on ourselves. For the time being, heart and mind are filled with a paeon of praise that comes tumbling out in poetic form.

Unfortunately, too few poetic writers realize that God has given them this gift not necessarily for publication in book or magazine form. The poetry itself may be just as valuable to him under lock and key in his desk as a diary is to its owner. The writer has experienced life—and verbalized it in written form. In so doing he reaps genuine benefits even though they may appear intangible.

A select few will be chosen by God to communicate to a wider audience, just as not many preachers or teachers are called by the average congregation. These few may share their poetry at special occasions in the local church, the women's group or the club. Their contribution will be appreciated and it will touch lives. Others may be called to share their poetry with a denominational publication—and the only pay check will be a comment or two from friends or relatives.

Even less will be called to share their poetry with the broad mass of people represented by radio, books and magazines. The fact that friends or relatives encourage you does not necessarily mean you have been called by the Lord Himself to have your poetry published. Nor is an inner compulsion to see your poetry in print necessarily evidence of God's call. Just as the Lord uses a church to call a preacher, so the Lord uses the public through an editor to "call" a poet into print.

**Changing tastes**

The editor, for example, will be aware of changing tastes in poetic forms. Today the poet may write rhyming verse for his diary, but if he wants to be published he probably will express himself through free verse and focus on contemporary, religious and social concerns. In fact, he may need to find an artist or photographer to illustrate his poetic expression before an editor will be willing to risk his publisher's capital.

Published collections of poetry may focus on a theme, respond to an event, or reflect a poet's experience of life. At all times he must reveal either deep sensitivity to beauty, inner conflict and victory, concern or judgment of contemporary expressions of life. The poet must experience more deeply, respond with greater concern, or react more vividly to rise above the everyday reactions of his peers. He must represent the ultimate in human awareness, concern and sharing to be read today and he must be filled with the Holy Spirit to communicate God's grace and mercy revealed through Jesus Christ.

# 66

# The how-to of writing poetry

JAN FRANZEN
Executive Editor,
*Christian Life* Magazine

Poetry, like other forms of art, is produced by combining talent and hard work. Few poems spring, full grown, from the poet's pen. But once the basic principles are learned they can be bent to fit the author's need. At times they even may be displaced by new ones. Here are a few things young poets should keep in mind.

**Ten principles**

1. A poet should have something to write about.

2. He should stick to one subject. Because he feels deeply on many subjects, he shouldn't try to cram all his ideas into one poem.

3. The idea should be crystal clear in the poet's mind before he begins to write. He can never achieve a unified effect unless he has thought through the subject himself.

4. Ideas should be written down in the most natural way. A strained effect is never good.

5. The poem should be grammatically correct. If there is any doubt about sentence structure, the use of a verb, etc., consult a dictionary.

6. Words should express exact shades of meaning.

7. The lines should be rhythmical, that is they should fall into metric feet when scanned. The most common metric feet can be classified as follows:

a. two-syllabled feet
   (1) iambic (last syllable accented as in *disMAY*)
   (2) trochaic (first syllable accented as in *AL-ways*)
   (3) spondaic (both accented as in *BRIGHT DAY*)
   (4) pyrrhic (both unaccented as *in the*)
b. three-syllabled feet
   (1) anapestic (first two short, last accented as in *as-cer-TAIN*)
   (2) dactyllic (first accented, last two short as in *CHRON-icle*)
   (3) amphimacic (first and last accented as in *NEV-er-MORE*)

These metric feet are used in two, three, four and five foot patterns. Probably the most common is the five foot pattern called iambic pentameter. The pattern of the majority of the verses determines the pattern of the poem. Perfect regularity, however, tends to produce a monotonous, sing-song effect and is usually avoided except in light verse.

8. The poet should know the various forms such as the sonnet and narrative.

9. Rhyming should be understood. The poet should be familiar with such terms as consonance, assonance, exact rhyming, off-rhyming, half-rhyming, etc.

10. The poet should make sure that the editor of his target publication uses poetry before he sends his manuscript to that magazine. It is usually wise to send four or five representative poems at once. Each should be on a separate piece of paper, typewritten, with the author's name and address on each page. A stamped, self-addressed return envelope should be enclosed. Accompanying letters usually are not necessary.

Sounds complicated? It's not, really. As you read widely, you'll absorb many poetic principles without being too conscious of it. And as you study you'll become better acquainted with this art form. Then as you apply the principles you learn, you'll begin to produce saleable poetry. When you do, the editors will be as happy as you.

## POETRY MARKETS

GATES (Dove Press), P.O. Box 67, Grand Rapids, MN 55744. Gail Harris, editor. (Q). Poetry and graphic art are encouraged. Poetry should be limited to three poems/submission. Deadline for each issue is 2 months prior to publ date. Graphic arts should be b & w, any media. Size should not exceed 10 x 12. Only poetry that exalts Jesus Christ and strengthens the body of Christ will be presented in Gates.

IDEALS PUBLISHING CORP., 11315 Watertown Plank Road, Milwaukee, WI 53201. Mary Jane Hooper Tonn, editor. (B). Homespun variety, inspirational, patriotic, religious, seasonal, family, childhood, nostalgic. Buys one-time rights. Will send sample copy on request. Prose 1500 wds max. Do not send your only copy. Pays $10 on publ.

# 67

# Your new product ideas can find a market

RON WILSON
Public Relations Director,
David C. Cook Publications

Somewhere in a dusty attic a bearded, wild-eyed genius sits surrounded by bales of wire, hieroglyphic filled notebooks and boxes of colored gadgets. He's an inventor. He really exists . . . and someday the world will hear his name and recognize his brilliant contribution to mankind.

Meanwhile, the down to earth salesmen, grandmothers, housewives, graduate students and the garden variety folks among us spin out new ideas such as the overhead projector, waterbeds, seat belts and pop-up books.

Publishers, producers and manufacturers turn out millions of dollars of new products each year. Many, if not most, of those come from someone who has bumped into a problem in his own church, home, school, work, etc., and sat down to find a solution to it.

If you fit this description and think you may have the greatest idea since sliced bread, the following suggestions may help you get together with a company or organization to produce it:

1. *Think it through thoroughly.*

**Think it through thoroughly**

Perhaps more new product ideas get turned down because someone whipped off half an idea to an editor or manufacturer. You had a flash . . . a brilliant thought. "Hey, what if . . . ?" The new product people need carefully thought through ideas, well detailed and thoroughly presented.

Have you tried it? Why is it an improvement over some other way? What problems has it solved? Why will anyone plunk down $1.79 or $15.95 for your idea? This initial description will determine much of the new product people's response, so, as you can see, it's critical.

**Define your audience**

2. *Define your market.*

Who is going to use this bright idea? How old are they? Where are they? How many of them are there? (If you have a red, white and blue baton for left-handed choir directors with trifocals, you probably don't have a large enough market.)

The company to whom you send your idea will have to determine channels of distribution. That is, how can they reach the greatest potential audience with the product? That's why your definition of the market is important. If you have any insights into how to reach buyers, include that with your description.

*Christian bookstores frequently handle many kinds of products in addition to books. Drop in and find out what is selling.*

**Count the cost**

3. *Count the cost.*

What's it going to cost to produce? Is the market big enough to produce enough quantity to bring the price low enough? And how much will the consumer pay for this answer to his problem?

Again, the marketing department will have to answer these questions, but you should give it as much thought as you can and include any helpful information you have. Under this category we should add that, if at all possible, you should develop a prototype of the idea and test it on as many people as you can.

**Keep trying**

4. *Finally, keep trying.*

There is, no doubt, much less agreement among new product people as to what constitutes a winner as there is, let's say, among book and magazine article editors. What one company may think is a wild idea, another may find feasible.

Meanwhile, what is that scream of joy from the attic, those flashing lights and smell of burning plastic . . .?

*Someone recognized the existence of a demand for products for Christian witness and identification. Christian jewelry has become an important business.*

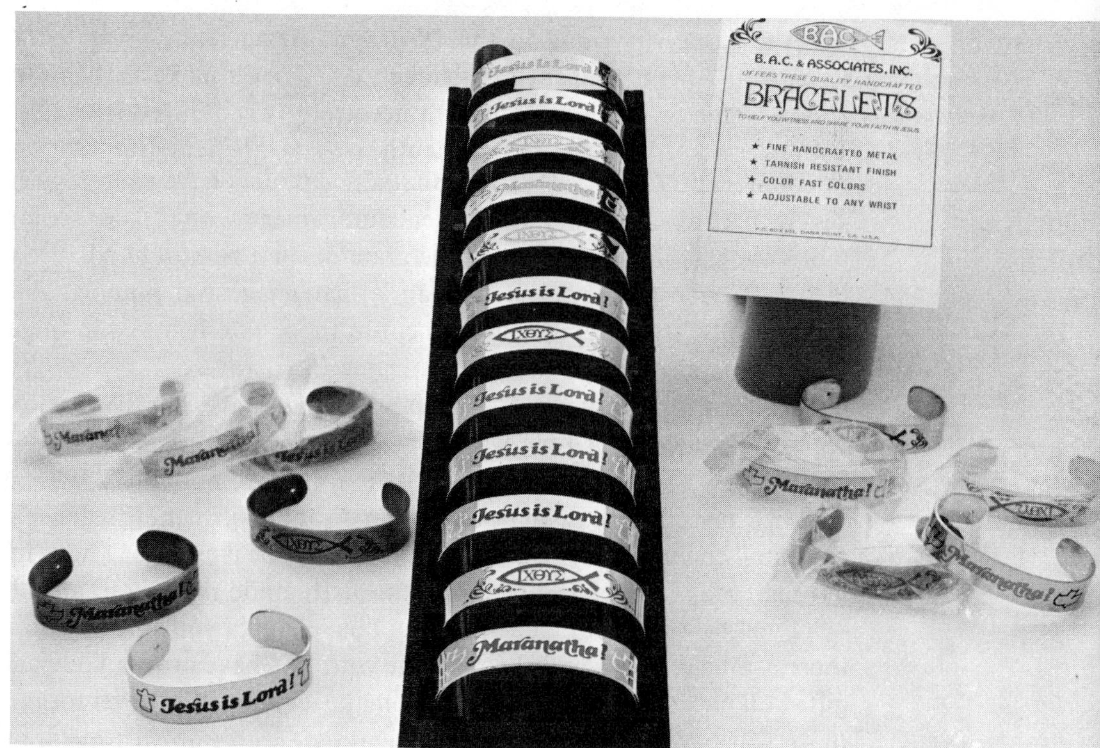

# 68

# The demands and rewards of teaching writing

JAMES L. JOHNSON
Author; Coordinator, Journalism Dept., Wheaton College Graduate School

Leslie Conger, writing in the *Writer* magazine recently quoted a statement, "If you need encouragement, you'll never make it. If you're good enough to make it, you don't need to be encouraged."

Conger admitted there is some truth to that statement, but went on to counter it by saying, "It's true that a few writers have risen to success with an absolute minimum of encouragement . . . but there are far more writers who have cause to be grateful for a helpful hand, a few pieces of good advice, even substantial patronage and support—or, more simply, the quiet encouragement of those who believed in them long before any official recognition came their way . . ."

And Truman Capote, as Conger pointed out, said, "The first person who ever really helped me was a teacher . . . who backed my ambitions in every way and to whom I shall always be grateful."

As for myself, I know that if it were not for my fifth grade teacher's continual encouragement, I would not have made it as far as I have in writing today. Before I passed into the sixth grade she said to me, "I want you to write as often as you can; I have taught you all I can, and there is much more I wish I could give you. You have proven yourself gifted on paper; now it is up to you to make it count . . ." I never forgot those words years later when I was tempted to give up writing.

Somewhere, some time, there is always a budding writer who needs a teacher—not simply for encouragement, but also for the discipline in structure and language that cannot be learned any other way. The teacher who shares all of that can know the fulfillment of creating new bards, many of whom will probably go on to connect with the destiny God intended for them. (Provided, of course, the teacher has led them into all of the dimensions of life necessary to excite them in what they write as well as help them know the keys to consistent production and faith in themselves.)

**Budding writers need teachers**

But not everyone can teach. In fact, not everyone who has become a successful writer should teach. It is fine to entertain that grand vision of all those creative, journalistic minds marching out of the classroom ready to become the new C. S. Lewis or Tolkien of our time. But when one faces reality, the vision does not come off quite that easily.

Teaching is a hard taskmaster; it demands discipline of time and effort, sometimes even more than writing itself; it means long hours organizing lectures and demands an ability to articulate the principles in such a way that students can get excited. Excited students learn the quickest, and they learn well. On top of that, it also means burning a lot of the midnight oil poring over papers that need grades and writing critiques that will give each student a reason for living (or not living) in a world of creative process.

**Demands of teaching writing**

But given the fact that a writer, who has gained enough publishing credits to feel somewhat confident, is concerned to give others encouragement and know-how, there are some areas to check off before taking the plunge.

One, and I emphasize it again deliberately, a teaching writer should be a published writer. That may seem obvious, but there are too many aspiring writers with college degrees who teach other aspiring writers strictly "from the book." Teaching writing is not the same as teaching spelling or the mechanics of English. There are no easy formulas for determining progress or even talent. It takes a writer who has "been there" to know what another writer is feeling or struggling with. Students respect teachers who have proven themselves in publishing; otherwise to them it is the "blind leading the blind" or the "bland leading the bland."

**A teaching writer should be a publishing writer**

That does not mean that there are no competent teachers who teach without publishing credits. But these have other gifts in the teaching field, the ability to hold a class spellbound by the power of speech and knowledge. But sooner or later, even these admit they need to be published for no other reason than to maintain their "credibility."

**Students want to learn how**

Secondly, students, especially writing students, want to *learn how* to make their material publishable. They are not interested *primarily* in the grand reasons for writing or the endless readings that go with so many writing classes where the professor, not having written himself, seeks to point to others who have. Students want to learn what *technique* is all about, how to get ideas expressed cogently without losing the flavor of their own writing. They want and even demand that the writing teacher take them to the practical dimensions of writing for publication.

Some writers who turn teachers are a bit put down when they find out that students are not content simply to listen to the "incredible journey" of their writer-teacher's rise to stardom. Students appreciate those experiences, but in the end they will say to that teacher, "Fine for you. But what about *my* material? What's good about it? What's bad about it? Is it publishable? What do I have to do to make it acceptable to publishers?"

To answer that takes time, patience and an understanding of how to put the form and structure of good writing back to back to that student's offerings. This means that writing students, above all others perhaps, are highly individualistic, even selfish about their own prose or poetry. They have high expectations in the learning process, and the writer-teacher who does not deliver can find the going rough with the restless, creative student.

**Writing must be thoroughly evaluated**

Thirdly, the teacher must recognize that he or she cannot simply grade writing but must also thoroughly evaluate it. Writing is a highly vulnerable act for people, especially the young. Students are sensitive about what they say on paper, more than in what they speak. Writing forces them to go down deeper into themselves, and in so doing, they reveal much more of themselves. They know it. And they are only willing to do that if the teacher handles that material with care, as if it were his own. Students lose interest quickly, even become depressed or critical, when a writer-teacher handles their written work with detachment, content merely to slap on a grade (which really doesn't mean that much in writing) without meaningful critique. The writer-teacher who is not prepared to do that for each student will simply be carrying out a forced drill. The fruit of such endeavor is practically nil.

**Share experiences**

Fourthly, and this is no contradiction to what was said earlier, the writer-teacher should share his experience in writing when he can, and the student expects him to. But in that sharing, there must be as much of the agony of that experience as the ecstacy. The writer-teacher who dwells on the high points only, the euphoric days, the successes, puts a heavy hand on the student who is nowhere near that yet. Students find writing exasperating, frustrating, pressurizing. If the teacher gives the impression that it's no more complicated than boiling a three minute egg, he is doing them and himself a disservice.

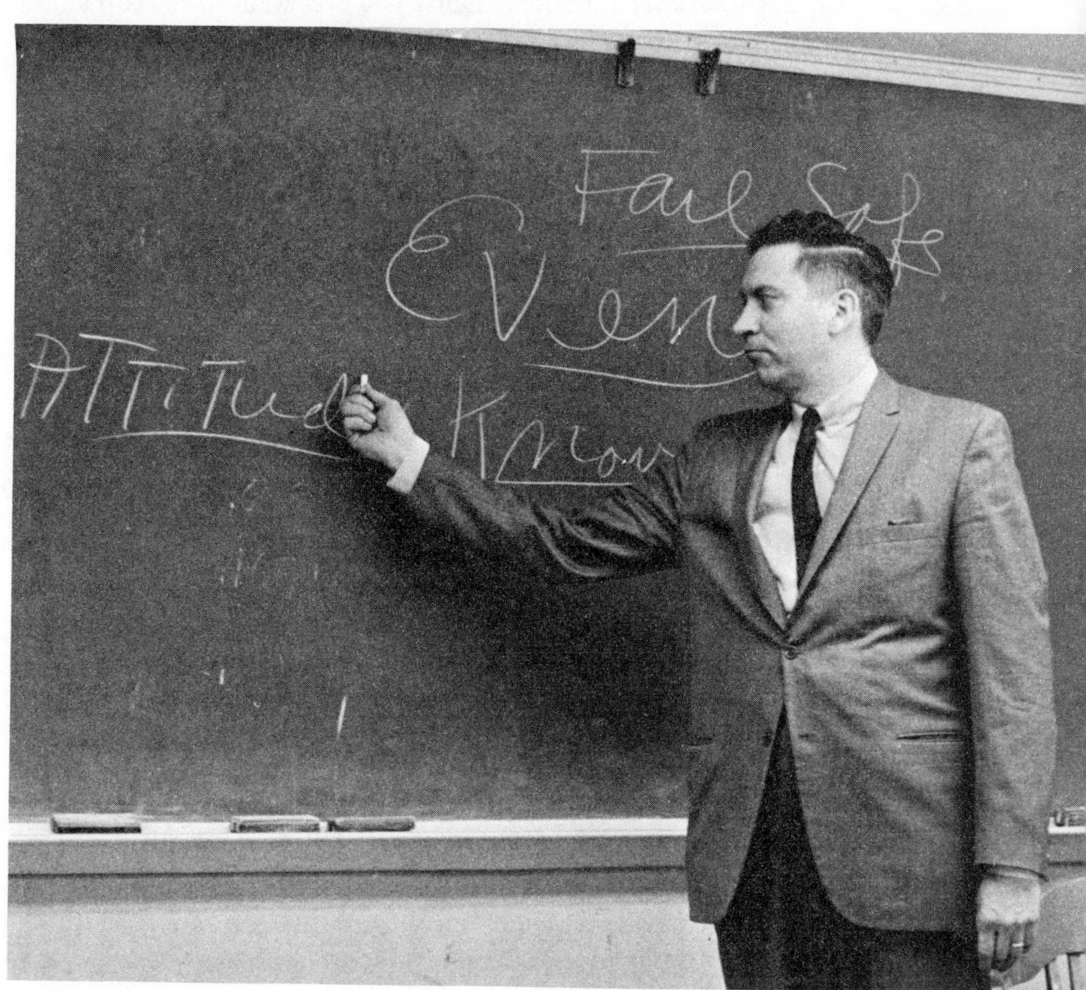


*Jim Johnson is one of many writers who owes some credit for his success to the encouragement of a teacher. Now he seeks to give this same kind of support to his own students.*

In fact, the published writer can teach more in sharing his or her problems in trying to get published than in the recounting of the glorious successes. This is true because the beginning writer, or even the advanced who has not yet published, feels alone in his suffering. Beginners feel they are the only ones who battle with writing block, rejections and the frustration of failure. A teacher who readily admits having experienced the same problems and yet finally made it can be a powerfully motivating force to a young writer.

When one student of mine dared in the middle of a class at Wheaton College to ask the question, "Don't you ever want to chuck it all?" I knew he was expressing a feeling that others in the class had. I realized then that I was not being honest enough or open enough about those days when I actually did feel like "chucking it." When I admitted there were times, and even recently, when I wondered if I was contributing anything to literature or changing any lives, a new sense of rapport, of understanding developed between my students and me. It was much easier after that to share the principles of success that I finally laid hold of and which I now wanted them to get hold of.

**Good teaching begins where the student is**

Good teaching begins where the student is, not where the instructor is, in other words. If that is not the attitude a writer-teacher takes with students, his classroom experiences can be frightfully defeating.

Joseph Heller, the novelist, said, "Teaching takes a lot of my time, and I enjoy it . . . a lot . . . The hardest thing to teach people is that writing is hard work . . . and hard work for everyone. I've got a doctor who wants to give up medicine, a lawyer who wants to quit the law. They read the finished, published work and think that's the way the writer dictated it. Well . . . they're wrong. The teacher must show the wrongness of this approach about writing while illuminating the right by his experience and the principles he teaches that make for success."

**Rewards of teaching**

But having faced up to these demands, one can also be assured that teaching writing has great rewards. Many times during my seven years of teaching college journalism and writing and conducting writing workshops have come those rich moments when a former student shows up with his or her byline in a magazine or on a book jacket. In one class of magazine writing alone nine students out of the fifteen published in a magazine *during their time of study*. What a teacher feels in those moments is beyond expression.

There is tremendous excitement in guiding young writers in finding themselves in what they write. There is a sense of eternal value in it, a feeling that one is shaping someone toward a writing career that will have long lasting effect on readers. In my time of teaching, I have shed tears with those who cried over their frustration; but I have rejoiced too with those who published or wrote something I felt was close to genius.

Of course, there are days when I wonder if it is worth it, if teaching, which takes so much time from my own writing, is really "my bag." There are days when I could cry over material handed in to me; days when I really wonder if writing can really be taught after all.

But then, at that point, there will come a note from someone across the country or even around the world that simply says, "I sold my first story to *Guideposts* today. Thanks, Teach!" It's at that point I realize that God is trying to tell me something, and I believe He says the same thing to every writer-teacher who comes to that point of uncertainty. What He is saying is what Henry Brooks Adams said once, "A teacher affects eternity; he can never tell where his influence stops."

Sometimes I tremble at that, but it also causes me to rejoice in my opportunity. Putting it all together then, a writer who can teach is surely doubly blessed in what he or she writes and in what others produce from their influence. It is quite a wonderful way to go!

# Section X
# Writing in the Field of Music

# 69

# A perspective on christian music

PAUL JOHNSON
Composer, conductor, arranger;
President—PJP, Petra Records

The Church has been deluged with a whole new kind of music. Youth-oriented Christian records are everywhere. Ten years ago, a contemporary sacred album was a collector's item. Today, a well done "traditional" sacred album is hard to find!

Everything from professionally-produced musicals to songs strung together into albums has saturated the market. But it's all refreshing inasmuch as it supplies clear evidence that Jesus' presence is changing things. Once again, He's expressing Himself to the secular culture in a new, meaningful way.

Like so many other things in the Church today, this new expression in music is growing out of the contemporary spiritual revival. Throughout the centuries, whenever the Holy Spirit has made a dramatic move into the world, He invariably has burst old wineskins and has given people the necessary vision to provide new ones.

**A problem of definition**

It also seems that there is always a struggle between the people with the new vision and the people with the rigid tradition. During the Reformation, the traditionalists, uptight that their definition of "sacred" was being profaned and secularized, labeled Handel's *Messiah* "too theatrical." Besides that, it sounded like his Italian operas and oratorios. Which is true! Martin Luther and Charles Wesley were both "guilty" of borrowing tunes from the pubs and putting sacred lyrics to them. Even John Calvin campaigned against pipe organs in churches because a worldly, secular instrument, he declared, didn't belong in God's house.

This is a bare sampling of the problem that definitions have continued to hold for Christian music. I think it's time to come to some conclusions about "sacred music." We need to define the purpose of music in our Christian lifestyle.

**Music serves three needs**

As I see it, music serves three needs:

1. Horizontal communication—message music for evangelism and teaching.
2. Vertical communication—worship and praise, confession and prayer to our Father.
3. Personal edification—God talking to us through music.

This last point bears on the whole "sacred or secular" issue. But how can sound be sacred or secular? Sound—which is what music consists of—is a physical phenomenon, like light or gravity, like birds or flowers. It was created in, through, and for Christ (Colossians 1:16). Therefore, it's perplexing that Christians, who would never dream of talking about secular and sacred birds or flowers, get so embroiled in silly quarrels over music. If we insist on continuing in that direction, the secular culture—which long ago gave sound and combinations of sounds their proper place among the natural sciences—will have all the more reason to think that Christians have their heads in sand.

Let's agree, therefore, that the following are true.

**Neither sacred nor secular**

First, music is neither inherently sacred nor secular; if anything, all tones and combinations of tones are an expression of the personality of the God who created them, according to Colossians 1:16.

**Reveals man's personality**

Second, music composition reveals man's personality seeking expression in a particular time and culture. Consequently, music changes from culture to culture and from century to century. Moreover, the discovery of new tonal relationships is inexhaustible. Therefore, music is and should be in a constant state of development as man continues to discover what God has already created.

**Nothing "holy" about sacred music**

Third, there is nothing "holy" about sacred music which may not change with the discovery of new tonal and rhythmic relationships. Church music's history continually bears this out.

*Paul Johnson (left) arranges the music for Tom Netherton's albums. They are shown here in a recording session.*

**Evaluation by another standard**

Finally, because much of today's "sacred" music was the "secular" music of centuries past, we must conclude that "sacred music" has to be evaluated on some other standard than sound or its combinations.

In the midst of our religious musical traditions, recall that Jesus' biggest task with religious people was to help them get over their religiousness! Jesus *never* congratulated anyone for protecting His sacred traditions. Rather, He was always a threat to their piousness because He knew the difference between being "spiritual" and being "religious" and they did not.

Throughout history, the Lord has continually burst old wineskins in order to keep His body on earth functioning properly in its witness to the secular culture. We Christians have always had a strange tendency to gravitate away from that culture rather than toward it. So

Jesus constantly raises up people and movements to steer the Church back into the world, to minister spiritual life where it's needed.

Perhaps we haven't properly understood what it is to be "in" the world, but not "of" it. One thing it must mean is that we have a responsibility to understand our culture and then minister to it with the tools that communicate best. We can't do that while we're hung up on sacred cows.

And certainly God is more concerned with getting His love and forgiveness to the dying than He is with "proper" musical taste. Most such taste has no scriptural basis and is purely an evolution of religious tradition—neither right nor wrong *until* it interferes with bringing spiritual life to the world.

Frankly, I'm confused. There is not one hint in Scripture that God created certain harmonies for church and others for the beach. In fact, the scriptural standard is quite the opposite. "Let everything that hath breath praise the Lord" (Psalm 150:6).

**A sacred function**

I think that a song takes on a sacred function when it is anointed by the Holy Spirit. Melody or time signature are not the issue. If God uses a song to bring conviction, repentance, assurance or forgiveness, then it has served a sacred purpose. The same song without the Spirit's anointing loses its sacredness. Jesus' words were "spirit and life" not because He had mastered the difference between sacred and secular words, but because the Holy Spirit anointed them to minister spiritual life. We've all known God's supernatural anointing on our inadequate speech to minister life to someone else. The ingredient that makes those experiences sacred is not our fine words, but God's anointing. The same truth gives us our standard for sacred music.

Where is music today, then? Frankly, I don't think it has ever looked so good! I think we're finally reaching the point where the Christian community can enjoy new things without guilt and older, traditional things with new appreciation. I find young people who are being edified as much by an 18th century hymn as a new Larry Norman tune.

This freedom was preceded by a stage in which musicians were preoccupied with "trying new things" in order to be "relevant." We followed after "hot chords," the bossa nova, folk music, and everything else. But, along with Jimmy Owens, Fred Bock and Otis Skillings, I agree that our previous fixation with keeping current was a necessary transition to the freedom of expression we enjoy today. I think we're over our need to prove how hip we are. As a result, I expect to see a lot

*This unusual bookstore display shows some of the varied types of Christian music available today.*

of good spiritual albums, with greater musical variety.

For those who still might have reservations about the usefulness of rock music rhythmics in sacred music, I'd like to suggest listening to the opening "Jesus Theme" from Jimmy Owens' musical "Show Me." Also listen to Ralph Carmichael's rock interpretation of the "Hallelujah Chorus" from the sound track of Billy Graham's film, "His Land." It's never sounded more exciting! In my own case, consider "The Four Spiritual Laws" on my *Sure Foundation* album; how else could it be put to music and not sound a little weird? For me, the rock rhythmics punch out the lyrics and make them happen. And the whole Gospel is spelled out step-by-step—something virtually impossible to do through a "traditional" sacred music idiom. On *Paul Johnson Voices, What's the Wayout,* 18 voices, singing a capella, demonstrate the power and excitement rock rhythmics can give to lyrics and melody.

**Quality lyrics**

However, I'm concerned about the quality of lyrics today. In centuries past, church music's pioneers have been alert both musically and theologically and we need that again now. Quite frankly, most of today's Christian music is so theologically shallow that it hurts. Part of the problem is that it is too evangelistically oriented. We need that, of course, but we also need music for discipleship and teaching. We've got a long way to go to meet the theological depth of Watt's "When I Survey the Wondrous Cross" and Toplady's "Rock of Ages." Otis Skillings and I collaborated on a new musical, *A Celebration of Hope,* with this need in mine. The albums current success indicates to me that the public is hungry for scriptural teaching, not just entertainment, in music.

Which all points to exciting days ahead. I predict a renaissance in Christian music in the immediate future—music that will have scriptural depth and doctrinal purity. Music that will help equip the Body of Christ to fulfill her mission on earth before the Lord returns.

(Reprinted from *Christian Bookseller*)

70

# How a folk musical is born

RALPH CARMICHAEL
President, Light/Lexicon

As I left my home in the sleepy township of Woodland Hills, Calif., to board the midnight plane for Waco, Texas (via Dallas), I tried to remember the number of times I'd made that flight. I couldn't: there were too many.

Why was I making another? To collaborate with Kurt Kaiser, musician/pianist/composer, on our first musical, *Tell It Like It Is.* And Kurt had made almost as many trips west. However, there is no substitute for long and careful preparation, testing and changing ideas, exchanging opinions, probing and praying. So that is what we'd been doing ever since Kurt and Billy Ray Hearn first got the notion that set the wheels in motion that launched *Tell It.*

Now I want to declare straight away that I'm no great authority on folk musicals. But I've been through the birth of enough of them to give you some actual behind-the-scenes experiences. They'll be based solely on my observations, though: Kurt may want to put his own feelings into an article some day. And let me say that during our years of working together, Kurt has maintained an unbelievably consistent level of spiritual motivation. Also as a craftsman, his reputation for technical excellence has a high gloss.

Now to the production of the musical itself. As I see it, God has not promised to bless folk musicals. Not that He couldn't, of course. But the fact is, He has only promised to "bless His Word." So, to be effective, a musical must have lots of Bible in it. Of course, it goes without saying that it needs nice melodies, tasty chords and catchy rhythms to be musical. It needs pacing and continuity, staging and lighting to be entertaining. But it can be effective and produce lasting results to the glory of God only if it has a good measure of God's Word. So the first order of business is that a musical have a message. That is easier said than done.

**An effective musical**

**Determine format**

After many meetings on our first venture (which turned out to be *Tell It*), we found that the songs fell into three categories. The first had to do with the reality and existence of God; the second introduced discrepancies that formed a credibility gap in the minds of some young people toward the establishment; the third emphasized the reality and relevance of Jesus Christ.

Looking back, I guess it was a blundering jump-in-and-try-to-swim attempt at writing a musical. Its only redeeming quality was that we did try to communicate the message of God's redemptive love.

Our second attempt had yet a different format. We ended up calling it *Natural High.* It was the story of John and Carol trying to share their faith with Murph and Jackie.

Our third musical, *I'm Here, God's Here, Now We Can Start,* has yet another format. It presents a dynamic, full-time awareness of the presence of God, and could and should completely revolutionize the quality, if not the quantity, of our Christianity.

Now the latest offering (written in collaboration with Keith Miller) is called *New Wine.* I've decided not to give you a synopsis because I wouldn't want to spoil it for you. But the point is, every musical needs a "peg," so to speak, upon which to hang the message of John 3:16. To sum it up, I personally approach my job much the same as a preacher preparing a sermon outline for his next Sunday pulpit appearance.

**Writing the songs**

After the format is determined, we start writing songs. It sounds easy but it's not—at least not for me. Of course I ask the Lord to help, but He is a very demanding partner. (I have a whole bundle of opinions regarding the use and misuse of the word "inspiration," but I'll save them for another time and place.) Discipline and long hours of writing induce a momentum so exhilarating that it actually produces visible physical manifestations. For example, my ability to concentrate is so intensified that nothing can distract; my endurance increases so that

*Ralph Carmichael, collaborator on the folk musical "Tell It Like It Is," conducts the orchestra during a recording session.*

*Musicians from Melodyland Christian Center, Anaheim, CA, present the folk musical "Show Me." The group took this musical on tour to Europe. (Gary Conniff)*

long hours of work seem the norm. (I have been interrupted by a sunrise and a chorus of birds and totally astounded at the passage of time.) It is also possible to become so emotionally involved in what I am writing that while sitting absolutely quiet I might break out with perspiration.

Finally, the songs are written and polished. (Sometimes lyrics first; occasionally lyrics and melody simultaneously; rarely melody first then lyrics.)

**The arranging**

The arranging is next. This is easy but very important. I have learned the hard way that complex and difficult are not synonymous with great and good. It may take some discipline, but "simple" can be "clever" and "sensible" can be "imaginative."

I like a musical to involve people—the more, the better: soloists, choirs (maybe more than one), narrators and/or actors . . . perhaps even the audience.

At this point, the songs are written, the arrangements are written and copied. (This includes not only the vocals but the orchestral arrangements.) Next we engage the studio singers and musicians. Then we record.

**Accompanying book**

But our work has really just begun (and the expenditures). We must have a choir book to accompany the album so, after the recording is complete, we launch the tedious job of "publication layout." After proofing, the manuscripts go to the engraver; after more proofing, the printer finally does his thing and, happy day, we soon have albums and books—with a five-figure investment.

But who needs them? Who wants them? Who, in fact, even knows about them?

We stood in bewilderment at this very spot with *Tell It.* It takes an eye-catching cover, a lot of advertising, and teamwork. We start with a premiere and invite some choir directors. We pray that the message will come through loud and clear; that young people will respond. We count on the backing of seventeen full-time sales representatives on the field calling on about 5,000 enthusiastic, dedicated book and Bible dealers, not to mention a record and publishing company that are willing to put their resources and reputations on the line.

The residual benefits of such a project are staggering. Thousands of choirs become "sharing machines" as they mobilize into a proclamation adventure. Young musicians are needed, and new choirs are organized. New and young writers—burning with something to say—spring into prominence. Soon we see an important happening that surely will leave a mark on the plus side of the ledger of "Kingdom Business."

Does God bless folk musicals? God can bless any thing, medium or vehicle that effectively communicates His life-giving message of redeeming love, that proclaims His Son, Jesus Christ, to be the Savior of the world, and that exhalts Him to His rightful position as King of kings and Lord of lords!

(Reprinted from *Christian Life*)

71

# Can you write gospel songs?

ALBERT S. WILLIAMS
President—Publishers,
Artists & Composers Service

"The song markets in America are closed to new writers," wrote a journalist in a national magazine recently. Perhaps his statement is true in the secular market, but not so with Gospel music. There is a growing demand for Gospel songs—good, unusual Gospel songs—and we editors are almost pulling our hair in a search for material that will fit into our publishing schedules.

After all, we are hired to find songs suitable for the catalogs and artists of our respective firms.

Each morning as I open my mail, I pray something like this, "Oh, Lord, please let me find a song in the morning mail that will be suitable for publication without too much re-work." But this so seldom happens that I sometimes wonder why more Christian writers (who have a fair to good knowledge of music) haven't turned to Gospel songwriting. The pay isn't very high, but the pleasure of seeing your song in print, of hearing it used in public and the possibility of reaching souls is indeed great!

**Writing the verse**

Each verse must have the same number of syllables, written in the same meter. A good rule to follow is to have the introduction of your subject matter in verse one, conflict (Satan?) in verse two and your climax (reward in heaven) in verse three. The burden of your songs

*One of the most prolific of contemporary Christian songwriters, Bill Gaither (seated) poses with the other members of the Gaither Trio, Danny and Gloria.*

goes in the chorus, and don't forget to repeat the title as often as possible.

It is best to submit your song in complete manuscript—both words and music, with four-part harmony. If this isn't possible, editors will examine lead sheets (melody line with words). Almost all editors will listen to demo records or tapes of new songs but they usually ask the writer to at least supply a lead sheet.

**Submit complete manuscript**

May I advise all aspiring writers to beware of songsharks. Never—NO NEVER—hire a firm to write the words or the music for your song. If you cannot write the melody down on paper, sing it on a tape and have a reputable musician make you a lead sheet. Publishers do not buy song poems, and you must have both words and music to your song.

Some subjects have been overworked. "The Cross," "Calvary," "Garden" and similar subjects have become threadbare. Look for new subjects to write about, or give a new twist to old ideas. My song, "Light From the Old Rugged Cross" (Zondervan Music Company), is a new slant to the standard "The Old Rugged Cross." I was privileged to do the arrangement for "Wings of a Dove" (hit record by Ferlin Huskey), and this song is a new slant to the country-sacred song, "The Great Speckled Bird."

Many of our Gospel songs have rhythm just as our modern music has today. But regardless of how we may feel about this new trend in the field of Gospel music, thousands of people are hearing and using Gospel songs who never enter a church door. They are hearing about Christ on records, television and radio through this new type of sacred music.

Don't worry if your first song isn't accepted. I have almost 300 published songs, but I also have a fine collection of rejection slips from my early days in the field. Be sure to include a stamped, addressed envelope. Some editors are slow in accepting or rejecting songs. Books are made up in a slow manner and if you don't get an early reply, perhaps your song is getting consideration for a Gospel songbook.

**Don't be discouraged**

The pay is not high; some of us give standard royalty contracts whereby you get paid only on sheets or records sold. This is your best bet.

But the idea behind the whole thing is personal satisfaction and winning souls for Christ through songs.

72

# How to write a song

DON WYRTZEN
Director of Special Projects,
Singspiration Music

I was sitting at home one night when my Dad, Jack Wyrtzen, the evangelist and camp director, called and told me he had a great idea for a song. In his devotions he had come up with three points (true to form as a preacher): "Yesterday He died for me, today He lives for me, and tomorrow He comes for me." He encouraged me to make a chorus out of his idea. So I sat down and wrote a song, a kind of 1940s jingle. I didn't like it! I threw it into my desk drawer and forgot about it.

Well, my Dad's a very dynamic and persistent person and he wanted to know where his song was. I took another shot at it and in about ten or fifteen minutes a second version of "Yesterday, Today, and Tomorrow" took shape. I juggled phrases, used a lot of repetition, added some rhyming and a final invitational verse. This became *the* version and one of the first Christian folk songs!

Is that the way to write a good song? Is a flash of inspiration the key? People continually bombard me with questions on how to write a song.

**No pat formula**

Well, let me assure you there is no pat formula—and "Yesterday" came not only with ten or fifteen minutes of work, but as a result of years of singing good songs, studying form and theory, endless piano lessons, a thorough knowledge of theology and doctrine and God's Word, and a deepening desire to communicate those truths in a fresh new way

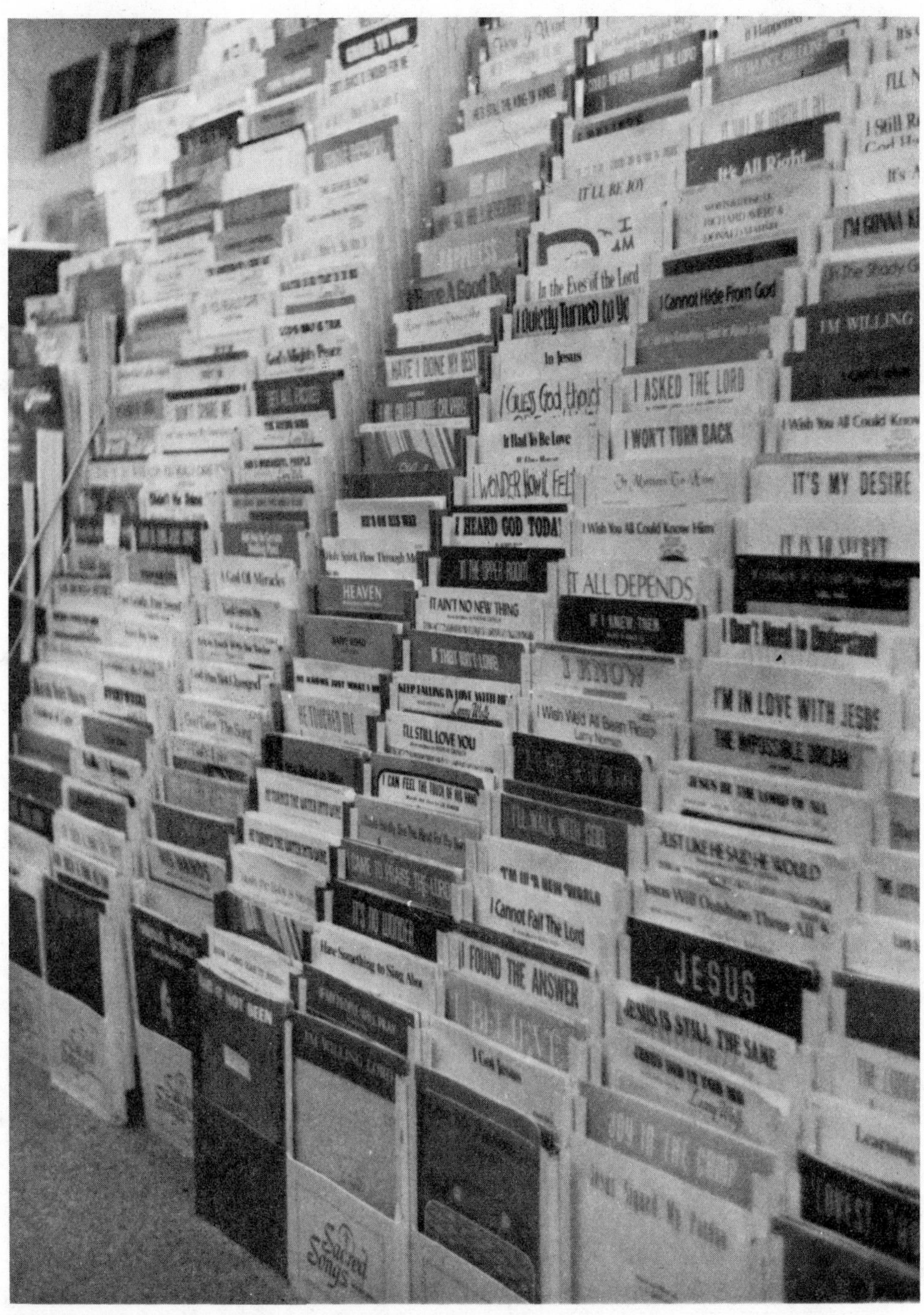


*Everybody's doing it—writing songs, that is. Or so it seems from the looks of this bulging display of Christian sheet music.*

through music. I've found that the more you get under your belt the better. Don't let the unpretentious simplicity of the well-known song mislead you.

I think most people have an inborn desire to create, and this natural bent often finds expression in writing songs. In the life of the Christian creativity can also be the logical consequence of being filled with the Word (Colossians 3:16) and coming under the control of the Holy Spirit (Ephesians 5:18-21). Almost anyone can potentially write a song. This is normal and natural. But the Christian in particular has a greater desire because God has placed a song in his heart, and this spiritual reality cries out to be heard.

Though anybody can write a song, very few people can write a really *good* song. To do this requires more than sincerity. It demands skill—and the development of skill requires discipline and education. Craftsmanship never comes easily. It involves time and hard work.

It is regrettable that the treasure of God's Word and the beauty of Christian truth are often presented with trivial lyrics and trite music. This is probably not done consciously but out of ignorance of the songwriting craft. All of us have heard similar stories about the hit song that was written in ten to twenty minutes. This occasionally happens. Sometimes the well-trained, seasoned writer gets it all together in a moment of inspiration. Or sometimes the beginner gets lucky. Yet, one would be a fool to build his craft on exceptions and anomalies. It is better to build one's craft on solid, time-proven guidelines.

This article will attempt to lay down some of the basic fundamentals of songwriting. Hopefully, it will help put beginning writers on the right track.

**What is a song?**

What is a song? A song is a short musical composition of words and music. Or in other words, the two basic components are lyrics and melody. The first part of our discussion deals with lyric writing.

The lyric is incredibly important in any song, but it is even *more* important in a sacred song. It is the lyric which makes a song Christian. If we remove the words from a song, we have no way of determining whether or not it is Christian (the only exception would be the familiar song or hymn tune with which we associate certain Christian words).

There are four characteristics discernible in good lyric writing: theological accuracy, logical consistency, personal sincerity, and technical mastery. Let's take a look at each of these characteristics.

**Four characteristics in good lyric writing**

*Theological accuracy.* One can divide sacred songs into three categories: (1) those built on the exact words of the Bible, (2) those built on the concepts of the Bible but written in the author's own words, and (3) those built on the author's own Christian experience. In the latter two categories the writer must make sure that his lyrics are biblically accurate and theologically valid. This would seem obvious—and yet an appalling number of songs today fall short of this standard. Few composers are Bible students, much less theologians. Many of the current hits are theologically thin, which will have highly regrettable consequences on our future hymnology. Sacred song lyrics *must* be in harmony with the Bible. This is of supreme importance!

*Logical consistency.* Each song should have one basic thesis or main idea. Every line of a song should tie in with this one central concept. Many songs that I review are like grocery lists of unrelated Christian ideas. They wander and weave and ramble lyrically like truant schoolboys. Maybe this reflects the general flight in our culture from literalism and rationalism in all artistic expression. It intrigues me that, in an age commonly called scientific, we are steadily becoming more indefinite and mystic. Study the well-known hymn, "Amazing Grace," and you will observe one main idea—grace. Each of John Newton's verses that we use today ties in with his grand concept—the grace of God. A writer would do well to emulate him.

*Personal sincerity.* This may well be the most important ingredient in the effectiveness of a song. A writer must learn to express his own convictions and feelings in the songs he writes. And these convictions and feelings must be in his own words. The natural tendency is to imitate, to say what successful songwriters have already said. It is fine to learn from the great writers and even to copy their form, but it is deplorable to use somebody else's words, pretending they are your own. That is where integrity and sincerity go out the window. A writer must learn to state sincerely, clearly and creatively what is at the bottom of his heart.

Bear in mind, however, that certain personal experiences—dreams, suffering, death in the family—may not be applicable to other people. Others may not be able to sing honestly about something that only you the writer have experienced. One must always keep his audience in mind.

Avoid also the tendency to be archaic. The influence of the King

James Bible has been colossal and beneficial. But how can we communicate God's truth in new songs unless we use the language of today! When we use archaic styles, cliche-ridden vocabulary and phraseology, we block communication with our contemporaries.

All of this may seem terribly obvious, but people tend to skip over fundamental things and grasp the superficial. State sincerely and clearly what is deep in your heart and say it in today's language!

*Technical mastery.* As important as sincerity is, it can never be a total substitute for skill. I would encourage you to take an introductory college course in poetry. Some of the rhyming dictionaries also contain much helpful information about technique. Let me just scratch the surface in this area.

**Poetic technique**

*INSPIRATION OR HARD WORK*— Inspiration is the moving of the intellect and/or the emotions. It is an enlivening, animating, and exalting experience. Most people think of inspiration as a magic spark to get them started. However, I have discovered that I get inspired *after* ideas come, and ideas usually come when I am *already* working. Don't wait for inspiration! Just work at songwriting every day. Don't be too easily satisfied with your work. Don't stop working if you can still make one small improvement. This painstaking approach to songwriting takes a lot of time. But any song that is easy to sing and requires little effort to listen to has been written carefully.

*RHYME OR BLANK VERSE*— I personally believe that theological content, highly imaginative phrases, and word pictures are more important than rhyme. However, I must admit that blank verse has really not taken hold in the sacred field. (It is of interest, however, that Hebrew poetry, such as the Psalms, builds not on rhyme but on symmetry and parallelism of thought.)

I maintain a moderate position between rhyming and blank verse. I agree with Oscar Hammerstein that rhymes should be unassertive and fresh. They should not stand out too noticeably and should be used when absolutely demanded to keep the pattern and cadences of the music. One can also use many substitutes for rhyme such as words that match, assonance, consonance, colloquialisms, and attractive combinations of words. When one does need a rhyming word, a dictionary of rhyme can be a help, though it should not become a crutch or a substitute for one's own ingenuity.

One word of caution. If you decide on the use of rhyme, be consistent! Don't have part of your lyric rhyme and part not rhyme. Formal metered lyrics need formal rhyme. Also, imperfect rhyming usually indicates laziness. Keep working until you are really satisfied with the organization and symmetry of your work.

*METER OR FREE VERSE*– Many young writers who play the guitar have been writing a kind of folk music which pays little or no attention to rhythm, accent, and meter. They seem unaware of the inexorable mathematics in music. There are only so many measures in a refrain and only so many beats in a measure. Much of the material now being written seems closer to prose than to poetry. Prose may have a kind of rhythm, but it is unorganized. Lyrics and poetry generally exhibit organized rhythm. I would encourage writers to count the number of syllables in each line. I would also encourage them to check where the accents fall. Line one in stanza one should match line one in stanza two in terms of number of syllables and the feel of the accents. This, of course, must follow throughout the lyric.

Many beginning writers are either unaware of meter or else they have become intoxicated with their freedom. There must always be a balance between the benefits of freedom and the benefits of confinement. Too much freedom inevitably leads to vague expression. On the other hand, slavery to form can cripple substance.

*ABSTRACT OR CONCRETE*– In my opinion concrete, down-to-earth expression in lyrics communicates better than abstract, generalized expression. Since the mind works best when it sees word pictures, lyric writing should be rich in similes and metaphors, and should be warm and personal. Cold, clinical terminology does not relate well to music.

Permit a personal illustration. Recently, I wrote a lyric based on Psalm One. I used the same word pictures that were already there, but went a step further and personalized the entire psalm in my lyric.

PSALM OF MY LIFE

*Like worthless chaff the wind blows away,*
*Scorched by the bright desert sun thru the day,*
*No root below, no fruit borne above,*
*My life was thirsting for rains of His love.*

*While roaming far away on my own,*
*I stood with sinners with hearts cold like stone;*
*I sat with scoffing cynics at play,*
*Until my life changed direction one day.*

*By meditation day and night,*
*His Word brought pleasure and highest delight;*
*It quenched my thirst and nurtured my soul,*
*It satisfied me and made my life whole.*

*Then like a lovely well-watered tree,*
*Nourished by rivers that flow endlessly,*
*Weighed down with luscious fruit from His hand,*
*My full life prospered for Him in this land.*



Use strikingly beautiful word pictures and your lyrics will sing themselves into the hearts of the people.

*SINGABILITY*— Every song that has a long life says something basic and says it in an appealing way musically and lyrically. Every song of this kind requires little effort to sing or listen to. The lyricist must have an understanding of the human voice and of the ease or difficulty with which various sounds are produced. Because certain consonants are virtually unsingable, one needs a working knowledge of phonetics. A line like "The gross-sized, much-touched scratch will itch" is nearly impossible to sing.

All vowels are easily sung. The broad *a,* long *o,* long *a,* and *au* are the easiest to sing. The soft consonants *m, n, l,* and *r* at the end of a word are comparatively easy to sing. The hard consonants *s, t, ch, sh* as terminals are sung with great difficulty, as we have seen in the illustration above. These phonetic characteristics should be very carefully observed on high notes and endings in particular. A word like *sweet* for a high note would be inappropriate—the *e* sound closes the larynx, and the *t* is a hard consonant which cuts the sound off. Many potentially favorite songs have been ruined because a singer was not able to really "sail" on the climax or ending. Even apart from the entertainment value, if a singer is to convey Christian truth clearly, the lyric must be natural and easy to sing.

*LYRICS OR POETRY*— I am of the school of thought which distinguishes lyrics from poetry. Songwriting has been grossly misunderstood and inordinately criticized at this point. I believe lyrics should be *underwritten.* When set to music, lyrics must be caught by the ear in time. One can read a poem at his own speed, but on the platform lyrics come at the audience and are heard but once.

Second, lyrics go with music, and because music is so "rich," a beautiful melody will greatly enhance the lyric. Therefore, lyrics should not be too complicated or sophisticated. They should be, as I said, *underwritten*. A lot of criticism of so-called trite lyrics errs at this point. I feel, for example, that many well-trained musicians utterly misunderstand the craft of songwriting in this context. There is an exquisite simplicity and grace in John Peterson's song, "It Took a Miracle."

In the five, simple, clear lines of that chorus is the very essence of the Gospel. In my mind, this is a masterpiece in the Gospel song tradition; and yet many well-trained musicians continue to criticize the Petersons, the Gaithers, and the Carmichaels because the critics themselves have little insight into the songwriting craft. Comparing songs with sonata is a little like comparing grapes with grapefruit. The public at large seems to have the greater insight!

We have seen that good lyric writing is dependent on theological accuracy, logical consistency, personal sincerity, and a technical mastery. Integrity and skill can go a long way in producing beautiful songs. And when the Holy Spirit gives those songs His special touch and breathes life into them, the results are incalculable!

The second part of our discussion concerns melody writing. I would be the first to admit that God gives certain people special gifts for writing both lyrics and melody. No amount of energy, education or craftsmanship can supersede this. Nevertheless, it is sad when a highly gifted person does not have the *discipline* to learn and understand his craft.

For the rest of us with no special gift, the following guidelines can help us greatly improve our songs. All exceptional songs have the effect of deft balancing between emotion and technique, sensitivity and virtuosity, and between feeling and craft.

**What is a melody?**

What is a melody? A melody is a succession of tones involving pitch, rhythm, and form. Stepwise melodies are much easier to sing than melodies made up of many larger intervals. A melody is simple if its pitches are easy to hear and if its rhythm is easy to feel.

Melodies also have an orderly arrangement which we call form. The smallest unit in a song is usually a phrase—or melodic fragment. A phrase is a group of notes, the last of which marks a natural resting place, either temporary or final. These natural resting places are called cadences. The usual length of a phrase is four measures.

*Andrae Crouch, popular Christian songwriter, also has his own singing group—the Disciples. The group performs here on the Johnny Carson show.*

Consider the old masterpiece, "When I Survey the Wondrous Cross." It contains four phrases of four measures each. Study it, sing it, play it. Note where the natural resting places or cadences are. These four smaller phrases can be combined into two larger phrases. The first phrase of eight bars ends on a temporary or half cadence. That is, the first eight bars do not give a feeling of finality, thus it is called an antecedent phrase. On the other hand, the second eight bars, which we

call the consequent phrase, do end on a final cadence marking the end of the hymn.

We can also classify phrases in terms of the rhythmic position of their first and last notes. Phrases beginning or ending on a strong beat or downbeat are said to be masculine phrases. Phrases beginning or ending on a weak beat or up beat are feminine phrases. There should be a certain consistency of pattern in the use of these two types.

The entire piece, "When I Survey the Wondrous Cross," can be called a musical period. Two large phrases combine to form a period. And a period may be either parallel or contrasting. If the two phrases in a period are similar, we call them parallel. This usually means the two phrases begin the same way. This, in fact, is the case with "When I Survey" (the first four bars of each phrase are identical). But when the two phrases of a period lack any specific similarity, we call them contrasting, as in the old hymn, "Sun of My Soul."

Now if all of this seems somewhat fussy or pedantic, remember these are the components of a good melody. Our Lord created a precise order in the universe. Our compositions and even our simplest tunes should reflect this orderliness. The Apostle Paul urges us to "let all things be done properly and in an orderly manner" (Philippians 14:40). The musical ineptitude and "schlock" abroad today do not please God!

While assuming that the gift of writing melody is from God, I still desire to present six special characteristics of a good melody. I'm also assuming that one can find beautiful melodies which do not display these characteristics. However, again, one should not build his craft on exceptions. I would prefer to call these suggestions guidelines rather than rigid rules. Some of the most successful songs stray far beyond the limits that restrict the well-made refrain. Yet common sense solutions to normal problems are the first thing to master.

**Six characteristics of a good melody**

Like keeping one's eye on the golf ball, these guidelines are so obvious they are unbelievably easy to ignore and forget. First, stepwise or scalewise progressions are always good. They make a melody easy to sing. But don't make too much of a good thing. Avoid more than five or six scale tones in the same direction.

Second, skips (intervals of a third or larger) should ordinarily be limited to not more than two skips in the same direction—after this movement the tune should progress in the opposite direction. An exception to this would be the fifth measure of "Onward Christian Soldiers," which has three skips and then progresses in the opposite direction. After a large skip (a fifth or larger) it is almost always best to change direction.

Third, repetition of smaller units of melody are effective. Repetition shapes a melody and gives it form. When repetition occurs at a new pitch level, it is called a sequence (sometimes a sequence is exact and sometimes it is slightly modified). A good melody is a subtle blend of unity and diversity, similarity and dissimilarity, and repetition and nonrepetition.

Fourth, every melody should have a climax note. This is the highest note in the melody, preferably in the last third of the piece near the end, and as such is exciting and effective. The climax note should not be repeated during the course of a musical period, for repetition would diminish its effectiveness. This same principle applies, though not as strictly, to the lowest note of a melody (the anticlimax note).

Fifth, the leading tone (the seventh degree of the scale) must be treated very carefully. As its name implies, it leads to tonic or home-base. In an ascending scale passage the leading tone has a strong tendency to progress to the tonic. In a descending passage the leading tone may progress either way.

Sixth, there are certain basic song forms. One is the musical period which we have been discussing. It is often called binary because it has two parts. Many of our hymns are binary in form: ("When I Survey," "Amazing Grace," "Jesus, the Very Thought of Thee," etc.). Another is the three-part refrain. This form, often called ternary, has a theme—A, a contrasting theme—B, and a return to A. Three part form is a little like a well-constructed sermon which has three points. Often, we use the alphabetic designations AB for binary and ABA for ternary. Examples of ternary form would be my song, "Love Was When," or John Peterson's song, "How Rich I Am," or Ralph Carmichael's "All My Life." A variation on ABA form is common such as in "Love Divine" where theme A is repeated twice before theme B. One could diagram that form AABA. Then, of course, there is the simple verse-chorus form which is really peculiar to the Gospel song tradition. A study of these examples with form in mind would be most beneficial in understanding song structure.

The ultimate test of a good melody is its singability. Since any melody can be rather easily played at the piano, playing it will not necessarily reveal defects. But if in singing there is an awkward interval or section, one should try to determine the cause and rewrite accordingly.

**Relating form to content**

Having now discussed lyric writing and melody writing, we must touch on the relationship of the form to the content. One does not depict a thunderstorm with a piccolo solo, nor does one sculpt a sunset in marble—the form would not relate well to the content. In much the same sense a certain lighthearted melody may not fit serious, heavy lyrics. Lyrics and melody must be compatible. The melody must underscore, elevate, and enhance the lyric mood of the song. This is particularly difficult to do in subsequent verses of a song, but *all* verses should match very closely the mood of the melody.

It has been my observation that many writers of sacred song flagrantly disregard this principle. I'm convinced that often when people react against so-called contemporary style, they're really sensing a poor marriage of lyrics and music. What is seen as an ethical problem is in reality an aesthetic problem. The song has been written in poor taste!

When I'm often asked how I write my songs, I'm inevitably asked which comes first—the words or the music. There is really no set rule here. It would seem more logical to write the words first since music is more flexible and less specific. However, if the music is written first, the lyricist has the benefit of the music to set the mood, to start a train of thought, and to be the creative spark for his imagination. Also, the very confinement of the musical meter can sometimes force a writer into a concise eloquence.

The main thing is to capture that germ idea which gets the ball rolling. Follow that with research. Then, the actual song is something like working a puzzle. Often I will hear a title that intrigues me and will write a chorus around that title. Subsequently, I will write verses leading up to the chorus.

Sometimes it is helpful to write songs backwards—arranging ideas in the order of their punch. The strongest lines should generally be last since they are the last for the ear to hear. Examples of this method of working would be Bill and Gloria Gaither's lovely song, "Something Beautiful," and Ralph Carmichael's famous song, "Something Good Is Going to Happen to You."

**Basic guidelines**

Finally, almost anyone who applies these basic guidelines to his songwriting can write a really good song and possibly get it published. In submitting work to a publisher offer only one or two songs at a time—editors become mentally bogged down when they are hit with a barrage of material. Second, make sure you send your material in lead sheet form—a melody with lyrics written underneath (most editors don't have time to transcribe your material from tapes). Third, trust reputable publishers with your material—they will not steal it, and they will advise you regarding contracts and copyrighting procedure.

Don't let a rejection throw you. Every composer and songwriter in the world has had rejections, and you will be in some excellent company! But don't expect editors to carefully analyze and critique your work—they are not in the teaching profession! It is your job to study your work, seek out professional help, and to demand personal artistic growth and development of yourself.

Then don't get money hungry. There are very, very few songwriters and composers in the world who make a substantial living writing music. Even if this were not true, making money would not be the basic motivation for writing. Mary Crowley, noted president of Home Interiors, Inc. used to tell me, "Do something because you love it so much that you don't care whether or not you'll make money, and you'll make money at it." The professional is in love with great songs and with the craft of songwriting. He is very busy writing, and the financial rewards come as a fringe benefit.

If you are just beginning, make songwriting your hobby. Then, see how the Lord may lead you—He *may* lead you into a full-time ministry writing music for the church. If He does, there is no more fulfilling life on this earth than to communicate God's truth in simple, appealing, and functional form. The songwriter must base his values on Philippians 4:8, "Finally, brethren, whatever is true, whatever is honorable, whatever is right, whatever is pure, whatever is lovely, whatever is of good repute, if there is any excellence and if anything worthy of praise, let your mind dwell on these things."

Jesus sang hymns when He was on this earth (Matthew 26:30). He sings in our assemblies today (Hebrews 2:12). And we will sing songs throughout all eternity (Revelation 5:12). Our Lord is the source of all music. As His life permeates our lives, may we write songs out of the overflow of a deep fountain of joy.

73

# How good should church music be?

PAUL JOHNSON
Composer, conductor, arranger;
President—PJP, Petra Records

Christians suddenly have been deluged with music materials in many varieties and forms. It can get to be confusing, particularly when record racks and music shelves are stuffed full of "goodies" which nobody has heard of.

Where did all of these products come from?

How do you distinguish between quality and quantity?

The obvious explanation for the mass production of sacred music today is that custom records are relatively easy to make. Virtually any soloist or singing group can cut an album on their own, and that's exactly what's happening.

Frankly, I'm really glad to see this. The result is a lot of new material from artists who wouldn't otherwise have a platform for their original contribution to today's sacred music. On the other hand, it has become hard for the average consumer to know what to purchase when he visits his local Christian supply store.

It is difficult to advise a general audience as to what they should or shouldn't appreciate when it comes to music, sacred or secular. Taste in music is a purely relative thing, and Scripture simply does not put limitations on individual preferences. God is primarily concerned with our spiritual edification as opposed to cultural aesthetics.

I'm well aware that many sincere Christians would like to debate that conclusion. But I am fully convinced that the Bible does not equate culture with spirituality. Neither does it equate education with spirituality. On the other hand, spirituality does not negate culture, or education, or the Christian's responsibility to produce art forms that have "quality," even if such "quality" is a purely cultural definition. I'd like to play with these concepts for just a minute.

In the second chapter of his first letter to the Corinthians, the Apostle Paul makes this remarkable speech: "Dear Brothers, even when I first came to you I didn't use lofty words and brilliant ideas to tell you God's message. For I decided that I would speak only of Jesus Christ and His death on the cross. I came to you in weakness—timid and trembling. And my preaching was very plain, not with a lot of oratory and human wisdom, but the Holy Spirit's power was in my words, proving to those who heard them that the message was from God. I did this because I wanted your faith to stand firmly upon God, not on man's great ideas" (Living Bible).

Now the remarkable thing about Paul's statement is that he was the most eloquent and culturally-educated man in the first century Christian movement. He was a highly skilled orator, as is shown by his speech in Athens to a culturally-sophisticated audience (Acts 17). His brilliance is evident in that his style of writing and usage of the Greek language is more intricate than that of any of the other New Testament authors, including that of Luke, the Greek physician. Paul was a highly trained debator. He knew how to "move" an audience by his eloquence. Yet he chose to relinquish his confidence in his own powers to a superior power—the power of Jesus speaking through him.

Paul was a living demonstration of one who had allowed his natural life to be crucified with Christ. The result was not a negation of his cultivated abilities, but a resurrection of his talents with a multiplied anointing of the Holy Spirit upon them. Though Paul ceased to depend on his eloquence, his eloquence wasn't canceled by the power of God in his life. It was multiplied!

The point is, submission to Jesus Christ doesn't cancel our cultivated natural abilities. It cancels only our dependence on them, our clutching at them for security and identity. And in the process of our "dying to them," we find that God resurrects, multiplies and anoints them with His Spirit.

Jesus said that by losing our lives we would find them. This principle

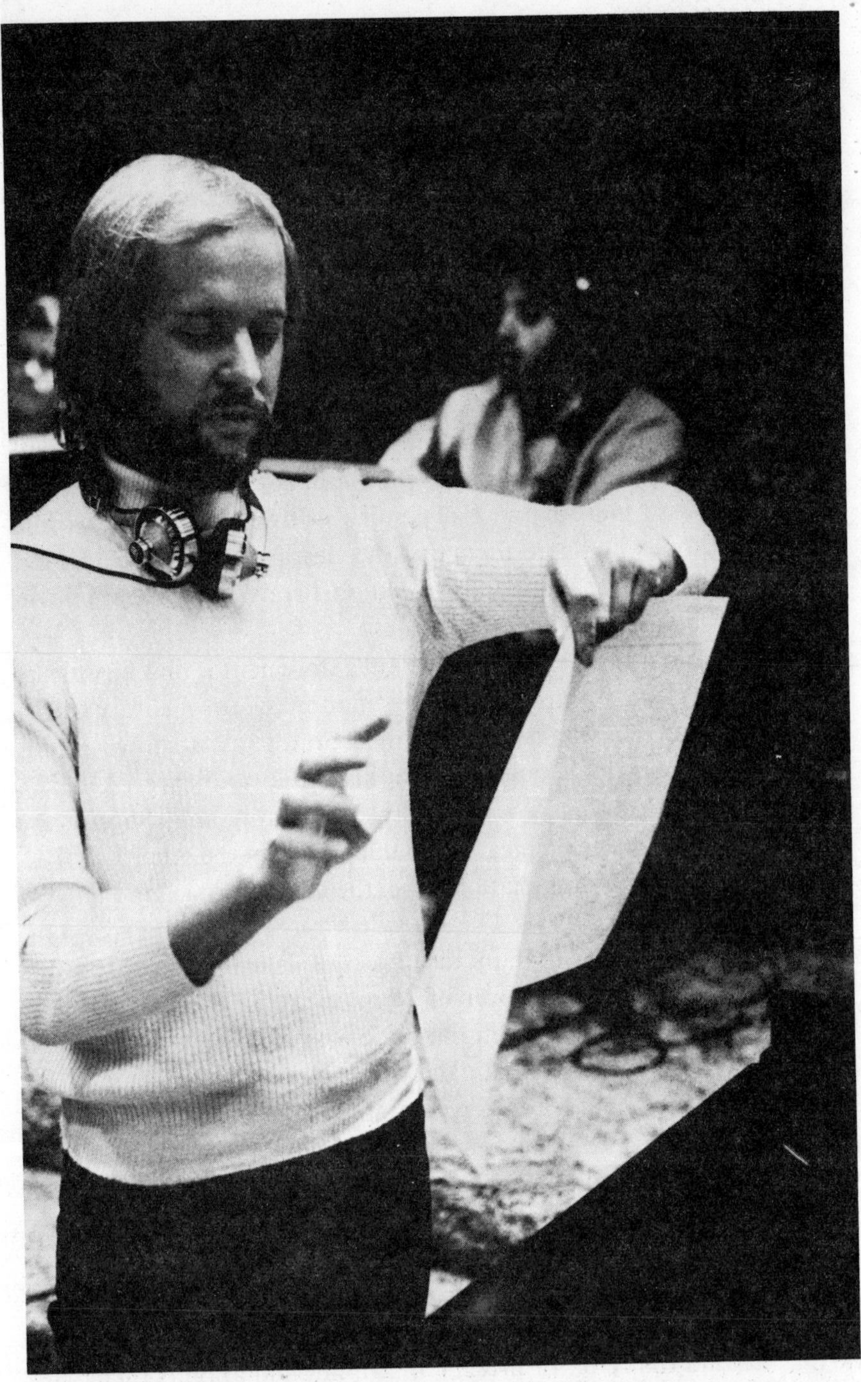

*Paul Johnson and the musicians work out some of the bugs in a musical composition—all part of achieving musical excellence. (Warren Sykes)*

applies to every area of our lives, including education, cultivated talents, and art forms of all kinds.

The Bible doesn't condemn the world's culture. God simply asks us to surrender to the lordship of Jesus all cultural ties so that we can be free to draw our security and identity from Him and not from our cultivated props. When we do that, our props aren't demolished. They're multiplied and expanded with His blessing.

**Two emphases**

There are two points I'd like to emphasize as a result of this discussion. One: spiritual communication does not draw its power from cultural props but from a dependence on the Holy Spirit to communicate through us as we surrender our abilities to Him to work through. Two: a dynamic and simple dependence on the Holy Spirit does not cancel our cultivated abilities or "props," but multiplies their use as we depend on "Him" and not on "them."

As a result of these spiritual principles, it is possible to have a culturally-weak but spiritually-powerful musical presentation (like a lot of homemade custom records), as opposed to a culturally-strong, spiritually-weak musical presentation (like a lot of professionally-made commercial records).

If that's really true, then is culture and quality important at all in Christian art forms?

If the magic ingredient is simply the anointing of the Holy Spirit, as opposed to cultural greatness, then why strain for quality and cultural perfection in Christian art?

These are profoundly significant questions. The church has tried for centuries to relate to art, the theater, dancing, popular music, etc. The easy way out has been to ignore it and/or label it "the world, the flesh, and the devil," and hope that kids won't be "contaminated" by such things. But it's precisely this attitude that has inhibited Christian art (and especially sacred music) from achieving any kind of cultural distinction for decades. I'm thankful that we are living in a time when God is delivering us from this wrong kind of thinking. He's helping us all to see that the world's definition of cultural art forms is immensely important to the Christian—not because God is impressed with good art but because He's interested in how well we relate to the world He came to rescue and save. It certainly is no credit to God, the Master-artist, when the world sees those who represent Him producing art that has bad quality, or is sloppy, in poor taste, or just plain tacky!

We need quality Christian art to communicate to a culturally-

*There is a type of Christian music for everybody's tastes and there is a message in every type. Shouldn't* you *be listening?*

**Quality in Christian communication**

minded secular society—art that's surrendered to the lordship of Jesus Christ and anointed by His Spirit. But that's not the only reason. We need quality art to communicate to the Church as well.

Even though Christians have been transferred out of the world's kingdom into God's eternal kingdom, they still operate in the world and benefit from the world's technology and culture. It's time for

Christians to realize that an appreciation for man's cultivated talents and abilities is not wrong or unspiritual. One thing that makes a Christian "different" is that he doesn't see these as being ends in or of themselves. Indeed he often can enjoy art and culture even more than the non-Christian because he views these things in proper perspective. He's not controlled by them. They are not his gods. He doesn't serve them. They serve him.

If anything, Christians should be the greatest artists (even by the world's definition of quality), for their inspiration comes from a higher order.

In light of this, let's encourage the production of amateur musical products, for this is a sign that Christian young people are trying to stretch culturally. At the same time, let's not be content with mass-producing inferior quality works. Let's learn all we can from the culture we live in, so that we'll not force new believers to commit cultural suicide in order to feel comfortable in the fellowship of believers. They have enough adjustments to make without having to make changes that aren't even Scriptural.

Let's also update the principles given in the New Testament book of Galatians and not demand "cultural circumcision" of new believers (or even old believers, for that matter). "For in Christ Jesus neither circumcision nor uncircumcision means anything, but faith working through love . . . For neither is circumcision anything, nor uncircumcision, but a new creation" (Galatians 5:6, 6:15, NAS).

(Reprinted from *Christian Life*)

74

# Music terms you need to know (part 1)

RALPH CARMICHAEL
President, Light/Lexicon

First, let me get something off my chest. In my travels I find a prejudice against the use of certain musical "names." It's as though their very utterance were an act of sacrilege. For example, in the old days it was all right to say "woodwinds" but not "saxes"; to say "percussion" but not "drums." Well, we've outgrown that silly obstacle and we now call the instruments by their "given" names. But we still have to cope with colloquialisms used to describe certain musical forms (their tempos and beats).

How often I have wished we could use the old-world glossary of musical tempos and forms, such as largo, andante, moderato, adagio, allegro, vivaci and prestissimo. I'm sure I'd then avoid raised eyebrows and whispered disapproval, but even I wouldn't know what some of these words mean. And they may not accurately describe today's music. So let us consider it proper to use the modern labels which denote the various kinds of music used today.

Second, let me acknowledge the fact that the definitions which follow may draw fire from some purists and/or specialists. However, in order to make the definitions understandable for the layman, we have to make some generalizations and simplifications. So here are the current music categories.

FOLK. Gentle, poignant, making use of acoustical instruments (gut string guitar, twelve string guitar and Spanish guitar) rather than electrical instruments, it usually involves some finger-picking, some strumming. It often has been called the music of a land people, and is descriptive of their way of life. Often earthy, almost spiritual, folk music has historically been written about experiences and traditions in home communities. It is life experiences set to music, and usually is written by untrained musicians.

**Folk music**

FOLK/ROCK. Here again the lyrics usually tell a story. While it is similar to folk, you will hear heavier accents. In the rhythm department there will be some amplification of the guitars, and the drums become more apparent. You might say that the musicians are utilizing a rock understructure to express folk music.

**Folk/rock music**

ROCK. In this category, a pretty heavy beat, making full use of amplified instruments, will run the full gamut from gentle rock to acid rock. In other words, rock encompasses everything from pretty sounds to electronic distortion. Electric guitars, the amplified Fender bass, and a strong drum beat come through loud and clear. Most generally even eighth notes are employed. Rock is energetic music; music that demands involvement on the part of performer and listener. Someone has said, the difference between plain music and rock music is similar to the difference between a placid speech being read at a graduation exercise and a fervent sermon being delivered with all its projection and animation. I'm not sure I'll stand behind that analogy all the way, but it does make a point. To sum it up, rock has drive, syncopation, makes use of electric instruments and, usually, simple basic chord structures.

**Rock music**

TRADITIONAL. This is straight-ahead music, written and performed conventionally. In the purest sense of the word, it is music that has been heard the longest. It carries with it the idea that it is a bit more classical in form and more sophisticated than the contemporary forms, but this is not necessarily true. Included are all those forms of music that do not provoke a raised eyebrow: hymns, anthems, well-known gospel songs performed very simply with a soloist, a small vocal group or a choir using the original harmonies and usually accompanied by a piano or organ, although some are sung a cappella. The man on the street might

**Traditional music**

think of traditional church music as "The Old Rugged Cross," "Beyond the Sunset," and "Abide with Me." Keep in mind that today's contemporary is tomorrow's traditional.

**Soul music** SOUL. To an arranger, this might mean the use of the Wa Wa guitar (an electronic attachment operated with a foot pedal to make a guitar actually sound like it is saying wa wa), and a spacey bass line. As the name implies, it is a music that emanates from the soul of a man. It really belongs to the blacks, but when the whites try to copy it, it can be referred to as "white soul." Another way of putting it: when the blacks sing it, it is soul; when the whites sing it, it is soul style (which is not necessarily all bad). When a lot of people think of soul singers, they think of Aretha Franklin. I think of Andrae Crouch.

**Spirituals** SPIRITUALS. I guess I would describe this as black folk music, originally sung a cappella. Spirituals grew out of travail and misery, and often were used as work songs with religious themes. Although the old-time spiritual crops up today treated every which way, it is still indestructible.

**Country music** COUNTRY. This kind of music often is thought of as pure American art form. The songs are of the rural people and express their feelings about themselves, their fellowman, their loves and life. Instrumentation always includes two rhythm guitars, which are strummed, not picked; a pedal steel guitar, and Floyd Cramer style piano. The vocal is usually a solo, not a group. Tempos are usually slow shuffles—but can be eighth notes. Chords are simple. Much of our country music bears the influence of the "Nashville" sound. For purists I might even point out that one of the guitars is usually tuned differently (the bottom three strings are up an octave).

COUNTRY AND WESTERN. The consensus is that this is the same as country.

**Western music** WESTERN. Western-style music is literally non-existent. Groups that used to call themselves western have sort of slipped their skin and are popping up as country groups.

POP COUNTRY. This would make use of all of the rhythm

*Kurt Kaiser (left) and Ralph Carmichael work together during a practice session. They have collaborated on several musicals.*

instruments mentioned under country, but would include violins and horns, or whatever is needed. The chords are slightly more sophisticated, the melodies more romantic. People like Charlie Rich, Glen Campbell and Ann Murray are in this category.

**Pop country music**

BLUEGRASS. Uses only acoustic instruments. Even the bass is acoustic, which we call a stand-up bass. There are no drums. Specifically, the instrumentation is one guitar, one violin, a five-string banjo, a mandolin, one dobro (a metal resonator guitar) and string bass. There are no fancy chords; just plain tonic, sub-dominant and dominant.

**Bluegrass music**

GOSPEL. This word has a cross use or is used independently to denote three separate kinds of music.

Gospel music

1. In the 40s and 50s the gospel song was simply a nice melody with a first-person testimony lyric. More often than not, it was sung by a soloist accompanied by a piano or an electric organ. Today the same songs appear with rather lush orchestral backgrounds. It is still gospel music.

2. Gospel in the secular sense has a heavy beat with roots traceable through rhythm and blues, all the way back to the black church. Usually a heavy left-hand piano comes through loud and clear, along with a dramatic organ and a predominant tambourine. It may be rousing with blistering tempos, or it may be slow—but it is always emotional.

3. Gospel quartets, originally a popular form throughout the South, are now popular everywhere. Two guys, Stamps and Baxter, are credited with introducing this style which the man on the street would probably describe as "old-time religion music."

Contemporary music

CONTEMPORARY. When I use the word "contemporary," I include a potpourri of many forms of music that are popular right now. It's like a combination pizza with whatever old and new flavors might please today's palate. Many influences are brought together, resulting in a sound that is labeled, "Here's what's happening right now."

In addition to all of the labels, handles, or monikers listed above, there are subheadings under each of the various forms. And if you came to one of my workshops, I might share with you the definitions of boog-a-loo, strut, shuffle, jazz, waltz or swing. But quite often I have to use my hands and funny sounds to be understood, so it just loses something when it is reduced to printin' and readin'.

In closing let me point out that all of the musical forms listed above can be performed authentically or can be reproduced in an enjoyable but rather unauthentic manner. The purists (who comprise a very small piece of any audience) want both their artists and background players to be authentic. However, most of us are perfectly happy to have just a flavor of folk or rock or gospel or country, or whatever. I guess what I am saying is that music is to be enjoyed, and that it is not necessary to be a specialist in order to qualify for the great inspiration and blessing that music of all kinds can bring.

(Reprinted from *Christian Life*)

75

# Music terms you need to know (part 2)

HELEN KIDD
Registrar,
Christian Writers Institute

Music is a universal language. People from greatly diverse cultures can understand the same musical work. Music has power to manipulate as well as to communicate.

During a prelude in a worship service, people tend to sit quietly awaiting what will happen next. When the postlude is played, everyone knows it's time to get up and leave. And when the Doxology is introduced, who would dare *sit* down and sing?

**Music, the international language**

What has made music an international language? Perhaps the following words and definitions will give some insight. When the following elements are used together in the right combinations, the result is a composition. A musical work will convey a story and/or message that the composer wishes to express. Music always conveys a message. These terms will guide you in understanding the composer's message.

Knowledge of these musical terms will also help you in your song writing. This knowledge can make your song more than an idea. It can become an expression of yourself and your beliefs.

A CAPPELLA — Vocal chorus without accompaniment.

ACCELERANDO — Gradually faster. Abbreviation is *accel.*

ACCENT — Extra strength given to a special note. >

ACCIDENTAL — Sharps and flats in the composition that are not found in the key signature.

ACCOMPANIMENT — Instrumental or vocal part designed to support or complement principal voice or instrument.

ADAGIO — Slow; leisurely.

AD LIBITUM — Played or sung at the pleasure of the performer. Abbreviation is *ad lib.*

ALLA BREVE — In duple or quadruple time with a beat represented by the half note. Sign used is ¢

ALLEGRETTO — Slower than allegro but not as slow as moderato.

ALLEGRO — Quick, lively.

ANDANTE — Moderately slow.

ANDANTINO — Faster than andante.

ARPEGGIO — Broken chord.

A TEMPO — In original time; after a modification.

BAR — Heavy line placed across the staff immediately before the measure accent.

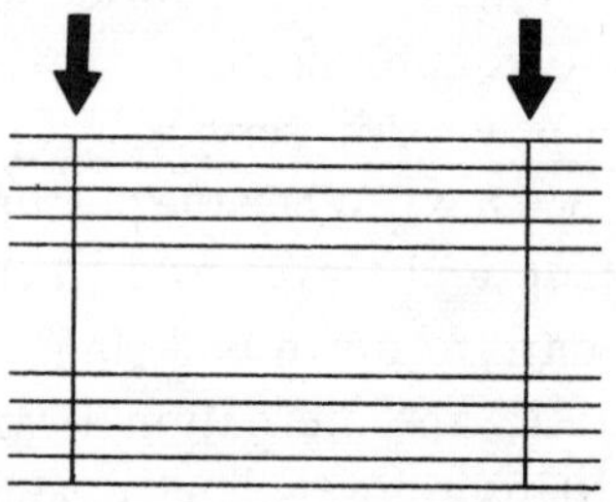

BASS STAFF — The five lower lines of the grand staff.

BREVE — The note that fills the time of two whole notes. Sign used is

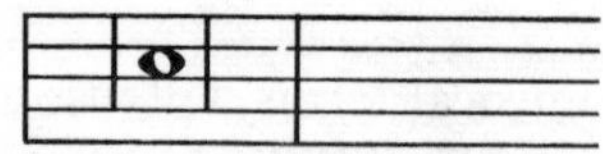

CHORD — Combination of three or more related tones.

CHROMATIC SCALE — Series of half steps, e.g. C C# D D# E F F# G G# A A# B C.

CIRCLE OF FIFTHS — Diagram showing the relationship between the major and minor scales.

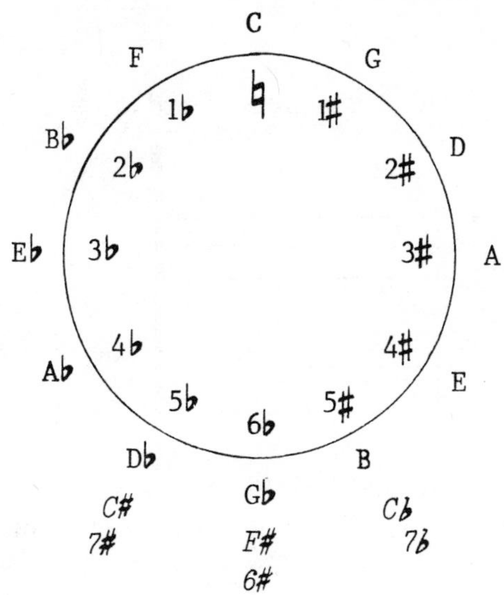


CODA — Concluding part of a movement. Also known as a "tail."

COMPOSITION — Result of arranging musical tones in proper proportion.

CONTRARY MOTION — Each hand going in a different direction.

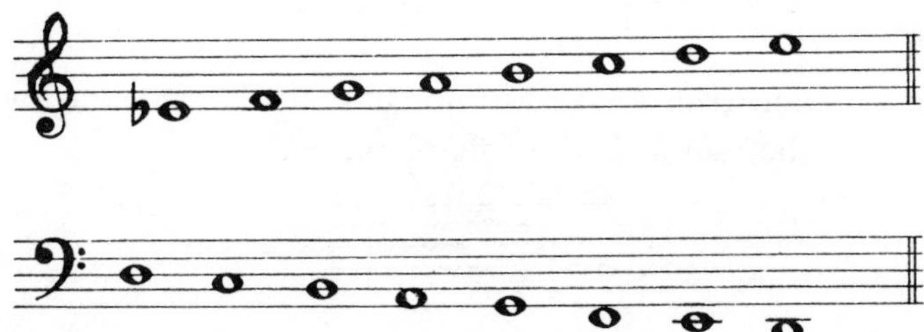

CRESCENDO — Gradually louder. Sign used is <

D.C. — *Da Capo;* Go back to beginning and play to Fine.

D.S. — *Dal Segno;* Go back to sign (𝄋) and play to Fine.

DECRESCENDO — Gradually softer. Sign used is >

DIATONIC SCALE — The stated key signature with no chromatic deviation.

DIMINUENDO — Gradually softer. Abbreviation is *dim.*

DOLCE — Sweet, soft.

DOTTED HALF NOTE — Usually gets three beats in a measure. The dot adds one-half of the note value.

DOUBLE BAR — Two heavy lines placed at the end of a piece of music.

DUPLE — A measure that has two beats.

EIGHTH NOTE — A musical note that gets half of a beat.

EIGHTH REST — Fills the time of an eighth note.

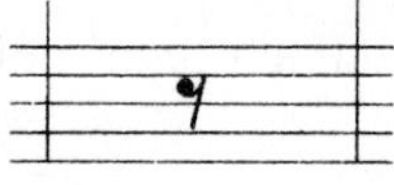

F CLEF — Another name used for the bass clef because the big dot starts on F and the two little dots guard the F line.

FERMATA — To pause or hold the note twice as long as the normal time value. 𝄐

FINE — Pronounced fee-nay. It means the end.

FLATS — The black keys when going down a half step. Sign used is (♭)

FORTE — Loud. Abbreviation is *f*

FORTEPIANO — Loud, then soft immediately. Abbreviation used is *fp*

FORTISSIMO — Very loud. Abbreviation used is *ff*

G CLEF — Another name for the treble clef because it crosses the G line four times.

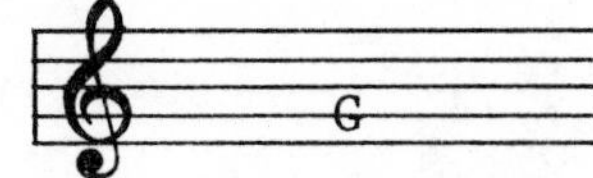


GRAVE — Very slow and solemn.

HALF NOTE — Note that gets two beats.

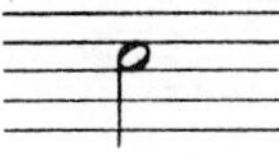

HALF REST — Rest that fills the time of a half note.

HALF STEP — Distance from any key, white or black, to the very next key. Example: C to C#.

HARMONIC MINOR — See definition of major scale. Difference is the lowering of the third and sixth notes.

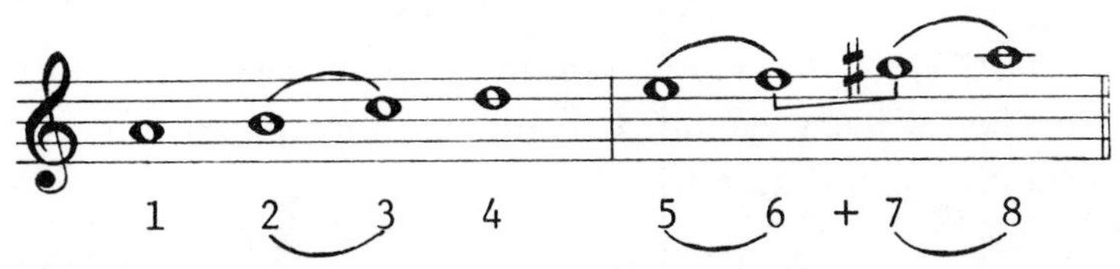


HARMONY — Two or more tones sounded together.

INTERVAL — The difference in pitch between two tones.

KEY SIGNATURE — Sharps and flats placed on the staff right after the clef.

LARGO — Slow, implying stateliness.

LEGER LINES — The added lines above and below the grand staff.

LENTO — Slow.

MAJOR SCALE — Series of eight tones, in alphabetical order, arranged in special pattern of whole steps and half steps.

MEASURE — The distance between two bars in which even groups of beats are placed.

MEASURE ACCENT — The strong beat at the beginning of the measure.

MEASURE SIGNATURE — The signature placed at the beginning of the composition to tell how to count music.

MELODIC MINOR — See definition of major scale. Here the third step is lowered when ascending the scale but remains the same as the natural minor when descending.

MELODY — The leading line of a composition of which the tones usually follow each other in an orderly and singable way.

METER — The name given to the working form of a measure.

MEZZO FORTE — Medium loud. Abbreviation used is *mf.*

MEZZO PIANO — Medium soft. Abbreviation is *mp.*

MODERATO — Moderate rate of speed. Abbreviation is *mod.*

MODULATION — The transition from one key to another by succession of related chords.

MUSIC — The science or art of incorporating intelligible combinations of tones into a composition having structure and continuity.

MUSIC THEORY — The study of music and its functions.

NATURAL MINOR — See definition of major scale. Difference is the lowering of third, sixth and seventh steps here.

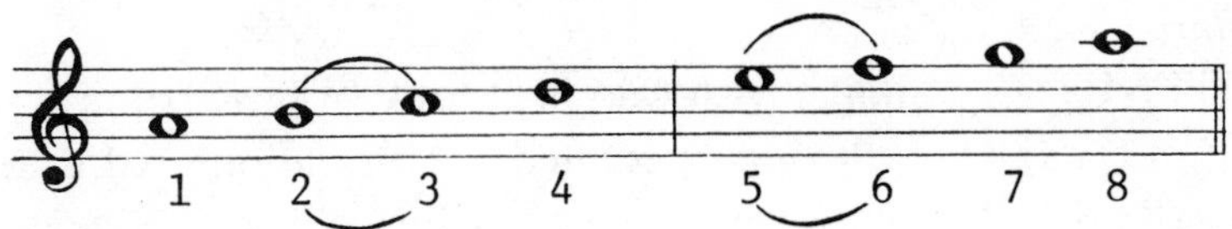


NATURALS — The white keys. The sign (♮) is used when, in the composition, the composer wishes to restore the sharp or flat to its natural note for that measure.

OCTAVE — The distance from one key to the next key with the same name, up or down.

OCTAVE SIGN — Sign used instead of adding leger lines and spaces. *8va,* Octave, eighth; to be played an octave higher

PERIOD — The portion of the composition most like a sentence in a story.

PHRASING — The separation of phrases to keep the musical ideas from running into each other.

PIANO — Soft. Abbreviation is *p*

PIANISSIMO — Very soft. Abbreviation is *pp*

PITCH — Highness or lowness of tones.

PIZZICATO — Plucked, as strings on a violin.

POSTLUDE — The after piece or concluding number of an event.

PRELUDE — The introductory music to prepare for an event. The purpose is to create atmosphere.

PRESTISSIMO — Fast as possible.

PRESTO — Very fast.

QUADRUPLE MEASURE — Measure that has four beats.

QUARTER NOTE — A note that gets one beat.

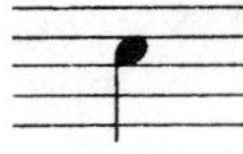

QUARTER REST — Rest that fills the time of the quarter note.

RALLENTANDO — Gradually slower. Abbreviation is *rall.*

RHYTHM — The arrangement of long and short tones.

RITARDANDO — Same as rallentando. Abbreviation is either *rit.* or *ritard.*

RITENUTO — Suddenly slower; held back. Abbreviation is *riten.*

SFORZANDO — Strongly accented. Abbreviation used is *sf.*

SHARPS — The black keys when going up a half step. Sign used is (♯)

STACCATO — Detached, separated tones signified by a dot.

STAFF DEGREE — Each line of a grand staff and each space between lines.

SWELL — Crescendo and decrescendo signs used together.

SYNCOPATION — Temporary displacement of regular metrical accent by stressing the weak beat.

TEMPO — Rate of speed.

TIE — A curved line joining two notes of the same pitch. The second note is not played but the time value is added to that of the first note.

TONE — Vocal or musical sound.

TREBLE STAFF — The five upper lines of the grand staff.

TRIPLE — A measure that has three beats.

TRIPLET — Three even notes used to fill the time of two notes of the same value or one note of the next longer value.

VIBRATION — A wave-like motion of the air which causes musical tones. Fast vibrations cause high tones. Slow vibrations cause low tones.

VIBRATO — Slightly tremulous effect imparted to vocal or instrumental tone for added expressiveness by slight and rapid variations in pitch.

VIVACE — Lively; faster than allegro.

WHOLE NOTE — Note that gets four beats.

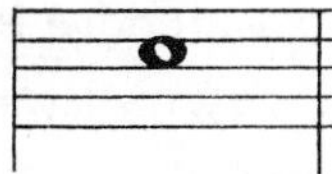

WHOLE REST — Rest which fills the time of a whole note.

Does knowledge of these words make you a musician? Hardly so. As with everything else in life, you need application and practice. Without these, theory has no relevance to human life.

**Apply and practice**

On the other hand, you need not be a master of all of these terms before becoming a musician. Irving Berlin could not read music and knew only how to play the black keys of a piano. Yet he wrote over eight hundred songs.

Know your talents as God gave them to you and use them to the fullest.

## MUSIC MARKETS

THE BETHANY PRESS, P.O. Box 179, St. Louis, MO 63166. Hymnal publisher.

THE CHURCH MUSICIAN, 127 Ninth Ave. N., Nashville, TN 37234. William Anderson, editor. (M). For Southern Baptist music leaders. Articles on Protestant church music. 1300 wds. Pays 2½¢/wd on acceptance. Use SASE.

CONCORDIA PUBLISHING HOUSE, 3558 South Jefferson Ave., St. Louis, MO 63118.

LORENZ PUBLISHING CO., Dayton, OH 45401. Publishes subscription choir magazines of anthems for every Sunday of the year. Wants anthem lyrics of 2-3 stanza. Also publishes short articles (not more than 500 wds) of interest to choirs and choir directors. Prices are in line with other buyers.

MASTER'S PRESS, 20 Mills St., Kalamazoo, MI 49001.

MUSIC MINISTRY, United Methodist Publ. House, 201 Eighth Ave. S., Nashville, TN 37202. H. Myron Braun, editor. (M). Intended for all persons in positions of music and worship leadership in church and church school. Articles dealing with any facet of the ministry of music in the life of the church are invited. 1200-1800 wds. Pymt approx 3¢/wd.

MUSIC & SOUND MERCHANDISER, Tinker's Turn, P.O. Box 1770, El Cajon, CA 92022. Gilbert Tinker, editor. (B). Feature articles on bookstore management related to music and sound communication. Articles about Christian artists (music), composers, speakers who record for resale, etc. Articles about Christian companies producing music and cassettes. Articles about music events of national interest.

SINGSPIRATION MUSIC (Zondervan Corporation), 1415 Lake Dr., S.E., Grand Rapids, MI 49506. Publishes sacred music exclusively. Nondenominational publishing house. Publishes for all age groups. Five editors on staff: John W. Peterson, Harold DeCou, John M. Rasley, Don Wyrtzen, and Norman Johnson.

# Section XI
# The Writer and Other Writers

# 76

# Reflections: christian writers conference

CHRISTINE FOUSER
Free-lance writer

Have you ever looked back on a blessing God has given you, and asked yourself, "Why did I fight it? Why wouldn't I accept it sooner?"

As I reflect on those exhilarating four days at the Christian Writers Conference in Wheaton, Illinois, I ask myself that question.

**The decision to go**

I'd been looking forward to the conference for a year—ever since a Christian friend suggested I might have a gift for writing—and I was depending on the conference to show me God's direction and guidance. Yet when the time came, I struggled with many questions.

"Will the kids and Tom be able to manage without me? Even if they can, is it right for a wife and mother to be away?"

My thoughts became prayers, "Lord, you know I've never driven that far alone. And when I get there, I won't even know anyone."

For weeks, fears of the unknown haunted me. In retrospect, it's obvious Satan did not want me to go. But the gentle voice of God persistently whispered away every objection the enemy presented.

The turning point in my dilemma occurred one morning at Bible study. I mentioned that I still hadn't decided whether or not to attend the conference.

Two friends exclaimed, "Go!" Knowing that the Lord often speaks through other Christians, I paid attention. And in faith, I prepared to go. God quickly showered me with blessings, as arrangements easily fell into place.

He even took care of my traveling fears, as one evening at dinner Cindy, our nine year old, asked, "Mommy, who's going with you?"

Still a little uneasy about the driving, I answered, "I'm going by myself."

My husband turned to Cindy and more aptly replied, "The Holy Spirit's going with her."

Wow! What better companion could a driver have?

The day of departure arrived, and as I drove out of town that afternoon, I smiled with confidence, thinking —*other travelers looking my way see a lady driving alone in a yellow VW van, but I know that really there are two of us, the Holy Spirit and me, flying off on a magic carpet of adventure.*

**Arriving**

When I arrived in Wheaton, a well-dressed gentleman, a professor perhaps, cordially showed me the way to the New Science Building where I registered.

That evening Pete Gillquist shared with the group his experiences and insights as a Christian author. He spoke on the art of writing in relation to walking with the Holy Spirit. He urged us to *walk* - not run - nor sit - with the Spirit. And he admonished us, "Don't try to run with the Spirit, or to be something big, for if God wants you to be a big hot dog, you will. If He doesn't. . . " We got the message.

**Beginning the day**

The following morning we assembled in the New Science lecture hall where Mark Fackler led us in devotional thoughts—how to begin, go through, and end the day as a Christian writer. The messages were informative and inspirational, but even more impressive to me was the prayer time which followed. Each day about ten people in the audience prayed briefly for those involved in various aspects of writing. One hundred fifty individuals, some perhaps with competitive feelings towards other writers, were being welded, through prayerful concern for others, into a body of dedicated servants.

That morning Bob DeVries of Zondervan spoke. He concluded his remarks with a statement that to me was awesome: "God may not allow a book to become a success," he said, "because it may be very bad for the author, killing his spiritual growth."

He explained that both believers and nonbelievers look to a successful Christian writer for leadership, and that writer must be able to handle the responsibility.

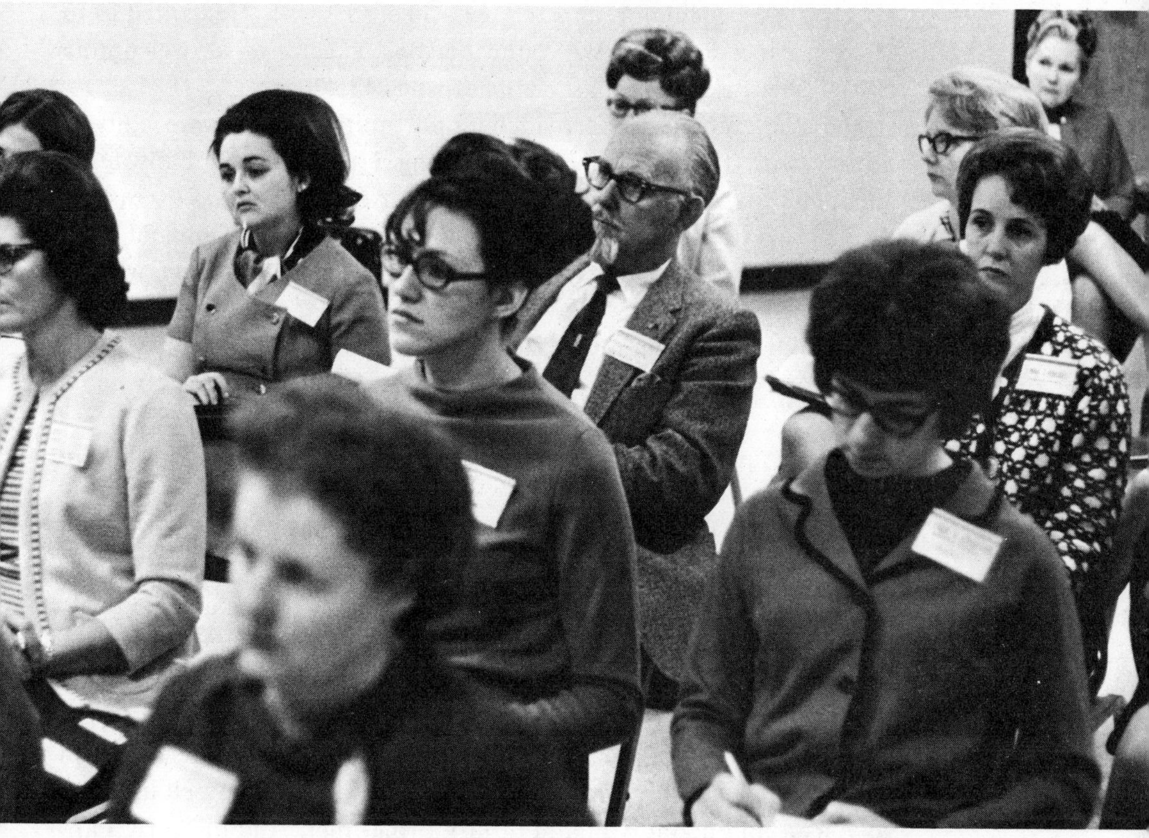

*A writers conference can give direction to your writing career as well as help you sharpen your writing skills.*

I wondered then, and still do—am I spiritually stable and mature? If God granted me success, could I handle it?

During that day and the following ones we enjoyed living-room-comfort talks by authors as well as instructional lectures by editors. Not only were we taught writing techniques, but more important, we were counseled as Christians.

Floyd Thatcher, publisher of Word Books, challenged us to be "Livers"! "Living fully is a prerequisite to being a writer," he stated, and went on to say that the problem in Christian literature is that "the writers don't live, and the 'livers' don't write! Too many Christians live in a beige-gray world, not willing to risk failure, because 'Christians don't fail,' but we've taken on the characteristics of fossilization . . . . However, Jesus was a 'Liver'! He was a person of passion, feeling, character."

Mr. Thatcher implored us to "feel - Feel - FEEL!" He invited us to awaken each day as new, young persons, eager to live, welcoming change, because "perpetual change fosters life!"

**The opportunities**

The conference also provided opportunities for private conversations with the speakers. One evening I paused in a hallway to commend an editor, and thus began a conversation which I treasure. While we talked about the conference, this busy, prominent man peered down at my name tag and pointedly asked, "Christine, why do you want to write?"

I quickly spilled out my friend's suggestion of a year ago, my writing endeavors since then, and my spiritual and mental search to know God's will.

When I quit talking, this stately man said softly, "I think you're hooked."

I'd come to the conference seeking direction, and this quiet simple statement jolted me. I privately asked, "Lord, is that you speaking?"

**Closing banquet**

The closing banquet was on Thursday night. I joined a line outside the banquet room. The gentleman next to me, a university librarian, asked what I did, occupationally. "I'm a wife and mother," I told him.

Then smiling inwardly, I recalled my qualms over coming to the conference, the hesitancy to step out of my roles. Yet after being in Wheaton for just three days, I realized that now I saw myself in a new way, as a unique individual, not just a role-filler. And instantly I appreciated this insight.

**"I'm hooked"**

Since being back in my accustomed roles, I've discovered that now I have something more than a desire to write. I also have a determination which continually drives me to the typewriter. As that editor put it—I think I'm hooked.

77

# To conference... to conference

JAN FRANZEN
Executive Editor,
*Christian Life* Magazine

There was a decided bounce to John's step as he headed for the Christian Writers Institute's annual conference and workshop. Under one arm was tucked a notebook, three ballpoint pens protruded from his shirt pocket—and in his heart was a song of thanks.

The big day had arrived and thanks to his Lord, he was there! Although this was an annual event, this was John's first trip East for it.

Suddenly, John noticed that the man ahead of him was toting a briefcase. This, John decided, was a pretty conclusive indication that he, too, was going to the conference.

John hurried, reaching the door labeled "Information" just as the other chap swung it open.

They matched smiles, and John made his first new friend of the day: Dick Wrightwell.

**Registration**

A minute later, squeezed between a dozen other happy, chatting writers, they elevated to the second floor. The elevator boy turned and smiled his second big welcome (John had received his first when he got on) and, presto, they were in the midst of a laughing, friendly registration line.

John and Dick went to the end of the line. The person ahead of them introduced herself. She said she hadn't missed a single conference since their start more than twenty-five years before, and added, "Each one is better than the last."

Ahead of her was a young lady. John stretched to get a composite picture of the group—but discovered that there was no way to categorize them. They were all ages, sizes, shapes, personalities—with a nice balance of men and women.

John relaxed. Next thing he knew it was his turn to receive the friendly greetings of the registrar and her helper.

"I recognize both of you from your pictures," John said, and realized that he had added two more friends to his list.

By that time, John began losing count of people—and forgetting names. But when he was handed a handy, good-sized name tag, he was reminded that every one has a problem remembering, and was glad that he had been provided with this memory-jogger.

John and Dick made their way to the big, airy classroom where the first session was to be held, and found seats together. A soft April breeze drifted in the window to their left. Blackboards across the front of the room promised some sort of "visual aids."

John began to compare notes with Dick: why they wanted to write, what they'd done, what they wanted to do, where they were from.

It seemed as though they had been talking only a few minutes when there was piano music and Robert Walker, President of the Christian Writers Institute, called the group to order.

Amazed, John looked around. The room was filled with at least 100 writers, and more were coming. He glanced at his watch. Just 8:50.

Walker welcomed them to the conference, explaining that the first day would consist of lectures, the second of workshops and the third of a variety of sessions, from panels to talk-backs.

**The workshops**

In preparation for the first speaker, John whipped out his notebook and a pen. He found it easy to put down a helpful outline of the speaker's talk which began with the statement "Interviewing is basic to all writing":

1. Before beginning your interview:
   a. Know your subject.
   b. Have a purpose or topic.
   c. Have a point for your interview.
2. Get all facts possible before your interview. Know why your subject is important. Don't do as the young cub reporter who

said, "What have you done lately that's important Senator?"

3. Present a good appearance in clothes and deportment—and of course, have a sympathy for the subject.
4. Develop a good method.

   a. Conduct your interview in person, if possible.

   b. Ask intelligent questions, not surface, superficial inquiries. Find out deeper instincts of the person and try to get him to talk about them.
5. Take notes.

   a. Don't let your subject start dictating. (Be careful about jargon that is peculiar to your subject's occupation, situation, etc.)

   b. Explain exact purpose of interview, theme, etc.
6. Get subject sympathetic to you.

   a. Tell him you heard his speech, read his article, etc.

   b. Find out hobbies, if possible, (to seize on something to make contact).

   c. Reveal a good deal of yourself.

   d. Show friendliness, hospitality.

   e. Explore his *feelings* as well as his knowledge of things, news, etc.
7. A reporter must know his own rights.

   a. Freedom of press.

   b. Right of public to know subject if in public eye. (This point pertains to news reporting.)

Types of interviews

1. Biography—straight statistics.
2. Profile—contains biographical material but designed to reveal personality of subject, anecdotes, incidents, etc.
3. Statement—enlargement on current event involving subject.
4. Technical—exploring new thought or discovery from expert in the field (explain terms back to subject in lay language).
5. Straight question and answer. (Have questions written ahead of time; give a copy to the subject.) Don't convey your own opinion, never argue, let him say what he has to say. Set time limit only if subject states so. To close interview, ask subject if he has anything to add.

At the lecture's conclusion, John joined in the hearty applause of the group (the talk had been downright enjoyable as well as helpful) then stood up with the others to stretch.

The second speaker was an author of both children's and adult books, now head of his own film company. John discovered that the discussion of how to add color to writing was very subjective, promoting quite a bit of self-analyzing. His notes weren't extensive, but he knew he'd be a better person (and author) as a result of this hour. He glanced back over what he had written:

There isn't much you can tell a person who wants to write: he has to learn it himself.

Depth in writing comes from being a Christian in depth.

Superficiality is too prominent in evangelical Christianity.

You must really walk with God if you intend to write.

Ask yourself, "What is my susceptibility to the deep meaning of life? What really motivates human beings? What do I see? What are my cultural interests?"

Study Hemingway as an author for color in manuscript vocabulary, tactical use of verbs. Also good are "This is My Best" and "Seas of Grass" edited by Whit Burdett.

Be an avid, insatiably hungry, student of the writing you want to do.

You have *time* to learn how to do it the right way.

Spend your words like money.

The third speaker followed his "fourteen reasons for rejection slips" with a five-step reading program for catching errors. John had to write quickly to get everything down—but he was able to follow the outline without difficulty:

A. Reasons for rejection slips:
   1. Bad organization of good ideas.
   2. Failure to establish significance of article.
   3. Extemporaneous material (irrelevant, side lines).
   4. Weak material that fails to convince.
   5. Awkward expression.
   6. Weak or missing transition.
   7. Lack of suitable illustrations.
   8. Lack of convincing documentation.
   9. Verbosity (big words, wordy).
   10. Pompous or technical language.
   11. Factual error or misinterpretation (meaning of words).
   12. Weak lead (weak end, sagging in mid-section) obscuring

luster of article.

13. Unrealistic dialog.
14. Overall stodginess (a dud).

B. Reread a manuscript six or seven times, each time with a specific thing in mind, a diagnostic reading. Let it "cool off." Reread.

First reading—rapid (as if I didn't write it). Ask, Is it interesting? Significant? Believable? Does it raise questions? Have blind spots? Don't make changes, just marginal notes.

Second reading—thought progression. Does it blend? Tighter sentences? Better wording? Simpler? More discipline? Transition logical? (More marginal notes.)

Third reading—lead or introduction. Valid? Strong note? Suitable climax? (More notes.)

Fourth reading—read for literal standpoint. Dates correct?

*Informal conversations around the dinner table or between sessions can also be of great help to a writer.*

Names? Spelling? Facts? (Check your material notes for confirmation.) Punctuation?

Fifth—ask someone else to read it. Watch for *initial reaction.* Probe, find what bothered him. If reaction is positive (wonderful or rotten), you got through.

Then get back to rewriting.

After the talk, John was amazed to see that the morning had gone! He was almost breathless. Three top-notch speeches already recorded twice: once in his mind, and again in his notebook.

He joined a group of six for lunch. More fun that way.

After a delicious get-acquainted meal in the cafeteria John hurried back to the classroom so he wouldn't miss a word of the fourth speaker.

The speaker was to talk on making Christian writing more realistic. John found it easy to take notes of this message, too:

1. Realism rejects pat answers. For example, Christians say "Jesus satisfies," but all problems are not solved by the act of salvation.
2. Realism makes its peace with alternatives. (Read Carnell's *Philosophy of Christian Religion.)*
3. Realism requires observation.
4. Realism requires research. (Read Dorton's *Split Level Trap.*)
5. Realism is relevance.
6. Realism requires theological understanding. (Read Strong's *Systematic Theology,* Hodge's *Systematic Theology,* and John Calvin's *Institute of Christian Theology.)*
7. Realism requires experience. (Read Lee's *To Kill a Mockingbird,* and Paton's *Cry The Beloved Country.)*
8. Realism requires forced study. (Good books are William Strunck, Jr.'s *Elements of Style,* Oxford Dictionary of Modern English Usage, Webster's New Work Dictionary, Webster's International Dictionary and Oxford English Dictionary.)
9. Realism requires evangelistic involvement. We must be men and women of broad knowledge, sharpened to a point.

The following speaker gave John a new challenge. John saw for the first time the variety of service open to him as the speaker presented four areas with which Christian writers should be concerned: (1) The church and religious publications, (2) The mass media, newspapers, etc. (3) The training of nationals to write and edit in their own language, and (4) A positive stand in opposition to obscene literature.

John was so excited that night, he hardly slept. He and a dozen other conferees had lingered for hours over their dinner, comparing notes and cementing friendships.

Because he had a number of sales to his credit, John entered the advanced non-fiction workshop which came next on the program. But he noticed that the beginning workshop was as large as his. He was glad he had sent a manuscript in for criticisms before the conference, for the leader read parts of it, and the entire group made helpful comments. When they had finished, John finally realized why the article hadn't sold. He was sure of an acceptance now!

John found the lunch hour and single lecture session before the afternoon fiction workshop to be just what he needed. And although he had long ago decided that fiction was not his forte, he was encouraged to apply short story techniques to a missionary adventure which he felt pretty certain he could sell, now that he knew how to dramatize it.

The Friday evening banquet was truly the highlight of the conference—just as he had read it would be. The speaker, a novelist, was practical yet inspiring. And the "Pilgrim's Progress" puppet show showed him another way he could use his writing talent: script preparation.

Saturday morning had just enough variety to be a fitting conclusion to three wonderful days. From a writer-editor panel he received answers to many questions that had been bothering him. From a former CWI student he learned the many rewards of this type of ministry.

**The farewell**

As he packed his bags for his jaunt back to the state of Washington, John felt that he had spent the most rewarding three days of his life. He had received specific help, encouragement, inspiration; had made new friends; and had dedicated himself to an enlarged ministry in the fascinating field of writing!

## WRITERS CONFERENCES

CAPE COD WRITERS CONFERENCE, Craigville Conference Center, Craigville (Cape Cod), MA 02636. Marion Vuellenmeer, agent and editor-in-residence. In Au, there are courses for fiction, nonfiction, poetry and juvenile writing each day. Noted authors address the members each evening.

CHRISTIAN WRITERS CONFERENCE, Warner Pacific College, 2219 SE 68th Ave., Portland, OR 97215. An annual three-day spring conference.

CHRISTIAN WRITERS CONFERENCE, 11405 Farnam Cr., Omaha, NE 68154. Mary Brite.

CHRISTIAN WRITERS INSTITUTE, Gundersen Dr. & Schmale Road, Wheaton, IL 60187. An annual four-day spring conference.

CHRISTIAN WRITERS WORKSHOP, 6853 Webster Road, Orchard Park, NY 14127. Don Booth.

CONFERENCE ON WRITING AND LITERATURE, Wheaton College English Department, Wheaton, IL 60187. Annual Conference usually held in Oc.

DECISION MAGAZINE SCHOOL OF CHRISTIAN WRITING, Box 779, Minneapolis, MN 55403. An annual three-day summer conference.

SCHOOL OF CHRISTIAN WRITING, Forest Home Conference Center, Forest Falls, CA 92339. One fall and one summer three-day annual conference.

WESTERN NORTH CAROLINA CHRISTIAN WRITERS CONFERENCE, 502 Lakey St., Black Mountain, NC 28711. An annual three-day summer conference.

WRITE TO PUBLISH WORKSHOP (Moody Press), 820 N. LaSalle St., Chicago, IL 60187. A two-week summer program at Moody Bible Institute for magazine or book writers with mss in progress.

78

# How to start a writer's club

CATHERINE BRANDT
Free-lance writer

There is nothing quite like a Christian writers' club to generate enthusiasm for top-flight writing. Workshop criticism, comparison of output and report of sales combine to encourage a writer, beginning or established.

The Minnesota Christian Writers Guild originated in 1954 when two Minneapolis writers met at the Christian Writers Institute conference in Chicago. Inspired by hearing about editors' needs and the variety of markets, they went home to launch a writers' club.

Notices were sent to local colleges, various churches and the newspaper. The first meeting brought out nine charter members. Today the group numbers forty-one, from various denominations, with an average attendance of twenty-seven. A number of published books and hundreds of published articles and short stories are the direct result of this fellowship.

Setting up a Christian writers' club need not mean that members will not write for the secular press. But such a name, along with beginning and closing the two-hour session with prayer, does screen out writers without integrity whose purpose may be far from that of inspiring others or honoring God. However, a writer should not think that the religious market is the place to unload old sermons or articles and stories that lack jet-away and depth. Top religious markets are as discriminating as secular markets, demanding good writing, clear thinking and current themes. The fact that a writer sells in the secular market means he is competing with the nation's top writers. This has the tendency to upgrade his writing for the religious press.

At the start the Minnesota Christian Writers Guild had a chairman and a secretary. Later, a treasurer and publicity chairman were added. The secretary notifies members by postal card of the monthly two-hour meeting. It is important to have a regular meeting place, centrally located, with tables or desks for note taking, and to begin and end promptly.

**Composed of selling writers**

To have a writers' club succeed, you should have several selling writers who know what it is to work hard, to use acceptable technique, to revise what they write and to study markets. This last is highly important. The more Christian magazines and papers the writer can become familiar with, the more likely he is to hit the target.

**Reports**

Also important is a round table report of what each member has sold during the past month, or what he has been working on. Hearing what others have done helps the rest to go home and get to work. It is best to limit reports to what a writer has done, not what he intends to do.

Besides the above, the Minnesota Christian Writers Guild has used the following interest-snaggers at monthly meetings:

1. Special speakers who are selling writers or authorities in the field of writing or literature.
2. Lectures and workshops led by experienced members of the group on the technique of fillers, articles, short stories, filmstrips and marketing.
3. Manuscripts written for workshop assignments have been criticized by a committee of experienced writers.
4. The larger group divides into several smaller groups to read and criticize manuscripts, later coming together to report.
5. Encourage members and visitors to attend writers' conferences, take writers' courses and other related adult classes.
6. Recommend books on technique, as well as current books that help the writer understand today's problems.

An outgrowth of the Minnesota Christian Writers' Guild is the small group meeting between monthly meetings, where four or five get together to read and criticize a worthy manuscript.

The object of a writers' club is not to be an admiration society, but to prune and weed and feed so that those writers who know the meaning of salvation can present it winsomely and acceptably in order that an editor will buy, the subscriber will read and the cause of Christ be advanced.

**Object of a writers' club**

## WRITERS CLUBS

ASSOCIATED BUSINESS WRITERS OF AMERICA, INC., P.O. Box 135, Monmouth Junction, N.J. 08852. W. R. Palmer, Exec. Director. Members are published free-lance writers, experienced in business journalism which covers advertising copy, public relations, ghost writing, books, reports, instruction manuals, etc. as well as business and technical magazines. ABWA publishes an annual directory profiling writers who are prechecked with editors to determine ability and dependability. Each is listed geographically, giving phone, area covered, photo skill, special industry knowledge (latter indexed at back) and alphabetically. Directory price is $5. List of members geographically arranged is free. Regular monthly bulletin goes to members; pages open to editors who desire special needs published for ABWA writers. Dues are $40/yr, payable semi-annually. ABWA is a professional organization of great value to writers who qualify for membership.

THE AUTHORS LEAGUE OF AMERICA, INC., 234 W. 44th St., New York, NY 10036. A national membership corporation to promote the professional interests of authors and dramatists, procure satisfactory copyright legislation and treaties, guard freedom of expression and support fair tax treatment for writers. The Authors Guild, Inc. (Tel: 212-695-4145). The Dramatist Guild, Inc. (Tel: 212-563-2233).

CANADIAN AUTHORS ASSOCIATION, 22 Yorkville Ave., Toronto, Ontario, Canada M4V1L4. Established in 1921. Its membership of close to 1000 is composed of writers of books, short stories, dramas, feature articles, poetry and of other people with a sincere interest in Canadian literature. It has no bias of race, color or creed. National membership fees are $25 a year; $37.50 for husband and wife.

THE NATIONAL WRITERS CLUB, 1365 Logan St., Denver, CO 80203. Founded in 1937 by David Raffelock. It serves free-lance writers throughout North America by making available to them information, advice and help in all matters relating to writing for various markets. The club mentors all services offered to writers and reports on those that are either competent and reliable or not to those that prey on writers. NWC maintains continuing products to improve writer-editor relations by informing writers of professional requirements and standards. The club intercedes on behalf of members when editors fail to report on mss or to pay for published material. A national workshop is conducted in early spring. Regular meetings are held only by the several chapters of the organization. There are two classes of membership: associate for which the annual fee is $17.50 and full or professional for which the annual fee is $22. An outline of the club's services and membership applications form may be obtained by writing the secretary.

NEBRASKA WRITERS GUILD, Lamar, NB 69035. Mr. Wayne C. Lee, president. Meets twice a year, Ap and Oc in different parts of the state. A bulletin is published annually listing names and addresses of all members and brief accounts of the sales made by members, books published and current writing activities. To be eligible, applicants must have sold something they have written. $5 annual dues.

OMAHA CHRISTIAN WRITERS CLUB, 11405 Farnam Circle, Omaha, NB 68154. Mary Brite. Meets monthly at Swanson Library. Beginning writers welcome. Annual conference in Oc.

MILDRED I. REID WRITERS' COLONY, Penacook Road, Contoocook, NH 03229. Annually from June 27-August 29. Tuition $75-$90 weekly. Students may come for any length of time—one or more weeks. Tuition includes breakfast, lunch, two private lessons each week, two roundtable classes each week. Some students may work for their tuition.

RHINELANDER SCHOOL OF ARTS, University of Wisconsin Extension, Prof. Robert E. Gard, Regional Writing Programs, 720 Lowell Hall, 610 Langdon St., Madison, WI 53706. Tel: 608-

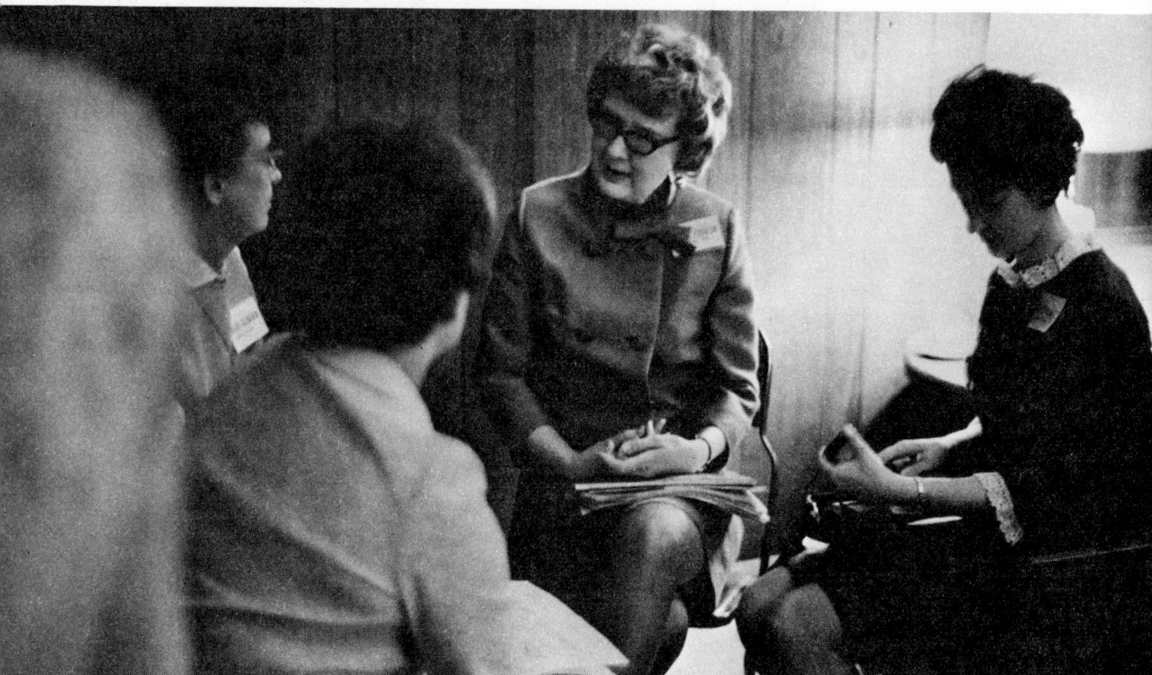

*There is nothing like a Christian writers' club to generate enthusiasm for top-flight writing.*

263-2954. Au 1-5, 1977, held in Rhinelander.

RHODE ISLAND WRITERS' GUILD, 139 Colfax St., Providence, RI 02905. Mrs. Muriel E. Eddy, president. Active, Associate, Shut-In, Junior memberships, $10 Active, $5 others. Members meet those who are interested in similar types of writing, such as hymns, fiction, nonfiction, poetry, etc. Referral services are available for help in technical aspects of publishing, promotion and personal attention.

WRITERS' CLUB OF WHITTIER, INC., 14560 Rimgate Dr., Whittier, CA 90604. Meets in separate workshops—fiction, nonfiction, juvenile, poetry and drama-TV—once or twice monthly at the Whittier Recreational Center solely to read and criticize each other's mss. Annual dues of $7 which entitles a member to attend all workshops for which he can qualify. Qualification for membership is publ in the field for which applicant applies, or submission of several mss considered acceptable by a reading committee.

# Section XII
# The Care and Feeding of Writers by Editors and Publishers

# 79

# How to find capable writers

The day will never dawn when imaginative people fail to dream of launching new magazines. To the old hand at publishing, however, these starry-eyed neophytes should spend a little more time at the drawing board before they rush to the printer with their copy. "The first issue is exciting," says one veteran editor who has been on the launching pad for a number of periodicals. "The second issue becomes somewhat less fun. After that you begin to realize you have a tiger by the tail."

Those who know their way around the periodical publishing profession agree that a magazine begins—not with the idea of making money, of producing a mouthpiece for an organization or simply as an extension of some person's ego. That is, a *successful* magazine does not begin for these reasons.

**A place to begin**

To succeed, an editor/publisher must begin with the certainty that there is a given market or group of people who are waiting to receive information on a given subject. This information can be incorporated in a magazine format. Once this is determined, then the editor/publisher is ready to begin.

As Jesus Himself pointed out, the first concern is to count the cost (for the man building the tower). Since this book deals only with the creative side, the next concern must be where to find capable writers to

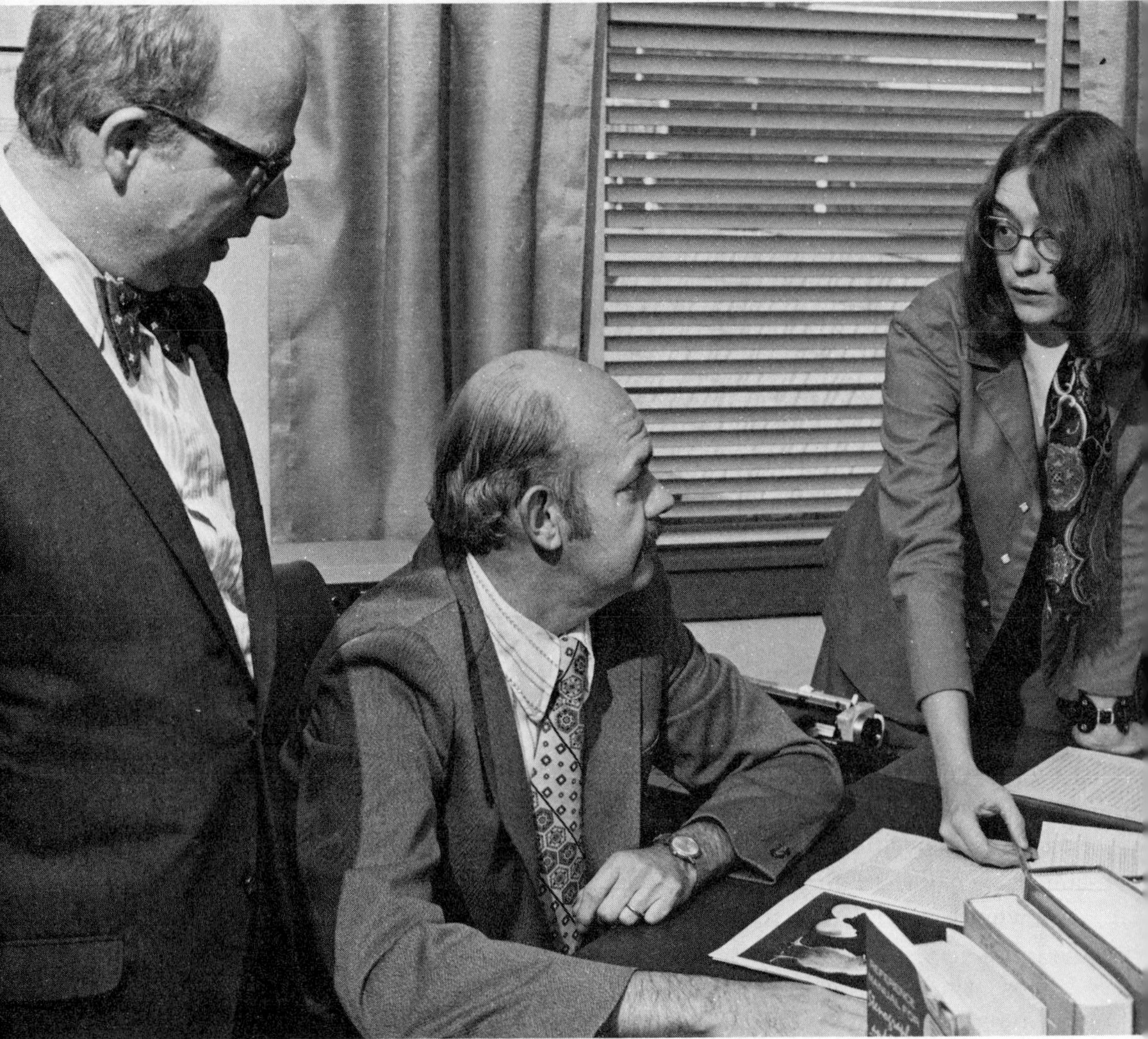

*Most religious periodicals rely on a combination of free-lance and staff-written articles. The* Good News Broadcaster *staff here evaluates the latest issue.*

present the information to the readers.

Basically, there are two ways to go. First, and perhaps the easiest, is to assemble a staff of writers. These are the trained persons who know how to write and who have some knowledge of and interest in the subject which the editor/publisher has determined will be the market focus.

With staff writers, obviously, the editor has better control over the quality of material published. Also, he has better control over deadlines. Regrettably, however, a staff of writers can be a sizable expense. Moreover, unless the editor/publisher has more than one periodical in his stable he may find his staff sitting idly at typewriters with not enough work to do between deadlines.

Thus, for most periodicals—particularly those in the religious field—editors/publishers are dependent on a combination of staff and free-lance writers.

**Scan other periodicals for writers**

The most logical source is other periodicals. Scan a few for writers whose ability appears to match what you desire. Book authors also are prospects. By compiling a list of potential authors and their addresses, you have a starting point because you know that these persons are producers.

*Producers* is an important word in the writing game. Many people dream about becoming successful authors. Too often the dream goes on and on but never bears fruit.

**Other sources**

For that reason other sources for free-lance writing talent must be considered with a jaundiced eye. Christian colleges or seminaries with courses in journalism or creative writing are a marginal possibility. Instructors sometimes can be motivated to send the names of their more talented pupils. By offering awards for acceptable manuscripts you may succeed in developing potential writers. Usually, however, this will depend upon the cooperation of the instructors.

Another source might be Bible teachers and/or pastors whose forensic ability has been demonstrated. The possibilities here for developing writers also have limitations. Too many successful speakers are unwilling to take the time to develop skill at writing. When you do find one who responds to your editing, cherish him. He is invaluable.

At the same time, however, don't lose heart completely with the pulpit personality who has demonstrated his ability to communicate orally but is unwilling to take the time to write. He can be interviewed by a writer and the interview published either under the byline of the well-known personality or as a "told to" interview giving the writer a piece of the action.

To get the best response from persons whom you wish to have interviewed, be sure to send a list of questions in advance. This will put the interviewee at ease and give him the opportunity to think through the answers. Such an approach also will help to eliminate the possibility of turn-downs from persons who might otherwise claim they were too busy.

# 80

# Training writers

Almost every editor wishes the manuscripts he receives were better. As surprising as it may sound to writers, editors simply don't like to return manuscripts. And often an editor will keep a manuscript—not because it is really what he wants—but simply because he has no choice. He wants an article on that particular subject and as inferior as it may be, this is the only manuscript available.

So the question becomes, "How do you improve the quality of manuscripts?"

Few editors are willing to go to the extremes of Harold Ross, founding editor of the *New Yorker* magazine, famed for its unique style of writing.

So the story goes, Ross determined that his writers worked best under pressure, so he invited free-lance writers to do the writing in the *New Yorker* offices. He provided the typewriters as well as paper. Not only did the magazine's weekly publication date put pressure on writers to meet exacting deadlines, but Ross provided another pressure of his own. His so-called "editorial policy" provided that something must always be happening in the editorial department. Either one wall was being torn down or another was being erected. According to some writers who worked under him, if Ross couldn't find a wall worth moving, he simply hired a man to stand around and pound nails into

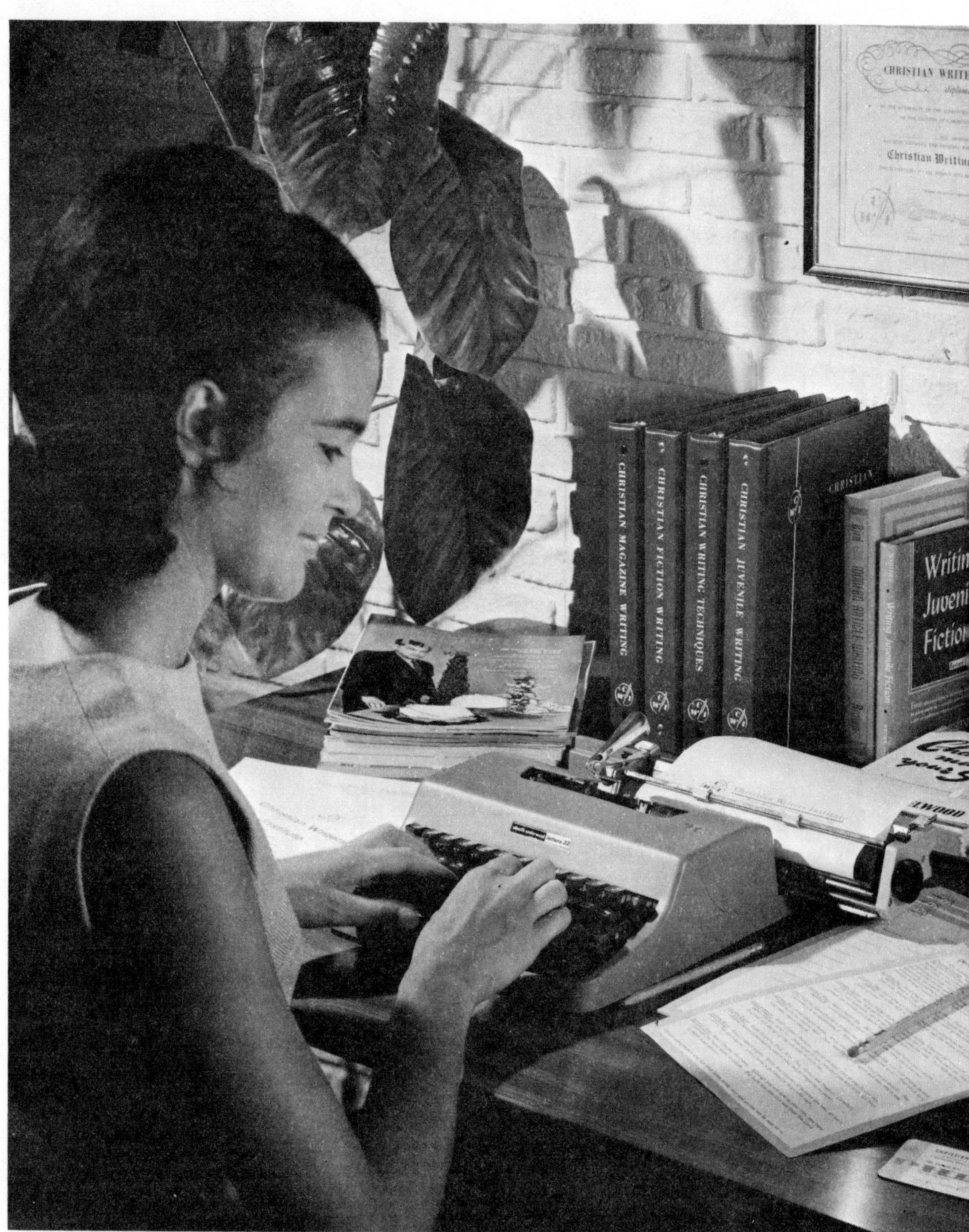


*Some writers have much potential but need guidance in developing it. A course in writing may be the solution. (Christian Writers Institute)*

The wonderful way of living . . . **Christian Life** PUBLICATIONS a division of Christian Life Inc.

• Christian Life Magazine
• Christian Bookseller Magazine
• Christian Life Marketing

GUNDERSEN DRIVE AND SCHMALE ROAD, WHEATON, ILLINOIS 60187 312/653-4200

Dear Author:

We appreciate the opportunity of reading your manuscript. Having material rejected always is disappointing. However, several hundred manuscripts are read in connection with the preparation of each issue. Many which have real merit must be rejected simply because they do not fit our needs at the time.

In regard to your manuscript, we offer the suggestions checked below.

___ We do not accept previously published material.

___ We prefer inspirational or devotional material developed around current events or the way in which the Holy Spirit of God is working today.

___ Your article needs to show what God is doing through individuals and groups instead of highlighting the personality or organization only. We should know what the individual thinks; we should hear him speak.

___ Your manuscript lacks the "in depth" treatment for which we are looking.

___ We prefer a "how-they (or we) -did-it" rather than a "how-to-do-it" approach.

___ Christian Life is not in the market for puzzles or quizzes.

___ This does not meet our current editorial needs.

___ Please study recent copies of Christian Life to see how articles are handled.

It is important that all articles slanted for Christian Life show how Jesus Christ works through people or programs rather than how individuals have achieved goals by their own ability. To understand how this is handled, it will be helpful to read current copies of the magazine. A sample will be sent upon request. If you will query before submitting longer non-fiction manuscripts, we will be glad to help you develop them to fit into our editorial program.

If you are interested in learning new writing techniques or in "brushing up," you may wish to enroll in a home-study course in Christian writing. Christian Writers Institute, a division of Christian Life Publications, offers correspondence courses in article writing, fiction techniques and juvenile writing. A catalog describing these courses is yours for the asking.

Cordially Yours,

The Editors

P.S. See reverse side for possible added comment.

WE USE THE FOUR WAY TEST: 1. Is it the TRUTH? 2. Is it FAIR to all concerned? 3. Will it build GOOD WILL and BETTER FRIENDSHIPS? 4. Will is be BENEFICIAL to all concerned?

*While not exhaustive, the* Christian Life *magazine rejection slip does give the reader some idea of the reason why his manuscript was turned down.*

blocks of wood. How else can you improve the quality of manuscripts submitted by your stable of free-lance writers?

**Improving the quality of manuscripts**

At least one publishing house in the Christian field returns manuscripts with a rejection slip which spells out the reasons why manuscripts do not make the grade. The editor checks the particular reason which applies to each manuscript. Obviously, different editors would have different reasons for the rejection. You can determine your own.

Other editors who are willing to spend the time with prospective writers have reported good success—when an idea appears to be worthy of developing—in rewriting the lead to the article. With this starting point the writers have been able to return much-improved manuscripts. Still other editors, willing to go the extra mile, have actually provided outlines on a subject which they wished the writer to develop and often include newspaper or other tear sheets as background material for the writer.

**Writers respond to encouragement**

Writers—like editors—are people. Usually they respond to encouragement. Hence, the editor who is willing to take the time and express his interest in a writer will be rewarded. Oftentimes, the editor may go to the extent of suggesting to the prospective writer that he enroll for instruction in writing—either in a classroom situation or in a correspondence school. In addition, some editors recommend to their writers that they attend Christian writers' conferences*—both for practical instruction and for fellowship with other writers and the opportunity of meeting editors and publishers.

Many writers have potential but need guidance to develop it fully.

*See listing of writers' conferences, pages 447-8.

81

# Making the assignment

The dream of every free-lance writer is to receive an assignment from an editor. And the dream of every editor is to receive from a writer a perfectly executed assignment.

Regrettably, too many writers expect to receive assignments when they have not demonstrated their ability to fulfill them properly. Few religious editors haven't received a letter that read something like this:

Dear Editor:

I will be leaving next month on a world tour. I will be visiting fifteen countries and will be able to furnish you with articles and pictures to your specifications.

Let me know how many subjects you wish covered and the length of manuscript desired.

Sincerely yours,

P.S. To help defray the cost of travel I will appreciate an advance. The amount is up to you but $100 would be acceptable.

**Handle an assignment with care**

Few editors can afford to take the time or the chance with unknown writers. Even with established performers, an assignment must be han-

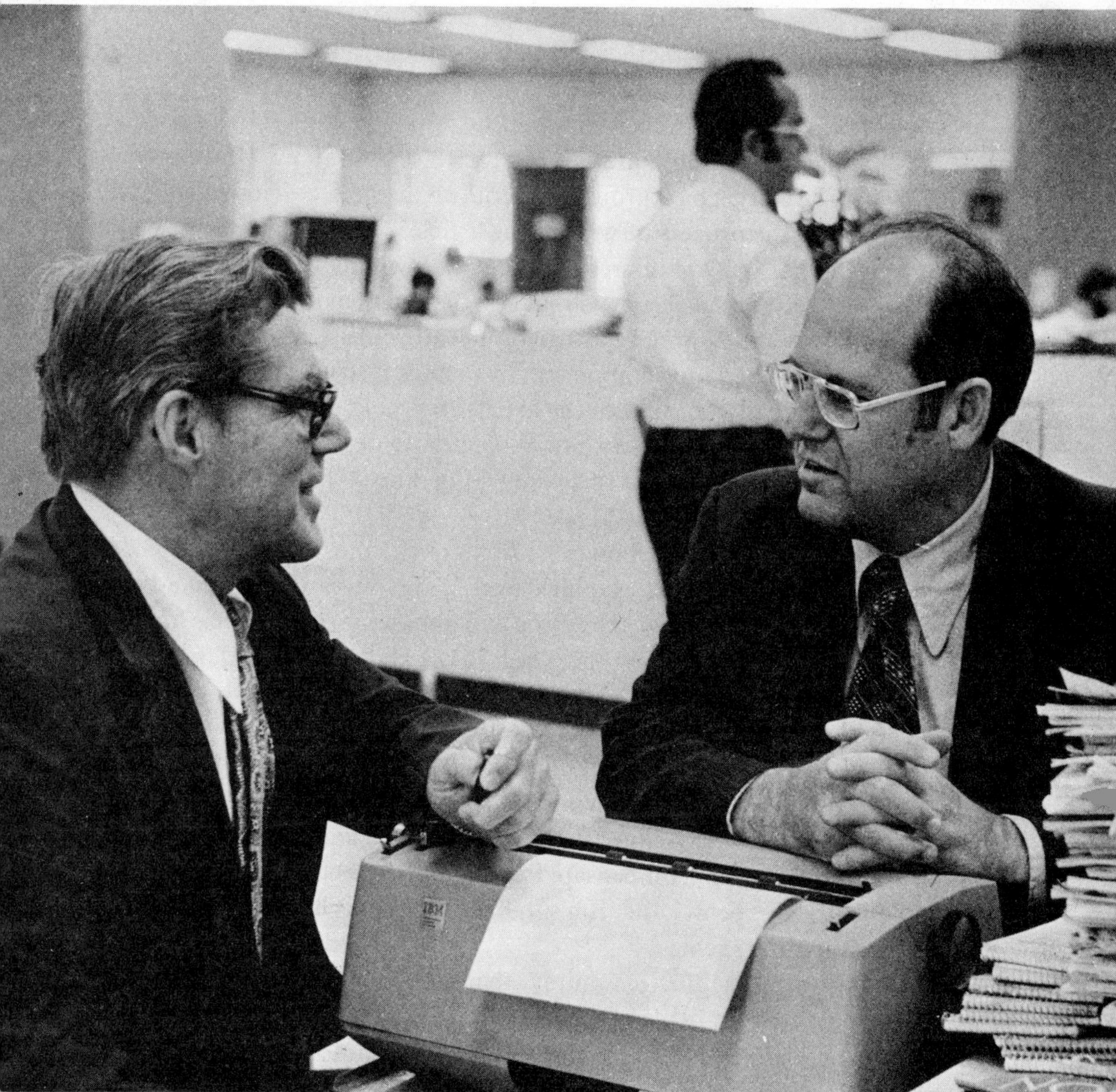

*Adon Taft (right) of the* Miami Herald *has proved his capability in handling assignments. Robert Walker of* Christian Life *magazine periodically calls on Taft for articles.*

dled with care. All writers have certain areas of proficiency.

First, it is important to know whether or not the writer to whom you wish to give the assignment is interested in the subject. If he is not, the chances are he will not do the best job.

Second, if a telephone call or a letter indicates he is interested, the next question is, "Can he meet your deadline?" At the same time you need to determine whether or not he is in the area to cover the subject or whether you are willing to pick up the travel tab.

Third, give the writer as much help as you can. If you have accumulated research material, be sure to send it along. If not, suggest where he can get background material on the subject. This will not only speed up the process of writing the article, but also help to make him realize that you are interested in him and willing to give him a hand.

Fourth, obviously you will suggest the length of the article and determine how many photographs you need to illustrate it.

Finally—and most important—you must instruct the writer as to the slant or pitch you want in the article. If you know the writer's ability well enough, you may wish to allow him to determine the slant. If so, then this should be stated plainly so he knows he has the latitude to determine the slant for himself.

In this connection, however, some of the most careful editors will take the time to do a rough "lead." This gives the writer advance knowledge of the way the editor would like to see the article handled. Few editors would insist that the lead actually be followed, but simply provide it as a direction which the writer should take.

**The risk of assignment writing**

As a postscript at this point, most editors assume that even though they give a writer an assignment, they are not bound to accept the manuscript. If after receiving the manuscript and reworking the idea with the author, an editor determines that the manuscript is altogether unusable, he can compensate the author for his travel, any other out-of-pocket expense, and, if his budget allows, perhaps offer a token fee for the time spent.

All of these factors imply that assignment writing is a risky business—both for the editor and for the writer. And that is correct.

# 82

# Handling problem writers

Writers come in all sizes, shapes—and problems.

Some insist that the Lord has told them to write and to submit their manuscript to the editor. The obvious implication is that the editor must publish it. An occasional honest editor has been known to reply, "How can this be? The Lord has told me not to accept your manuscript."

Other writers can be identified as "cry babies." They object to tough editing and threaten not to submit again unless the editor agrees not to edit so rigorously. Most editors are glad to have them carry out their threat.

Still other writers will claim that the editor has either invited them to submit and/or given them an assignment; therefore, their manuscript cannot be rejected. Most editors take the precaution when responding to an inquiry to add, "We cannot guarantee to accept your manuscript in advance," or, "All manuscripts are reviewed on a free-lance basis."

**Suggestions in handling difficult authors**

Still, there are those writers who obviously have a good idea and/or a measure of talent. But they are difficult to handle. Granted, most editors shy away from them, but how can you work with them? Here are a few suggestions.

1. Be specific. Make it abundantly clear that the manuscript must be submitted only on speculation. You cannot agree to accept the manuscript before you have seen it.

2. Be exact as to the length of the manuscript and the number and type of photographs desired.

3. Indicate clearly the slant you wish the article to take. Perhaps even say how you do *not* want it to be handled. You might even write a hypothetical lead and send it along to the writer. In the lead make clear the direction you wish the article to take.

4. Finally, if you think it will help, give the writer an outline of how you wish the subject to be handled. And since at this point you must be sold on the ability of the writer to do the job, you may wish to include tear sheets on the subject which will be helpful to him in developing the idea.

In all human relationships nothing is better than a face-to-face confrontation. Thus if you have a prospective writer whom you would like to develop, invite him to lunch. Here you will have the opportunity of making clear to him the type of articles you desire and of clearing up any misunderstanding he may have regarding the editorial format of your publication. Such a meeting will soon determine whether or not the writer can be molded into the kind of writer on whom you can depend.

# Section XIII
# Writing Religious News

# 83

# Pleased to meet you, mr. editor

The newspaper in your community is usually an institution claiming wholesome respect.

This makes the editor an important man.

If you are going to write for your local newspaper, you are going to work for the editor. One of the most important things for you to do first, therefore, is to meet your boss.

**Meet your boss**

Many people who attempt to write for their local newspaper shrink from this. Failure to get to know your editor is courting disaster.

If you are unwilling to meet your editor you will never know exactly what he wants.

Editors are normal people. Like you they are interested in children, flowers, dogs, and other people. Approach him when he is least occupied and you will find him easy to meet and talk with.

On an afternoon newspaper schedule you call after 3:00 p.m. On a morning newspaper make it the first thing in the morning.

If the editor is busy on your first call, don't become discouraged. Try him at another time.

**Establish yourself**

When you introduce yourself, tell him plainly that you are interested in helping him get more religious news in the newspaper. Tell him that you are interested because you believe that he and other community leaders realize the significance of religion today. Don't preach. Simply observe that because religion is popular you would like to report on it from your local church point of view to start.

After you have established yourself as a reliable reporter for your local church then you may be able to tackle larger assignments.

**Learn to be Helpful**

Learn to be helpful to your editor. Suggest article ideas to him in addition to those you write up. He will appreciate your thoughtfulness and alertness.

This "casting your bread upon the water" device may also pay out real dividends to you. Before long you may find the editor passing on to you tips for stories which you can dig up yourself.

Simply stated, the principle of "meeting your editor" means this: If you are sincere about wishing to serve the Lord in the field of Christian journalism in your local newspaper field, make yourself useful to your editor. Don't become discouraged if he at first appears indifferent. He has a lot on his mind. Many different people are attempting to wheedle favors from him. If he discovers you are sincere, your efforts will be rewarded.

In a small Midwestern city a local newspaper possessed the reputation of being antagonistic toward religion. Church news appeared sparingly. Virtually no other religious stories ever appeared.

A young man who had caught the vision of using the newspaper for presenting the claims of the Gospel decided he would see what he could do to break the ice.

He was amazed when he spoke to the editor. "Yes, we would like to carry more religious material," was the reply. "But we don't know how to get it, and no one seems to be interested in giving it to us."

The young man went to work. In a matter of several months most of the stories on church activities which he wrote were appearing regularly in the newspaper.

In another Midwestern town a pastor who had recently taken a church in the community was told that the only way church material could appear in the newspaper was through the advertising columns.

Fellow pastors in the ministerial council confirmed the report. "The editor is simply not interested in religion," they said.

Picking a time when he knew the editor would have a little leisure the pastor walked into the newspaper office. Introducing himself as the new pastor of the community, he said, "A number of events occur in our church which I believe would be of interest to the community. If they appeared in your newspaper, I am sure many of our people who do not now read your newspaper would find it necessary to do so. This would help you and it would help me too."

The pastor went on to explain that he had done a little newspaper writing before and would be glad to help the editor in any way possible.

The response came as he expected it would. "You send in any item that you think is news worthy," said the editor. "You are the first minister who ever offered me any help. The other ministers in town always want me to do something for them. They can't understand why I get tired of doing it."

# 84

# Getting off on the right foot

The key to the successful newspaper article is proper organization. The most important factor in proper organization is a good *lead.* Second factor is the *body* of the article.

**Definition of a newspaper lead**

By *lead* we mean the opening of the article. In some cases the lead may be covered in the first paragraph. More likely it will include the first two or three paragraphs.

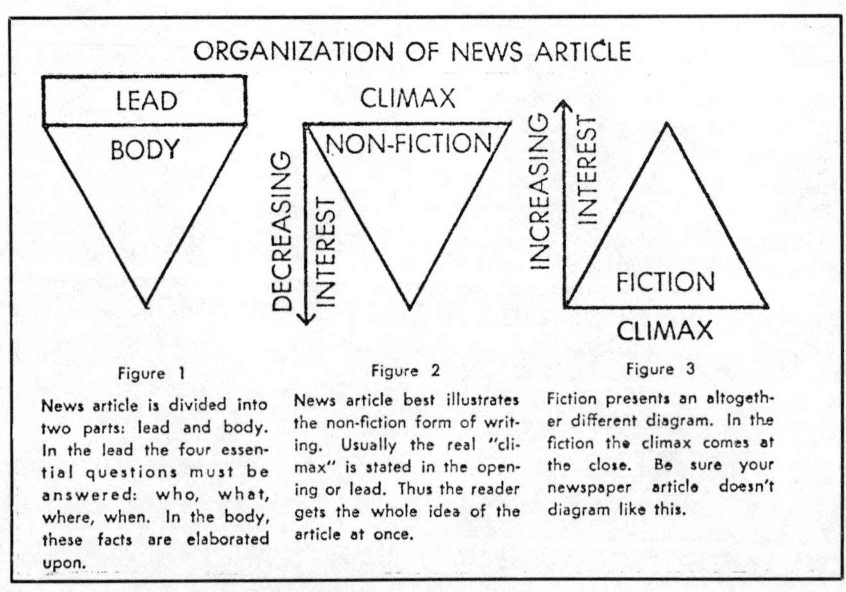


Figure 1

News article is divided into two parts: lead and body. In the lead the four essential questions must be answered: who, what, where, when. In the body, these facts are elaborated upon.

Figure 2

News article best illustrates the non-fiction form of writing. Usually the real "climax" is stated in the opening or lead. Thus the reader gets the whole idea of the article at once.

Figure 3

Fiction presents an altogether different diagram. In the fiction the climax comes at the close. Be sure your newspaper article doesn't diagram like this.

The definition of a good lead may be best summed up as the answers to four basic questions. These questions are:

*Who* is it?

*What* happened?

*Where* did it happen?

*When* did it happen?

How these individual subjects are treated is of tremendous importance to the success of your story. Therefore, it is necessary for us to consider each one of them separately.

## TELL WHO IT IS

Names are a newspaper's most important commodity. Names make news.

**Names make news**

For this reason the "who" in your newspaper story is of prime importance. Be sure you get as many names into the story as are important to it. But don't load up your articles with meaningless names.

Be sure the name is correctly spelled. Be sure also the name is complete with first name and initial.

Your failure here means a black mark against you in the mind of the editor. If he comes to distrust you because of carelessness in this department, your progress in serving that newspaper will be limited.

Always identify properly the name used. Don't guess at the office held or the address you give. Be sure.

Likewise, be careful in giving proper titles to your individuals. Correct way to write a pastor's name is important.

Incorrect: Rev. Doakes, Pastor of the First Baptist Church
Correct: Rev. Joe E. Doakes, pastor of the First Baptist Church

Above is the proper way a pastor's name should appear first in your article. Second mention and all mentions thereafter are also important. Most newspaper style books call for the following:

Incorrect: Rev. Doakes
Correct: Mr. Doakes

Some pastors and evangelists prefer to be identified as "Dr. Sam Smaltz." If so, be sure that your story identifies him in this way. In second mention of this title, the same form is followed as that above: "Dr. Doakes."

## SAY WHAT IT IS

**Clarity claims a premium**

In newspaper writing clarity claims a premium.

The "what" of your story must be said plainly, simply. Best way to do this is to keep your sentences short. Use two simple sentences rather than a complex or compound sentence.

The "what" must also be significant. If it isn't, perhaps the whole item is not worth the space in the newspaper that you intend to give it. Help your editor by saving him the trouble of throwing it in the waste basket: throw it there yourself.

Incorrect: The city council juvenile delinquency sub-committee urged an immediate school building program and stepped-up park improvement program to help halt a disgraceful, spiraling increase in juvenile delinquency throughout the city and county.

Correct: The city council juvenile delinquency sub-committee today called for "a halt to the disgraceful spiraling increase in juvenile delinquency in the city and county." The committee urged an immediate city building program and stepped-up park improvement plan for the community.

## WHERE IT OCCURRED

**A basic principle**

If the scene of the action is not located the lead is incomplete.

This is basic to the successful news story. Always remember it.

Even if the location appears unimportant to you, put it in. No editor will accept the story unless the location is identified or clearly implied.

Only exception to this is where two locations might be unnecessary.

Incorrect: Mrs. Robert Hurtz last night was elected president of the Womens Missionary Society of the First Presbyterian Church for the coming year at a meeting in the church parlors.

Correct: Mrs. Robert Hurtz last night was elected president of the Womens Missionary Society of the First Presbyterian Church for the coming year. She succeeds Mrs. Alfred Stevenson.

There are times, however, when both locations are necessary. This occurs when both are pertinent to the sense of the story itself.

Correct: A dime per day per person is being put away during Lent by 1,750 members of Glenview Community Church to help underwrite the cost of keeping a full-time Protestant chaplain at the large and growing county hospital.

AND WHEN

**The element of time**

In the fast pace of life today the time element becomes more imperative than ever. Be sure not only that you include the time element, but that your article itself is as timely as the newspaper that carries it.

*Member of the Washington, D. C. Bureau of United Press International, Wes Pippert also reports frequently on national affairs in Christian periodicals.*

Most newspapers want the news no later than the day it happens. Exceptions of course, would come in the case of a bi-weekly or weekly newspaper.

The magic word in the newspaper article is today. Never forget this. Adroit use of this word will often pull up an otherwise ordinary story enough to make it score for you.

Ordinary: Mary Nelson, 346 Elm Street, has been named queen at the Sunday school at the First Presbyterian Church. Announcement was made by Rev. Peter Cartwright.

Better: In a dramatic announcement today, Rev. Peter Cartwright answered the question foremost in the minds of members of the First Presbyterian Church. "Who will be Sunday school queen?" etc.

At the same time don't overlook the value of an advance story. Editors are eager to secure these as well. Also, they offer you a tremendous advantage in giving the subject more complete coverage. But if for some reason or other the event fails to take place, be sure to notify the editor immediately. You, and you alone, are responsible for this.

**Why and how**

In addition, two other questions occasionally can be answered. They should be whenever they contribute materially to the sense and meaning of the material. Those two questions:

*Why* did it happen?

*How* did it happen?

The test as to whether or not it is necessary to answer these questions depends upon the significance of the facts. In the example below the *why* is obviously important to the meaning.

Incorrect: The congregation of Jackson Boulevard Christian Church has accepted the offer of the First Congregational Church to worship in that church's chapel.
Service will begin at 8 a.m. etc.

Better: The congregation of Jackson Boulevard Christian Church, *which was destroyed by fire Tuesday,* has accepted the offer of the First Congregational Church to worship in that church's chapel.
Service this Sunday will begin at 8 a.m. etc.

Here you can see by answering the *how* the facts of the article take on new significance. Without them the whole point of the story is lost.

Poor: As a result of Tract Distribution Week, sponsored by the First Baptist Church last year, 500 reports including one from Dover, England were received, according to Rev. Frank Doddsworth, pastor.

Better: A tract placed in a bottle and tossed into the harbor during the First Baptist Church's Tract Distribution Week last year was picked up and read by a fisherman on the beach at Dover, England. Reviewing the 500 reports of tracts received, Rev. Frank Doddsworth, said etc.

# 85

# What's going on here?

You have just learned that your news story lead must answer the questions, *who, what, where,* and *when.*

Now we come to the question, "Which comes first?"

This is where many would-be newspaper writers fail. As a result their articles are either rejected or rewritten so completely they don't recognize them.

The answer to this question involves the whole matter of organization of a newspaper article. Many people don't realize this. They think they can simply start anywhere and write until they're finished. That's where they make their big mistake.

**Newspaper writing is a craft**

Newspaper article writing is a craft. It is not a difficult one to learn. The principles are simple. Once they are learned they are practiced by the experienced writer almost without thinking.

But to get back to our question which comes first: The *who,* the *what,* the *where,* or the *when.*

The answer to this question lies in the situation itself. To determine which it is you must simply ask yourself the question, "Which is *the most important?*" You must answer this question carefully. What are your reasons for the answer?

Let's take a simple situation and see how we might handle it under different circumstances. Suppose your church has just completed a $100,000 educational unit. A dedicatory service has been arranged for Sunday, October 1, at the time of the regular Sunday morning service. The pastor will deliver the dedicatory message.

With these facts of the situation in hand clearly, the most important fact is, *what*. Thus, your lead might read:

> *Dedicatory services for the new $100,000 educational unit* just completed by the First Baptist Church will be observed at the regular morning service, Sunday, October 1. The Rev. J. P. Small, pastor, will preach the dedicatory sermon.

Now let's add another ingredient. Suppose this dedicatory service were scheduled on the day which the church would observe the 25th anniversary of its founding. Now, a new element has been added, and we have the opportunity of emphasizing the *when* as the most important fact:

> *Next Sunday morning,* on the 25th anniversary of its founding, the First Baptist Church will dedicate a new $100,000 educational unit. Dedicatory sermon will be delivered by Rev. J. P. Small, pastor.

Or another situation might exist which would give us still another opportunity. Let's say, for instance, that your church invited the governor of the state to take part in the dedicatory service. It might also be some other outstanding personality such as a well-known evangelist, a denominational official, a famous missionary, etc. In this case, obviously, the *who* becomes the most important factor. Therefore, it must be played up in the lead.

> *Governor A. B. Blowhard* will take part in the dedicatory services at the First Baptist Church Sunday. Services will be conducted in the auditorium of the new $100,000 educational unit just completed, etc.

Still another approach might be necessary if our facts indicated that the *where* was more important. This might occur if the building site held such especial interest. In such a case our article might read as follows.

*On the site where the first school house in Kane County was built,* the First Baptist Church, Sunday, will dedicate a new $100,000 educational building. Rev. J. P. Small, pastor, will deliver the dedicatory sermon.

**Evaluate the facts**

Your job in each case is to evaluate the facts. Take every angle into consideration. And be careful not to be prejudiced by personalities. Instead, think in terms of what would be of the greatest interest to the greatest number of people in your town or community. If you use this as a measuring stick, you are not likely to fail.

Now, what comes next?

You have written your lead, answering the four questions: *who, what, where* and *when?* You have begun your news article by answering the most important question first. To do this job as it has been outlined, it may have taken you one, two, or three paragraphs.

After the lead comes the body of your news article.

In the body you do nothing more than expand on the answers you have given to the questions appearing in the lead. After all, these are the essential factors of the situation which you are describing. Logically, you would develop these in their degree of importance. It is important to do this because of the very nature of a newspaper.

After the newspaper article has been set in type and it goes to the make-up table, it may need to be cut. If you have organized it in this way, the less important paragraph will be cut first.

This means the newspaper article must be so stringently organized that the reader can catch at a glance the sense of the meaning of the article. How important this is can be seen in a moment in the diagrams on page 483.

In Figure 1 you can see how a nonfiction action article looks when it is reduced to a diagram. The lead answers the questions: *who, what, when* and *where.* In the body these facts are simply enlarged upon.

In Figure 2 you can see how another type of newspaper article looks when diagrammed. This type of article is best suited for the great bulk of newspaper items.

In both these types, note that the lead is complete in itself. Later paragraphs carry only further details beyond the bare statements of fact. These are the "more details" that give the article body and substance.

Keeping this whole matter of organization in mind, you can see now

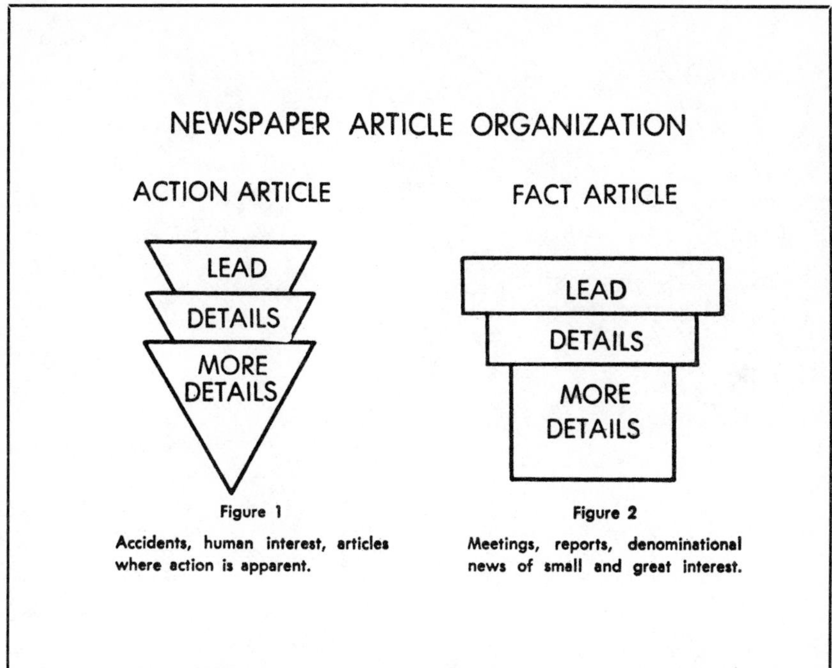


Figure 1
Accidents, human interest, articles where action is apparent.

Figure 2
Meetings, reports, denominational news of small and great interest.

**Organize correctly**

why it is important. And if the article is not written in this way the editor may think it is not important enough to rewrite and reject the whole item. Or, if he believes it is important it will be necessary for him to rewrite it himself.

You can become a friend of editors by organizing your newspaper articles correctly. You can also become a successful newspaper writer by doing so.

# Appendices

# Appendix 1

## Abbreviations used in this book

### MONTHS

| | | | |
|---|---|---|---|
| JA | January | JU | July |
| FE | February | AU | August |
| MA | March | SE | September |
| AP | April | OC | October |
| MY | May | NO | November |
| JN | June | DE | December |

### STATES AND PROVINCES

| | | | |
|---|---|---|---|
| AL | Alabama | FL | Florida |
| AK | Alaska | GA | Georgia |
| AZ | Arizona | HI | Hawaii |
| AR | Arkansas | ID | Idaho |
| CA | California | IL | Illinois |
| CO | Colorado | IN | Indiana |
| CT | Connecticut | IA | Iowa |
| DE | Delaware | KS | Kansas |

**Abbreviations Used in This Book**

| | | | |
|---|---|---|---|
| KY | Kentucky | TX | Texas |
| LA | Louisiana | UT | Utah |
| ME | Maine | VT | Vermont |
| MD | Maryland | VA | Virginia |
| MA | Massachusetts | WA | Washington |
| MI | Michigan | WV | West Virginia |
| MN | Minnesota | WI | Wisconsin |
| MS | Mississippi | WY | Wyoming |
| MO | Missouri | CZ | Canal Zone |
| MT | Montana | DC | District of Columbia |
| NE | Nebraska | GU | Guam |
| NV | Nevada | PR | Puerto Rico |
| NH | New Hampshire | VI | Virgin Islands |
| NJ | New Jersey | AB | Alberta |
| NM | New Mexico | BC | British Columbia |
| NY | New York | MB | Manitoba |
| NC | North Carolina | NB | New Brunswick |
| ND | North Dakota | NF | Newfoundland |
| OH | Ohio | NT | Northwest Territories |
| OK | Oklahoma | NS | Nova Scotia |
| OR | Oregon | ON | Ontario |
| PA | Pennsylvania | PE | Prince Edward Island |
| RI | Rhode Island | PQ | Quebec |
| SC | South Carolina | SK | Saskatchewan |
| SD | South Dakota | YT | Yukon Territory |
| TN | Tennessee | LB | Labrador |

## OTHER ABBREVIATIONS

| | | | |
|---|---|---|---|
| B&W | Black and White | max | Maximum |
| / | Per | exec | Executive |
| wd | Word | ¢ | Cents |
| wds | Words | publ | Publication |
| mss | Manuscript(s) | SASE | Self Addressed Stamped Envelope |
| pymt | Payment | | |
| yr | Year | pix | Pictures |
| + | and up | approx | Approximately |
| min | Minimum | M | Monthly |

| | | | |
|---|---|---|---|
| B | Bimonthly | S | Semimonthly |
| W | Weekly | Q | Quarterly |
| BiW | Biweekly | | |

Example:

B&W pix should accompany mss. Approx 2500 wds. Pymt 2¢/wd+.

Explanation:

Black and white pictures should accompany manuscript. Approximately 2500 words. Payment two cents per word and up.

# Appendix 2

## Proofreader's marks

### SIZE AND STYLE OF TYPE

| | |
|---|---|
| *wf* | Wrong font (size or style of type) |
| *lc* | Lower Case letter |
| *lc* | Set in LOWER CASE |
| ≡ | capital letter |
| *caps* | SET IN capitals |
| *caps + lc* | Lower Case with Initial Capitals |
| *sm. caps* | SET IN small capitals |
| *caps + s.c.* | SMALL CAPITALS WITH INITIAL CAPITALS |
| *rom* | Set in roman type |
| *ital* | *Set in italic type* |
| *ital s.c.* | *ITALIC SMALL CAPITALS* |
| *ital caps* | *ITALIC CAPITALS* |
| *LF* | Set in lightface type |
| *bf* | Set in **boldface** type |
| *bf ital* | ***Boldface italic*** |
| *bf s.c.* | **BOLDFACE SMALL CAPITALS** |
| *bf caps* | **BOLDFACE CAPITALS** |

Superior letter or figure[b]
Inferior letter or figure$_2$

## POSITION

Move to right
Move to left
Lower (letters or words)
Elevate (letters or words)
Straighten line (horizontally)
Align type (vertically)
tr Transposes pace
tr Transpose enclosed in ring matter
tr Transpose (order letters of or words)
tr Rearrange words of order numbers in
center Put in center of line or page (ctr)
run over Run over to next line. (A two-letter division should be avoided)
run back Run back to preceding line. (Such a division is improper)
reset—12 picas A syllable or short word standing alone on a line is called a "widow"; it should be eliminated
The nearly blank line is a "quad line"

## INSERTION AND DELETION

OUT see copy Insert matter omitted; refer to copy (Mark copy *Out*, *see proof*, *galley 00*)
the Caret. Insert marginal addition
Dele. Take out ~~(delete)~~
Delete annd close up
e/ Correct litter or word marked
stet Let it stand—(all ~~matter~~ above dots)

## PARAGRAPHING

¶ Begin a paragraph
no ¶ No paragraph.
run in Run in or run on

| | |
|---|---|
| □ ¶ | Indent the number of em quads shown |
| flush | No indention |
| hang in | Hanging indention. This style should |
| one em | have all lines after the first marked for the desired indention, either separately or by means of a bracket, as shown |

## SPACING

| | |
|---|---|
| solid | Means "not leaded" |
| leaded | Additional space between lines |
| ⁀ | Close up entirely; take out space |
| # | Close up partly; leave some space |
| ✓ or ‿ | Less space between words |
| ✓ or eq # | Equalize space between words |
| hair # | Hair space between letters |
| thin # | Thin space where indicated |
| l/s | LETTER-SPACE |
| # | Insert space (or more space) |
| space out | More space between words |
| en quad | ½-em quad (nut) space or indention |
| □ | Em quad (mutton) space or indention |
| □□□ | Indent number of em quads shown |
| ld in | Insert lead between lines |
| ℊ ld | Take out lead |
| 2 pts # | Insert space (amount specified) |
| ℊ 1 pt | Take out space (amount specified) |

## DIACRITIC MARKS; LIGATURES; SYMBOLS; SIGNS

| | |
|---|---|
| ü | Diaeresis or umlaut |
| é | Accent acute |
| è | Accent grave |
| â | Circumflex accent or "doghouse" |
| ç | Cedilla or French c |
| ñ | Tilde (Spanish); til (Portuguese) |
| ⁀ | Use ligature (œ—oeillade; ffi—affix) |
| = | Sign of equality |

/ Virgule (separatrix; solidus; stop mark)

⁂ Asterism ⁂ Leaders . . . . . . .

⊙□⊙□⊙ Ellipsis___or * * * or . . . . .

*/†/‡/ Order of symbols: *†‡§‖¶#; then double

## PUNCTUATION

⊙ Insert period

,̂ or ,/ Insert comma

⊙ or :/ Insert colon

;/ Insert semicolon

∨' or ∨ Apostrophe or 'single quote'

∨“/∨” Insert quotation marks

?/ Insert question mark (eroteme)

!/ Insert exclamation point (ecphoneme)

-/ or =/ Insert hyphen

1/en or |en| En dash

1/em or |—| One-em dash

|2/em| Two-em dash

(/) Insert parentheses

[/] Insert brackets

## MISCELLANEOUS

e/⊗ or × Replace broken or imperfect type

9 Reverse (upside down type or cut)

⊥ or ⊥ Push down a space that prints

(SP) Spell out (twenty (gr.)) grains

(G?) Question of grammar

(F?) Question of fact

Qy or (?) Query to author

(Qy Ed) Query to editor

⌐ Mark-off or break; start new line

# Appendix 3

## Glossary of terms

*All rights* - publisher takes complete responsibility for material. Author can make no other use of material.

*Bimonthly* - every two months

*Biweekly* - every two weeks

*Blind Lead* - lead that does not identify subject immediately

*Blue-penciling* - editing of a manuscript

*Blurb* - descriptions of book on book jackets

*Byline* - name of author printed just below title of article

*Clean copy* - manuscript free of errors, smudges, etc.

*Cliche* - overused or trite expression

*Closing date* - deadline on which copy must be submitted

*Column inch* - all type contained in one inch of published material - whether newspaper or magazine

*Copy* - manuscript before set in type

*Copyright* - presently protects for twenty-eight years with one renewal for twenty-eight years

*Credit line* - name of photographer or illustrator

*Feature* - indicates a lead article in a magazine

*Filler* - short item used to "fill" a page, e.g. joke, puzzle, light verse, etc.

*Format* - general make-up of a publication

*Formula story* - typical story with typical plot structure, e.g. boy meets girl

*Gagline* - cartoon caption

*Ghostwriter* - writer doing manuscript based on another person's ideas or knowledge

*Glossy* - black and white photograph with a shiny surface

*House organ* - company publication. Can be for employees only or can be for members of a specific denomination.

*Illustrations* - highlights the manuscript: photographs, artwork, etc. Usually paid for separately.

*Lead* - first sentence or paragraph of article or news story

*Lead-in* - provocative beginning to an article usually set in different type and preceding article

*One-time rights* - after use of story, author may sell article elsewhere

*Outline* - summary of contents usually for a book

*Payment on acceptance* - editor pays for article as soon as decision is made to publish it

*Payment on publication* - editor decides to publish article but doesn't pay author until published

*Photojournalism* - feature story told through medium of photography

*Public domain* - material never copyrighted or copyright has expired

*Quarterly* - every three months

*Query* - letter written to editor to inquire of possibility of article or book

*Rejection slip* - notice that editor has turned down your article for publication

*Runover* - continuation of article in back of magazine

*Second rights* - publication after article has appeared elsewhere

*Semimonthly* - twice a month

*Semiweekly* - twice a week

*Serial* - published periodically

*Slant* - approach used in an article to fit requirements of a specific magazine or audience

*Speculation* - editor reads manuscript without promising to publish it

*Style* - way in which author writes

*Subsidiary rights* - all rights in addition to publishing book: paperback, book clubs, movies, etc.

*Subsidy publishers* - (Vanity publishers) charges author for publishing own book

*Tabloid* - newspaper format

*Tearsheet* - pages from a magazine or newspaper

*Think piece* - magazine article from intellectual approach

*Third world* - reference to underdeveloped countries of Asia and Africa

*Trade magazine* - magazine whose audience is in a specific trade or business

*Transparencies* - positive slides

*Unsolicited manuscript* - material presented to editor he did not ask to see

# Index

## M



## N

## O



## P



## Q



## R